Scandinavia

A new geography

Scandinavia

A new geography

Brian S. John

Longman
London and New York

Longman Group Limited
Longman House, Burnt Mill, Harlow
Essex CM20 2JE, England
Associated companies throughout the world

*Published in the United States of America
by Longman Inc., New York*

© Brian S. John 1984

First published 1984

British Library Cataloguing in Publication Data
John, Brian S.
    Scandinavia.
    1. Scandinavia – Description and travel
    I. Title
    914.8   DL11

    ISBN 0-582-48950-4

Library of Congress Cataloging in Publication Data
John, Brian Stephen.
    Scandinavia: a new geography.

    Bibliography: p.
    Includes index.
    1. Scandinavia – Description and travel – 1981 –
I. Title.
    DL11.5.J63   1983   948   82-24930
    ISBN 0-582-48950-4

Set in 10/12 pt Linotron 202 Times Roman

Printed in Singapore by
Selector Printing Co (Pte) Ltd

Contents

Contents

Acknowledgements

This book would not have been written but for the encouragement and help of many friends both in this country and in Scandinavia. I am happy to acknowledge the kind help of the following, who have all read through pieces of my text and provided many helpful comments and corrections: Bergliot Svanholm, Bo Petersson, Jan Linzie, John Button, John West, Hans Aldskogius, Gunnar Hoppe, Stig Jonsson, Jan Mangerud, Marit Orheim-Mauritzen, Borghild Orheim, Thomas Lundén, Sölve Göransson, Michael Alexander, Brian Roberts, Lotte Möller, Lars Sjögren, Stig Jaatinen, Lauri Hautamäki, Jens Christian Hansen and Christopher Jensen Butler. I am grateful to Maureen Williams, Liz Williams, Caroline Kedward and my wife Inger for all their help with typing and retyping sections of the manuscript.

I owe a great debt of gratitude to the following for providing specific information, research literature and photographs, and for allowing me to quote from published and unpublished material relevant for the chapters of my book: Jämtland-Härjedalens Turistförening; the National Swedish Institute for Building Research; Stockholms Läns Landsting; Waxholmsbolaget; Energisparkommittén (Swedish Industry Department); Uddeholm AB; Saab-Scania AB; Rauma-Repola OY; Wärtsilä AB; Swedish National Tourist Office; Nordmanns Forbundet; the Editor of *UNESCO Courier*; The National Swedish Board of Agriculture; the Finnish Power Producer's Coordinating Council; the Royal Danish Fisheries Department; the Swedish Embassy (London); the Royal Norwegian Department of Fisheries; the Royal Norwegian Embassy (London); det Danske Selskab; the Norwegian Water Resources and Electricity Board; NORDEL; the Iceland Tourist Board; the Editor of *Iceland Review*; the Chief Editor of Anders Nyborg A/S; the Embassy of Finland (London); Lantbruksstyrelsen (Jönköping); the Swedish Institute (Stockholm); the Royal Danish Embassy (London); Danish Agricultural Producers; the Nordic Council; the Swedish Forest Service; the Finnish Forestry Association; the Icelandic Ministry of Fisheries; the Icelandic Tourist Bureau (Reykjavik); Vattenfall (Sweden); Norsk Hydro A/S; Danfoss; Huhtamäki-Yhtyma AB; SKF (Göteborg); Serlachius OY (Mänttä); ASEA (Västerås);

Yhtyneet Paperitehtaat OY; OY Fiskars AB; Finncell; Atlas Copco (GB) Ltd; Volvo (Göteborg); Skanska Cementgjuteriet; Tandbergs Radiofabrikk A/S; Årdal og Sunndal Verk A/S; the Editor of *Sweden Now*; the Editor of *Danish Journal*; the Editor of *Denmark Review*; Copenhagen Handlesbank; Scandinaviska Enskilda Banken; Svenska Turistföreningen; the Central Association of Finnish Forest Industries; the Finnish Institute of International Affairs; the Swedish Natural Environment Protection Board; the Editor-in-Chief of *Look at Finland*; EFTA; the Finnish Foreign Trade Association; Naturgeografiska Institutionen and Kulturgeografiska Institutionen, Stockholm University; Dept of Maritime Studies, UW-IST, Cardiff; the Editor, *Faroes in Figures*; Faroese Tourist Information Office; Stockholm Information Service; Finnish Tourist Board.

Among the individuals who have kindly advised me and given freely of their time are Hans Holtedahl, Per-Erik Tonnell, Thorleifur Einarsson, Vibjorn Karlén, Sigurđur Thorarinsson, Aage Kampp, James Coull, Olav Orheim, Sigfus Jonsson, Robert Mednis, Gudmundur Karlsson, Bolli Kjartansson, David Sugden, Erling Lindström, Bo Strömberg, Leif Wastensson, Bill Mead, Joannes Rasmussen, Nini Svanholm, Gunnar Østrem, Björn Berglund and Joh. Ludv. Sollid.

Many of my visits to Scandinavia were organized from the Department of Geography at Durham University, and I am happy to acknowledge the generous help received at all times from Professor W. B. Fisher, my colleagues on the teaching staff, technical staff, research students and undergraduates. Various parts of this book are based on a course on Scandinavia which I taught for eleven years with my colleague Michael Alexander. Other parts are based on student project work and research projects in Iceland, the Faroes and Norway, and I thank the following in particular for allowing me to use their collected data and analyses: Michael Alexander, Eggert Larusson, Peter Rafferty, Geoff Clarke, Pat Copland, John Holme, Graham Butcher, Philip Ogden, Steve Benson, Bernard Mitchell, Andy Wood and David Hollington.

Many others have provided me with information, hospitality and help during my travels in Scandinavia; and I offer all of them my grateful thanks. My studies of the countries dealt with in this book have been coloured by my friendly contacts at all sorts of different levels. My incomplete and very personal impressions of the personality of Scandinavia have been shaped by conversations with friends as much as by sights and scenes, and I hope that those who know Scandinavia far better than I will enjoy this very personal geography.

Finally I thank my wife Inger, who has done more than anyone else to awaken and cultivate my interest in Scandinavia. She has provided endless encouragement and has put up with the traumas of research-writing, proof-reading and indexing with only a few complaints! She has also helped with typing, proof correction and many other essential tasks, and has corrected many errors in her readings of the text.

Brian John
September 1982

We are grateful to the following for permission to reproduce copyright material in the form of maps and diagrams: National Gallery, Oslo, for Fig. 2.4; W. R. Mead for Fig. 2.5, Fig. 12.5, and Fig. 16.1; J. Gjessing for Fig. 3.4; H. Holtedahl for Fig. 4.3; T. Einarsson for Fig. 4.8; R. Millward for Fig. 5.2; J. W. Cappelens Forlag for Fig. 5.4, Fig. 6.6 and Fig. 8.1; Nordic Statistical Secretariat for Fig. 8.5, Fig. 8.11, Fig. 17.4 and Fig. 22.3; Nordel for Fig. 9.4; Skandinaviska Enskilda Banken for Fig. 10.1; United Paper Mills for Fig. 10.5; Swedish Council for Building Research for Fig. 11.1; Willy Breinholst for Fig. 12.1 and Fig. 22.1; Longman Group Ltd for Fig. 12.7; Royal Swedish Ministry of Foreign Affairs for Fig. 14.4, Fig. 14.6 and Fig. 16.3; E. Ödmann for Fig. 15.2; International Federation for Housing and Planning for Fig. 16.4; Royal Danish Geographical Society for Fig. 22.4.

Most of the illustrations not listed above are the copyright property of the author. *However, we have been unable to trace the copyright owners of a number of other illustrations, and we take this opportunity to apologise to any copyright holders whose rights we may unwittingly have infringed.*

Preface

Scandinavia: a new geography started to take shape in my mind over
a decade ago when I was involved in the teaching of a regional
geography course on Northern Europe at the University of
Durham. During the 1960s and 1970s I visited Scandinavia on many
occasions, learning to know Norway and Sweden particularly well
and culminating in a year as a Royal Society European Fellow at the
University of Stockholm in 1973–74. Visits to Finland, Denmark
and the Faroe Islands followed, and Iceland became a regular summer base during the years 1973–77. The personality of Scandinavia
has been imprinted on my consciousness, and its spirit has pervaded
me in a way that defies scientific explanation. This book is one consequence of my Scandinavian obsession; other consequences include a Swedish wife, an inordinate affection for a small patch of
land on the coast of a small Swedish island, and a strange longing for
a remote and barren basalt peninsula in the north-west of Iceland.
My personal view of Scandinavia is full of passions and prejudices,
subjective assessments and value judgements. If you, the reader,
feel that such things have no place in modern geography, you may
find this book subversive. If you feel that geography is a subject
which seeks explanatory statements which are as universal as possible, and that true explanation can only be achieved through scientific methodology, you may find the book reactionary. However, I
ask you to accept that this is an *honest* book. It is a book which
represents geography as I see it, incorporating a multitude of internal contradictions and structural weaknesses and yet imbued with a
fatal fascination for those who must ask questions about the face of
the earth. My version of Scandinavian geography contains no reaction against the status quo, and neither does it represent an attempt
to be 'radical'. Rather, it is a forward-looking affirmation of a set of
values which are going to demand more and more attention from
geographers during the remainder of this century. Of these values,
more in a moment.

The organization of the book

The book is organized into five parts, which deal in turn with the

Scandinavian environment (physical and cultural); spatial express-
sions of human economy; regional inequalities; local landscapes and
sample studies; and unity and stress. There are no chapters specifically devoted to individual countries, although certain countries
feature large in the sections of the text which deal with historical,
social and economic topics. For example, Chapter 7, on the theme
of 'The Viking tradition today', is concerned almost entirely with
the cultural geography of the Faroe Islands because this seems to
me to be completely appropriate. Similarly Chapter 9, on 'Mineral
resources and their exploitation', is concerned largely with case studies from Sweden and Norway. The book begins with a brief introduction to the philosophy of regional geography and a brief analysis
of the region's geographical setting. In the 'meat' of the text much
prominence is given to geology and geomorphology. There are two
reasons for this. In the first place, the basis of the physical landscape
is, to my mind, very inadequately treated in other texts on Scandinavian geography, and something more substantial is required at
the present time if the territory of regional geography is not to
appear as if inhabited by human geographers alone. In the second
place, as a geomorphologist myself, I believe I have something original to offer in this field, and Chapters 3 and 4 contain a great deal
of material previously unpublished in a regional geography text.

In Part I of the book I have also placed considerable stress on the
cultural environment, interpreting this term in the 'humanistic' and
even spiritual way which is proving increasingly attractive to geographers. Part II, which is the longest part of the book, deals with the
human geographer's familiar ground. The terminology is familiar
and many of the concepts considered are well tried and tested.
Primary, secondary and tertiary economic activities all demand, and
are given, separate treatment. I have tried to give a reasonably
strong emphasis to the service sector, which seldom features in regional geography texts, and arising from this I include three chapters on the impact of the urban-industrial mentality on patterns of
living. Rural settlements, urban settlements, and the modern hybrid
recreational settlements are all affected by the priorities of the individual in his or her choice of work, in capital and property acquisi-
tion, in the choice of lifestyles, and in the stresses and strains associated with bureaucracy and personal mobility. In Chapters 12, 13
and 14 there is an examination of the difficulties experienced by
national governments and local government authorities in determin-
ing the 'best' course of action either in the countryside or in the city.
Words like 'pollution', 'protection' and 'conservation' must figure
largely in this debate.

The topic of actual and potential conflict between national and
community interests is extended into the third part of the book. In
Chapters 15, 16 and 17 I examine regional inequalities, looking at
the shifting priorities and loyalties of individuals, corporations,
communities and national governments to territories which they

perceive as over-endowed or deprived, remote or familiar, politically important or politically expendable. In considering concepts such as heartland and core, periphery and transitional zone, pioneer fringe and frontier, value judgements abound, and the reader will recognize that the term 'territorial value' has so many different meanings that geographers, just like economists and politicians, have found solutions to the problem of regional inequality almost impossible.

Part IV of the book consists of four brief sample studies. These are, quite deliberately, on a small scale, and they are based partly upon the work of research students or undergraduate groups undertaking field projects. The sample studies are, inevitably, variable in their style of approach and their degree of sophistication. The study of Vestfirðir (Ch. 20) is relatively broad-based, dealing with the social and economic difficulties facing a remote province of Iceland. The study of Rödlöga Skärgård in Sweden (Ch. 18) is on a much smaller scale, dealing with a single archipelago community facing up to the problem of an obsolete lifestyle and a tourist take-over. All four of the sample studies are rural and all of them are from marginal areas; these are the areas which seem to hold the greatest fascination for students, and they are easier to understand than urban areas or 'metropolitan farming areas' where people have less and less control over their own destinies in the face of national planning regulations, centralized finance and remote decision-making in all fields of economic activity.

The final part of the book (Part V) deals with some of the characteristics of life in Scandinavia which arise from cooperation and competition between those states which see themselves as parts of the Nordic world. There is an examination of the cooperative institutions which have been established, and of the complicated web of relationships – at many different levels – which binds the Scandinavian peoples together. There is also a look at the sources of stress which undoubtedly exist, especially in such matters as military strategy, political sovereignty and economic affairs.

It is not expected that anyone will wish to read this book as they would a novel, from cover to cover. It is, above all else, a student textbook, and as in all student texts there must be a clear separation of topics and a grouping of related themes. While I have attempted to give the book a strong individuality I have resisted the temptation to make it a product of author's self-indulgence. The user of the book should be able to find those parts of the text which are required reading by referring to the contents list. As far as possible, the five Parts of the book, and their constituent chapters, stand on their own merits and should be comprehensible to the reader who is simply 'dipping' into the book. For more detailed research I have included a comprehensive index, and I hope that teachers and students will get into the habit of using this in a constructive way in their attempts to understand the intriguing personality of Scandinavia.

Small is valid

After writing this book I felt that I had still not properly identified the philosophical undercurrent which had carried me from beginning to end. True, the book had been carefully planned, meticulously researched and painstakingly written. At the outset I had decided to attempt a portrayal of the landscapes of Scandinavia and to capture something of the personality of landscapes and communities at a variety of different scales. The twenty-three chapters were written with a number of very specific and recurring themes in mind: environment and culture, resource evaluation and economic activities, patterns of living, and regional inequalities. A glance through the contents list will show that the book, like most other regional or human geography texts, is concerned with geographical or spatial relationships, problems of scale, interactions and hierarchies, relative location and spatial diffusion, land use and rural/urban relationships, decision-making and state intervention, and so forth. Inevitably the centre of attention is Scandinavia and its component parts, but the reader might be excused for wondering, as in other regional geography texts, whether this large region is simply being used as a convenient laboratory for the testing of an assortment of modern and trendy hypotheses from the field of human geography.

Some of the sections of the book as it stands have been well treated in other texts; others have not. This book is no encyclopaedic reference work, and other texts will be easier to use for those who wish to concentrate their minds on the geography of specific states. That this is a 'new' geography cannot be doubted, for it is certainly very different from the other Scandinavian geography texts on the market. But what is its *raison d'être*, and where does its message lie?

On considering the comments of the many friends who have read parts of the manuscript prior to publication, I realized, quite suddenly, that many of them have looked at the book from a standpoint which typifies not only modern geographical thought but also the prevailing thought patterns of our urban-industrial world as a whole. In the first place, a number of friends have criticized the *balance* of the book, arguing that it places a very great emphasis on areas known to me personally (for example, the Swedish east coast, Copenhagen, the Faroes, N.W. Iceland and the Norwegian fjord country) to the exclusion of detailed studies from other areas which have greater 'relevance'. Secondly, some have argued that there is too much geology and geomorphology in the book and not enough historical geography or cultural geography or urban geography. Thirdly, some have said that there is too much emphasis in the text on rural matters and too little on the complexities of Scandinavian city regions and urban hierarchies. It is implied that the book is too folksy and too descriptive, and that it lacks a 'proper' content of scientific analysis. Fourthly, various colleagues have commented that the book concentrates unhealthily on the smallest-scale communities and landscapes which are, by implication, lacking in validity because they do not demonstrate universally applicable geographical laws.

This brings us to the crux of the problem. What is regional geography *for*? Is it simply a part of a scientific geography in which facts are sacred and opinions profane? Is it simply a field of study in which the new breed of scientific geographers, trained in the 1960s and 1970s, can go through the mechanical motions of scientific methodology? Must we *always*, as some would argue, keep in the forefront of our minds the need for hypothesis formulation, observation and description, classification, hypothesis-testing and so forth, and aim towards the ultimate construction of great and noble laws? Should we *always* be concerned with models of 'reality' and with the theory of scientific explanation? In their influential book called *Spatial Organization*, which grew out of the scientific euphoria of the 1960s, Ronald Abler, John Adams and Peter Gould undertook a careful study of the role of science in geography. They recognized that science is, and always was, a highly formalized and institutionalized ordering system, possessed of a formidable forward and upward momentum. The three authors referred to science as 'an outstandingly successful enterprise'; they claimed that it was essential if we were to answer the basic geographical question 'Why are spatial distributions structured the way they are?' They saw science as *the* way of explaining experience, predicting future events, calculating consequences, and manipulating space and spatial distributions. These were, so they thought, the geographer's greatest contributions to human welfare. Science, they said, would enable geographers to accelerate their output of useful knowledge about human spatial behaviour and its consequences, and they invested this activity with a high moral and social purpose. This was the philosophy of the New Geography. It was, perhaps, an inevitable product of the urban-industrial world in which we live – assertive, manipulative and masculine, devoted to the ideals of growth and progress, dedicated to the crude philosophy of environmental conquest and the management of personal and group behaviour. Is this the Brave New World of the modern generation of geographers? Clearly it is not, and in the writings of authors such as Yi Fu Tuan, Anne Buttimer and Jay Appleton we can discern an increasing concern for personal and spiritual values in geography.

My geography, which has evolved somewhat during the writing of this book, is based upon a set of values which may be unfamiliar in a regional geography context. It is based upon the related assumptions that subjectivity is as valid as that unattainable commodity called 'objectivity', that spiritual values have a place in geography, that a personal perception of the world is not the lowest thing on the scale of experience but the highest. In common with a growing number of academic geographers, I have little respect for the near-

sacred values of our urban-industrial society; and the vision of a
technocratic society (in which political authority, to an increasing
extent, is based upon a mystique of scientific expertise) fills me with
horror. Together with geographers like David Lowenthal and Anne
Buttimer, I am increasingly attracted by a geography which places
its emphasis on authenticity and personal experience – and on the
recognition and appreciation of personality. These words, by the
chemist Thomas Blackburn, sum up my feelings exactly:

> By replying lopsidedly on abstract quantification as a method of
> knowing, scientists have been looking at the world with one eye
> closed. There is other knowledge, and there are other ways of
> knowing besides reading the position of a pointer on a scale. The
> human mind and body process information with staggering
> sophistication and sensitivity by the direct sensuous experience of
> their surrounding (*Science*, 4 June 1971).

In his book *Person/Planet* the historian Theodore Roszak links
urban imperialism with a range of planetary ecological emergencies.
He is concerned about the fetish of bigness, the worship of the intel-
lect, and the pursuit of material growth. He writes of a world 'where
cities grow bigger and bigger and where urban intellectuals grow
smarter and smarter'. He writes of the urban exploitation of the
resources of the planet, and of urban naivety concerning 'the
rhythm of the seasons, the ways of the soil, the language of wild
things'. As solutions he sees the necessity for ecological sensitivity,
the recognition of the rural lifestyle as valid and even dignified, and
the rediscovery of small communities as the best guardians of
planetary health. In arguing against scientific reductionism, Roszak
frequently refers to the appropriate scale for human understanding,
but he argues that the choice before the present generation of students is not essentially a choice between big and small. It is, instead,
a choice between 'a society dominated by mystification and a society
open to self-discovery'. This thinking can be extended from the field
of personal psychology to the field of geography. Roszak looks to a
world 'less urbanized, less dominated by the compulsions of industrial productivity, more characterized by small-scaled localized operations, by personal and participative relationships in government
and the economy'. This is the world to which I subconsciously refer,
again and again, in the pages of this book. It is not an imaginary
world. It exists in people's minds, and it exists in many rural areas
which are conventionally described as 'rural' or 'marginal' or 'deprived'.

I did not discover Roszak's book until the text of my own book
was complete. But the way in which my writing echoes his thinking
will be obvious to the reader, particularly in the later chapters. To
my mind the most valuable part of my book is the postscript to the
final chapter, where the words of Jon Jonsson, Icelandic farmer and
sage, speak to us with the wonderful directness of his own *personal*
geography. I assume, therefore, that personal experiences and

personal judgements are valid, even if they are coloured by naivety and distorted by prejudice; I assume that small communities are no less worthy than large ones and that they are inherently much more interesting; I assume that the city region and the urban bias it produces are sources of regional inequality and community and personal stress; and I assume that national interests are often in conflict with, and even destructive of, the interests of the community and the individual. In short, I believe that *small is valid*. As a consequence of this belief, two articles of faith have been woven into the fabric of this book:

(a) rural life and small-scale communities are relevant and even vitally important subjects of geographical concern; and

(b) a geographical methodology which involves students and teachers in 'the direct sensuous experience of their surroundings' is more valid than a methodology based upon the accumulation and analysis of second-hand data.

These articles of faith are closely interrelated, even though one concerns philosophy and the other methodology. By keeping them in mind I hope that you, the reader, will enjoy this book. I make no apologies for the book's lack of science and lack of respect for some of the values of modern society. If you reach the end of the book feeling that you have gained some understanding of the personality of Scandinavia and some respect for its people, I shall be well satisfied.

Part I The Scandinavian environment

Chapter 1 Introduction: Regional geography guidelines

That branch of geography known as 'regional geography' has assumed a number of forms over the course of the past fifty years. However, geography texts about Scandinavia have varied only within surprisingly narrow limits with respect to both their contents and the philosophies adopted by their authors. Most of the standard English-language texts on Scandinavian regional geography employ a 'dual approach', in which part of the book is concerned with a systematic treatment of topics such as agriculture, fisheries, fuel and power, and transport at a Scandinavian scale, with the remainder devoted to more detailed studies of the individual nation states (Fig. 1.1). This is the approach used by A. C. O'Dell in his text *The Scandinavian World* and by R. Millward in his *Scandinavian Lands*. Other books, such as *Scandinavia* by B. Fullerton and A. F. Williams and *The Geography of Norden* edited by A. Sømme, have brief introductions to the physical, social and economic background of Scandinavia, with the greater part of each book devoted to national studies. F. J. Monkhouse, in his intermediate geography text called *The Countries of North-Western Europe*, devotes only 4 pages out of 527 to analysis and synthesis at a large or supra-national scale. This is not an unusual balance for a school geography text.

Two books stand out as radically different. W. R. Mead's *Economic Geography of the Scandinavian States and Finland* (1958) and his *Historical Geography of Scandinavia* (1981), both intended for a more advanced readership, adopt a broad approach; there are no chapters on individual countries, and the emphasis in both books is on the region as a whole. However, the author did not conceive of either book as a regional geography. When the *Economic Geography* first appeared in 1958 it was acclaimed for its novel and exciting approach to the geography of Scandinavia, and after twenty-five years it is still as stimulating and refreshing as ever. That this should be so is a credit to Mead's originality and foresight; but it is also a sad reflection upon the 'state of the art' as far as regional geography is concerned. While other branches of the subject have evolved at such a pace over the past twenty years that some of them are now hardly recognizable, regional geography has remained

3

Fig. 1.1 Map of the Scandinavian world, showing the five countries and two self-governing territories dealt with in this book.

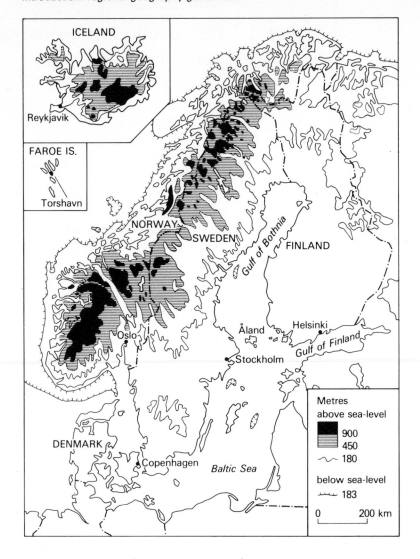

largely static. Somehow it has failed to attract its geographical philosophers, and somehow its texts have remained rooted in tradition.

This chapter examines some of the brands of regional geography on the market, some of the special difficulties which regional geography has to face, and some of the themes which this book treats as priorities.

Approaches to regional geography

What is the purpose or theme of regional geography? It is not enough to say that regional geography should be concerned with regions, for regions are all things to all men. In 1938 H. W. Odum and H. E. Moore collected together forty careful definitions of the word 'region', and there have been a multitude of published definitions since then. In my view the most satisfying definition is that of the Oxford geographer A. J. Herbertson: 'a complex of land, water, air, plants, animals and man regarded in their special relationships as together constituting a definite, characteristic portion of the earth's surface'. This definition was applied to the concept of the 'natural region', and while it has been criticized for not being anthropocentric enough, it demonstrates a certain ecological awareness which is entirely appropriate in this day and age. And yet, while there is no consensus on its meaning, the region undoubtedly exists as a focus of attention in academic geography. For the moment, it may be suggested that the much-debated 'problem' of regional geography is more apparent than real; it is not that it is difficult to recognize regions, but that it is difficult to define them.

A glance at the learned texts enables the reader to discern two major approaches to regional geography: (1) descriptive regional geography and (2) thematic regional geography. Clearly, these are neither all-embracing nor mutually exclusive, but they are worthy of brief examination.

Descriptive regional geography

Descriptive regional geography attempts to describe an area as completely as possible. Commonly, after an exercise in regional subdivision, a study of this type covers systematic topics under headings like structure, geology, landforms, climate, history, agriculture and communications. At its worst this approach is fact laden, educationally stultifying and concerned largely with half-digested trivia. At its best it can give a rational and orderly description of an area. The approach plays an important role if geography is regarded, following R. Hartshorne, as being concerned with *areal differentiation*; it is marked by its concern for the unique and the reasons for uniqueness. This approach to regional geography may be admirable as a classificatory tool but it does not necessarily help in the search for widely applicable principles of spatial arrangement. Hence it can be criticized on the grounds that it curtails the discovery and development of theoretical principles.

It is easy to recognize the inadequacies of descriptive regional geography, even if not all of it qualifies for the label of 'catalogue geography'. Also, it is all too easy to become cynical about the inadequacies of an approach that stresses the *need* for the delimitation of regions as an academic exercise. Although regions have to be devised and delimited at an applied (or planning) level, the process of regional delimitation for its own sake can become artificial and sterile. It must, therefore, be motivated by something more worthy than academic game-playing.

Thematic regional geography

Under this heading the following can be included:

(a) Regional geography in which the author highlights the links between man and physical environment (for example, Katherine Scherman's *Iceland – daughter of fire* or Ogrizek's *Scandinavia*).

(b) Regional geography in which the author selects the local theme which seems most relevant to his particular region (for example, agricultural development, industrial growth or rural depopulation). The book *Winter in Finland*, by W. R. Mead and H. Smeds, is an example.

(c) Regional geography in which a selected theme of geographical importance is examined at regional level (for example, overpopulation, racial conflicts or the distribution of wealth). T. Miljan's *The Reluctant Europeans* is an example.

(d) Regional geography in which individual systems (for example, conurbations or hydrological systems) are compared and contrasted with the aid of specific regional case studies. A good example is *Urbanization in Sweden* by E. Ödmann and G.-B. Dahlberg.

Thematic regional geography has the attraction of being interesting, contemporary and, at first sight, satisfying. However, it is open to three fundamental criticisms from the point of view of the geographer. First, the themes require subjective choice and the deliberate rejection of large volumes of data which may be deemed by the author (but not necessarily by anybody else) to be irrelevant. Second, the approach has no recognizable methodology. Third, and most serious, a thematic regional geography may not turn out to be geography at all, but sociology, or demography, or economics, with example from the chosen region. All of the above-mentioned books are fascinating to read, but are they *geography books*? The reason for this dilemma is that there may be nothing inherently spatial in a theme or a problem; it is all to easy for an author to be diverted into a consideration of a problem *per se* and to encroach on another discipline. Again, therefore, the geographer may be depressed by the inadequacies of thematic regional geographies which may be novel for novelty's sake and which may fail completely to help him in his attempts to understand regions or regionalism.

Now it is easy to criticize, and it is acknowledged that most regional geography authors have, deliberately and conscientiously, been attempting to formulate a regional geography 'recipe' which will be interesting, stimulating, intellectually satisfying, and at the same time reliable and well balance. And clearly it is no bad thing that there should be a variety of recipes at the student's disposal.

In the influential early writings of the sometime 'geographical theoretician' W. Bunge, he states that in his view regional geography should be relegated to a classificatory role and used mainly for the storage of facts which can be studied by the systematic branches of geography; it thus becomes no more than a data bank or a field laboratory for specialists. But this would be to side-step geography's central concern, namely the *search for order in the complex interaction of numerous functioning and relict systems which go to make up reality on the surface of the earth.* What is needed, according to P. Haggett, is a rigorous, spatial method of analysing areas. He argues, with the global ecologists, that the phenomena on the earth's surface comprise one complex system with interactions between every component. A rigorous analysis of the spatial components of the system (points, lines and areas) and their functional relationships could, it is suggested, form the basis for a regional study. To put it another way, this could be referred to as a study of the systematics of regional location. A new regional study of Scandinavia could have such headings as movements, networks, nodes, hierarchies, and surfaces. This would perhaps be novel and stimulating, but there is a suspicion that it might prove overwhelmingly difficult to cope with in practice. More serious is the suspicion that the preoccupation with *location* inherent in this approach would lead to the neglect of geography's traditional and more valid concerns with landscape and with people/place relationships.

The search for regionalism

Another possibility is worth discussing. Should regional geography be about regionalism rather than regions? The implication here is that there should be a shift of emphasis from the concrete world of hard fact and solid lines to the abstract world of regional consciousness. Is this feasible? Undoubtedly it is, although in any reliable regional geography the presentation, examination and classification of relevant data must according to tradition precede the processes of synthesis and wide-ranging analysis. This must mean that regions still have to be identified and studied during our attempts to understand the concept of regionalism. Perhaps regionalism is best understood by making sure that any exercise in regional geography has two parallel objectives:

(a) an examination of the interactions which exist between temporal process and spatial form, as suggested by P. Haggett and other modern geographers; and

(b) a recognition of 'personality' or 'character' in regions, as suggested by E. W. Gilbert and other geographers who are often thought of as romantics or traditionalists.

These objectives can be considered in turn. Under (a) it may be suggested that the examination of *temporal process* involves a close look at the variations in process which affect landscape evolution

(a)

(b)

Fig. 1.2 (a), (b) Artistic impressions of Scandinavia. These demonstrate the artist's preoccupation not only with the portrayal of landscape but also the recognition and portrayal of regional personality or character. The artist not only sees landscape; he also *experiences* landscape with all his senses and attempts to transfer this experience to the canvas in a way which will evoke an emotional response in the viewer. Great landscape photography achieves a similar effect. (Photos: National Gallery, Oslo and the Göteborg Art Gallery)

through time, historic or prehistoric. When *spatial form* is examined the foci are areal distributions and linkages, which in turn provide us with information on spatial *structure*. Landforms and landscapes, both natural and man-made, have to come under close scrutiny. This all involved a study of the surface of the earth, seen in terms of structures and processes. In many cases there is no obvious relationship between observed structures and measured processes; hence the observer may be dealing either with processes which have ceased functioning, or with relict structures. Or both. If there is a readily apparent relationship between present process and present structure, then the observer may be justified in asking 'What *stage* has the interaction reached?' This leads to a statement which will come as no great surprise to a historical geographer; namely, that *process and structure can only be correctly interpreted if both are set in the dimension of time*. This statement is beautifully illustrated in W. R. Mead's *Historical Geography of Scandinavia*, in which the author examines the Scandinavian scene and its formative influences at six different 'cross-sections through time'. Perhaps the great god of regional geography should not be the definable region, but a holy trinity of regional structure, process and stage. In all this the geomorphologist will notice more than a hint of the ideas of W. M. Davis.

In studies of structures, processes and stages it will be readily acknowledged that scientific techniques can be employed with advantage. The geographer can make maps; he can measure and record accurately; he can describe mathematically and analyse statistically; he can argue on the basis of his accumulated evidence; he can reach rational conclusions. In his examinations of interactions he is making use of techniques, both mechanical and intellectual, which appeal to his scientific inclinations. Some geographers are, of course, more inclined than others; some, over the last two decades, have been known to lean over backwards. But whatever his degree of tilt, the geographer must ensure that he does not get involved in the futile and tortuous exercise of 'drawing lines that do not matter around regions that do not exist'. This is difficult enough to do even when standing upright. There is a need to look beyond the limits of the region to the *principles of regionalism*. In part this involves the search for order; more specifically, it involves the search for widely applicable principles of spatial and temporal arrangement.

The recognition of regional personality as a geographical goal is less fashionable. In his attempts to recognize personality or character in a region the geographer is attempting to define the indefinable, to recognize regional distinctiveness, to find regional idiosyncrasy. To a certain extent he is, with R. Hartshorne and others, engaged in a search for *uniqueness*, although he should be careful that this search does not become the sole objective of his regional geography. In the pursuit of regional personality, techniques are used which are difficult to define scientifically. Personality is experienced rather than measured, and the methods of recognizing personality are essentially artistic rather than scientific. These methods arise out of man's *emotional involvement with landscape* (Fig. 1.2).

If regional geography concerns itself on the one hand with the interactions which exist between temporal process and spatial form, and on the other hand with the recognition of regional personality, it seems that it can provide a link between the geographer's own scientific and artistic inclinations. It *can* be deeply satisfying, for this very reason. More often, however, it is neither deep nor satisfying. This is a sad commentary on the methods normally employed in the writing and teaching of regional geography.

On the appreciation of scale

Scale is one of the traditional preoccupations of the geographer. Certain scales are more meaningful than others, and the somewhat mysterious satellite imagery of the earth is far less easy to comprehend than the imagery of 'conventional' aerial photography. At the very large scale (i.e. where the level of resolution is high) the geographer may be concerned with the nature of gravel particles or the specific characteristics of a tuft of grass. At the very small scale (i.e. where the level of resolution is low) the focus of concern may be the moon as a planet, or the Milky Way. But the geographer tends not to be entirely happy with either of these levels of resolution. To quote from D. Harvey (*Explanation in Geography*: 484): 'the geographer tends to filter out small-scale variation and large-scale variation and to concentrate his attention upon systems of individuals which have meaning at a regional scale of resolution.' This regional level of resolution can be thought to lie approximately midway between the very high and the very low.

Hence it can be assumed that *the geographer has a natural preference for the regional viewpoint*. This is not because he happens to be a geographer, but because he is a human being. Most humans have a medium-scale range of experience; most are frustrated by areas which are too small and intimidated by areas which are too large. It was not always so. Some of the fathers of geography (for example, A. von Humboldt, A. J. Herbertson and H. Mackinder) were capable of a global view; they saw the world as a whole at a time when academics could, with some safety, leap across inter-disciplinary boundaries and scatter generalizations which could be picked up and chewed over by succeeding generations. Times have changed, and the volume of geographical data now available is so great that no geographer can hope to grasp more than a small proportion of it.

Fig. 1.3 The Norwegian city of Bergen, viewed at two different levels of resolution: (a) part of the old commercial district at Bryggen; (b) an oblique air photograph of Bergen. (Photos = author (a) and Widerøés (b))

(a)

(b)

It follows from all this that *what is seen in the landscape varies according to the level of resolution employed* (Fig. 1.3). At a high level of resolution the geographer may be preoccupied with the description and interpretation of a drumlin or a suburban shopping centre. As the level of resolution is lowered these features become individually indiscernible and his attention is attracted by a whole zone of glacial depositional landforms or by a whole conurbation of which these elements form a part. As the level of resolution is lowered even further a viewpoint is obtained which enables only the first-order features of the earth's surface to be discerned: the continents and the oceans.

For many years geographers have been recognizing the distinctions between regions of different dimensions. There are many hierarchies of regions in the literature, and geographers have coined the terms macro-region, region and micro-region. If quantitative measures are applied the geographer can use much more closely defined hierarchies. It can be suggested that the activities of man are only worthy of investigation at a specific level in the hierarchy of regions. The description of man-made forms and structures has little relevance either at the highest or the lowest levels of resolution. *It is only at the regional scale that the geographer's attention is attracted by the manifestations of man's occupation of the earth*: his roads, his cities, his forest clearances, his mosaics of cultivation. Thus, since geographers are concerned above all with what they can see in the landscape, it is especially at the middle level of resolution that the elements of the 'cultural landscape' must be considered. But man and his spatial organization must not occupy a disproportionate amount of the geographer's time, for at certain scales the features of the natural landscape are of far greater importance than the cultural.

The argument can be pursued further. Almost inevitably *the processes operating upon the landscape will assume varying importance according to the level of resolution employed*. At a high level of resolution the geographer may be preoccupied with erosion by raindrops. Lower down the scale this process will not be discernible, but the observer will note the effects of runoff concentration in rills and gullies. Lower still, and well into the 'regional' scale of resolution, the processes associated with rivers and river systems demand attention. Again, at this scale it is essential to consider the role of *man as an agent* in landscape modification. By the time the observer looks at the earth from an altitude of, say, 2,000 km, he sees no rivers and no river systems; he sees only continents and oceans, and it could be claimed with some validity that the only processes worth considering at this very low level of resolution are those connected with continental drift and sea-floor spreading.

Finally, the argument can be extended into the dimension of *time*. At the largest scale, short-term variations in process over time are of tremendous significance. A pit formed by a falling raindrop in a fraction of a second may be obliterated by the debris from another raindrop pit only a fraction of a second later. Both the creation and the destruction of a surface form may be observed within the time-span of a second. Conversely, at the smallest scale, millennia or even geological eras will be the only time units with any meaning. For example, a continental land-mass may be ravaged by a succession of earthquakes, cyclones, volcanic eruptions, meteorite impacts and civil wars and will show little, if any, trace of these events when seen at a sufficiently low level of resolution. But at the intermediate or regional level of resolution these processes, measurable in days, weeks or years, will assume great significance, and it will be possible to conceive of their effects in terms of a readily appreciated time-scale. In short, these effects can be thought of in terms of *stage*, with some areas more drastically affected than others if they have been affected by the relevant process over a greater length of time.

Regional guidelines

The thoughts outlined on the foregoing pages are too briefly argued to point a convincing 'new direction' for regional geography. This is not the place for the pursuit of such an ideal. However, this brief introduction is intended to provide a number of useful guidelines and to isolate a number of meaningful themes for regional geography. These themes are used implicitly and explicitly in the chapters which follow, although it is of course just as difficult as ever to achieve a fully integrated and coherent approach to the geography of a region as large and as complex as Scandinavia. To summarize:

1. Self-evidently, descriptive regional geography is too preoccupied with descriptions and regional delimitation. Thematic regional geography is too preoccupied with themes. It is therefore wisest to hold in mind the concept of regionalism but to forget about the delimitation of regions as a prime objective of regional geography.
2. Regional geography should have as parallel objectives: (a) the study of interactions between process and form, seen in terms of both time and space; and (b) the recognition of regional personality. The former objective must be pursued via scientific means, and the latter via artistic means.
3. The importance of scale must always be borne in mind in studies of regional geography. Interest and enthusiasm can be maintained through constant shifts of scale. Geographers should be involved in a search for the principles which underlie the spatial organization of regions seen at different levels of resolution. These principles are most easily discerned at the micro-regional scale, and a strong emphasis on local sample studies is entirely justified.

Another potential 'unifying hypothesis' for regional geography is that landscapes reflect accurately the amount of energy (both natural and human) expended in their formation. Again, it could be argued that the the traditional 'reductionist' scientific methodology (data collection → synthesis → generalization) should be turned upside down as an aid to simplification and understanding; this is another regional hypothesis for future debate. But these are hypotheses for others to play with. As outlined in the Preface, this book is a product neither of geography's 'quantitative revolution' nor of its more recent concern with social relevance. It is, rather, written out of a concern for global ecology and for the self-esteem of small communities; it is a book about the relationships of people and landscapes and about the appreciation of 'geographical personality'.

Suggested reading

Regional geography

Abler, Adams and Gould 1972; Bunge 1962; Buttimer and Seamon 1980; Davis 1909; Dickinson 1976; English and Mayfield 1972; Eyles and Smith 1978; Eyre and Jones 1966; Gale and Olsson 1979; Gregory 1978a; Hartshorne 1960; Herbertson 1905; Jacobsen 1976; Johnston 1978, 1979; Minshull 1967; Relph 1981; Robinson 1953; Roszak 1981; Turnock 1967; Whittlesey 1954.

Regional personality

Anderson 1954; Appleton 1975, 1979; Connery 1966; Gilbert 1960; Hirn 1970; Linden and Weyer 1974; Lowenthal and Prince 1965; Mead 1958, 1981; Nyquist 1977; Ogrizek 1952; Pocock 1981; Sauer 1963; Simpson 1966; Voksø 1980, 1966; Spate 1966; Tuan, Yi-Fu 1974, 1980.

NB Full details for further reading at the ends of chapters are given in the consolidated bibliography at the end of the book pp. 345–358)

Chapter 2 Scandinavia and its geographical setting

Scandinavia, the fundamental regional unit of north-west Europe, has proved over the years to be notoriously difficult to define. It was first referred to by the Roman Pliny about the year AD 70 and it was later spelt variously *Scatinavia*, *Scadinavia* and *Scandia*. Originally it was used as a name for the Danish archipelago and southern Sweden; only later did the corrupted term *Scandinavia* become used for the wider region enclosing the Baltic Sea. While the compound word *Scadinavia* is generally accepted as being of Nordic origin, there is no agreement as to its precise meaning. The most likely explanation of the name is that it comes from the two words *scatin* (meaning 'darkness, shade, fog') and *aujo* (old Norse for 'island'). Hence *Scatinavia* is interpreted as 'island of fog' or 'island of darkness'. This is quite reasonable in view of the region's northerly latitude and its oceanic west-coast climate, and in view of the fact that the Northlands were always assumed by the ancient writers to be insular in nature. Not until the sixteenth century was it widely appreciated that there was a Scandinavian *peninsula* (Fig. 2.1).

According to F. Isachsen, the name *Scandinavia* should strictly be used only for the three countries Denmark, Norway and Sweden taken together. More particularly, Norway and Sweden together should be designated the Scandinavian peninsula. There is, however, no consensus among English-language authors about the extent of Scandinavia. A. C. O'Dell includes not only the three 'true' Scandinavian states but also Finland, the Faroe Islands, Iceland and Greenland. R. Millward includes only Denmark, Norway, Sweden and Finland in his book, as do B. Fullerton and A. Williams in theirs. The latter authors, however, include a few words on the Faroe Islands and Svalbard. W. R. Mead includes Iceland and Finland in his 1958 book, but argues that Finland is not culturally a part of Scandinavia; hence his title *An Economic Geography of the Scandinavian States and Finland*. On the other hand in his book *Scandinavia*, written with Wendy Hall, he *does* include Finland in Scandinavia, and the same is true in his recent *Historical Geography of Scandinavia*. In *The Geography of Norden*, written entirely by Scandinavian authors, Iceland and Finland are discussed

Fig. 2.1 A view of the Scandinavian world during the sixteenth century. By this time it was realized that there was no connection between the Baltic Sea and the Arctic Ocean, although many maps continued to show an archipelago or a group of peninsulas with large inland seas instead of the main Scandinavian peninsula.

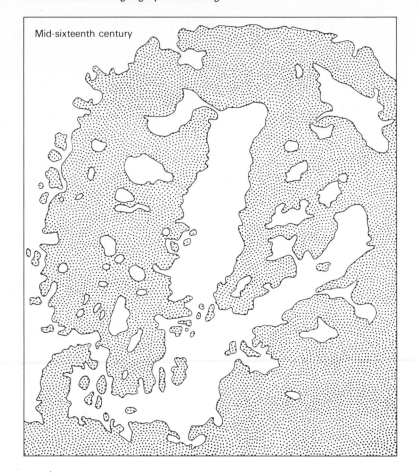

Mid-sixteenth century

alongside Denmark, Norway and Sweden, and there are also brief sections on the Faroe Islands, Åland, Svalbard and Greenland. However, the title of the book is significant, for the authors and editor use the comprehensive label *Norden* (meaning simply 'the North'), which is now widely used in academic circles within the countries concerned.

Would it not therefore be more appropriate to use the term 'Norden' in the title of this book? The countries of Norden have strong cultural ties and a shared history; they have many common points of concern in matters of economics, social policy and politics; and in recent decades they have cooperated closely in the field of international affairs. On the other hand the term 'Norden' is no signpost to geographical uniformity or unity. Finland and Greenland do not share the cultural heritage of the other countries, and both may be claimed (not least by their own people) to be racially distinct also. The racial origins of the Finns can be traced to south-central Russia, and they have relatives in the Soviet Baltic republics. Their language belongs to the Finno-Ugrian group and sounds quite different from the other Scandinavian tongues. The Greenlanders rejoice in the fact that theirs is an Arctic territory, and that their culture has more in common with the Eskimo or Inuit cultures of Canada and Alaska than with Denmark. Again, the Arctic territory of Svalbard has little in common with the Scandinavian mainland although it has political links with Norway.

In spite of the fact that the term 'Norden' is now widely used within the five countries concerned, it is not entirely acceptable from the point of view of an English-speaking readership. W. R. Mead considers the term to be both artificial and ambiguous – artificial because it was invented for the purpose of demonstrating the cultural unity of the northern lands, and ambiguous because 'The North' is no more accurate as a geographical label than 'The South'. While the adjective 'Nordic' may be useful in linguistic and literary studies, it is still linked in many minds with the crude racial theory and the politics of superiority of the Second World War. The term 'Scandinavia' is sufficiently flexible and sufficiently well known to outsiders to continue in use.

Another useful term which is commonly encountered in the Scandinavian literature is *Fennoscandia*. This was coined as a geographical term by W. Ramsay, a Finnish geologist, in 1898. Later it became popular with geologists when referring to the north European area of crystalline Pre-Cambrian rocks (Fig. 2.2), and it is still thought of basically as a *geological* label. Some geologists used the term extensively for the area where the rocks of the Baltic Shield outcrop at the surface, while others included in Fennoscandia the Caledonian Mountains of Norway and Sweden and the areas where the Shield rocks are deeply buried by later sedimentary deposits in Denmark and Skåne. Some geologists included the Pre-Cambrian outcrops of north-western USSR, while others excluded them. Others used the terms 'Scandofennia' and 'Baltoscandia' instead, thereby compounding the confusion.

In this book the term *Fennoscandia* is used extensively. It refers, in the author's mind, specifically to the four Scandinavian states located on and around the peninsula, based upon the Baltic Shield, and having a direct interest in the Baltic Sea and its outlet. These states are Finland, Sweden, Norway and Denmark. The region also includes Åland, which is a near-autonomous province of Finland. Besides their historical, cultural and political links these countries are related geologically and also from the point of view of landscape. Although the basement rocks of Fennoscandia are immensely old, many of its landscapes are geologically young, having been created during the last few hundred thousand years. The ice of the Scandinavian ice sheet has affected the region on several occasions during the present Ice Age; landscapes have been deeply eroded by glacier ice in the uplands, and in the lowlands there are thick accumulations of glacial drift. There are similarities in soils, climate and vegetation. And each country has experienced the effects of isostatic depression and uplift as a consequence of the

Fig. 2.2 The main structural units of Fennoscandia. The feature which gives the region its coherence is the Baltic Shield, an extensive and stable 'craton' of Pre-Cambrian rocks.

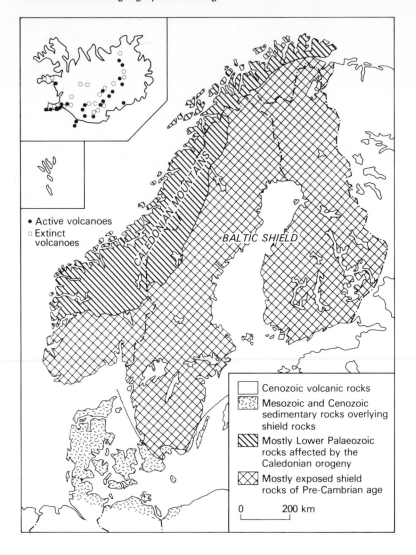

• Active volcanoes
○ Extinct volcanoes

CALEDONIAN MOUNTAINS

BALTIC SHIELD

☐ Cenozoic volcanic rocks

▨ Mesozoic and Cenozoic sedimentary rocks overlying shield rocks

▧ Mostly Lower Palaeozoic rocks affected by the Caledonian orogeny

▩ Mostly exposed shield rocks of Pre-Cambrian age

0   200 km

crustal load exerted by the Pleistocene ice sheets. According to F. Isachsen, the 'marine' sedimentary lowlands of Late-glacial and Holocene age are of fundamental importance not only in terms of the Fennoscandian landscape but also in their effects upon human geography. And this is what A. C. O'Dell writes about the significance of the Pleistocene legacy: 'The presence of rock-basin lakes, morainic drift, thin soils, over-deepened valleys and kindred phenomena of a glaciated terrain profoundly affect the ways of life and the outlook of a people living within such an environment.' Undoubtedly the term 'Fennoscandia' deserves to be used from a geographical as well as a geological point of view; in this book it is used as it was almost a century ago, for an easily comprehended geographical region, even if it is somewhat ill-defined.

One part of Scandinavia which is especially difficult to define is

Lapland, that mysterious northern territory which has no frontiers of its own but which exists in the minds and souls of those who live there. It includes parts of the provinces of Troms and Finnmark in Norway, Norrbotten in Sweden and Lappi in Finland, and it extends eastwards into Murmansk Oblast in the USSR. The Lapps (or *Sami*, as they call themselves) number less than 50,000, which is less than 5 per cent of the population of the northern provinces, and yet they have a sense of place and sense of territorial freedom which are difficult to accommodate within the concepts of the nation-state and the sovereign territory. Lapland is looked at in more detail in Chapter 17.

To summarize, the term 'Scandinavia' is used throughout this book with respect to the five countries of Finland, Sweden, Norway, Denmark and Iceland. It also includes the two self-governing dependencies of the Faroes and Åland. Greenland, Svalbard and Jan Mayen are excluded, in spite of the fact that they are conventionally included in Norden, for even though they have political links with Denmark and Norway they belong physically to the polar world. (It will be apparent that in the mind of the present author the terms 'Scandinavia' and 'Norden' are not interchangeable.) The five independent states dealt with in the chapters which follow do, of course, have a wide range of environments and landscapes, and large differences are apparent when one compares the Atlantic islands of Iceland and the Faroes with the states which are anchored to the mainland of Europe. However, in spite of these physical differences, both Iceland and the Faroes are firmly wedded to Fennoscandia from a cultural point of view, and their ancient languages and many surviving traditions are reminders that they have cherished their Viking heritage even more proudly and more carefully than the four mainland states. Isolation has been partly responsible for this; but it would also be true to say that small nation-states, vulnerable as they are to the influences of the outside world, protect their cultural identity more energetically than large states which may have long histories of trading and other contacts with adjacent countries.

The setting

The geographical setting and physical environment of Scandinavia can be conveniently studied under three main headings. The remainder of this chapter is concerned with matters of location and with land–sea relationships. The next two chapters deal with landscape and its evolution through time, and especially with the influence of past processes upon the features of today. Chapter 5 deals with the present-day climatic environment and its relations with soils and vegetation. These chapters, taken together, should provide the reader with some appreciation of the 'natural landscape' – the face of the land as it might appear without the influence of man. They should also help the reader to assess the extent to which the natural environment has shaped the destiny of the Scandinavian peoples.

There is no attempt to preach old-fashioned 'geographical determinism' in this book, but most authors who have written on Scandinavia have remarked upon its remote location, upon the harshness of its environment, upon the stimulus (or the stress) felt by the Scandinavian peoples particularly during the long winter season, and upon the links between natural environments and national temperaments. These themes are examined again in Chapters 8, 14, 16 and 17, but at this stage it is worth recalling the concept of 'environmentalism'. According to this concept, human activities are directed and conditioned but not actually determined by location and environment. With their access to modern technology and abundant capital, humans can undertake virtually any activity they wish in virtually any setting. Tomatoes can be grown at the South Pole; lakes can be created in deserts; and mountains can be literally removed if they happen to be made of iron ore or some other valuable mineral. The Scandinavians have the technology and the capital to undertake large-scale alterations of the environment if they so wish; but environmental controls dictate that many activities which may strictly be *possible* are in fact *uneconomic* or *environmentally undesirable*. For example, the small returns from various types of farming activity in marginal areas such as the Norwegian uplands or the interior desert of Iceland, cannot justify the great investment of capital and time required to initiate and maintain them. In terms of the concept of environmentalism, *the environment presents a range of opportunities and constraints which vary according to the level of technology and degree of motivation.* The greater human technological skill, the greater the range of opportunities. But the Scandinavians have learnt over the centuries to respect the constraints of their environment, and they have acquired a degree of sensitivity in environmental management which will become apparent in later chapters of this book. The respect felt by the Scandinavians for the art and science of ecology is entirely in accord with the sentiments expressed in the Preface. The three chapters which follow should not be interpreted as the basis of a crude determinism; they should be seen instead as a prerequisite to the proper study of the relationships between people and place.

Where is Scandinavia?

In the global context, Scandinavia occupies the Atlantic fringe of

Fig. 2.3 The winter freeze in the Gulf of Bothnia. It is not uncommon even today for vessels to be locked in thick ice, and for bicycles and even cars to travel about freely on the ice surface. (Photo: Keystone)

Arctic and subarctic Europe. From the point of view of its physical geography there is inevitably a close juxtaposition of Atlantic or maritime influences and Arctic influences, and this is reflected both in the climate and in the landscape features of the countries concerned. The greater part of Scandinavia is bound by snow and ice into the Arctic world during a long winter season. On the other hand Iceland, western Norway and the Faroe Islands are profoundly affected by the sea, with marine influences also penetrating, on a less dramatic scale, to almost all other parts of Fennoscandia.

As seen in Fig. 2.2, there are very few areas which are more than 200 km from an oceanic or Baltic shore. Norway is affected by the waters of the North Sea, the Norwegian Sea and the Arctic Ocean; its west coast is warmed by the waters of the North Atlantic Drift, while the coast of Finnmark is cooled through the year by the proximity of pack-ice in the Barents Sea. Denmark is affected by North Sea water to the west and Baltic Sea water to the east, with a complicated mixing of waters in the currents of the Kattegat and Skagerrak. This area of mixed water also affects the south-west coast of Sweden, keeping it much warmer during the winter than the Swedish eastern coastline. This coast is affected by the sea which the Swedes call Östersjön (the Eastern Sea). South of the Åland archipelago the waters of the Baltic are quite saline and relatively warm, but the coast of the Gulf of Bothnia is affected by water with low salinity and very low winter temperatures. Much of the surface of the Gulf of Bothnia remains frozen during the winter and spring (Fig. 2.3), and this reduces or even eliminates its potential ameliorating influence upon climate, allowing the surrounding lands to be cooled by polar continental air-masses from the east. In contrast, the Swedish uplands are close enough to the Atlantic west coast to feel the ameliorating influence of the North Atlantic Drift. Finland is affected by its proximity to the Barents Sea in the north, but it is really a part of the Baltic world flanked to the west by the Gulf of Bothnia and to the south by the Gulf of Finland. In Karelia it is also affected by its proximity to the White Sea. Each of these water bodies is ice covered during the winter, but because the component parts of the Baltic Sea are so shallow (mostly less than 100 m deep) and because tidal movements are minimal they warm up during the summer and exert an ameliorating influence upon the 'interior' climate of Fennoscandia during the autumn in particular.

The land-masses of Scandinavia are dominated by peninsulas, islands and archipelagos. The Scandinavian peninsula is split into two near its southern end; Finland occupies a peninsula bounded by the Gulf of Bothnia and the Gulf of Finland; and the Danish peninsula projects northwards from the European mainland. These main peninsulas, and many smaller ones, have acted as both bridges and barriers over many thousands of years of evolving landscapes. The same may be said of the Scandinavian archipelagos and larger islands. In the oceanic west the islands strung along the Norwegian Atlantic seaboard have protected the mainland coasts from the worst effects of the oceanic swell and storm waves, and the relatively sheltered waters of the Norwegian 'Inner Lead' have played a great part in the historical development of the state by permitting easy sea travel along virtually the whole length of the coastline. The islands of the Danish archipelago have been stepping-stones between the Scandinavian heartland and the other countries of western Europe, while the archipelagos of south-west Finland, Åland and the Stockholm region have been stepping-stones during centuries of contact between Finland and Sweden.

If we enlarge the field of vision to take in the whole of Europe, Scandinavia is seen to occupy the north-western corner of the continent. Lying a great distance from the ancient cradles of civilization of the eastern Mediterranean, and even remote from the main cultural and industrial axes of western Europe, the region might appear to suffer from considerable locational disadvantages. However, a comparison with Alaska shows that Scandinavia is by no means badly off either from the point of view of environment or resources. Both Alaska and Fennoscandia are peninsulas at the north-western extremities of continental land-masses. Both straddle the Arctic Circle, and they are broadly similar in latitudinal and longitudinal extent. They have similar types of climate, associations of landforms, and vegetation types, although Alaska has more extensive tundra vegetation. Both areas were profoundly affected by glaciers during the last glaciation, although much of northern Alaska remained ice-free. In contrast, the northern and western shores of Alaska are caught in the grip of pack ice for much of the year, and on the coast of the Chukchi Sea pack ice is present all the year round. Alaska has a great extent of permafrost or permanently frozen ground. While the states of Fennoscandia have been settled intensively for over 1,000 years, most of the settlement and economic development of Alaska has occurred within the last 100 years or so. Centuries before the 'opening up' of Alaska, Fennoscandia had developed a distinct culture and a distinct political identity, with centres of settlement, agriculture and industry, and with patterns of routeways which have remained largely unchanged to this day. Fennoscandia has approximately twenty times the population of Alaska, while at latitudes affected by continuous permafrost in Alaska the Scandinavian states have elegant cities and thriving ports. The comparisons could continue; but the most important locational fact is that Scandinavia enjoys an environment which is, from the point of view of human habitation, anomalously favourable when one considers its location on the fringe of the Arctic world. To summarize the points made above, three factors are responsible for this:

1. the penetration of the warm waters of the North Atlantic Drift into the Norwegian Sea and the Barents Sea;
2. the location of the region within the belt of westerly winds which transport both warmth and moisture from the Atlantic Ocean;
3. the complicated distribution of both land and sea in Fennoscandia, allowing marine influences to penetrate to the very heart of the region.

A matter of latitude

In one of his geographical moods Willy Breinholst once wrote: 'The geographical position of the North is so northerly that even the Northerner will be surprised to hear how far to the North he lives.' Other authors have written, more seriously, about the overwhelming influence of latitude and the profound impact of the northern winter upon the Scandinavian way of life. Medieval cartographers referred to the Scandinavian countries as 'the Midnight Lands'. Many of the early travellers in Scandinavia were both impressed and frightened by the terrible winters which they encountered and by the incessant darkness of the winter months. Darkness and cold occupy special places in the mythology of the northern lands, and the prolonged winters still make a psychological impact which it is difficult for the inhabitants of the middle latitudes

Fig. 2.4 A Norwegian troll-hag, typical of the gloomy characters which inhabit the world of Scandinavian folk-tales. (Drawing by Theodor Kittelsen)

to understand. The Norwegians suffer from a complaint which they call 'dark sickness', and the Finns, the Swedes and the Icelanders know all about it too. Depression and gloom figure prominently in folk-tales (Fig. 2.4), in the works of many modern Scandinavian novelists, and even in learned academic texts. In their book called *Winter in Finland*, W. R. Mead and H. Smeds use the theme of winter as the core of a study of Finnish economic geography.

Most of Scandinavia lies to the north of 56 °N, and the Norwegian North Cape lies at a latitude of 71 °N. Copenhagen, the most southerly of the capital cities, lies at approximately the same latitude as Edinburgh. The other mainland capitals lie well to the north of the northernmost tip of Great Britain. Stockholm, at about 59 °N, lies at approximately the same latitude as the southern tip of Greenland. Oslo and Helsinki lie at about 60 °N, and Reykjavik (about 64 °N) prides itself on being closer to the Arctic Circle than any other capital city in the world. Another important feature of the three largest Scandinavian states is their great latitudinal extent. Norway extends over 13 ° of latitude; Sweden extends across 14 °; and Finland extends across 10 °. This means that no simple generalizations can be made about the climatic characteristics of these three states, and many authors have preferred to write of broad east–west climate zones, especially comparing and contrasting the environmental characteristics of Lapland or 'Nordkalotten' (literally, the North Cap) with those of the balmy south.

The distribution of daylight and darkness through the year is of course related to latitude. Denmark has approximately the same distribution of daylight and darkness as northern England, but further north there is a rapid diminution of winter daylight and a lengthening of summer daylight. For example, the city of Stockholm experiences $18\frac{1}{2}$ hours of bright daylight at midsummer and only 2 hours of real darkness. At the same time of year Lapland experiences 24 hours of daylight, with the sun never dipping beneath the horizon. In contrast, midwinter is a time of prolonged darkness in northern Scandinavia. On 21 December Stockholm enjoys only $5\frac{1}{2}$ hours of daylight and endures 16 hours of total darkness. In Lapland there are $19\frac{1}{2}$ hours of total darkness and only $4\frac{1}{2}$ hours of twilight. The sun does not appear at all in the extreme north (say, at 70 °N) between mid-November and mid-January.

The distribution of seasons through the year is influenced by air and sea temperatures as well as by latitude, and climatic characteristics are considered in more detail in Chapter 4. At this stage, however, it should be noted that the Scandinavian countries experience prolonged winters and relatively short summers. Many visitors to Scandinavia have remarked that spring and autumn are so short that they hardly deserve to be thought of as seasons at all. Summer seems to grow organically out of the death of winter, and in August or September the first frosts and early snowfalls seem to signal a sudden shift back into winter. In Lapland summer does not start until mid-June, and it is over by mid-August. In the extreme north winter may last for almost 300 days of the year. Even in those parts of Scandinavia which lie south of the Arctic Circle the 'meteorological year' is punctuated with events which are related to winter, to darkness, and to snow and ice. W. R. Mead and H. Smeds analyse these events in their book *Winter in Finland*, discussing summer frosts, the leaf fall of deciduous trees, the arrival and departure of the period of lasting frosts, the appearance and disappearance of lake and sea ice, the advance and retreat of the snow

Fig. 2.5 The impact of winter. Four measures of the winter climate. (a) Average dates of arrival of the period of lasting frost; (b) the advance of the snow frontier or boundary of lasting snow; (c) duration of the period with mean daily temperatures below 0 °C; (d) average dates of disappearance of lake ice. (After Mead and Smeds 1967)

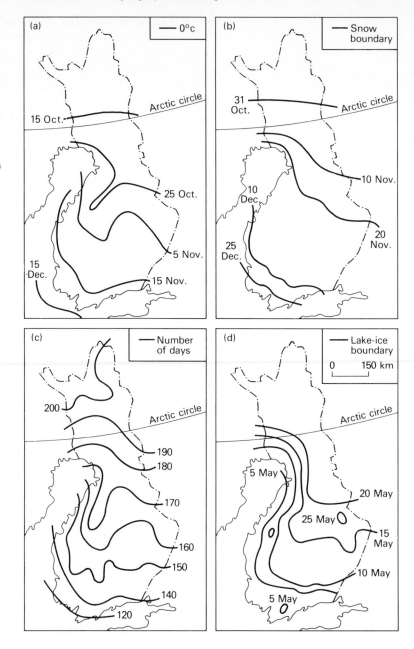

frontier, the freezing and thawing of the ground, the disappearance and reappearance of the sun, and many other factors (Fig. 2.5).

Without being too deterministic the student can ask himself whether an understanding of the Scandinavian setting and environment helps in an understanding of Scandinavian society. Can artistic and other creative activity be related to the rhythm of seasons and the seemingly interminable winter darkness? Why do the Scandinavian peoples, in their festivals and folk customs, place so much emphasis upon *light*? Again, is the Scandinavian 'flight to the sun' (in the shape of package deal holidays to the Canary Islands, southern Spain and North Africa) a product of modern affluence or a deep-seated psychological and physical need for sunlight and warmth during the dismal days of winter? These are themes which will be recalled later in the book, and especially in Chapter 14.

Suggested reading

Environment and environmentalism

Eyre 1964; Huntingdon 1927; Lewthwaite 1966; Martin 1951; Minshull 1970; Montefiore and William 1955; O'Riordan 1983; Semple 1911; Spate 1957.

The geographical setting

Church et al 1973; Fullerton and Williams 1972; Isachsen 1961; Jordan 1973; Malmström 1965; Mead 1958; Mead and Hall 1972; Millward 1965; Ogilvie 1957; Sømme 1961; Whittlesey 1949.

Chapter 3 The physical environment: the foundations of landscape

The natural landscapes of Scandinavia make a profound impact upon visitors and local people alike. Impressions of regional personality are not by any means created by the impact of winter harshness alone, for writers through the ages have been equally if not more impressed by the elemental or primeval features of the Scandinavian landscape. Oceans of coniferous trees submerging the rolling hills of central Sweden contrast with the harsh ranks of ancient treeless mountains and plateau remnants that make up the Norwegian skyline. In Finland there are thousands of square kilometres of landscape dominated by barren tundra in the north, and vast areas dominated by a mosaic of lakes, forests, peninsulas and islands in the south. In Iceland there are lava deserts and ice-caps, and in the Faroe Islands there are bleak treeless slopes plunging seawards on the flanks of fjords and sounds. For those who know Scandinavia a multitude of images spring to mind at the very mention of the word 'landscape' and most of these images can be translated into words which have an uncomfortable ring about them. Marcel Brion (Ogrizek 1952: 155, 156), writing about the landscapes of Norway, expresses his feelings as follows:

> This is the land of the boundless. Everything is different from conditions in other European countries. There are huge mountain masses, separated by deep valleys, almost entirely cut off from one another and ending in dominating snow-covered plateaux, cliffs overhanging the winding fjords that pierce their way into the land like writhing dragons. . . . This all-powerful scenery requires our total submission and complete union, without which we shall never gain a knowledge of Norway.

Such phraseology is not uncommon in writings about the other Scandinavian countries as well, although the landscapes of Denmark and southern Sweden inspire warmer and gentler sentiments among writers. The determined determinist could claim that there is a perfectly good reason for this, for the extreme south of Fennoscandia is the only area where extensive Mesozoic and Cenozoic sedimentary rocks outcrop at the surface. In general, these are fertile lowland areas which look quite different from the ancient rocks and ancient landscapes of the greater part of the region.

Structure and bedrock geology

There are four basic geological units in Scandinavia:
1. The Baltic Shield, a Pre-Cambrian feature which is the structural 'core' of Fennoscandia.
2. The Caledonian Mountains, formed for the most part of folded Lower Palaeozoic rocks and stretching from southern Norway to Lapland.
3. The region of Mesozoic and Cenozoic sedimentary rocks in Denmark and Skåne.
4. The Cenozoic volcanic islands of Iceland and the Faroes.

The boundaries between these units are generally, but not always, quite distinct (Fig. 3.1). For example, the western edge of the Baltic Shield is clearly defined in Sweden between Östersund and Kebnekajse, but in southern Norway the Caledonian Mountains contain Proterozoic rocks of widely differing ages in addition to Lower Palaeozoic rocks. In southern Fennoscandia the boundary between the shield rocks and the Cretaceous rocks of Jylland is marked by the Kattegat, but near the southern tip of Sweden the edge of the Mesozoic rocks is difficult to pick up in the landscape. If we concentrate upon the characteristics of the geological units themselves, rather than upon the boundaries between them, we can recognize clear correlations between structure, geology and landscape, and it is worth examining the important features of each unit in turn.

The Baltic Shield

The rocks of the Baltic Shield are found in Finland, Sweden, Norway, and on the Danish island of Bornholm. The oldest rocks are gneisses which outcrop in the north-eastern part of the shield, and radiometric dates show that they were deformed and metamorphosed some 3,000 million years ago. Probably these rocks are part of the original structural core of Europe, created at a time when there was hardly any oxygen in the earth's atmosphere, no life on land and hardly any sign of life even in the great 'world ocean' which encircled the globe. These ancient rocks are overlain by a sequence of buckled and metamorphosed rocks which were originally shales, sandstones, greywackes, lavas and ashes; most of them in their altered state date from about 2,600 million years ago. The shield rocks of southern Finland, largely granites and gneisses, are for the most part more than 1,700 million years old, and they

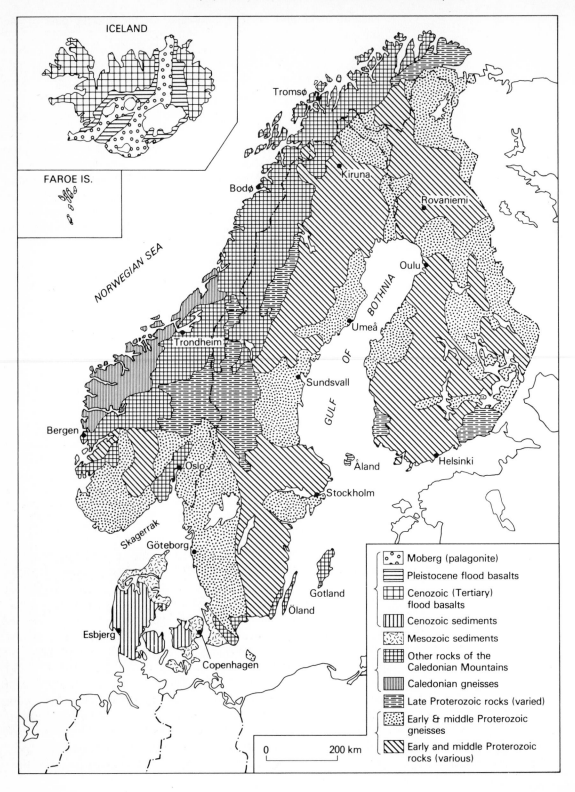

ICELAND

FAROE IS.

NORWEGIAN SEA

Tromsø

Kiruna

Bodø

Rovaniemi

Oulu

GULF OF BOTHNIA

Umeå

Trondheim

Sundsvall

Åland

Helsinki

Bergen

Oslo

Stockholm

Skagerrak

Göteborg

Gotland

Öland

Esbjerg

Copenhagen

	Moberg (palagonite)
	Pleistocene flood basalts
	Cenozoic (Tertiary) flood basalts
	Cenozoic sediments
	Mesozoic sediments
	Other rocks of the Caledonian Mountains
	Caledonian gneisses
	Late Proterozoic rocks (varied)
	Early & middle Proterozoic gneisses
	Early and middle Proterozoic rocks (various)

0   200 km

Fig. 3.1 A simplified geological map of Scandinavia showing the main structural and geological units.

Fig. 3.2 An exposure of Baltic Shield rocks in the Finnish archipelago. Here the rocks are for the most part granites and gneisses; and the colouring is striking, with reds, pinks, whites and greys predominating. (Photo: Finnish Embassy)

are now classified as Lower Proterozoic in age (Fig. 3.2). The granites and gneisses of south-eastern Sweden are younger still (1,300–1,700 million years old), while those of south-western Sweden and south-eastern Norway are occasionally as young as 800 million years old. Thus the shield rocks become younger towards the south and west, showing that the 'Ancestral Europe' of Pre-Cambrian times was growing westwards and southward for at least 2,000 million years.

The early period of continental growth was a period of great crustal instability; it seems to have been interrupted by at least four major episodes of mountain-building with widespread igneous intrusions and volcanic eruptions, and by many prolonged episodes of denudation. During the later part of Pre-Cambrian time there was at least one Ice Age. This time of global cooling, represented by tillites and other glacial sediments in the Eocambrian rocks of southern Norway and northern Lapland, is generally referred to as the Varangian Ice Age after the classic 'type localities' of Varanger Fjord on the shores of the Barents Sea. This Ice Age may have lasted for over 20 million years, and it is dated to about 600 million years ago.

At the top of the Pre-Cambrian rock sequence there are many sedimentary rocks such as sandstones, quartzites and shales, as well as slates, dolerites and igneous intrusives. The sediments thicken towards the western edge of the shield, and they show that eroded materials were beginning to accumulate in deep water in a great geosyncline along the contact between ancestral Europe and ancestral North America before the onset of the Phanerozoic eon. The processes of continental drift and plate tectonics must already have been under way. Where the bedded rocks are resting upon thick igneous and metamorphic rocks of the ancient shield they are not greatly deformed, and over wide areas (for example in the valley of Västerdalälven west of Lake Siljan) they are protected by sheets of dolerite. Probably the 'core of Europe' has remained broadly stable for something like 600 million years. Furthermore, there seems to have been a prolonged period of denudation at the end of the Proterozoic era, for Cambrian rocks rest unconformably upon an undulating and yet well-developed peneplain. This is called the 'sub-Cambrian peneplain', one of the most important of all the landscape features of Fennoscandia. Another important feature of the shield is the central 'downwarp' which is now occupied by the Baltic Sea and its northward extension into the Gulf of Bothnia. This downwarp, similar to that on the Canadian Shield which is occupied by Hudson Bay, may have originated during the Caledonian orogeny with the uplift and distortion of the western shield rim. Alternatively, it may be due to progressive sinking during the Hercynian and Alpine orogenies as a result of some deep-seated plate-tectonic process.

The Caledonian mountain range

This mountain range, variously referred to in the literature as the 'Caledonides', the 'Scandes' or simply the 'Scandinavian mountains', is one of the most carefully studied of the world's ancient fold-mountain chains. It stretches for some 1,600 km along the western edge of the Baltic Shield, owing its origin to the compression and uplift of great thicknesses of materials in the Caledonian geosyncline. In early Palaeozoic times this geosyncline stretched all the way from Svalbard to the southern Appalachians in North America. From studies of continental drift and plate tectonics we know that there was a closing sea here in Cambrian times, and it is now clear that the Caledonian mountain range was originally created as a result of a continental 'collision' between ancestral North America and ancestral Europe. That part of the geosyncline stretching from southern Ireland to Svalbard contained up to 10,000 m of shale, quartz sandstone, greywacke and conglomerate, as well as some limestone and volcanic rocks. The bulk of the sediments were produced through the erosion of the sub-Cambrian peneplain on the Baltic Shield, although deposition in the great deep-water trench continued in Cambrian, Ordovician and Silurian times also. These younger 'Cambro-Silurian' deposits are exposed at the surface throughout the length of the mountain range. On the other hand there are extensive areas (especially in western Norway) where Pre-Cambrian rocks have been metamorphosed during the Caledonian orogeny; the resulting gneisses can be seen along the sides of Sogne-fjord from Balestrand and Vik all the way to the fjord mouth, and they are known to Scandinavian geologists as 'Caledonized' rocks.

The process of mountain-building referred to as the Caledonian orogeny occupied more than 250 million years. There were a number of different episodes of uplift and deformation during the Early Palaeozoic, and these culminated at the end of the Silurian with the terminal phase of mountain-building which brought to an end marine sedimentation in the old geosyncline. As uplift proceeded there were repeated extrusions and intrusions of igneous materials. Folding was accompanied by the creation of great overthrusts and by shearing of the harder rocks on a vast scale; in central southern Norway and throughout the Swedish part of the mountain range there are complicated systems of overthrust sheets or nappes which are not yet mapped in any detail. Sometimes great slabs of Pre-Cambrian rock were broken from the basement and carried by overthrusting into areas of younger rock. Throughout the various episodes of deformation metamorphism occurred at depth, especially beneath the surface layers subjected to folding and shearing. In general, metamorphism increases from east to west, and it seems to have been most severe along the west coastal strip of Norway south of the Arctic Circle. This was the actual 'buffer zone' subjected to the most intense deformation during the process of plate margin collision.

At the end of the Silurian period the Caledonian mountain range must have been an immensely impressive upland barrier with innumerable complicated ridges, deep structural troughs, and probably with many frost-shattered peaks more than 5,000 m above sea-level. Since the beginning of Devonian times the sea has hardly affected this area at all, and geological evidence suggests that there was an extremely rapid breaking down of the elevated land surface by the processes of denudation. Frost shattering and wind action must have played a part, but most of the Devonian and later rocks point to the occurrence of fluvial erosion on a large scale. Thick beds of conglomerate and sandstone dominate the Devonian sequence in western Norway, and there are other freshwater sediments (accompanied by lava beds and igneous intrusions) in the Permian sequence of the Oslo area. In general, however, one of the most impressive features of the mountains is the scarcity of rocks less than 400 million years old. Ever since the end of of the Caledonian orogeny erosion has dominated the Fennoscandian scene, reducing the land surface to but a fraction of its former altitude and in the process exposing the roots of the uplands. We can only assume that most of the resultant rock debris has been transported seawards, both towards the west and eastwards towards the Russian platform. The last two mountain-building episodes to have affected north-western Europe were the Hercynian orogeny (during Permian times) and the Alpine orogeny (during the Tertiary period), and both of these affected the uplands to some extent. During the Hercynian earth movements there was a substantial amount of faulting in the mountains, and local fault-bounded uplift may have been considerable. The Norwegian Channel is thought to have formed at this time, and various gaps through the mountains may have been created by down faulting. During the Alpine orogeny there was little violent disruption of the rocks, but the whole mountain range was subjected to a dome-like uplift with the greatest increase in surface altitude in the extreme west. The uplift in western Norway may have been more than 1,000 m.

The Sognefjord region of western Norway provides an excellent example of the range of rock types to be found within the Caledonian uplands (Fig 3.3). In the south-east of the region there is a detached mass of Pre-Cambrian gneiss, flanked by schists of Cambro-Silurian age. Then there are gabbros, anorthosites or granidiorites extending across a broad band of country south-westwards from Jotunheimen. Further west there is a vast area of gneiss, and finally in the extreme west Devonian conglomerates and sandstones are exposed on Solund and on other islands off the mouth of the fjord. The structures exposed in this rock sequence, as elsewhere in the Sognefjord – Hardangerfjord area, are extremely complicated, with abundant folds, faults, thrusts and nappes.

The region of Mesozoic and Cenozoic sediments

On the margins of Fennoscandia Mesozoic rocks are found above the basement rocks, and these are especially well preserved in Denmark and Skåne. In southern Skåne there are sandstones and clays of Triassic age, and there are also some Triassic coal deposits. The Jurassic rocks of Skåne are mostly sandstones, shales and mudstones. The most widely exposed Mesozoic rocks of southern Sweden are Cretaceous limestones, but there are also many exposures of Cretaceous sandstones and clay deposits. In Denmark many of the Mesozoic rocks are overlain by superficial materials related to the stages of the Quaternary Ice Age. However, they are known to be over 1,000 m thick in some areas, and exposures of them can be seen in northern Jylland, on Sjaelland, Møn, Falster and Lolland. In the central parts of Denmark Tertiary sediments overlie the Mesozoic rocks, and these include the old delta and beach swamp deposits, lignite beds, sands and soft clays. There are also layers of volcanic ash derived from volcanic eruptions in the vicinity of the Skagerrak.

In general the Mesozoic and Cenozoic rocks are not greatly

Fig. 3.3 A geological map of Sognefjord region of western Norway, showing the great range of rock types to be found in the western part of the Caledonian mountain range.

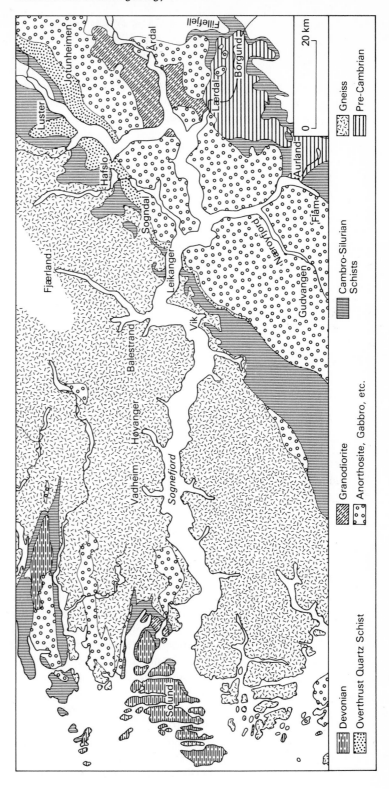

distorted. The Alpine orogeny, which culminated in Mio-Pliocene times around 10 million years ago, did not affect Denmark beyond causing some uplift, faulting and mild flexuring of the gently dipping strata. The overall dip of strata from the north and east towards the southwest was preserved in Jylland, but there was greater disturbance in Skåne as many ancient faults in the Pre-Cambrian basement were reactivated. At the same time a number of basaltic volcanoes were active the area around Ringsjön.

For many years geologists have discussed the possibility that there was once a more extensive cover of Mesozoic (and possibly Tertiary) rocks over the interior parts of Fennoscandia. It is now considered unlikely that such rocks were ever widespread in the northern parts of the Baltic Shield or in the Caledonian Mountains, but there are a few signs of Mesozoic sediments well away from Denmark and southern Skåne. On the Norwegian island of Andøy there is a small area of down-faulted coalbearing slates and sandstones of Jurassic and Lower Cretaceous age, and in the zone of Pre-Cambrian rocks in northern Skåne Cretaceous rocks are also preserved in down-faulted depressions. Cretaceous rocks are also to be found on the floor of the Skagerrak and Kattegat and in the southern Baltic. It is therefore likely that a 'Cretaceous cover' existed above the Pre-Cambrian and Palaeozoic rocks in at least some of the peripheral parts of Fennoscandia, before the onset of the Cenozoic era. Fluvial erosion during the Tertiary and erosion by ice during the Quaternary period has ensured that most of the veneer of sediment has been removed and been replaced by till and other materials related to the melting of the Scandinavian ice sheet.

The Cenozoic volcanic islands

From a geological point of view the Faroes and Iceland are quite distinct from the rest of Scandinavia. Both are of Cenozoic age, and both were formed as the result of outpourings of basaltic lava during the splitting and widening of the Atlantic Ocean. The Faroes lie well to the east of the Mid-Atlantic Ridge, having now been carried on the crustal 'conveyor belt' away from the scene of contemporary volcanic activity; but Iceland still straddles the ridge and is by far the largest of the Atlantic islands which have developed on its crest. It is being split down the middle by sea-floor spreading, and the widening of the country is being accompanied by faulting, earthquakes and intermittent volcanic eruptions which transport new crustal material to the surface.

The twenty or so islands of the Faroes, with a total land area of only 1,300 km^2, were formed during the dissection of the broad submarine ridge which connects the Scottish and Icelandic sections of the great 'Brito-Arctic' igneous province. Gently dipping basalt layers are typical of this part of the province, and they are exposed in three distinct series which are associated with tuffs and also some sedimentary strata sandwiched between the basalt flows. All these deposits are shown by palaeomagnetic investigations, by isotopic dating and by studies of fossil plants to be of early Eocene age – that is, about 50–54 million years old. At this time the Faroes lay close to the Mid-Atlantic Ridge and the Norwegian Sea was being widened by sea-floor spreading. Some sills and dykes which have been intruded into the basalt sequence are much less than 50 million years old and the whole basalt mass was gently buckled during the Alpine earth movements of later Tertiary times.

Because Iceland is still located astride the Mid-Atlantic Ridge it has a much greater variety of rock ages. Some of the rocks in the extreme east of Iceland may be about the same age as those of the Faroes, but for the most part the basalts of the eastern and western plateau districts are Miocene and Pliocene in age, dated radiometrically to 16 million years or less. In the north-west peninsula of Iceland, one of the classic areas for the study of plateau basalts, the lava 'pile' is several kilometres thick, made of a multitude of lava flows which vary in thickness from less than 1 m to over 10 m. Here, as in Iceland's eastern basalt province, the bulk of the lavas were extruded along volcanic fissures, carried to the surface along 'feeder dykes'. Elsewhere, there are traces of shield volcanoes similar to those which are still active in the Hawaiian Islands. A third type of eruption was associated with the 'central volcanic complexes' which can be found in the basalts here and there; these complexes are geologically very varied, introducing andesites, rhyolites, gabbros, granophyre and also a great deal of tephra into the basalt sequence. New central volcanoes are being discovered all the time, for the geology of the plateau basalt areas is still not very well known. The three types of eruption, working together over a period of 10 million years or more, gradually built up the surface of the basalt plateau, layer by overlapping layer. In between the basalt layers there are weathered horizons and also soils bearing traces of plants; from the fossil remains it appears that the landscape of Tertiary north-west Iceland was probably covered with coniferous forest with some interspersed areas of deciduous woodland.

The two plateau basalt districts of Iceland are separated by a belt of newer rocks exposed in a broad sweep from the north-east to the south-west. These rocks are referred to as the *Palagonite Formation*, and they are for the most part of Pleistocene age. The most characteristic rock in the formation is a tuff breccia rich in brownish hydrated glass known as palagonite; its Icelandic name is *Moberg*. Probably it was formed during volcanic eruptions beneath a thick Pleistocene ice cover. These subglacial eruptions formed two main types of mountains – long serrated ridges (formed during fissure eruptions) and table mountains (made for the most part of Moberg but capped with basalt lava flows). The landscape of the palagonite areas is quite different from the plateau basalt landscapes referred to above; here there are vast open expanses of undulating volcanic terrain with blankets of tephra, lava flows, glacial deposits and also areas of wind-blown sands. Here and there table mountains and postglacial volcanoes rise out of the plains. The land surface is broken up into broadly parallel fissures and small escarpments, as in the area to the east of Myvatn and at Thingvellir. These features are the result of the contemporary rifting which is occurring on the crest of the Mid-Atlantic Ridge, in the process splitting Iceland down the middle at a rate of 1 cm per year.

Since the wastage of the last Icelandic ice sheet, which commenced about 15,000 years ago, volcanic activity has been concentrated in two broad belts. About 200 volcanoes have been active during this period, and 30 of them have erupted since the beginning of settlement about 1,100 years ago. The Holocene lava fields are of two main types: *apalhraun* lava has a clinkery, rough and irregular surface which is difficult to traverse, while *helluhraun* lava is comparatively smooth with a ropy surface structure. The lava which is extruded during an eruption can make a magnificent and frightening impact upon the landscape, as around Myvatn and in the country south-east of Reykjavik. However, much more ructive from a human point of view is the tephra thrown into the air during explosive eruptions. When the Laki fissure eruption occurred in 1783 the gases and tephra which accompanied the lava flows poisoned the grasslands over a vast area and caused a terrible famine. When Askja erupted in 1875 a fall of rhyolitic tephra caused great damage, and several of the fourteen recorded eruptions of Hekla have also been accompanied by widespread tephra falls. In recent times the eruption of Eldfjell on the south coast island of Heimaey caused the evacuation of a town of 5,000 people, and about a third of the town was buried or burnt by tephra and lava.

Where volcanic eruptions occur beneath the surface of a snow-field or ice cap great floods are an inevitable consequence and these can devastate low-lying areas around the foot of a volcano. Such floods are called *jökulhlaups*, and they occur in conjunction with the eruptions of Oraefajökull, Katla, Grimsvotn and other volcanoes in the centre and south of the country.

The pre-glacial landscape

Tertiary landscape change in Fennoscandia

In Fennoscandia the most significant events of the Tertiary period were concerned with the denudation of the landscape. Although there may have been quite a thick cover of sedimentary rocks above the sub-Cambrian surface in Sweden and Finland virtually all of this was removed, and in many respects the landscape was transformed to create the basic outlines of the regional landscape of today.

Geological reconstructions suggest that during the early Tertiary (in Eocene times) the central and eastern parts of Fennoscandia were extensive lowlands crossed by abundant rivers flowing from the old Caledonian mountains. Then there was a prolonged series of 'uplift episodes' which coincided with the Alpine orogeny of southern Europe; each phase of uplift was followed by a period of very active erosion and dissection of the land surface. The greatest uplift occurred in the west, where the Caledonian mountain axis served as the axis for this most recent series of earth movements. The old and denuded roots of the mountain chain were uplifted by at least 1,000 m and the denudation which followed, especially in Norway, created a landscape of broad erosion surface remnants separated by deep erosional gashes. Norwegian geomorphologists now think that there were at least fifteen different 'erosion cycles' during the Tertiary period in western Norway, although other parts of Fennoscandia may have had quite different histories of denudation.

Two distinct types of landscape are found on the Baltic Shield sections of Finland and Sweden. The first of these is the 'Norrland terrain' which extends from near Lake Vänern to the far north of Sweden and eastwards across the Finnish province of Lappi. This vast morphological region, otherwise known as the Limes Norrlandicus, is a gently sloping undulating foreland. It has a relatively uniform river pattern and altitudes are in the range 20–500 m. In some areas there are wide plains with groups of monadnocks; elsewhere, as in central Sweden, there is a more broken type of landscape with distinct uplands and closely spaced deep valleys. Here the relative relief is sometimes greater than 300 m, in contrast to the wide open plains of Lappi where relative relief is generally less than 50 m. The second type of shield landscape is the *sprickdalslandskap* (fissure-valley landscape) which characterizes much of southern Sweden and the south coastal strip of Finland. Over thousands of square kilometres the land surface is broken by a network of narrow intersecting valleys and broader hollows flanked by steep straight slopes. Valleys and hollows are generally filled with lakes or clay deposits, and the intervening blocks of higher land are often plateau-like with wide exposures of bare rock. The landscape has an angular pattern, although this angularity is difficult to discern where the land surface slopes below sea-level; in the immensely beautiful archipelagos of south-west Finland, Åland and Stockholm only the high points break the water surface. The origins of the fissure-valley landscape are diverse, but it is certain that Alpine rejuvenation of an ancient fault pattern played an important part in breaking up an older erosion surface. Here, as with the gradual tilting of the Norrland terrain during the Alpine orogeny, the impact of Tertiary tectonics is apparent.

On the Baltic Shield areas of Sweden and Finland denudation by streams continued throughout the Tertiary period, although the low-lying areas of Skåne and Denmark were transformed by the deposition of sand, silt and clay. This was the material eroded from the highlands and transported across the shield rocks towards the south and east. As mentioned on p. 34, as the Tertiary sediments in Denmark built up their weight was sufficient to depress the land surface even while adjacent areas were being uplifted tectonically.

Most of the studies of Tertiary landscape change concern the uplands, where there are three distinct and easily recognizable pre-glacial landscape elements:

1. Extensive undulating erosion surfaces such as that which underlies the Jostedalsbre ice-cap in western Norway;
2. Prominent residuals or upstanding hill masses such as Dovre and Jotunheimen in south-central Norway; and

Fig. 3.4 Map of the surface contours of the pre-Pleistocene 'Paleic surface'. (After Gjessing 1967)

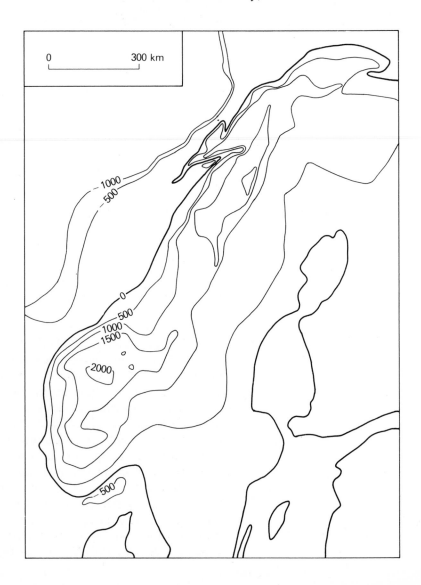

3. Deeply incised river valleys such as those associated with the fjord country of the Norwegian west coast.

These three elements were created for the most part by fluvial processes operating under a warm, moist climatic regime. Episodes of downcutting or valley incision coincided with phases of land surface uplift, while episodes of valley widening and erosion surface planation coincided with phases of land surface stability. The main erosion surface of Tertiary age is referred to by Norwegian geomorphologists as the 'Paleic' surface. In 1948 K. Strøm suggested that the Paleic surface is in reality composed of two surfaces: a high one (represented, for example, in the Jostedalsbre area at 1,800 m) of Miocene age, and a lower and younger surface (found in south Norway at 1,100–700 m) of Pliocene age. Other authors (notably German geomorphologists who have worked in Norway) have recognized a whole staircase of surfaces rising in steps from the Norwegian west coast to the high fjells. In 1967 Just Gjessing brought together a great deal of evidence to show the distribution and overall slope of the Paleic surface in Norway and Sweden, and his map (Fig. 3.4) is considered to be one of the basic source documents in the interpretation of the scenery of Fennoscandia.

It should not be imagined that the Paleic surface was ever *flat*; even at the time of its most perfect development it was undulating, with hill masses and isolated residuals, broad depressions, deep valleys and rolling lowlands. The highest residuals could not be removed by fluvial processes during late Tertiary times, but the greater part of the landscape was affected and altered quite substantially. At the end of the Tertiary period the final pre-glacial episode of river downcutting led to the creation of deeply incised trenches or river gorges which are clearly much younger than the Paleic surface; often remnants of the 'old' surface remain as high terraces or benches above the 'new' steep valley sides.

Tertiary landscape change on the volcanic islands

As indicated on p. 36 the land areas now known as Iceland and the Faroe Islands probably did not exist at the beginning of the Tertiary period. In looking at the landscape evolution of the Tertiary plateau basalt areas, therefore, geomorphologists have a neat 'age framework' into which they can fit their theories. These theories are not well treated in other Scandinavian texts, and they are worth looking at here in the context of a small-scale study. In the Faroes the denudation of the plateau basalt surfaces has had some 50 million years during which to operate, while in north-western and eastern Iceland (the Tertiary basalt 'provinces') the processes of subaerial erosion have operated for some 20 million years at the most. Large parts of north-western Iceland have basalt sheets as young as 10 million years, and in these areas denudation has been operating over what is, geologically speaking, a relatively short period of time.

In the Faroes the Tertiary basalts dip gently towards the south-east, and this was also the direction of dip of the plateau surface following the earth movements of the Alpine orogeny. Most of the original eruption fissures were also aligned NW–SE, together with the main 'lineations' and fractures in the basalt sequence. It was inevitable that the main river valleys of late Tertiary times should be aligned in the same direction, so initiating the process of splitting the plateau into a series of broad ridges or interfluves separated by deep river valleys. The highest part of the plateau was in the north-west, with large areas above 700 m and a few broad summits over 800 m. Gradually, through the operation of fluvial processes inland and marine processes on the coast, the basalt plateau has been broken up. The magnificent cliffs of the north and west coast show that the coastline has retreated under the constant battering of the North Atlantic breakers almost as far as the position of the original watershed between those streams flowing south-eastwards and those flowing north-westwards. It is impossible to decide how far the coast has retreated, but it would not be unreasonable to suggest that it was originally some 20 km further to the north north-west than it is now. The cliffs of the Faroe Islands are among the scenic glories of Scandinavia; many are over 400 m high, and the highest rise sheer from the stormy waters of the North Atlantic for more than 600 m Enniberg, on the island of Viđoy, is a breathtaking 725 m high.

There are now few traces of the original Tertiary basalt plateau of the Faroes. Dissection by fluvial and glacial processes has reached such an advanced stage that the islands stand up for the most part as old interfluve ridges between drowned river valleys which have become the fjords and sounds of today. The highest erosion surface remants occur in the north, with large areas of undulating topography above 400 m. On the other hand, the largest of the southern islands (Sandoy and Suđuroy) are more subdued and lower in altitude, as one would expect from the overall south-easterly dip of the original plateau basalt surface. In places the mountain-tops are broad and undulating. but elsewhere the structural control of the flat-lying or gently dipping basalts is evident in the stepped appearance of steep slopes. This type of landscape used to be called 'trap' by the geologists of the last century. The exposed edges of individual lava flows are called *hamrar*, and they alternate with the grassy rock-strewn shelves which coincide with the intra-basaltic tuffs or weathered layers.

In the Tertiary basalt districts of Iceland much more extensive areas of the old plateaux remain, especially in the north-west peninsula *Vestfirđir*. Originally much of this district was an undulating volcanic plain with an occasional shield volcano or steeper volcanic cone standing above it. There were a few down-faulted depressions and downwarps in the lava surface, and these may have held lakes. From the evidence of plant remains in the few sedimentary layers that can be found between the lava flows, the climate was relatively warm, with a mean annual air temperature close to 9 °C. The mean air temperature of the warmest month was as high as 15–20 °C, and sub-zero temperatures were uncommon. Annual precipitation was in the order of 1,000 mm. The vegetation was not unlike that of the eastern United States at the present day; coniferous forests were widespread, but there were extensive areas of deciduous woodland also. Direct runoff of rainfall was very limited; the fresh basalt lavas were extremely permeable, causing surface water to infiltrate the rocks and reappear in depressions or as springs on slopes. There was a very low drainage density, and most rivers seem originally to have been small ones with only a small capacity for erosion.

Eventually, as is the case with all plateau basalt surfaces, the basalts became impermeable. Runoff increased and fluvial erosion commenced on a large scale. The orientation of the main river valleys was not greatly influenced by the tilt of the basalt layers themselves (which dip gently towards the south and the south-east over most of Vestfirðir) but rather by the slope of the ground surface. This old surface seems to have been gently warped, forcing

Fig. 3.5 Map of the fjord pattern of the north-west peninsula of Iceland – a pattern which reflects the ancient drainage lines which developed on the Tertiary plateau surface.

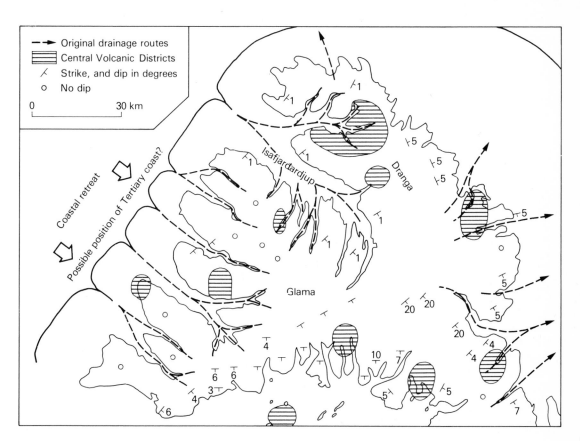

most of the main rivers to flow towards the west or north-west. The precise alignments of the valleys were greatly affected by the fracture pattern of the basalt plateau, and the majority of valleys were controlled either by N.W.–S.E. fractures or N.E.–S.W. fractures. The largest river valleys by far were created on the western flank of the peninsula, and these valleys have been broadened and deepened by ice to create the magnificent fjord pattern of today (Fig 3.5). As in the case of the Faroes, it can safely be assumed that the Tertiary coastlines lay well to the north and west of those of today.

The plateau surfaces of Vestfirđir at the present day lie at an altitude of 500–800 m although individual peaks rise to almost 1,000 m. The plateau remnants of Glama and the area south-east of the small ice-cap of Drangajökull are wide undulating surfaces with depressions and broad open valleys; occasional broad domes and stepped hill masses stand above the general plateau level. In these areas, well away from the sea and inland of the heads of the glacial troughs created during the Pleistocene, the Tertiary basalt plateau seems to have changed hardly at all since its formation more than 10 million years ago. If one looks beyond the mosaic of snow patches and lakes and through the blanket of frost-shattered rock debris which covers most of the bedrock surface one can see a landscape which is, in Icelandic terms at least, extremely old.

Suggested Reading

Structure and Geology

Ahlmann, 1919; Bailey and Holtedahl 1938; Bergsten 1976; Einarsson 1954–1962, 1971; Holtedahl, H. 1975; Holtedahl, O. 1960; Jacobsen 1960; Kjartansson 1969; Kristjansson 1974; Magnusson *et al.* 1957; Preusser 1976; Rudberg and Bylund 1957; Sømme 1961; Strand and Kulling 1972; Strøm 1960; Thorarinsson *et al.* 1959.

Pre-Glacial Landscape

Ahlmann, 1919; Barđarson 1976; Dons 1960; Gjessing 1967; Rudberg 1954, 1965; Schwartzbach 1971; Steindorsson 1962; Strøm 1949, 1960; Sund 1960; Thorarinsson 1937, 1956; Thoroddsen 1905–6.

Chapter 4 The physical environment: Quaternary landscape evolution

Towards the close of the Tertiary period there was a sharp deterioration of world climate, and this culminated in the series of glaciations which we refer to as the Cenozoic Ice Age. Most of these glaciations occurred during the Quaternary period, but the evidence from northern Iceland shows us that in some areas glaciation began very much earlier, more than 4 million years ago. By about 2 million years ago (the date usually accepted for the beginning of the Quaternary period and the Pleistocene epoch) intermittent glaciation was probably occurring over the greater part of Scandinavia. At the peak of each glacial episode Fennoscandia was affected by a single vast ice sheet, while Iceland and the Faroe Islands supported a number of smaller ice-caps. The effects of glaciation were quite different in the various parts of Scandinavia, and on the pages which follow we examine the 'Pleistocene legacy' in the uplands, the lowlands, the coastal districts and the volcanic islands in turn.

Glaciation of the uplands

A number of factors contributed to the large-scale glaciation of the Fennoscandian uplands, and it seems that climatic circumstances combined with pre-existing landscape elements to attract heavy snowfall and also to allow the thickening and spread of glacier ice through a number of stages of ice expansion. These stages appear to have been approximately as follows:

Stage 1. Onset of glaciation. The Caledonian mountain range is ideally situated for the receipt of heavy snowfall during a 'glacial' climate, for it combines both high latitude and high altitude with a position on the oceanic border of a large land-mass. At the beginning of each glacial episode moisture-laden winds from the Atlantic brought abundant precipitation in the form of snow, and mean annual air temperatures in the heart of the mountains were low enough to ensure that a good proportion of the snowfall was able to persist from one year to the next. Hence there was a gradual thickening of snow-banks, leading in turn to the creation of snow-fields and upland glaciers.

Stage 2. Mountain glaciation.   The flanks of the highest summits in the mountains, and also the heads of the deeply entrenched valleys of late Tertiary age, were ideal for the initial build-up of snow-banks, snowfields and cirque glaciers. Probably the early part of each glacial episode was characterized by a type of mountain glaciation similar to that of parts of northern Iceland or Spitsbergen at the present time.

Stage 3. Ice expansion.   As climatic conditions became more severe during each glacial episode, the extensive erosion surfaces of the mountains (such as the Paleic surface and the sub-Cambrian pene-plain) proved to be ideal for the build-up of plateau ice-caps. As these developed and expanded over the edges of plateau remnants, the deeply cut valleys of western Norway favoured the direct drainage of excess ice towards the Norwegian Sea, but the outflow of glaciers was more restricted towards the east. This led to a gradual thickening of ice on the leeward side of the Caledonian mountains.

Stage 4. The growth of the ice sheet.   Eventually the gently sloping land surface of the Baltic Shield allowed the growth of large pied-mont glaciers and ice-caps which coalesced to form a huge ice sheet. The axis of the ice sheet shifted towards the east from its original position over the mountain range, eventually stabilizing approx-imately along the western coast of the Gulf of Bothnia.

Stage 5. Ice over all.   It should be remembered that at the times of greatest ice expansion during the Pleistocene world sea-level was at least 100 m lower than it is now. At such times there would have been no North Sea. At the peak of each glaciation the Scandinavian ice was able to flow uninterruptedly southwards into the Nether-lands, north Germany and Poland, and eastwards into the USSR. The ice extended westwards towards the east coast of the British Isles and northwards into the Barents Sea. Some geomorphologists now believe that the Scandinavian ice sheet was joined along its northern and eastern margins to two other ice sheets, referred to as the Barents Sea and West Siberian ice sheets (Fig. 4.1).

It is still not known how many times the great Scandinavian ice sheet affected the landscape of the countries around the Baltic Sea. Evidence from Iceland and from other parts of the world suggests that there may have been at least twenty distinct glacial episodes during the Pleistocene epoch, but there is stratigraphic evidence for only three (or four) such episodes around the fringes of the Scan-dinavian ice sheet. These have been given the following names:
1. *North European terminology*: Weichselian, Saalian, Elsterian, 'Glacial A'.

Fig. 4.1 Map of the maximum extent of the Scandinavian ice sheet and its neighbouring ice sheets.

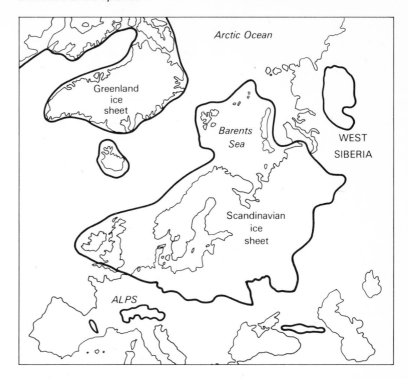

2. *Alpine (European) terminology*: Würm, Riss, Mindel, Günz.
3. *British terminology*: Devensian, Wolstonian, Anglian.

Glacial deposits from various of these glaciations have been found in the Netherlands, Denmark, North Germany and Poland, but away from the southern margins of the ice sheet nearly all of the deposits are of Weichselian age. The last glaciation of the central parts of Fennoscandia was powerful enough to ensure that ancient glacial and interglacial deposits had little chance of survival. Animal bones, lake deposits and plant remains have been discovered here and there in and beneath the deposits of the last glaciation, but the story of early and middle Pleistocene events in Scandinavia has so far proved impossible to piece together.

The glacial landforms and landscapes of the Fennoscandian uplands can be related satisfactorily to an unknown number of glaciations which occurred more than 100,000 years ago. During the Saalian glaciation there was very intensive erosion by ice. On some of the high plateau areas where the ice was relatively thin the base of the ice sheet may have been frozen to its bed, so that the old erosion surfaces were hardly modified. But this type of 'glacial protection' was unusual. Most of the plateau surfaces and most of the undulating parts of the uplands were very drastically affected by a set of processes known collectively as 'areal scouring'. Large masses of thick glacier ice flowed across the whole land surface, moving on a film of meltwater and removing all loose material such as soil, old lake deposits, organic remains, and all periglacial accumulations such as talus cones and ramparts, blockfields and soli-fluction terraces. In many areas the bedrock was also deeply eroded to create an undulating landscape of rock hollows and knobs, *roches moutonnées* and smoothed hills and valleys. The bare bones of the landscape were revealed, with bedrock fractures, faults and other geological structures exposed in spectacular fashion through the erosive work of ice.

By far the most impressive results of glacial erosion in the uplands are the deep fjords of western Norway and the multitudes of glacial troughs and basins found throughout the areas of ice dispersal. As a glaciological principle, where there is an excess of ice in the uplands there is always a tendency for it to flow towards the lowlands or the coast as directly as possible, exploiting old valleys or lines of geological weakness and flowing in concentrated 'ice streams'. Thus the outlet glaciers of the early glaciations used pre-existing river valleys, many of which had been deepened and widened by small valley glaciers during previous glacial episodes. Occasionally, as in the case of Naerøydalen in western Norway, glacial troughs were cut by outlet glaciers flowing in the opposite direction to the original river drainage; and where the regional direction of ice movement was opposed to the slope of the land surface (as, for example, near the peak of each glacial episode when the ice shed or ice-sheet summit lay well to the east of the Caledonian Mountains) completely new glacial troughs and glacial breaches were formed. Sometimes deep gashes were cut by ice across old watersheds, and the resultant troughs are still very spectacular features of the landscape in parts of Lapland and western Sweden.

The fjords of Norway are justly famous from a scenic point of view, and if they are examined as geomorphological features they are both fascinating and instructive. Each fjord displays a number of interrelated features, as shown in Fig. 4.2. Most of the important features are related to the operation of glacial processes, with the processes of large-scale glacial erosion of paramount importance. In a typical fjord the long profile of the glacial trough provides most of the clues to the efficiency of glacial erosion at various points

Fig. 4.2 The main features of the fjord landscape of western Norway. The landscape over many thousands of square kilometres was transformed by glacial action.

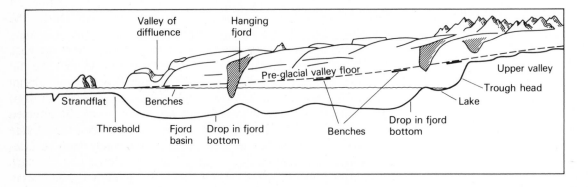

between the outlet glacier source area and the trough exit at the coast. Sognefjord provides a perfect example. This impressive and very beautiful fjord is really a whole complex of glacial troughs extending almost 200 km from the west coast into the heart of the mountains. The branching fjord pattern (Fig. 3.3, p. 35) clearly owes its main features to an ancient river system. The tributary fjords are seldom more than 300 m deep, but the bottom of Sognefjord proper is deeper than 800 m for most of its length. At its deepest point the floor of the trough lies 1,308 m beneath sea-level. The two most important features of the fjord, from a geomorphological point of view, are the submerged trough head (about 210 km inland) and the submerged threshold which is about 50 km inland from the open coast.

In a definitive article published in 1967 Hans Holtedahl showed that the efficiency of glacial erosion in outlet glacier troughs such as those of western Norway could be accurately related both to the volume of ice to be discharged and to the amount of constriction in a particular part of the trough. The submerged trough head was created by a great mass of ice from the main Sognefjord valley and from its tributary troughs. This ice was probably 3,000 m thick, and it must have been melting on its bed. Since there was no possibility for it to escape except in the main trough, it eroded deeply into the bedrock and created a well-adjusted channel. Further along the trough other tributary glaciers joined the main Sognefjord Glacier, and each increase in discharge led to a further increase in basal melting and erosion and in a further deepening of the trough floor. This erosion continued as long as the ice in the trough was unable to escape by 'diffluence'. Closer to the coast, the land surface on the flanks of the trough was at a lower altitude, and some ice from the huge glacier was able to spill over and escape seawards by a variety of different routes. This resulted in a sharp reduction in the glacier's erosive capacity; it no longer had to deepen its trough in order to discharge the ice from the highlands, and so the trough floor rose very steeply to the submerged threshold at a depth of only 100–300 m. This analysis of the Sognefjord landscape is summarized in Fig. 4.3; similar analyses can be made for all the fjords of western Norway, and they help the student to understand how the Pleistocene outlet glaciers have contributed to the character of the Norwegian landscape.

Studies of the main glacial features of the Fennoscandian uplands indicate that they are probably of great antiquity. Troughs such as Nordfjord, Sognefjord and Hardangerfjord were not cut by valley glaciers such as those that are found in the Alps at the present day; they were cut by huge ice streams at a time when the *whole* of the Fennoscandian land surface was thickly covered by glacier ice. In addition, glacial erosion seems to have been specially effective during prolonged glaciations characterized by great thicknesses of temperate or warm-based ice. The last (Weichselian) glaciation was

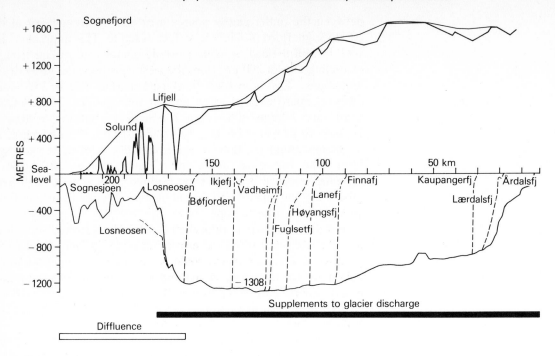

Fig. 4.3 Long profile of the Sognefjord glacial trough, showing how trough depth is related to glacier discharge. (After Holtedahl 1967)

not of this type, and it lasted for only about 60,000 years. Most geomorphologists now believe that the Weichselian glaciers were not responsible for the creation of the glacial landscapes of the uplands; it is certain that troughs were deepened and that the upland plateaux were eroded on a small scale, but the glacial landscapes of today are, in their essentials, probably at least 150,000 years old. Even the cirques and upland valleys which still hold glaciers at the present day are probably of great antiquity.

Glaciation of the lowlands

In attempting to understand the landscape of the Fennoscandian lowlands we must concern ourselves above all else with events which occurred at the end of the Weichselian glaciation, and around 8,000–10,000 years ago. At this time the last Scandinavian ice sheet was melting and breaking up catastrophically, exposing large numbers of freshly created morainic features and leading directly to the creation of fluvioglacial landforms and landscapes in favourable areas. This is not to say that *erosional* landforms are absent in the lowlands; they are well developed in many areas where active ice flowed across the landscape, as shown by the ice-scoured surfaces of the Pre-Cambrian rocks of the Stockholm Skärgård and Åland, and the deeply eroded lake basins of Lapland and Småland. But the lowlands of the Baltic Shield provide us with many classic examples of moraines, eskers and a host of other features, and they deserve more than the passing reference which they are accorded in most texts on the geography of Scandinavia.

The oldest glacial and fluvioglacial deposits in Fennoscandia occur in Denmark. Here there are two types of drift landscape. In western Jylland there is a subdued drift landscape of Saalian age, much of it submerged beneath Weichselian fluvio-glacial 'outwash'. In eastern Jylland and the Danish Archipelago much more recent landscapes fashioned from Weichselian glacial deposits are prominent. The contact between these two types of landscape is marked by a great belt of end moraines running more or less north–south along the length of the Jylland peninsula. Any traveller on routeway E4 between Esbjerg and the Little Belt bridge is bound to notice the transformation of scenery from the gentle flatlands of the west to the hummocky and hilly moraines of the east. The glacial deposits of Denmark are of great thickness; even the Saalian drifts of Jylland are in places 30 m thick, and the thickness of tills and other Pleistocene materials in the archipelago is on average over 50 m. If it were not for the presence of these Pleistocene deposits a great deal of Denmark would lie well beneath sea-level. The drift landscapes of Denmark have been carefully described by Axel Schou, and his immaculate block diagrams of sample landscape types are well known to generations of geography and geology students. The map in Fig. 4.4 gives but a simplified impression of the features that can be discerned.

The drift landscapes of the Baltic Shield are related closely to the gradual northward retreat of the ice-sheet margin from its outermost position in Denmark and north Germany. Ice wastage probably began about 14,000 years ago, and the most prominent depositional features were related to the following ice-margin stillstands or 'retreat stages':
1. The Gothi-glacial stage of about 13,000 years ago;
2. the Fini-glacial stage of about 10,300 years ago; ice margin referred to the Ra stage in Norway and the Salpausselkä stage in Finland;
3. the Late-glacial stage of about 9,000 years ago; ice margin well defined in some areas but not in others.

The positions of the ice margin at the times of these stages and at intervening intervals was plotted quite accurately by the Swede Gerard De Geer in 1912. His work was based upon the counting and correlation of annual sediment layers or varves in ancient proglacial lakes. His so-called 'varve chronology' was remarkably accurate, and modern varve studies accompanied by radiocarbon dating have given rise to revisions of only about 200 years over a total time-span of 12,000 years.

By far the most important of the halt stages of the ice margin was the Ra–Salpausselkä stage which is believed to have lasted for some 800 years. The resulting landforms consist not so much of

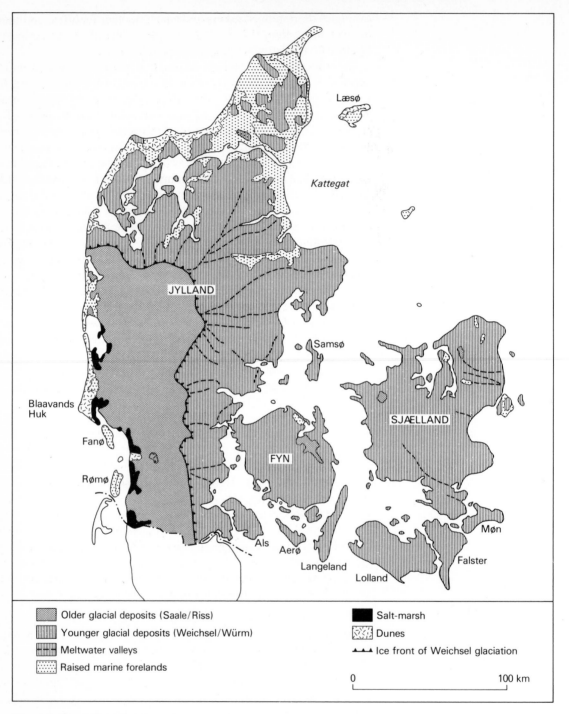

Fig. 4.4 The drift landscapes and related features of Denmark.

moraine and till as of masses of fluvioglacial materials. In parts of central Finland there are huge accumulations of these materials, some of them marking the position of the ice edge and others apparently showing the positions of subglacial, englacial and supra-glacial streams where they reached the ice edge. There are lake infills of sands and gravels, kames and kame terraces, and a multi-tude of eskers. Many of these eskers are found on the Central Lake Plateau of Finland, but there are thousands of others elsewhere in the country. For the most part they show the direction of meltwater drainage at the end of the last glaciation; this direction may or may not coincide with the alignment of drumlins and other 'streamlined' features made of till which are interspersed with the fields of fluvioglacial landforms.

Many other types of drift landscape can be found in the low-lying parts of Finland, Sweden and Norway. There are till plains and drumlin swarms, large expanses of delicate morainic ridges called *De Geer moraines*, litters of erratics and patches of till, and other special types of morainic landscape. Close to the eastern fringes of the uplands there are chaotic landscapes of dead-ice or hummocky moraine, landscapes of *Rogen moraine* ridges, landscapes of fluted moraine, and areas of special landforms such as *Kalixpinnmo* and *Veiki moraines*. These and many more features are described in the writings of Gunnar Hoppe and others.

Isostasy and eustasy

On p. 46 reference was made to the fact that world sea-level drops very sharply during an episode of global refrigeration and ice expan-sion. This is because ice sheets, as they expand, 'trap' huge quan-tities of moisture in the form of snow and ice on the land surface. This moisture has to come from the oceans, and sea-level must fall as the volume of ice increases. Conversely, when a glacial episode comes to an end moisture in the form of glacial meltwater is released. As it returns to the oceans the sea-level returns to its interglacial position. This interplay of sea-level and ice sheet behav-iour is referred to as glacial eustasy, and it is the main mechanism responsible for the sea-level movements of the Pleistocene period. It is believed that during the Saalian glaciation sea-level dropped to about −140 m, and it fell to at least −110 m in the Weichselian glaciation. During interglacial episodes sea-level normally stabilizes at approximately its present position or a little higher. Some earlier interglacials seem to have experienced sea-levels at least 5 m higher than at present.

Another important mechanism which must be taken into account in any attempt to understand the Fennoscandian landscape is *glacial isostasy*. Here the focus of attention is the vertical movement of the land surface rather than the sea surface. When a large ice sheet builds up on a continental land-mass the sheer weight of ice is sufficient to depress the land surface. A simple rule is that every 3 m of ice will depress the land surface by about 1 m. Hence, in Scandinavia, an ice sheet 2,000 m thick is capable of depressing the earth's crust by more than 650 m. When the ice melts the isostatic load is gradually removed, and the land surface rises or 'rebounds' to its former position.

As far as the implications of this process are concerned, the onset of a glacial episode is a time of land-surface depression and sea-level reduction, whereas the close of a glacial episode is marked by a land-surface and sea-level rise. It would be unnatural for the movements of land and sea to remain completely in step even though there is a remarkable similarity in the patterns of isostatic and eustatic recovery. In general, the fastest rates of recovery (both isostatic rebound and sea-level rise) occur during the early stages of deglaciation when catastrophic ice melting is characteristic. At such a time a depressed land surface may rise at a rate of 9 m per century, although sea-level seldom if ever rises as quickly as this. As deglaciation proceeds the rate of land uplift falls off exponentially, and 20,000 years may elapse before recovery is complete. On the other hand, sea-level may attain its interglacial position within 6,000 years, thereafter oscillating only very slightly in step with small-scale increases and decreases in global temperatures.

This preamble provides a basis for an understanding of one of the fascinating facts of Scandinavian life – namely the ever-changing interrelationship of land and water which continues with the uplift of many land areas even at the present day. The land uplift of the present interglacial period has profound geographical implications which are examined in Chapters 6 and 18. For the moment, however, what matters is the interpretation of the natural landscape, and in particular the complicated sequence of land- and sea-level changes which occurred within the Baltic basin between 12,000 and 7,000 years ago.

As the ice of the last Scandinavian ice sheet melted two very unusual geographical circumstances influenced the pattern of landscape change. In the first place, the position of the 'natural' watershed near the extreme western edge of the Scandinavian ice sheet caused most of the meltwater from the decaying ice to flow eastwards and south-eastwards, towards the centre of the Baltic depression. In the second place, the Danish islands and peninsula of Jylland created a very effective dam across the natural outlet of the Baltic Sea, holding back huge quantities of meltwater. This led to the creation of a series of lakes and inland seas which persisted for varying lengths of time as glacial melting proceeded and as the rates of isostatic rebound and eustatic sea-level rise varied.

The first of these great meltwater lakes is referred to as the *Baltic Ice Lake*, which persisted from about 11,000 to 10,000 years ago.

At this time the Scandinavian ice sheet was still very large, and the rate of isostatic uplift was not great. The increasing volume of meltwater in the Baltic basin eventually led to a catastrophic overflow at Billingen in Sweden. As the wastage of the Scandinavian and other ice sheets proceeded at an ever-increasing rate sea-level began to rise rapidly, leading to a transgression of the sea through the Swedish Central Lakes depression. This brought sea water into the Baltic and formed the *Yoldia Sea* which persisted until about 9,500 years ago. With further ice wastage the rate of isostatic rebound increased to a point where it was faster than the rate of eustatic sea-level rise, and the Yoldia Sea was cut off from the open waters of the Kattegat and North Sea. In this way the *Ancylus Lake* was formed. It persisted for something like 2,000 years, during which time the Scandinavian ice sheet disintegrated and retreated until there were only a few small remnants left in the uplands. As ice wastage came to an end the rate of isostatic recovery gradually declined. The rate of eustatic sea-level rise was now faster than the rate of land rise in the southern parts of the Baltic, and around 7,500 years ago the sea flooded through the meltwater outlets of Öresund and the Danish Great Belt to create the *Littorina Sea*. Since then there have been a number of changes in the dimensions or coastal configuration of the water bodies of the Baltic basin, and continuing land uplift (especially in the Gulf of Bothnia) has caused a steady advance of the coastline in very many coastal districts. Between 6,000 and 4,000 years ago the waters of the Littorina Sea were warmer than at any time before or since. With the cooling which occurred at the end of this 'climatic optimum' about 3,800 years ago the Baltic Sea as we know it today came into existence.

The foregoing description of the sequence of Baltic water bodies is of more than academic interest, for the geographical implications of these land–sea–lake changes are considerable. Some of the most significant consequences of isostatic and eustatic change in Fennoscandia are as follows:

1. Raised sea beds and lake floors are now found around many of the coastal districts of Fennoscandia. Often these old water-lain deposits are of fine sand, silt and clay; in south-west Finland, south-east Norway, and in many of the coastal districts of Sweden and the Danish Archipelago they are of great agricultural importance. In western Norway raised deltas are found all over the fjord country. They normally consist of sand and gravel, and they provide superb sites for settlements and for agricultural activities. Normally the terrace tops are higher in the inner parts of the fjords than they are near the fjord exits, since isostatic uplift has been much greater inland. For example, the marine limit near the mouth of Sognefjord is only about 50 m above sea-level, whereas it rises to about 150 m at the fjord head.
2. Many of the moraines and fluvioglacial materials of Finland and Sweden were laid down in the sea or in lakes, and for hundreds

Fig. 4.5 Map of the highest strandlines and contours of uplift (in metres) for Fennoscandia.

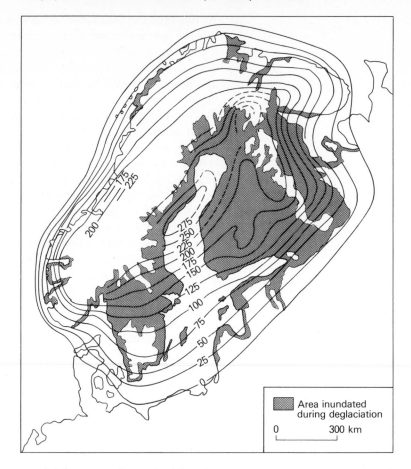

of kilometres the retreating ice-sheet margin was grounded in shallow water. The significance of this fact has still not properly impressed itself on glacial geomorphologists and geologists outside Scandinavia who are used to thinking of ice-sheet wastage on dry land; and the peculiarities of many of the Fennoscandian ice-wastage deposits can often be explained by reference to their watery origins. The map in Fig. 4.5 shows just how great an area was inundated by water at the end of the last glaciation.

3. Even in those areas where 'normal' glacial and fluvioglacial landforms were created on dry land, later inundation often led to the creation of characteristic 'washed' landscapes. In such areas, especially around the shores of the Gulf of Bothnia, wave action has removed a great deal of fine till and other loose material from hill summits and valley sides, leaving behind a clean bedrock surface covered with a litter of erratic boulders and stones. Often in quite unexpected locations perhaps 150–200 m above sea-level and more than 100 km from the coast, the traveller in eastern Sweden or central Finland can find marine deposits and other traces of wave action in clearings in the coniferous forest.

4. Actual shorelines abound throughout the inundated area shown on Fig. 4.5. In some areas the highest shoreline or marine limit coincides with a 'washing limit' above which normal till and fluvioglacial features still exist and beneath which the rock surface is washed and cleaned. The limit may be shown by a change in vegetation, with healthy deep-rooting trees growing on the thick till above the washing limit and smaller stunted trees struggling for a precarious foothold around the boulders and in rock crevices beneath the limit. In Sweden hills which are capped with till above a clearly defined washing limit are called *kalottberg*. Even where there is no clear washing limit Swedish and Finnish geomorphologists can discover the altitude of the highest shoreline by identifying features such as old storm-beaches in favourable localities. The lines of equal uplift on the map show that at least 290 m of isostatic uplift has already occurred in part of Ångermanland. In southern Finland and in the Central Lakes depression of Sweden the highest shoreline occurs at about 150 m, and in southern Skåne marine traces can be found up to an altitude of about 50 m. In the Danish archipelago the raised marine forelands referred to above (p. 55) are normally only a few metres above present sea-level.

5. The effects of isostatic uplift are still spectacular, especially in the northern part of the Gulf of Bothnia. The map in Figure 4.6 shows that the area around Luleå, Skellefteå and Oulu is rising at a rate of almost 1 m per century. In the Stockholm archipelago the rate of land rise is about 50 cm per century, and the rate falls off to zero in Skåne and Denmark. Along most of the Swedish east coast and along the whole coastline of Finland, the rate of land uplift can easily be perceived within the span of a human lifetime as old straits disappear, offshore islands become peninsulas, and as shallow embayments rise to levels at which they are beyond the reach of storm waves, thus allowing them to be used for agriculture.

A particularly interesting feature which is apparently related to the changing levels of land and sea is the *strandflat*. This is a wide rock terrace which occurs along the western coast of Norway and along parts of the Icelandic coast at or a little below present sea-level. Many of the Norwegian skerries are part of the strandflat, and in the Lofotens and elsewhere there is a very sharp break of slope between this low undulating rock terrace and the steep rock cliffs and hills affected by glacial and marine processes. The origin of the strandflat has exercised the minds of geologists and geomorphologists for well over a century. Some authorities have suggested that the strandflat was cut by 'fringing' glaciers which formed close to sea-level during one or more of the Pleistocene glaciations; others have suggested that frost-shattering under a periglacial climate was responsible; and yet others believe that the strandflat is an old river-cut feature formed at a time of lower Tertiary sea-

Fig. 4.6 Map of contemporary uplift rates in Fennoscandia (mm per year).

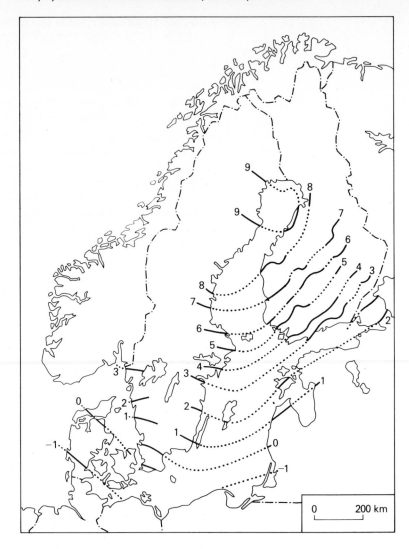

level. Nowadays most geomorphologists who have studied the strandflat seem to favour a composite origin. Since the rock terrace extends along the shores of Sognefjord and other fjords it may be at least partly of interglacial age; possibly it was cut by marine abrasion at a time of slightly higher sea-level and then further extended and abraded by the piedmont glacers that occupied the Norwegian west coast zone beyond the fjord exits during the Pleistocene glaciations.

Independent centres of glaciation

The glacial history of the Faroe Islands and Iceland is less well documented than that of Fennoscandia. Nevertheless, both Iceland and the Faroes were inundated by Pleistocene glacier ice and their landscapes bear abundant traces of both erosion and deposition.

It may safely be assumed that on several occasions during the Pleistocene the Faroes supported a small ice-cap fed by the moisture-laden winds of the North Atlantic. Features of glacial erosion abound in the islands. On the northern islands of Vagar, Streymoy and Eysturoy large parts of the uplands have been scoured by overriding glacier ice, and it is most likely that the watershed breaches that created the sounds or straits between the islands were cut by glaciers. These glaciers flowed towards the south-east from an ice-cap axis which was more or less coincident with the position of the present north and north-west coast. Much of the ice-cap rested upon a land surface which has now been worn away by marine erosion. The sounds are not the only glacial watershed breaches in the Faroes; other examples are Kollarfjarðardalur, a deep trough which runs across the island of Streymoy from Kollafjörður towards Kvivik, and the through valley that runs south-eastwards from the town of Klaksvik on Bordoy. The island of Eysturoy is almost sliced in half by yet another through valley aligned N.W–S.E.

In addition to the features created beneath a thick ice cover, there are innumerable cirques in the Faroe Islands. These show up spectacularly on the aerial photographs of Vagar and Streymoy; they occupy a wide variety of sites, and they vary considerably in their orientations and altitudes. On the eastern side of Eysturoy, near Fuglafjörður, there is a row of huge cirque basins along the edge of the upland; their bases coincide with the altitude of a spectacular coastal terrace at about 100 m. Elsewhere old cirque basins are found at sea-level, and some of the Faroese cirque glaciers have eroded their bedrock hollows beneath present-day sea-level. Here and there marine erosion on the north and north-west coasts has left only remnants of cirque headwalls and sidewalls as reminders of the work of Pleistocene glacier ice.

There are very few landforms of glacial deposition in the Faroes, although ridges of medial and lateral moraine can be found here and there on the flanks of glacial valleys. Much of the land surface is covered with a veneer of stony till, but in the present moist climate of the islands most of this glacial material has been redistributed by the processes of solifluction and slope collapse. There may well be spreads of glacial and fluvioglacial materials in the outer parts of the main glacial troughs; but because there has been very little isostatic uplift on the islands the sea-level rise of the past 10,000 years or so has caused the deep submergence of these key areas.

The youthful island of Iceland did not exist in its present form until the Pleistocene epoch was well under way. And yet the effects of glaciation are apparent on all sides. As in the Faroes, there are many features which can be related to the work of a large ice-cap which probably covered the whole land area, and there are many more features such as cirques and valley glacier troughs which can be explained by reference to 'local' glaciation.

In several localities in western and northern Iceland ancient tills or *tillites* are interbedded with lava flows, and the dating of these lavas indicates that glaciation has been in progress for at least 3 million years. The most famous of the tillite sequences are at Tjörnes in north-east Iceland and at Husafell in western Iceland; at both sites the evidence suggests that there have been at least ten glacial episodes, although it is not known how many of these were full-scale glaciations and how many were of local importance only. Even if large-scale glaciation has only affected Iceland for the last 2 million years or so (i.e. since the beginning of the Pleistocene period as it is generally defined by geologists), the accumulated results of glacial erosion are striking. The satellite image in Figure 4.7 shows part of the Eyjafjörđur district in northern Iceland. The huge glacial troughs that have carried ice towards the coast are easily picked out on the photograph, and we can see how the original dendritic pattern of Tertiary river valleys has been modified by ice. The large outlet glaciers which have used these troughs have truncated the interfluves between the main tributary valleys and have widened the main or 'trunk' valleys to a marked degree. The result is a remarkable and somewhat distorted type of dendritic channel pattern which is very characteristic of large-scale erosion by outlet glaciers. This type of channel pattern may have been

Fig. 4.7 Satellite image of part of the landscape of northern Iceland. The fjord is Eyjafjörđur. Note the dendritic pattern of glacial troughs, particularly in the upland area called Tröllaskagi. (Photo: NASA)

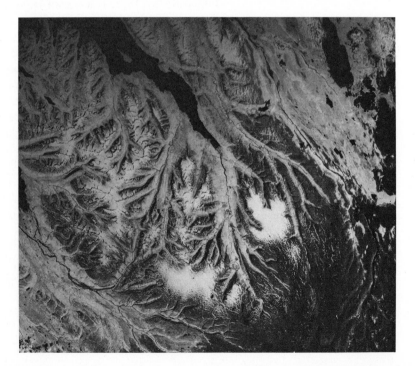

created during a time-span of less than 2 million years; from the dating of volcanic rocks on the flanks of glacial troughs elsewhere in Iceland we know that completely new valleys 700 m deep can be cut by active ice in less than 1 million years.

As in other parts of Scandinavia, Iceland has supported its own ice-cap on at least two occasions during the last 250,000 years. The counterparts of the Saalian and Weichselian glaciations were probably both very important from the point of view of landscape change. Again, as in the case of Norway, there are signs that the main elements of the glacial landscape (such as the fjords and main cirque basins) were already in existence at the onset of the Weichselian glaciation; furthermore, these features were not greatly modified by the work of Weichselian ice. Thus as in the case of Fennoscandia, the main erosional features of Iceland are probably of Saalian or greater age, while the main *depositional* features were created at the end of the Weichselian glaciation.

An interesting area for the study of glacial erosion in Iceland is Vestfirðir, a peninsula which is somewhat remote from the main centre of the Icelandic ice-cap and which probably supported its own thick ice cover during the Saalian glaciation. This is an area which is famous for its multitude of cirques, but of much greater importance in the landscape are the features linked with the cutting of fjords which are ranged around the whole of the Vestfirðir coastline. There are three main types of glacial landscape on the peninsula:

1. Alpine landscapes with steep-sided ridges, mountain peaks, deep cirques and valley glacier troughs. Such landscapes are found mostly on the peninsulas of the west and north.
2. Fjord landscapes with 'amphitheatre' collecting-grounds. These amphitheatres are like broad, enlarged cirques, and they seem to have been cut by glacier ice descending from the old Tertiary basalt plateau in the interior parts of the peninsula.
3. Fjord landscapes with very steep trough heads cut by large outlet glaciers descending from the main plateau ice-caps.

The types of features to be found in any particular part of Vestfirðir, and the extent to which the old plateau surface has been destroyed by glacial erosion, can be related to the amount of local ice which had to be discharged towards the coast. The alpine landscapes, with their small glacial valleys and fjords, represent a high density of small or moderately sized glaciers. Coalescing ice streams in the main amphitheatres have been responsible for the elimination or truncation of old drainage divides, and the evidence shows that in such locations a great deal of ice had to be disposed of. For the most part the ice was converging towards the heads of the main outlet glacier troughs, and the amount of downcutting in these troughs was sufficient to create sizeable fjords. But by far the most impressive fjords of Vestfirðir are the wide and steep-sided troughs of Arnarfjörður, Dyrafjörður, Isafjörður and Jökulfirðir.

Arnarfjörður is about 40 km long and the Isafjörður fjord system is about 75 km long. These may not seem very impressive when compared with the lengths of Sognefjord and other Norwegian fjords, but in the Icelandic context they represent very great modifications of the landscape by glacier ice. These troughs were undoubtedly cut by large volumes of ice draining directly from the old plateau remnants of Glama and Dranga. These were the two main areas of Pleistocene ice accumulation in Vestfirðir, and the Dranga plateau still has a small ice-cap at the present day. If we examine the distribution of the troughs shown on Fig. 3.5 (p. 43) we can see that there is a gradual northward diminution in the dimensions of troughs both on the western coast of Vestifirðir and in the Isafjörður fjord system. The largest troughs are those that drained the largest areas of plateau; the smallest are those that drained but small remnants of the original plateau. All of these features, large and small, illustrate the enormous erosive capacity of ice flowing in concentrated 'ice streams' or outlet glaciers.

One other type of erosional landscape exists in Vestfirðir; in the southern and south-western parts of the peninsula thick active ice appears to have been flowing across the whole of the landscape. The land surface has a 'scoured' appearance, and the processes of erosion seem to have lowered the old plateau surface by at least 200 m in this area. In contrast, some of the old plateau surfaces further north, which were the source areas of the ice that flowed into the main glacier outlet troughs, appear to have been *protected* rather than lowered by the thick ice cover which rested upon them during more than one Pleistocene glacial episode.

During the Weichselian glaciation ice again covered the whole of Iceland. There is some debate about ice-free 'plant refuges' in the peripheral parts of the country, and some authorities have argued that various high peaks and remote peninsulas were never completely covered by glacier ice. (Fig. 4.8). Recent evidence from many of these key areas shows that the Icelandic ice cover *was* complete, with ice flowing for some distance on to the surrounding offshore shelf in all directions. While the ice cover was still thick there were many subglacial volcanic eruptions, giving rise to the palagonites referred to on p. 37. Later on, about 14,000 years ago, the ice began to retreat. The isostatic depression of the island was considerable, and as the ice margin retreated across the coastline the sea flooded in to affect many coastal districts. The marine limit has now been plotted in many parts of Iceland, and in some areas raised marine deposits are found more than 120 m above sea-level. Allowing for the eustatic sea-level rise that has occurred during the last 13,000 years there has been an isostatic rebound of at least 230 m.

As in other parts of Scandinavia, the most important Pleistocene deposits in the coastal districts are the raised marine terraces of sand

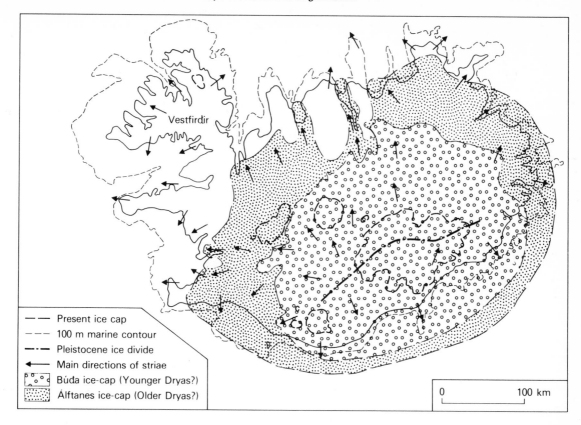

Present ice cap
100 m marine contour
Pleistocene ice divide
Main directions of striae
Búda ice-cap (Younger Dryas?)
Álftanes ice-cap (Older Dryas?)

Vestfirdir

0   100 km

Fig. 4.8 Some important Pleistocene features in Iceland. (After Einarsson 1971)

and gravel. Some of these are prominent landscape features, and they grade into thick spreads of outwash gravels in the main river valleys. In addition, impressive terminal moraines and other morainic features are found in many of the coastal valleys that carried outlet glaciers during the wastage of the Weichselian ice sheet. Many of the terminal moraines and masses of dead-ice moraine are difficult to date, and many of them may have been formed during local oscillations of the ice margin during the long period of deglaciation between 13,000 and 8,000 years ago. However, one Icelandic moraine is of national importance, being found throughout the northern and western parts of the country. This is the so-called Budi moraine, represented by huge elongated mounds of till and fluvioglacial materials near Myvatn, in the Thjorsa valley near Reykjavik, and in many other localities (Fig. 4.8). The moraine has been correlated with the Ra moraine of Norway and the Salpausselkä moraines of Finland, and it shows that there was a prolonged stillstand of the ice margin (or even a glacier re-advance) about 10,500 years ago. Following the Budi stage the ice-cap margin in Iceland retreated steadily, finally breaking up into the smaller ice-caps such as Langjökull and Vatnajökull which still exist today.

The present interglacial

The present interglacial (which is often referred to as 'the postglacial period') has lasted, so far, for about 10,000 years. During this time the landscapes of Scandinavia have evolved steadily, at first largely under the influence of natural processes, and in recent centuries increasingly under the influence of man. The pattern of environmental and landscape change has not by any means been simply controlled by a regular warming up of the climate following the end of the Weichselian glaciation. On the contrary, the events of the past 10,000 years or so illustrate both the instability and the variability of the Scandinavian environment.

Table 4.1, which has been constructed from a number of sources, shows the main environmental changes that have occurred in Scandinavia during the Flandrian or Holocene interglacial. The stages referred to on the table are labelled according to the conventions of pollen stratigraphy, being based on the changes on the pollen content of organic or lake deposits. The assumptions are always that the character of the 'pollen rain' gives a good indication of the character of the local vegetation at any particular time, and that the local vegetation reflects accurately the nature of the local climatic environment. Hence a stratigraphic change from a deposit rich in birch pollen to another deposit rich in pine and hazel pollen may be taken to indicate a climatic warming; conversely a reduction in oak and elm pollen and an increase in pine and birch pollen in a succession of deposits may be taken to indicate a climatic deterioration.

During Pollen Zone III (also called the Younger Dryas) the deglaciated parts of Fennoscandia were gradually colonized by tundra plants such as dwarf willow, dwarf birch, mosses, lichens and cotton grass. In a few areas, especially in Denmark, there were quite large wooded areas in which birch, pine and willow were the main tree species. As the climate warmed during Zones IV, V and VI (referred to as the Pre-Boreal and Boreal episodes), the ice of the Scandinavian ice sheet retreated to the mountain fastnesses of the far north and the Ancylus Lake grew to its greatest extent. More and more land became available for colonization by plants, and as the zone of tundra vegetation moved northwards and into the mountains so the mixed forest spread over much of the land area of the Baltic Shield. By the time of the Atlantic period and the Littorina Sea the climate of Fennoscandia had warmed up so much that mean annual air temperatures were higher than those of the present day. The 'Atlantic' conditions of Zone VII were so warm that they have been referred to by Scandinavian botanists as the 'climatic optimum' or the 'Hypsithermal'. At this time the mixed coniferous forest of southern Sweden was replaced by a forest in which deciduous trees such as oak, elm and linden were common, and deciduous species also became very common in the boreal

B.P.	Stages of ice retreat	Pollen stratigraphy (southern Finland)	Stages in the development of the Baltic Sea (generalized)	Cultures	Years AD/BC
1,000–					–1,000
2,000–		IX Sub-Atlantic (spruce, pine)	Iron Age — Baltic Sea		–0
3,000–		VIII Sub-Boreal (birch, pine, spruce, elm, oak, linden)	Bronze Age		–1,000
4,000–				Kiukainen Culture / Boat-Axe Culture / Degenerate Comb-Ceramic Culture / Typical Comb-Ceramic Culture	–2,000
5,000–	Holocene (Flandrian)	VII Atlantic (birch, pine, elm, oak, linden)	Littorina Sea	Early Comb-Ceramic Culture	–3,000
6,000–					–4,000
7,000–				Suomusjärvi Culture	–5,000
8,000–		VI	Stone Age — Ancylus Lake		–6,000
9,000–		V Boreal (pine)		Askola Culture	–7,000
10,000–	Salpausselkä III / Salpausselkä II / Salpausselkä I	IV Pre-Boreal (birch)	Baltic Ice Lake		–8,000
11,000–	Gothiglacial	III Younger Dryas (tundra)	Late glacial Yoldia Sea		–9,000
12,000–		II Alleröd / I Older Dryas			–10,000

Table 4.1 Vegetational change and pollen zones in Fennoscandia during the past 12,000 years. (After various authors)

forest of southern Finland. About 4,000 years ago the climate deteriorated and rainfall totals were somewhat reduced. This was the Sub-Boreal episode also referred to as Zone VIII. About 2,500 years ago moister conditions returned and the resulting Sub-Atlantic climatic regime (Zone IX) has persisted. The vegetation of Fennoscandia took on its present-day character, with mixed deciduous forest in the south, boreal or coniferous forest over most of the Baltic Shield area, and park tundra and true Arctic tundra in Lapland and in the highest parts of the Caledonian Mountains. In recent times human interference has altered the character of the natural vegetation in many ways; agricultural clearances, tree-felling for urban and industrial developments, afforestation projects and many other activities have left their mark over very large tracts of southern Fennoscandia in particular.

Superimposed on the broad environmental changes referred to above and on pp. 54–63 there have been many smaller-scale climatic oscillations lasting for centuries or for just a few decades. The most important of these oscillations are referred to by geomorphologists as 'Neoglacial' oscillations, because several distinct but short-lived coolings of climate appear to have resulted in readvances of the glaciers of the Caledonian Mountains and Iceland. Neoglacial advances in Norway and Sweden seem to have occurred at about the following times: 8,000 years ago, 5,000 years ago, 2,500 years ago and during the last 300 years or so. The 'periodicity' of about 2,500 years has been hotly debated by glacial geomorphologists during the last few years, and it may indeed be more apparent than real, since the differentiation and dating of the various Neoglacial advances are still matters of dispute.

The most recent of the Neoglacial episodes is referred to as the Little Ice Age. This was a time of marked climatic cooling and strong glacier advances in many of the glacial valleys of Scandinavia, and it was a time during which glacial history helped to fashion the corporate personality of the Scandinavians. The impact of this episode on the farming communities of the Norwegian valleys was dramatic; harsh winters and cold rainy summers caused hardship and even famine, particularly around 1750 and around 1850, when advancing glaciers and floods of meltwater destroyed many of the higher pastures in the valleys of the Norwegian fjord country. In the seventeenth and eighteenth centuries the spectre of famine was never far away from the peasantry of Norway, Sweden and Finland, and an overpopulated countryside could not produce enough food to maintain the farming community. Thousands of animals and thousands of people died as a result of runs of cold rainy summers accompanied by crop failures; when the opening up of the New World presented the opportunity of escape in the later part of the nineteenth century, mass emigration was an inevitable consequence. This is a theme which is treated in more detail in Chapter 12.

The impact of the Little Ice Age was particularly tragic in Iceland. During the early Middle Ages the climate of Iceland was relatively warm, and the agricultural community prospered. Then, around 1400, the climate began to deteriorate. Harvest failures became commonplace and sea ice began to appear around the Icelandic coast even at the height of the summer. In the 1700s and 1800s there were a number of glacier advances, and catastrophic meltwater floods and volcanic eruptions caused widespread famine and greatly reduced the morale of the population. Many thousands of farm animals died. The population of Iceland was decimated by famine, and written records show a reduction by 50 per cent between 1600 and 1850. As in the case of the other Scandinavian countries, thousands of country people fled to the New World, desperate for a life which could be lived away from the threat of climatic decline and glacial and volcanic catastrophes.

By 1950 the climate had improved again, and the Little Ice Age seems to have come to an end. But the events of the last few centuries have made a deep imprint upon the folk memory of Scandinavian people, and the Little Ice Age serves as a timely reminder that the environment of the countries discussed in this book is seldom constant but always harsh.

Suggested Reading

Quaternary Glaciation

Ahlmann 1919; Andersen 1965; Andersen and Sollid 1971; Åse 1979; Bout *et al.* 1955; Dahl 1946; Einarsson 1971; De Geer 1912; Gjessing 1966; Glückert 1974; Holtedahl 1967; Hoppe 1959, 1971, 1972; John and Sugden 1962; Lundqvist 1965, 1972, 1974; Mangerud 1976; Mangerud *et al.* 1974; Mannerfelt 1945; Okko 1955; Østrem *et al.* 1973; Østrem and Ziegler 1969; Schou 1949; Schytt 1959; Sund 1960; Thorarinsson 1969; Virkkala 1963.

Eustasy, Isostasy and Climatic Change

Bergthorsson 1969; Denton and Karlen 1973; Einarsson 1963; Evers 1962; Eythorsson and Sigtryggson 1971; Holtedahl and Sellevoll 1972; Jones 1977; Karlén 1973; Mangerud 1970; Nilsson 1960; Rudberg, 1961; Scherman 1976; Smeds 1950; Steindorsson 1962; Thorarinsson 1944; Vasari *et al.* 1972.

Chapter 5   The physical environment: present-day conditions

The physical environment of Scandinavia is made up of a multitude of interrelated elements. Taken together, these elements comprise an environmental system; separately, they can be identified as components of the five main 'spheres' that affect the surface of the earth:

1. *the lithosphere* or surface layer of rocks and sediments, mostly of non-organic origin;
2. *the atmosphere* or envelope of air which surrounds the planet;
3. *the hydrosphere* or sphere of water represented by oceans, seas, lakes and rivers;
4. *the cryosphere* or sphere of frozen water that affects the high latitudes in particular;
5. *the biosphere* or sphere of living things (plants and animals) which inhabit parts of the other spheres.

The main characteristics of the lithosphere have already been examined in Chapters 3 and 4, and mention has already been made of certain of the climatic and vegetation characteristics of the Scandinavian countries. However in this chapter it is worth bringing together in a rather more organized way some of the essential information that the student needs if he is to understand the contemporary physical environment of Scandinavia and the problems and potentials that arise from it. The text will concentrate for the moment upon the lithosphere, the atmosphere and the biosphere, for these are the spheres of greatest importance both from the human standpoint and from the point of view of regional personality.

The lithosphere: Scandinavian landscape zones

Most geographers hold, in their mind's eye, images of 'typical' Scandinavian landscapes. When they think of Norway they think of deeply cut fjords and snow-capped peaks; when they think of Iceland the image is one of barren deserts with grotesque lava formations, or perhaps of large ice-caps and erupting volcanoes;

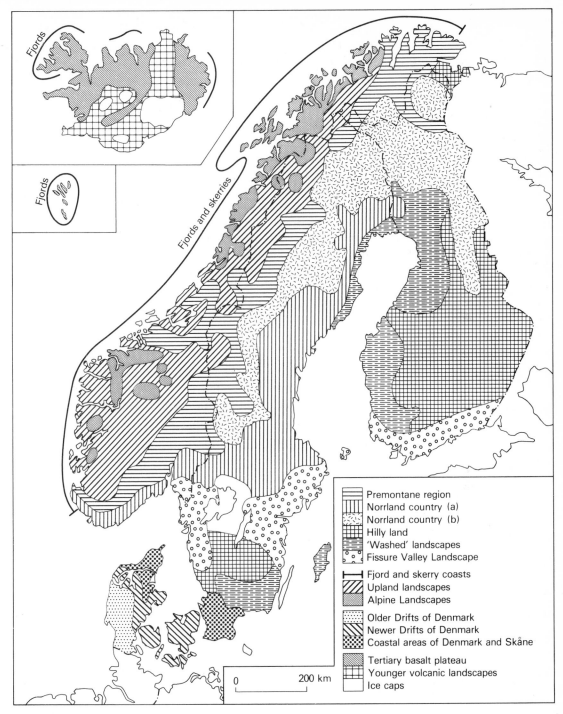

Legend:

Premontane region
Norrland country (a)
Norrland country (b)
Hilly land
'Washed' landscapes
Fissure Valley Landscape

Fjord and skerry coasts
Upland landscapes
Alpine Landscapes

Older Drifts of Denmark
Newer Drifts of Denmark
Coastal areas of Denmark and Skåne

Tertiary basalt plateau
Younger volcanic landscapes
Ice caps

Fiords

Fiords

Fiords and skerries

0   200 km

Fig. 5.1 Map of the main landscape zones of Scandinavia. These zones are related for the most part to the geological units described in Chapter 3.

they imagine Finland as a land of lakes and forests; and their image of Denmark is perhaps one of a man-made landscape full of efficient dairy farms and carefully managed fields. These images are partly based upon fact, but they are also based upon mythology and tourist propaganda, and those who are interested in the geography of Scandinavia need to know something of the range of landscape types and their distribution if they are to acquire a framework for an understanding of the region's cultural and economic 'character'.

The map in Fig. 5.1 shows the distribution of the main landscape zones of Scandinavia. The classification is based upon both geological and geomorphological criteria, and it differs in many respects from other published classifications. It could be elaborated through the creation of many more subdivisions; but it is adequate for the purpose of this book. Perhaps the most striking feature which emerges is the incredible juxtaposition of the very old and the very new in the Scandinavian landscape. By far the most important parts of the geological time-scale from the point of view of landscape evolution are the Pre-Cambrian and the Cenozoic eras, separated by a 'gap' of over 500 million years. The following are the main points of interest.

A. Baltic Shield landscapes

1. *Premontane region.*   Here the landscapes are composed of hills or plateau sections separated by deep valleys which sometimes contain finger lakes and Pleistocene drift landscapes.

2. *Norrland country.*   As described on p. 39, this is a vast expanse of hilly land. Scandinavian geomorphologists often subdivide this landscape type on the basis of relative relief 'categories', but the main subdivision is between (a) the undulating hill and valley terrain which is particularly widespread in southern Norrland, and (b) the monadnock and plain landscape of northern Norrland and Lappi, with widely dispersed mountains rising sharply above the surrounding country. Large parts of these landscapes are covered with relatively unmodified glacial and fluvioglacial features.

3. *Hilly land.*   In parts of southern Sweden and especially in the Lake District of Finland there is an open landscape of broad swells and hollows with a relative relief of less than 100 m. A notable characteristic is the almost total lack of clearly defined valleys.

4. *'Washed' landscapes.*   Around the Gulf of Bothnia, in the centre of the Baltic Shield downwarp, there are a number of different landscape types including morainic and fluvioglacial features modified by higher sea and lake levels. In some areas the exposed bedrock surface is hilly; elsewhere, especially on the Finnish shores of the Gulf of Bothnia, there are wide plains of bedrock or alluvium.

5. *Fissure-valley landscapes.*   These landscapes, especially wide-

spread in southern Sweden and south-western Finland, have already been described on p. 39. Glacial scouring is a feature of bedrock surfaces, and submergence and emergence have resulted in the widespread occurrence of washed bedrock hills with intervening narrow clay vales.

B. Caledonian Mountain landscapes.

1. *The Norwegian fjords and skerries.* The fjord coast extends from the far north to the far south of Norway. Many of the fjords extend deeply into the heart of the mountain country. Some of the skerries and offshore islands are parts of the strandflat, which is especially well marked around the Lofotens and along the fjord coast to the south of the Arctic Circle.

2. *Upland landscapes of glacial erosion.* Large parts of the uplands are composed of ice-scoured erosion surfaces and deep glacial troughs. In the southern parts of the uplands there are especially extensive glaciated plateaux with glaciated valleys and high residual mountain peaks. Relative relief is sometimes less than 200 m, but adjacent to trough heads and steep mountains it can be as high as 1,500 m.

3. *Alpine landscapes.* Here there are steep peaks, arêtes, cirques and valley glacier troughs. This type of scenery is found in parts of Norway, Sarek and other areas of Swedish Lapland, and also in the Lofotens off the Norwegian west coast. In some areas 'local' or mountain glaciation has affected the landscape more drastically than ice-sheet glaciation.

C. Landscapes of Denmark and Skåne

1. *The Older Drift landscapes of Denmark.* In Jylland, landscapes of subdued and denuded glacial drift are broken up by old meltwater courses. There are some newer fluvioglacial channels and sheets of outwash deposits beyond the edge of the Weichselian terminal moraine in Jylland.

2. *The Newer Drift (Weichselian) landscapes of Denmark.* Hummocky morainic drift, meltwater channels and masses of fluvioglacial sands and gravels can be found in eastern Jylland, and throughout Fyn and Sjaelland.

3. *Coastal areas of Denmark and Skåne.* Here there has been slight uplift of marine sediments as a result of isostatic recovery. In the Danish literature these areas are referred to as the 'postglacial marine plains'. Other plains are found in Skåne and in the granite districts of Blekinge.

D. The Cenozoic volcanic islands.

1. *Landscapes of the Tertiary basalt plateaux.* Broad plateau

surfaces and deeply cut fjords and sounds are typical. Examples of these 'trap' landscapes can be found in north-western, northern and eastern Iceland and in the Faroe Islands.

2. *Volcanic landscapes of central Iceland.* These were created for the most part during the Pleistocene period. Volcanic cones, lava fields and deserts are widespread; in many areas there is little surface drainage, and wind-eroded forms such as dunes and stripped surfaces can be found, particularly in conjunction with areas of ash or tephra.

3. *Ice-cap landscapes.* These occur in parts of western and southern Iceland, in particular. In addition to the main ice-caps themselves (e.g. Langjökull, Vaknajökull and Hoffellsjökull) there are associated outlet glaciers and broad *sandar* (plains of fluvio-glacial sands and gravels) created from meltwater stream deposits. Most of these *sandar* are on the Icelandic south coast; they are periodically inundated by great meltwater floods called *jökulhlaups*. Some of these are connected with volcanic eruptions beneath the ice, and others are connected with the very rapid and short-lived glacier advances called *surges*.

The soils of Scandinavia

The soils of the Scandinavian countries are influenced to a great extent by the nature of the superficial deposits dumped by ice or meltwater at the end of the last glacial episode. Of these deposits, tills of various types and fluvioglacial sediments such as sand and gravel are by far the most widespread. Silt and clay deposits are found in particular where fluvioglacial materials have settled out of suspension in glacial lakes and in areas submerged by the great water bodies referred to in the previous chapter. Other uplifted marine deposits form the basis for soils in some of the coastal districts of Denmark and western and northern Norway. In the higher mountain areas there are great expanses where frost-shattered bedrock and other periglacial materials blanket the ground surface, and in Iceland lava, volcanic ash and wind-blown sediments are the soil-forming materials in the younger volcanic districts in particular.

In spite of their 'youthful' nature, Scandinavian soils can be differentiated on the basis of their pedological or soil-profile characteristics. The greater part of Fennoscandia is covered by podsols – soils which are formed under continental subarctic conditions and which are typical of the north European *taiga* or coniferous forest zone. Away from the coniferous forest areas, podsols are also found in western Jylland, especially on the Older Drift landscapes. In southern Sweden most of the low-lying areas experience a milder climate and where the forest cover is of mixed deciduous and coniferous species the process of podsolization is less marked. Some pedologists refer to the soils of this region as *brown earths*, and others as *grey–brown podsols*; they are characterized by freer drainage and less acid surface conditions than the true podsols, and they are best developed in Skåne and eastern Denmark. In the uplands of Norway and Sweden, and in the coastal lands bordering the Arctic Ocean, *tundra soils* are common. Such soils consist for the most part of broken rock fragment; they are relatively thin, and lacking in organic material. Most of Iceland supports tundra soils, but here they are immensely varied as a result of the volcanic, glacial, fluvioglacial and periglacial materials which occur at the surface. Other 'special' soils, which cover restricted areas only, are the *calcareous upland soils* of north-western Norway (found especially in the coastal districts between Namsos and Tromsø), the salt-marsh soils found in western Jylland, and the bog or peat soils of south-western Iceland and the Lofotens.

The relatively simple picture of soil types given above can be misleading, for the traveller in any part of Scandinavia affected by Weichselian glacial processes will be struck by the immense range of surface conditions that confront him. In central Finland, for example, the chances of finding 'ideal' podsols over a wide area are rather slim: within any given area there may be bare rock outcrops, patches of clay till or ground moraine, drumlins with a surface cover of stony till, eskers or more extensive sheets of sand or gravel, and patches of lacustrine silt and clay. In the hummocky areas of dead-ice moraine large boulders and stones may litter the surface. And almost everywhere minor topographical irregularities give rise to myriads of small shallow lakes, peat bogs and wider expanses of open water. Even if such areas support thick coniferous forest the podsols are thin, poorly developed and immensely variable in their profile characteristics. Little wonder that in some parts of Scandinavia pedologists prefer not to use the terminology of the major soil groups at all.

The climatic environment

In Chapter 2, in the consideration of Scandinavia's geographical setting, some stress was placed upon the influence of location and latitude in the climatic environment. Mention was made of the environmental and psychological impact of darkness and light, cold and warmth, and the chapter introduced the idea of Scandinavia as a world dominated by winter. At this stage it is necessary to look in more detail at the climatic characteristics. The most important climatic generalizations are as follows:

1. Over the year the amount of solar energy received at the surface

is smaller than the amount of energy transmitted into the upper atmosphere and into space. In other words, Scandinavia has a negative annual radiation balance.

2. The energy deficit is compensated for by the horizontal transport of air (advection) particularly from the south-west and west, and by latent heat released by condensation.

3. There is a moisture surplus. On average, the Scandinavian countries receive 200–300 mm more precipitation per year than is lost by evaporation.

4. The atmospheric circulation is of a 'westerly' type, with relatively warm, moist air transported across the Atlantic Ocean bringing anomalously warm conditions to the maritime parts of Scandinavia during the winter half-year.

5. The movement of air across the North Atlantic and Scandinavia involves a great deal of turbulence. Partly this is a result of cyclonic activity, with frequent depressions and their associated fronts passing across the countries concerned. Partly the turbulent conditions result from the topographic barrier presented by the Caledonian Mountains, leading to exaggerated windiness and increased precipitation on the western flanks of the mountains and decreased windiness and precipitation to the east.

6. The contrast between the maritime and continental sections of Scandinavia results not only from latitude and location but also from the characteristics of water bodies such as the North Atlantic, the Norwegian Sea and the Baltic Sea. The flow of the warm North Atlantic Drift is, of course, the factor of greatest importance in the west, while the tideless Baltic acts during the autumn and spring as a reservoir of summer heat and then of winter cold to increase the continentality of climate in Sweden and Finland in particular.

Most of the climatic statistics (for example, those concerning temperatures, precipitation and wind) are related to these points, as are the day-to-day changes in atmospheric circulation which we refer to as weather.

Temperature variations

In the maritime areas of Scandinavia there are no great excesses of either heat or cold (Fig. 5.2). In south-eastern Iceland the difference between the mean temperature of the coldest month and that of the hottest month is less than 8 °C, and along most of the Norwegian west coast the difference is less than 14 °C. In Bergen, for example, the mean temperature for July is 14.2 °C, while the mean for January is 1.7 °C. Further to the south and east Copenhagen, in a more continental situation, has a July mean of 16.7 °C and a January mean of 0.4 °C. The variation in temperature amplitude is controlled by longitude much more than by latitude, and maritime influences seldom find their way to the east of the Cale-

Fig. 5.2 Maps showing the distribution of air temperatures in Fennoscandia during (a) January and (b) July. Note that temperature extremes are much greater in the continental east than they are in the oceanic west. (After Milward 1965)

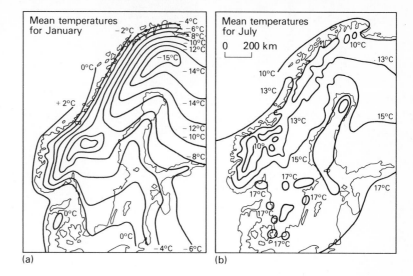

(a)

(b)

donian Mountains. Where the mountain barrier is low, for example in the Storlien Pass between Trondheim and Östersund, maritime influences can penetrate almost as far as the Gulf of Bothnia. Östersund has an amplitude of monthly means of only 22 °C, compared with 24–26 °C at the same latitude in central Finland.

The maps in Fig. 5.2 show that temperature extremes are much greater in the eastern part of Fennoscandia, where polar continental air-masses make their influence felt. In northern Finland January mean temperatures are commonly below –15 °C, and in some areas as low as –20 °C; and even in the eastern parts of the Finnish Lake District January means can be below –10 °C. No part of Finland has a January mean which is above 0 °C. To compensate for the excessive cold of winter these areas have unexpectedly high summer temperatures. It is by no means unusual for daily maxima in July and August to rise above 25 °C and even 30 °C, and in south-eastern Finland the July mean temperature is higher than anywhere else in Scandinavia, over 18 °C. The July mean at the head of the Gulf of Bothnia is 16 °C, higher than the July mean in Esbjerg more than 1,500 km to the south-west. To a very large extent the influence of warm continental air at this time of year, combined with the local effect of continuous daylight and long hours of sunshine, compensate for the relatively low position of the sun in the Arctic summer sky.

Precipitation

Precipitation is controlled above all else by the prevailing westerly winds of Scandinavia, so that the western and seaward coasts receive far more precipitation than the more continental areas further east. In the west most precipitation falls during the winter half-year, and mostly it is associated with cyclonic activity

Fig. 5.3 Winter in Finland: snow-clearing operations in the streets of Helsinki. (Photo: Finnish Embassy)

in the atmosphere. In the east, however, the wettest months around the Gulf of Bothnia are July and August. The wettest parts of Scandinavia are the high mountain areas of western Norway, where snowfields and glaciers receive over 4,000 mm of precipitation per year. The greater part of western Norway receives over 1,000 mm per year, in contrast to large parts of Lapland and the coastal districts around the Gulf of Bothnia which receive under 500 mm per year. The driest part of Norway lies to the east of Jotunheimen, where in the rain-shadow zone the annual precipitation is only 300–400 mm per year. Similarly low totals may occur in parts of the western fjord country, in low-lying valleys adjacent to uplands which receive over 2,000 mm per year.

During the winter months much of the direct precipitation falls as snow; at Engabreen, for example, one of the outlet glaciers of Svartisen, about 3,000 mm of the annual precipitation total of 4,000 mm falls as winter snow. In Finland the thickness of the winter snow cover is considerable; for example at Sodankylä, just inside the Arctic Circle, the snow-pack may be more than 60 cm deep from October through to mid-March. When temperatures are well below 0 °C much of the snow-pack may be redistributed by drifting during blizzards (Fig. 5.3).

Other factors

A number of other climatic parameters are dependent upon the relations between temperature and precipitation. For example, the annual duration of the snow cover is clearly related to both air temperatures and precipitation, and Fig. 5.2(a) shows how altitude is also a factor. Snow lies throughout the year above the firn line and in the vicinity of glaciers, for more than 220 days per year in the mountains of Swedish Lapland, and for more than 200 days per year in other parts of Lapland. In the highlands of south-western Norway the ground is snow covered for more than 180 days per year, for altitude tends to counteract the benefits which may derive from southerly latitude and from the effects of mild Atlantic air. Most of southern Sweden experiences a snow cover of less than 100 days per year, and the Lofotens, far to the north of the Arctic Circle, have no more than 120 'snow-days'. Denmark, the Faroes and southern Skåne have fewer than 40 days per year when snow lies on the ground.

The distribution and duration of sunshine through the year are influenced by temperatures and cloudiness, and sunshine totals are highest in those areas which have the least precipitation. The sunniest parts of Scandinavia, with totals over 2,100 hours per year, are south-eastern Norway, the western coasts of the Gulf of Bothnia, northern Finland and south-east Sweden. The islands of the Baltic Sea also have quite high sunshine totals, since they escape for the most part the cumulus clouds which commonly build up over land during the summer months. Some sheltered areas inside the Arctic Circle benefit from the long daylight hours of the summer months. The areas with the lowest sunshine totals are the rainy coastlands of Trøndelag in Norway and the windward slopes of the southern Swedish highlands, with only 1,400–1,600 hours per year. Iceland also suffers from its stormy, cloudy climate; although it has a climate lacking in extremes, it is also somewhat lacking in sunshine.

Another climatic factor of critical importance for the human geography of Scandinavia is the length of the growing season. This is related above all else to the period during which daily mean temperatures remain above 3 °C. In Lapland the growing season may last for no more than 130 days; for example, in Karesuando in northern Sweden all planting, cultivating and harvesting needs to be completed between 18 May and 24 September in an average year. In contrast the growing season is over 180 days in most of southern Sweden and western Norway. On the island of Fanø, Denmark, the growing season lasts from 24 March to 5 December.

Here the risk of frost damage to growing crops is slight, but it should be borne in mind that even well within the growing season inland districts of Lapland and central Finland in particular may still be liable to crop damage by frost. In general, however, the northern-most areas reap the full benefit of continuous daylight and high air temperatures during the early and most critical part of the growing season.

Vegetation

The main vegetation regions are shown in Fig. 5.4. The boundaries between successive woodland zones are highly generalized, for the

Fig. 5.4 Map of the main vegetation types of Scandinavia. (After Sømme 1961)

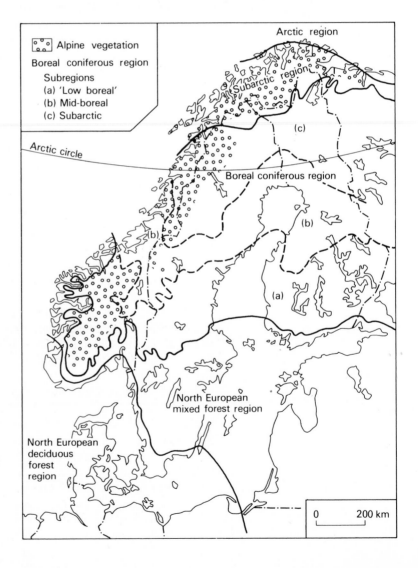

gradations between one vegetation type and the next are subtle in the extreme. By and large, however, the control of latitude over vegetation is quite strong, except in the west of Fennoscandia where maritime influences and altitude have marked effect upon the distribution and abundance of plant species. For example, the arctic–alpine plant *Dryas octopetela* is found even in the southern-most parts of the Norwegian mountains, while maritime influences allow beech (*Fagus silvatica*) to exist on the coast of western Norway somewhat north of its normal range.

In the far north the vegetation is dominated by Arctic tundra, with a predominance of low hardy dwarf shrubs (mainly Ericaceae) grasses, mosses and lichens. Locally, where there is abundant mois-ture and sunshine and a good depth of soil, vegetation is luxuriant. Elsewhere barren rock surfaces or periglacial blockfields predomi-nate. In some boggy areas there are patches of permafrost, and *palsas* (ice-cored mounds of peat) and other features demonstrate the presence of ground ice. On the tundra there are striking changes of surface texture and hue from the short-lived technicolour extra-vaganza of summer flowers to the flaming reds, yellows and browns of autumn and the sterile whiteness of winter. Similar changes of scene can be seen among the high peaks of the Caledonian Moun-tains, where the alpine vegetation of southern Norway has many species in common with the Arctic tundra proper.

As far as woodland types are concerned, Fennoscandia is domi-nated by the western part of the Eurasian taiga or boreal coniferous forest belt. It grades northwards into a type of 'forest tundra'; here there are treeless areas of barren rock or subarctic tundra inter-spersed with stands of conifers and also the birch species *Betula tortuosa*. These trees grow further north than any other tree species, extending into the Arctic tundra proper and forming a dense tangle of 'scrub forest' in sheltered valleys.

On the southern edge of the boreal coniferous forest there is a wide belt of mixed deciduous–coniferous forest. It is best repre-sented in southern Sweden, although it extends into southernmost Norway and south-western Finland also. In this region the forest is more variable in character and disturbed to a much greater extent by human activities over the centuries. In some areas conifers make up over 75 per cent of the tree species, but there are increasing numbers of the following deciduous trees towards the south: beech (*Betula*), alder (*Alnus*), aspen (*Populus*), mountain ash (*Sorbus*), willow (*Salix*), lime (*Tilia*), elm (*Ulmus*), ash (*Fraxinus*), oak (*Quercus*) and hazel (*Corylus*). In south-western Sweden and in Denmark the mixed forest gives way to pure deciduous forest. In some of the luxuriant woodlands of Denmark the beech is the most widely dispersed tree (Fig. 5.5), and yew, holly and ivy are also characteristic. In many areas there are extensive heather heaths, mostly resulting from deliberate forest clearance by grazing and burning.

Fig. 5.5 One of the beech woodlands of southern Sweden. Most of these woodlands are not 'natural' but planted; most of the original mixed deciduous woodland of Denmark and Skåne has long since been removed. (Photo: Domänverket, Falun)

Fig. 5.6 A photograph which for many people typifies the vegetation of Scandinavia. The coniferous or boreal forest covers vast areas of Sweden and Finland in particular; the most common species are Norway spruce and Scots pine. (Photo: Leif Öster/Domänverket, Falun)

The taiga proper, which extends across at least 600,000 km², gives Scandinavia one of its most enduring popular images. In Norrland and central Finland the forest blankets the landscape, subduing its irregularities and eliminating colour variation through the constancy of its greenery. However, the apparent uniformity of the taiga is illusory (Fig. 5.6). Although the coniferous forest of Finland and Sweden is poorer than any other part of the taiga in its range of tree species (most of the trees are of two species only – Norway spruce and Scots pine), birch and other broad-leaved species make up 13 per cent of the forest area even in Norrland. In addition there are wide expanses of peatlands; about 30 per cent of the area of Finland and northern Sweden is covered by bogs and fens of different types, and some of these wetlands are particularly rich in plant species. In some areas lakes and wide, slow rivers dominate the scene, and where ice-scouring has left a bare rock surface few trees are able to find an adequate foothold. On the shores of Lake Rogen there is a grotesque landscape of living and dead Scots pines,

tilted and twisted and fallen, a few of them still rooted precariously in shallow soil and in rock crevices between hugh erratic boulders. This sort of variety in the forest can be seen by those who are prepared to look, for the taiga is in places young healthy and elsewhere in a state of decline. It often requires management, and management usually means harvesting and replanting. This is where man comes in; as indicated in chapter 8, the taiga is not so much a dreary wasteland as a cherished resource.

The vegetation of Iceland and the Faroes shows much less diversity than that of Fennoscandia. Trees are scarce; although species such as birch, rowan, juniper, dwarf willow and conifers can thrive out of the reach of salt spray and sheep, the flora of the Faroes is dominated by grassland with heather in drier locations and mosses and sedges where damper conditions prevail. In Iceland grassland and *myri* vegetation (with mosses, cotton grass, sedges and rushes) predominate in the lowlands whereas inland, in the semideserts, and at altitudes above 200 m or so there are areas of subarctic tundra. On the ice-caps, on the shifting sands and gravel plains of the coastal *sandar*, on the sterile precipitates of the hotspring districts, and on the great sheets of lava and ash around the main volcanoes, there are the real Icelandic deserts. In these areas low temperatures, lack of nutrients or lack of moisture often create conditions in which not even the hardiest of lichens can survive.

Suggested reading

Landscape zones

Ahlmann 1976; Jacobsen 1976; Malmström 1958; Naturgeografisk regionindelning av Norden 1977; Preusser 1976; Rudberg and Bylund 1959; Schou 1949; Smed *et al*. 1966; Smeds 1960a.

Soils, climate and vegetation

Ångstrom 1958; Eythorsson 1949; Hultén 1950; Kiilerich 1928; Ostenfeld 1901; Ostenfeld and Gröntved 1934; Rutherford 1982; Sjörs 1956; Steindorsson 1935–37; Tamm 1950; Wallén 1961.

Chapter 6 The cultural environment: settlement, politics and regional personality

The settlement of Scandinavia commenced about 11,000 years ago, while the Weichselian ice sheet was melting away and as more and more land became available for human occupation. As the ice edge retreated northwards and westwards small groups of Palaeolithic hunters followed it, living for the most part in the scanty forests near the coasts of the Baltic Ice Lake, the Yoldia Sea and the Ancylus Lake. Other groups of hunters reached Arctic Norway by following the coast westwards from Siberia. Later, as the forests spread northwards, these Stone Age people learned to live a nomadic life based upon intermittent forest-burning and animal husbandry, and by Neolithic times (about 5,000 years ago) there was some permanent settlement. The Neolithic peoples created the first villages and tribal centres, and for the first time land was cleared specifically for the cultivation of crops such as wheat and barley.

As the outlines and levels of the Baltic water bodies fluctuated so the pattern and process of settlement changed. Throughout Fennoscandia several different cultures overlapped. Since most of the inward migration was through Finland and Denmark these were the earliest 'centres of culture' in Scandinavia; later on tribal groups settled in Bohuslän in Sweden, and in the Oslo area in Norway. The Neolithic culture which developed in the eastern part of Denmark spread to northern Jylland and eastwards into much of southern Sweden. This phase can be recognized through innumerable traces in the landscape, including longhouses, half-circular houses, field boundaries and dolmens such as the Troldkirken near Limfjorden, Denmark. In Finland there was a succession of cultures during the Stone Age, beginning with the Suomusjärvi culture around 9,000–7,000 years ago and culminating in the 'boat-axe' culture of about 4,000 years B.P., so called because of the finely polished boat axes made by a seafaring or coastal people. Whereas earlier groups of Stone Age people were quite widely scattered, those who carried the boat-axe culture concentrated almost exclusively on the emerging clay plains of southern and western Finland as the land gradually rose isostatically out of the sea. These plains probably provided ideal conditions for the introduction of animal

Fig. 6.1 Tollund Man, one of the Iron Age 'bog people' whose wonderfully preserved corpses were found in Tollund bog in Jylland, Denmark. He had been sacrificed to Mother Earth, strangled with a rope before being cast into the bog. (Photo: National Museum of Antiquities, Copenhagen)

husbandry. The pastoral way of life was supplemented by hunting, fishing and gathering.

The technology of the Bronze Age reached Fennoscandia rather late, just over 3,000 years ago. New metal ornaments and tools came into use in many areas, but the spread of Bronze Age culture was very erratic and for centuries there was a complicated mixing of Neolithic groups who survived on hunting, other nomadic groups who cultivated small patches of land, and more sophisticated and organized Bronze Age settlers who kept herds of semi-domesticated animals and who practised a more permanent form of agriculture. In the far north the Arctic Stone Age continued, with a sparse population concentrating entirely on hunting and fishing. With the onset of the Iron Age about 2,500 years ago the use of iron tools, domestic items and weapons spread throughout southern Fennoscandia. There was a great increase in population, and distinct tribal groupings began to appear. Many Iron Age people lived in villages, and we know something about their racial characteristics from 2,000-year-old corpses found in bogs at Tollund and elsewhere (Fig. 6.1).

Fennoscandia was spared many of the troubles of the early Christian era. The area was never incorporated into the Roman world and had few contacts with Roman civilization. Among the most powerful peoples at this time were the Goths, who spread their influence from Götaland and Gotland by widespread colonizing operations around AD 350. The chaos which reigned on the North German Plain following the break-up of the Roman Empire largely bypassed Fennoscandia; the region experienced no major folk migrations and little of the strife and famine which gave this period of history its 'Dark Ages' label. Settlements spread and trade increased. In relative peace the distinctive cultures of the Norse world began to develop.

At first the Baltic was the centre of Norse culture. The tribes of Finland, originally dependent upon trading links with the east and south-east, began to involve themselves more and more in the Baltic world; and in the other settled parts of the region tribal groupings centred upon early 'core areas' were brought under the control of a number of ruling dynasties after AD 700. About AD 800 the tribal rivalries of Sweden subsided when the Svear people conquered the rest of the southern Swedish tribes, laying the foundations for a common development of tribal organization, economy and culture.

The Viking expansion

This is not the place for a discussion of Viking culture and territorial organization; both of these topics are well covered in the huge literature about the Vikings and their way of life. A number of points are, however, of great importance from a geographical point of view in a consideration of the 'Viking era' which lasted from approximately AD 800 to AD 1100.

1. The Vikings were by no means a single homogenous people with a common culture and tribal organization, although they were closely related through language. After two centuries of linguistic evolution the people of Scandinavia all spoke variations on the 'Danish' tongue; they could communicate with one another, and this made joint enterprises easy and emphasized some sort of common identity.

2. The Vikings were not as brutish as much of the early literature on the Viking age might suggest. Recent research on the Vikings reveals that they were as much farmers, seamen, merchants, poets and artists as they were warriors (Fig. 6.2). And they were no more 'barbaric' than any of the other tribal groups of the early Middle Ages.

3. There were no nation-states during the early part of the Viking age. The most effective political unit was the *land* or province. sometimes under the control of a single leader, sometimes part of a federation, and sometimes split by tribal dissensions. The lack of national loyalties is demonstrated by the fact that some of the first Norsemen abroad referred to themselves as 'men of Hordaland' or 'men of Vestfold', rather than as Norwegians.

4. The Vikings were for the most part farmers who supplemented their food supplies through hunting and fishing. As they organized themselves into larger communities during the period AD 800–1100 and as villages and towns such as Hedeby, Birka and Kaupang were created, more and more people made their living by trade and commerce. Trading links became important, especially in Denmark and Sweden; and always the sea was the great trading highway.

5. Viking society functioned through the consent and cooperation of free men. Their main interests were self-preservation and prosperity. The standard unit of society was the extended family or the kinship group; slaves were of great importance in providing labour, and at the other end of the scale there were chiefs and kings who demanded loyalty from their subjects but who were nevertheless dependent upon the consent of the free men for their authority. Respect and loyalty were keywords; profit and loss, honour and shame, were all shared, and common efforts were needed if a community was to aspire to the good or eliminate the bad. There were no written laws, but society placed its own constraints upon the individual and provided him with his motives.

Even before AD 800 Viking groups had begun to range far and wide throughout Europe. Their famous and infamous expeditions have been referred to variously as piratical raids, trading enterprises, or serious attempts at organized colonial expansion. Prob-

Fig. 6.2 A rune stone at Ledberg, Östergötland, Sweden. Most of the runic inscriptions, which are both literary and artistic, are found in the historic 'core' areas of the Fennoscandian states; in Sweden there are more than 3,000 of them. (Photo: Antikvarisk Topografiska Arkivet, Stockholm)

ably they were all of these things, and there is much evidence that the motives of expedition leaders were immensely varied. Probably the period of Viking exploration and settlement owed much more to personal initiative and local tribal circumstances than to any centralized and organized drive towards territorial expansion.

The first phase of expansion took the Vikings to the Netherlands and to northern Britain. Later they reached the Celtic coasts of western Britain and all the other coasts of western Europe. In many cases the earliest contacts between the Vikings and other peoples were in the form of pirate raids; later these were replaced by trading activities and later still, in many areas, by semi-permanent or permanent settlement. The literature of the period AD 800–1000 is full of references to the dreaded Northmen or Norsemen. Even in west Wales, which was very remote by sea from Fennoscandia, records show that the mother church of Welsh Christianity at St David's was ravaged ten times by Norse pirates within the space of just a few years. Large Viking fleets wintered not far away from St David's in the great natural waterway of Milford Haven, and the coast of west Wales acquired a multitudes of Norse place-names (such as Skomer, Skokholm, Ramsey, Grassholm and Musselwick) which demonstrate that the Viking sea-rovers were thoroughly familiar with the west Wales coast. Large settlements were established in northern England, on the Isle of Man and in the Dublin area of Ireland. In France, Normandy was another centre of settlement, and it is not often appreciated that the Normans who conquered England in the eleventh century were the direct descendants (only two or three generations removed) of the Viking colonists of northern France. There were many Viking expeditions (particularly by the Swedish tribes) south-eastwards towards the Volga and to the Slavonic territories of the Danube basin. Quite often these expeditions penetrated as far as the Black Sea and the Mediterranean, and it is now believed that the Vikings also became familiar with the coasts of Spain and Portugal and with the coastline of West Africa.

As their confidence and maritime prowess increased the Vikings ranged further and further afield in the North Atlantic, eventually drawing the Faroes, Iceland and Greenland into the Scandinavian world. Between AD 820 and AD 900 a sizeable Norse colony was established in the Faroes, mostly by family groups from western Norway. They settled in coastal sites throughout the archipelago, and by AD 900 had achieved a sufficiently stable society to establish a *Løgting* or parliament at Torshavn. At the same time the peopling of Iceland was in full swing. In Icelandic history this period is referred to as the *Landnam* period. By about AD 950 nearly all of the feasible settlement sites around the coast had their own small farming communities, and in AD 975 the first Icelandic parliament was organized at Thingvellir. By AD 877 the Vikings had reached Greenland and established their colonies on the west coast; and around AD 1000 Leif Eriksson reached North America. At this time the Vikings had the free use of all the seaways of the North Atlantic, and they held undisputed control of much of the land-mass of western Europe. In terms of global influence this was perhaps the greatest period in Scandinavian history.

There have been many analyses of the reasons for these two centuries of Viking expansion. According to historians, demographic, political, climatic, psychological and technological factors all played a part. In the first place overpopulation was a problem in the main tribal centres of Fennoscandia. The 'population explosion' of the seventh century had led to a great deal of new settlements in the mountain valleys and forests of Norway, and the seafaring instincts of the Vikings must also have prompted many family groups to seek fresh farming land abroad. Community life was also disrupted by internal dissensions and a frequent lack of political stability. It was often necessary for young noblemen to go into exile or to 'prove' themselves on pirate expeditions or voyages of exploration. The warrior chieftains of western Norway were those with the least fertile farming lands and the smallest opportunities for trade; some of them took up a way of life based on plunder, piracy and conquest, and before the reign of King Harald Finehair (AD 872–930) there was no one to control their excesses.

During some decades bad harvests, animal deaths and famine prompted the emigration of family groups in search of virgin territory with a more secure basis for food production. This factor may have been particularly important in eastern Sweden where harsh winter weather and severe sea-ice conditions may have had a damaging effect upon some Viking settlements which were dependent upon farming or fishing.

Many Viking communities had a strong regard for mercantile activities. Piracy was the cheapest way of acquiring exotic foreign goods, but very often conventional trading links were forged with overseas communities and continued over many decades of mutual respect. In addition there was a great deal of internal trade, and the commercial centres referred to above catered as much for local needs as they did for foreign merchants.

The Viking character placed great emphasis upon the virtues of adventure and self-determination. According to Johannes Brøndsted 'their disposition was proud, adventurous, with a

Fig. 6.3 Lindholm Høje, a Viking cemetery near Aalborg, Jylland. The Vikings were not afraid of death, and they often practised very elaborate burials. (Photo: National Museum, Copenhagen)

yearning for glory, a desire to excel in battle, and a scorn for death. These qualities of heroism, combined with their mercantile skills, made them a powerful and dangerous race' (Fig. 6.3). As the Viking age progressed there was also an 'exploration mentality' which excited the peoples of Denmark, Norway and Sweden. Stories of great deeds and great men were handed down and no doubt elaborated, causing young men to leave home determined to emulate if not outdo their predecessors in their search for glittering prizes.

The final factor behind the Viking 'explosion' was related to maritime technology. The shipbuilding developments of the Viking age and in particular the wonderfully graceful and seaworthy qualities of their exploring and trading vessels (Fig. 6.4) have been widely cited as fundamental causes of their trading and colonizing sucess. According to Michael Kirkby, 'without the peculiar perfection of these vessels, the whole seething upsurging manifestation of sheer energy which we call the Viking movement would probably have boiled itself away inside Scandinavia . . .'. The Viking ships were slender and flexible, clinker-built, with symmetrical ends and a true keel. There were various types of vessel, but generally they were of very shallow draught; a 20 m ship drew less than 1 m of water. They could be sailed or rowed; they could be landed on open beaches through heavy surf, and they could be taken up shallow estuaries which were inaccessible to the ungainly craft in use by the other seafaring European peoples.

The roots of inequality

The spread of population through the Scandinavian states during prehistoric, Viking and later times can be interpreted in terms of the concept of 'cores and peripheries'. This concept is considered in greater detail later in Part III of this book, but the main concern of this chapter is the idea that the 'territorial imperative' or the sense of place of a population is of fundamental importance for that population's initial occupation of a landscape, its economic priorities, its feeling of cohesion or national identity, the density of its settlements and so forth. The sense of place is also intimately connected with regional personality, as discussed in the Preface of this book.

The *core* is that section of the nation's territory where most of its historical relics (and hence its cultural roots) are located, where its centre of government lies and where its most important towns and cities are established. It is the area of greatest agricultural productivity, the area on which its manufacturing and trading wealth is founded and the area of greatest population density. It is also that part of a state over which national control is most easily exercised,

Fig. 6.4 The Oseberg Ship, built in the early ninth century, was a burial ship – more ornate and a little smaller than the exploring and trading vessels which mastered the harsh conditions of the North Atlantic. The ship is now in the Viking Ship Museum in Oslo. (Photo: Universitetets Oldsaksamling, Oslo)

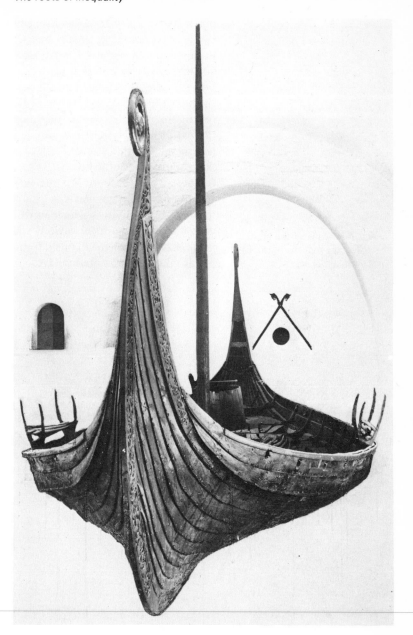

and in times of war it is the territory most energetically defended. In contrast, the *periphery* of a nation-state or a tribal territory is that part of it which lies at some distance from the centre of authority. It has a lower cultural significance than the core area because it is settled later; the rule of law is more difficult to impose; population density is generally lower than within the core area; and the periphery tends to have fewer large urban centres and fewer manufacturing and trading functions. At the same time agricultural productivity is lower, and surpluses of all sorts which are produced by the people of peripheral areas are more difficult to dispose of because of remoteness from the main centres of population. And yet these very population centres, because they are the centres of power, can turn the peripheries into economic dependencies through the use of a number of different techniques. This causes resentment, so the people of the peripheral area tend to be more radical in politics than the people of the national core areas, and less satisfied with the machinery of state control. They are also spiritually more self-sufficient. In general, those parts of the periphery furthest from the core are the last areas to be absorbed into the state; and the periphery is gradually colonized as a result of 'pioneering' activities which move outwards from the centre and gain their impetus from various state initiatives and incentives.

Fig. 6.5 Maps of the main settlement regions of the five Scandinavian states.

Basically, then, in a consideration of cores and peripheries the geographer is concerned with regional inequalities, relative wealth

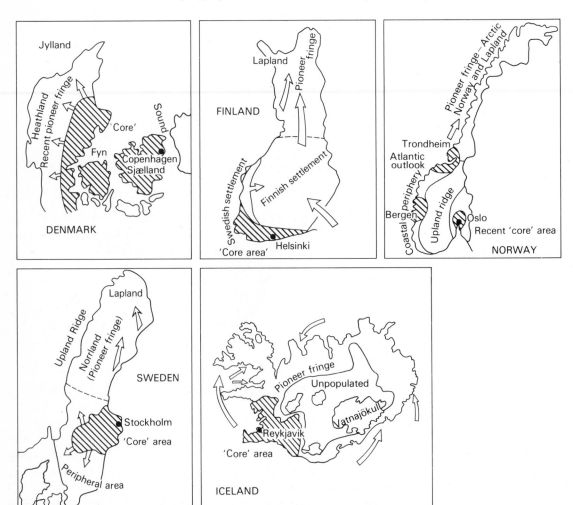

and relative poverty, accessibility and remoteness, comfort and hardship. These are not simply matters of historical interest; as is demonstrated in Part III of this book, the problem of regional inequality is one which still demands solutions from the politicians of the five Scandinavian states.

The earliest and most stable of the cores shown in Fig. 6.5 were those of Sweden and Denmark; this is reflected in the long political rivalry of these two states, although it must be remembered that their present-day territorial extent was not defined until quite recent times. The political development of Norway suffered from that country's lack of physical cohesion; its early growth centres were widely separated by difficult stretches of coastline and by mountain barriers inland, and so it took a long time to acquire nationhood. Finland also emerged as a state in relatively recent times, having been for centuries virtually a colonial territory of Sweden. Iceland and the Faroe Islands, which were not properly settled until the Viking era, were colonized very rapidly, and real inequalities between cores and peripheries did not appear until the last few centuries. The following paragraphs summarize the main features of the historical development of the component parts of Scandinavia and provide some insight into the workings of the 'territorial imperative'.

Sweden

The Swedish core area came into being before Viking times as a result of the combined power of the Svear and the Goths. There was a dense and settled agricultural population by AD 800, and in Östergötland and Uppland (Fig. 6.6), agricultural villages had already developed on the fertile clay plains. The forested upland blocks between these settled areas acted as barriers, and the lack of contact between various tribal groups resulted at first in intense rivalries. Eventually, however, trading links were established through the use of the lakes and rivers of the region, and a sense of common identity began to grow.

During the Viking era the frontier of settlement was pushed northwards and westwards into the dense forest, and scattered clearings were made for agriculture in Småland, Dalarna and southern Norrland. During the fourteenth century the rate of colonization slowed down, partly as a result of the Black Death and of a temporary deterioration of climate. In some areas there was even a retreat from the margins of the settled territory.

During the fifteenth century Sweden was linked intermittently with Denmark, but the Swedish independence movement culminated in the final restoration of home rule under Gustav Vasa during the 1520s. Subsequently there was a phase of aggressive territorial expansion which culminated in the 'golden age' of Sweden. This commenced under the rule of Gustav Adolf between

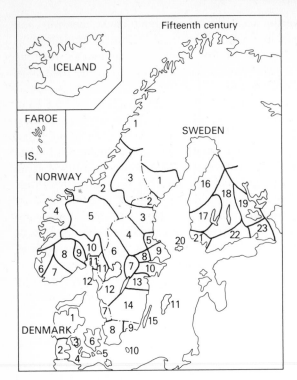 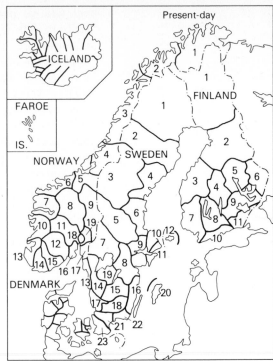

Fig. 6.6 Maps of the administrative divisions of Scandinavia.

The Faroe Islands were, as at present, administratively a part of Denmark. Each province was called a *landskap*. At present each Icelandic and Faroese county is called a *sysla*; the Danish county is called an *amt*; the Norwegian county is called a *fylke*; each Finnish county is called a *lääni*; and each Swedish county is called a *län*. (After Sømme 1961)

The modern administrative divisions of Denmark, Iceland and the Faroe Islands are too small and too numerous to be shown at this scale.

(a) Fifteenth century

Norway 1. Hålogaland 2. Trondheim 3. Jämtland 4. Bergen 5. Oplandene 6. Stavanger 7. Agder 8. Skiensyssel 9. Tunsberg 10. Oslo 11. Borgarsyssel 12. Viken

Denmark 1. Jylland 2. Sønder-Jylland 3. Fyn 4. Lolland 5. Falster 6. Sjaelland 7. Halland 8. Skåne 9. Blekinge 10. Bornholm 11. Gotland

Sweden – Finland 1. Ångermanland 2. Medelpad 3. Hälsingland · 4. Dalarna 5. Gästrikland 6. Värmland 7. Närke 8. Västmanland 9. Uppland 10. Södermanland 11. Dal 12. Västergötland 13. Östergötland 14. Småland 15. Öland 16. Österbotten 17. Satakunta 18. Tavastland 19. Savolax 20. Åland 21. Egentl. Finland 22. Nyland 23. Karelen

(b) Present-day

Norway 1. Finnmark 2. Troms 3. Nordland 4. Nord-Trøndelag 5. Sør-Trøndelag 6. Møre og Romsdal 7. Sogn og Fjordane 8. Oppland 9. Hedmark 10. Hordaland 11. Buskerud 12. Telemark 13. Rogaland 14. Vest-Agder 15. Aust-Agder 16. Vestfold 17. Ostfold 18. Oslo 19. Akershus

Sweden 1. Norrbotten 2. Västerbotten 3. Jämtland 4. Västernorrland 5. Kopparberg 6. Gävleborg 7. Värmland 8. Örebro 9. Västmanland 10. Uppsala 11. Stockholm 12. Södermanland 13. Göteborg och Bohus 14. Älvsborg 15. Jönköping 16 Kalmar 17. Halland 18. Kronoberg 19. Skaraberg 20. Gotland 21. Kristianstad 22. Blekinge 23. Malmöhus

Finland 1. Lappland (Lappi) 2. Uleåborg (Oulu) 3. Vaasa (Vasa) 4. Mellersta Finland 5. Kuopio (Kuopio) 6. Nordkarelen 7. Åbo och Björneborg (Turku and Pori) 8. Tavastehus (Häme) 9. Sankt Michel (Mikkeli) 10. Nyland (Uusimaa) 11. Kymmene (Kymi) 12. Åland (Ahvenanmaa)

1611 and 1632. Various of the old Danish territories were brought under Swedish control. Skåne, an ancient exclave of Denmark on Swedish soil, was finally taken during the Thirty Years War, and under Gustav Adolf and his daughter Christina the Swedish state extended its political control over a number of territories on the southern shore of the Baltic. Under Karl Gustav (1654–60) the Swedish Empire attained its greatest-ever extent.

By 1700 a number of different settlement types could be discerned in the landscape of southern Sweden. One of the most important was that associated with the economic development of Bergslagen, based upon the discovery and exploration of various mineral ores and upon the clearance of the forest. In addition, the old tribal centres with their long-established villages, the later areas of dense agricultural settlements and the small clearances and homesteads of the pioneer fringe all contributed to the development of regional character.

While all this was going on in the south there was a quiet colonial expansion into Norrland and Finland. Settlers were encouraged to move north in order to stabilize the political control of the state, and there was also much new settlement well to the south of the pioneer fringe. Eventually Lapland was brought under effective control, and by the early 1800s the extreme north of Sweden was the home of a mixed community of struggling farmers, smallholders and traders in hamlets and small villages, nomadic Lapp reindeer herders, hunters and trappers, and miners and their families. After 1850 Lapland acquired great economic and strategic significance with the exploitation of the iron-ore reserves of Kiruna and Gällivare. In more recent times the state has invested a great deal in forestry projects and hydro-electric power schemes, but to-day the northern part of Norrland is still a 'problem area'. Its remoteness and its harsh physical environment make it far less attractive to modern settlers than other parts of Sweden, and there is considerable emigration. Subsidies and incentives are required if firms and individuals are to make the move to the north in order to stabilize the population. There is considerable affluence in parts of northern Norrland today, but many outsiders argue that it is an artificial and subsidized affluence.

The map of Sweden in Fig. 6.5 shows the following four settlement zones:

1. The ancient core area of Svealand.
2. The peripheral area of southern Sweden, settled for the most part before 1600.
3. The 'pioneer fringe' of Norrland, which has subsequently become a 'problem area' instead.
4. The upland ridge. The Swedish mountains are unimportant from a settlement point of view except for occasional mining, hydro-electric power and recreational developments.

Denmark

The history of settlement in Denmark is closely linked with the natural division of the country into Older Drift and Newer Drift landscapes, although it would be a mistake to interpret the Newer Drift margin as a sharp settlement boundary. Stone Age settlement was widely distributed, but later development took place for the most part in the Newer Drift areas. In some coastal districts, as in Vendsyssel and around the shores of Limfjorden, fertile plains provided the basis for successful Iron Age farming; elsewhere undulating morainic topography provided shelter for animals. By the time of Christ there were village communities in addition to the scatter of isolated homesteads. There was a particularly dense settlement pattern in Sjaelland, eastern Fyn and northern Jylland. As noted above, several of the Danish Iron Age communities have acquired great modern renown through the discovery in peat bogs of wonderfully preserved human corpses about 2,000 years old. Tollund Man is the best known of these (Fig. 6.1), but at least 165 other pickled Iron Age inhabitants have been dug up from Danish bogs.

During the Dark Ages the Danish tribes began to develop their maritime interests, and fishing and trading activities grew in importance. Local rulers began to capitalize upon the growing economic importance of the Sound, and as they realized the full strategic value of controlling the Baltic Sea exit more and more settlement occurred in Fyn, Sjaelland and Skåne. The core region of Denmark stabilized on the western and southern coasts of the Kattegat; the old trading centre of Ribe, on the North Sea coast of Jylland, gradually gave way in importance to Hedeby at the base of the Jylland peninsula and then to Viborg, Aalborg, Århus and Lund.

During the Viking era Denmark entered into a phase of aggressive expansion. Harald Bluetooth unified the Danes and his successor Svend Forkbeard incorporated Norway and most of England into his kingdom. King Canute completed the process of expansion by taking over the Swedish crown. In 1035 Denmark was the centre of a far-flung empire, and although it contracted somewhat in later centuries it remained the most powerful of the Scandinavian states. Its economic wealth was based upon fishing, farming on the fertile soils of Sjaelland in particular, and trading. Its military strength was based upon its historic position astride the crossroads of northern Europe and especially upon the determination of a succession of rulers to maintain the strategic control of the Sound. Military encampments such as Trelleborg were used as garrisons for maintaining control over home territories and also as bases for foreign expeditions.

The three centuries between 1100 and 1400 were devoted, militarily at least, to the conquest of new Danish territories on the southern Baltic shores and to the recovery of Norway and Sweden.

This was achieved in 1397 when the annexation of Sweden by Queen Margaret was confirmed by the Treaty of Kalmar. After 1400, however, with the intermittent rise of Swedish power and the decline of Danish influence abroad the Danes entered upon a phase of home-based development. Most of this development took place within the traditional Danish core area. The seat of power was moved in 1445 from Roskilde to Copenhagen, and thereafter the latter city was to grow into the greatest commercial, administrative and political centre of the Baltic Sea arena. Most of the advances in the Danish economy now took place in the east, and the heath-lands of western Jylland suffered from relative neglect. On the North Sea coast there were few settlements of any size, and Ribe and Ringkøbing suffered from many decades of neglect.

In the year 1864 the Danish state lost Schleswig-Holstein to Germany. The province had contained some of the country's best farmland, supporting a population of 200,000 Danes. The trauma of this defeat led to an episode of introspection in Denmark, and one of the results of this was a determination to conquer the peat bogs and barren sandy heaths of western Jylland. Under the auspices of the Danish Heathland Society drainage schemes were commenced in the wetlands while the dry heaths were transformed by shelter belts of conifers and subjected to careful schemes of soil improvement. Special agricultural techniques were pioneered; planned villages were established in previously unsettled locations; and urban life also flourished as the sleeping countryside was stirred into action. Between 1880 and 1950 the greater part of the heath-land disappeared. Denmark's pioneer fringe, smaller and less remote than the pioneer fringes of the other Fennoscandian states, was thus conquered in one quiet yet determined national assault.

Finland

The early evolution of the Finnish settlement pattern is best seen in terms of the country's shifting relationships with Sweden in the west and Russia in the east. Medieval Finland was an appendage of Sweden, brought under control during the crusades of the twelfth, thirteenth and fourteenth centuries and confirmed in 1362 with the legal recognition of the seven Finnish provinces (Fig. 6.6) as the equal of the Swedish provinces. Thereafter the Swedish – Finnish union was almost unbroken until the beginning of the nineteenth century, in spite of nationalist unrest within the Finnish provinces and two short episodes of Russian occupation around 1720 and 1740. As the strength of Sweden waned the Russian tsars saw Finland as a rich territorial prize; and in 1809 pressure from Russia culminated in military conquest and the creation of a Grand Duchy tied to Russia but enjoying a considerable measure of independence in administrative, economic and social affairs.

Throughout the greater part of the post-Viking era the personality of Finland has been shaped by three complementary influences. These have emanated from the stable Swedish-speaking territories of the south-west, the unstable Finnish territories of Karelia and the east which have always been the subject of Russian ambitions, and the areas of restless pioneering in the centre and north of the country. Finnish settlement history is as complex as its political history, but the pioneering theme is a common one, and many authors have remarked upon the persistence of pioneering as a way of life until quite recent times. Basically the story is one of expansion northwards from an old core area and of consolidation or 'infilling' in those areas (such as the Finnish Lake District) already settled.

As mentioned above (p. 83), the early settlement of Finland occurred in a series of erratic episodes, particularly along the south-western coast as it emerged isostatically from the sea. This area, close to Sweden and easily accessible via the skerries and the Åland archipelago, was also agriculturally productive. By 1155 (the year of the first Swedish crusade) the south-west quarter of Finland was the home of a stable agricultural community with but a loose political organization. As Swedish influence increased, the coastal district around Åbo (Turku) became the country's first clearly defined core region. Gradually the Swedes extended their control northwards and eastwards, and Swedish immigration was concentrated particularly on the Finnish south coast and on the coastal plain in Österbotten. The immigrants coexisted, for the most part amicably, with the Finnish-speaking peoples of the area to give Finland its distinctive dual personality which has persisted to this day.

Åland is part of the Swedish-speaking realm which has a unique settlement history. The earliest settlement occurred about 6,000 years ago, although most of the prehistoric features in the landscape date from the Bronze Age and Iron Age. The latter lasted in Åland until Viking times, when the island group was incorporated into the Swedish culture area. There was considerable immigration from the Swedish mainland, especially following the introduction of Christianity, and by the year 1400 Åland was well defended by the mighty fortress of Kastelholm and also by other fortified structures. The islands thrived on farming, fishing and sealing, and trading links with the Baltic ports were well established by the end of the Middle Ages. Åland was important to Sweden as a stepping-stone on the route to the Swedish settlements in Finland, and in later centuries its maritime traditions were enhanced through trading operations between the Baltic and the North Atlantic ports. The port of Mariehamn was founded in 1859. During the eighteenth and nineteenth centuries Åland was subjected to all sorts of pressures through the decline of Swedish authority, and it experienced military action on a number of occasions. During the twentieth century its status has been much disputed. Although it was traditionally looked on as a province of Finland its cultural affinities were undoubtedly Swedish. During the period 1809–1917 it was a part of the Grand Duchy of Finland, and hence effectively under Russian control, but during the First World War the sovereignty of the islands evolved into a debate between the Swedes, the Finns and the Ålanders themselves. In the end Åland became neither an independent state nor part of Sweden; Finnish sovereignty was confirmed by the League of Nations in 1921, but the islanders were granted a large degree of autonomy.

Most of the inland settlement of Finland during the Middle Ages was by Finns. Later there was a sixteenth-century push northwards and eastwards in response to directives from the state and as the population of the core area increased. The first tentative movements into the southern part of the Lake District of central Finland had been based upon fur-trapping, fishing and hunting, but as the forest trails were used more and more intensively small trading posts had evolved into centres of settlement and pioneer farming. By 1600 larger clearings were being made in the forest, and farming communities were springing up particularly in the provinces bordering the Gulf of Finland, with the support and encouragement of the Swedish–Finnish state.

The push to the far north, into the harsh marginal lands of Lapland, took place only very slowly, but with the upsurge of Finnish nationalism during the seventeenth century there was an awakening of territorial consciousness and colonial settlers pushed further and further into the territory of the Lapps. There was a further great surge of pioneering activity during the nineteenth century. In the remote districts more and more permanent fields appeared. Farms were planted in the border country of north-eastern Finland, for now pioneering was not only a way of life but a political and strategic necessity; even under the relatively benign control of the Russians Finnish nationalism was growing, and the Finns were determined to demonstrate their economic and spiritual dependence upon their cold and stony soil. They recognized, too, that the wilderness held some economic resources of value, and the exploitation of both forest and mineral resources for industry was well under way by the year 1900.

The twentieth-century exploitation of the timber resources and water power of the northern part of Finland has brought many people into the area as settlers, but Lappi is somewhat deficient in the great mineral resources which might provide a sound economic basis for intensive settlement. So the successes and failures of the colonial process were based largely on forest clearance, marginal agriculture and, recently, renewed afforestation.

The Second World War was a time of political confusion, wavering national purpose and spiritual trauma for the Finns. They lost Karelia in the east and the Petsamo Corridor in the north, and Lapland was devastated by the Germans. Karelian refugees flooded

Fig. 6.7 Notodden stave church in western Norway. This is one of the best preserved of the Norwegian stave churches. (Photo: Norwegian National Tourist Office)

into a battle-scarred Finland. They had to be settled on Finnish soil, and this resulted in an episode of pioneering on a scale unparalleled anywhere else in north-western Europe during modern times. This pioneering effort was concentrated not in the 'empty' lands of the north but in the forested centre and south of the country, in areas supporting an established agricultural population. As a result of the Karelian resettlement, overpopulation became a problem in many farming districts during the 1950s and 1960s; and the Finnish government subsequently had to introduce a policy to reduce the number of forest farms. As a result much of the land laboriously reclaimed and brought into agricultural production in the post-war years was replanted as forest.

The three main settlement zones of Finland are as follows:
1. The old core of Swedish settlement in the south-west and along the shores of the Gulf of Bothnia and the Gulf of Finland.
2. The area of Finnish settlement and Karelian resettlement in the centre and east of the country.
3. The pioneer fringe of north-central Finland and Finnish Lapland.

Norway

From the map of Norway on Fig. 6.5 it is apparent that the country has three historic core areas, widely separated and differing in character. This situation arose because of the lack of physical cohesion in Norway. From the earliest days of settlement the coastal configuration and physical characteristics of Norway have not encouraged a feeling of unity among its people; the west-coast districts have always had an Atlantic outlook, while the Oslo district has always maintained close links with the adjacent coasts of Denmark and Sweden. Even today there is a strong feeling of rivalry between Bergen and Oslo, two of the traditional trading centres of the country. It can be argued that there are very sound environmental reasons why Norway, having lost her independence in 1319, did not again become an independent state until 1905.

Some of the earliest centres of settlement were in the Oslo area, but there was also pre-Viking settlement around Bergen and Stavanger and in other west- and north-coastal districts. During Viking times there were strong tribal territories centred on Oslo, Bergen and Trondheim. These groups had relatively little contact with one another, for while the Oslo tribes enjoyed trading and cultural links with the peoples of Denmark, the Low Countries and the British Danelaw, the west-coast tribes were in constant contact with western Britain, Iceland, the Faroes and the Greenland colony. Norway was unified to some degree under Harald Fairhair in the tenth century and again between 1014 and 1030 with the introduction of Christianity by Olaf Haraldsson. The 'early Christian era' which followed was notable for the building of Norway's beautiful stave churches, as at Borgund, Urnes, Notodden and Fantoft (Fig. 6.7).

Trondheim was the first of Norway's core areas to enjoy a position of pre-eminence. It was founded by Olav Tryggvesson in AD 97, and as the centre of a fertile and sheltered farming district with strong trading traditions it held a leading place in Norway's economic and political life until the end of the fourteenth century. It was also a great ecclesiastical centre, and its archbishops built the city's cathedral from tithes and trading revenues. Bergen, further south but devoid of any fertile hinterland, was a daughter of the sea. Following its founding around 1070 it was no more and no less than a trading outpost of the Hanseatic League. It flourished at Trondheim's expense in the Middle Ages, and its prospered while other parts of Norway suffered through economic exploitation, a deteriorating climate and a succession of plagues. The town's strength was reinforced by the passing of the crown to Denmark in the late fourteenth century. Now that the control of the state had been removed far to the south Bergen reached the peak of its prosperity, holding a monopoly on the fish trade of the whole of northern Norway. The Hanseatic warehouses of Bryggen are a reminder of this period (Fig. 1.3(a), p. 11). Later Bergen entered into a slow decline, and with the ending of the Hanseatic trading monopolies sixteenth-century Bergen could no longer survive on special privileges.

In 1380 King Olav V shifted the Norwegian capital from Trondheim to Christiania, later to be called Oslo. Gradually administrative institutions were moved to the new centre, which already enjoyed great advantages of location and natural resources. Its fertile farmlands were already intensively cultivated, and it had, in the Middle Ages, strong trading links with the other ports of the Kattegat and the Sound. It was, however, subordinate to Bergen, in both size and importance, until the middle of the last century. Thereafter it grew rapidly during its union with Sweden which lasted until the declaration of independence in 1905. The lowlands around Oslofjord, and the city of Oslo, have now become the undoubted economic core of Norway, with prosperous agriculture and industry and a growing population drawn from every province of the state.

In Arctic Norway, the country's pioneer fringe, the basic settlement pattern of scattered fjordside communities , isolated homesteads and small fishing villages has remained unchanged for centuries. Probably the region's greatest relative importance was at the time of Trondheim's dominance in Norwegian affairs. Most of the colonization of the coasts and inland valleys occurred during the eleventh and twelfth centuries, but thereafter, for 500 years or more, this territory was a political no man's land, subject intermittently to Danish, Hanseatic and even Russian interest but for the most part left to its own devices. The population suffered from neglect and famine; settlements and fields were abandoned, and for long periods these Arctic coasts seem almost to have disappeared from the Norwegian consciousness. It was not until the end of the eighteenth century that a new phase of settlement commenced.

During the 1800s the Norwegian Arctic settlements survived, precariously, on fishing, supported by the products of an imported mid-latitude agricultural system on the very limits of its physical range. During the present century fishing has continued as the main pillar of the local economy, and small centres such as Hammarfest have grown considerably. Industrial and hydro-electric power developments have brought with them new towns such as Mo i Rana; but the region is still remote, deficient in natural resources, and 'marginal' from many different points of view. It is *still* a pioneer fringe.

Norway's four settlement zones are as follows:
1. The Oslo district, which is the most recent of the three core areas but now the industrial and agricultural centre of Norway.
2. The Stavanger–Bergen–Trondheim coastal belt, where the Atlantic maritime tradition is still strong.
3. Arctic Norway and Norwegian Lapland, an economically marginal area which still has many of the characteristics of a pioneer fringe.
4. The Norwegian uplands, where isolated hydro-electric power and tourist developments coexist with a few scattered farming communities.

Iceland and the Faroe Islands

The settlement geography of these two Atlantic territories has many features in common. Both were settled relatively late (during the period of Viking expansion in the North Atlantic) and also relatively rapidly. By about AD 950 most of the available coastal sites of both Iceland (Fig. 6.5) and the Faroes had attracted settlement, and the later immigrants from western Norway found that there was little land left for them to occupy. Both the Icelandic capital of Reykjavik and the Faroese capital of Torshavn developed in Viking times as political and commercial centres, but their growth was retarded during the Middle Ages by outside domination of the affairs of state. Under the provincial rule of Norway, and then the joint Norwegian–Danish state, and then Denmark alone, there were almost eight centuries of neglect and economic stagnation in Iceland. In the Faroes the Danish trading monopoly of 1662–1856 had particularly severe effects, but the abolition of the monopoly brought with it a period of modest economic advance. Within the last century both Reykjavik and Torshavn have grown rapidly, and now, somewhat belatedly, they dominate the economic life of these two Atlantic outposts of the Scandinavian world.

Iceland and the Faroes are unusual in Scandinavia in that they were almost completely settled within a century of the arrival of the first immigrants. Certainly they have their uninhabitable areas and their territories which are so marginal that they have been inter-mittently settled and intermittently abandoned; but the spatial extent of settlement in both countries has hardly changed for almost 1,000 years.

Settlement themes and regional consciousness

The above brief survey of Scandinavian settlement history demon-strates the complexity of the region's internal relations over thou-sands of years. A good proportion of the story is concerned with the territorial imperative – the animal instinct that attaches people to places. This instinct may be strong, but it is also variable in its quality and liable to be suppressed or even destroyed by changing economic or political circumstances. Much of the history of Scan-dinavia can be seen in terms of personal or national ambitions for power or wealth; the multitude of territorial changes which has produced the present-day political map of Scandinavia demon-strates that no territory is bound with sacred ties to a particular group of inhabitants or a particular nation-state. Many factors can lead to changes in the territorial status quo, but in general the longer a territory is occupied the stronger is the territorial imper-ative of its people. A solidly based population, feeling that a spirit of place has entered its corporate soul, will not easily be displaced; if it *is* displaced (like the population of Karelia at the end of the Second World War) its sense of loss is difficult to comprehend, for the loss is measured in spiritual rather than material terms.

Another point of interest concerns the shifting perceptions of territorial value which characterize the relationships between people and places. As mentioned on p. 90, the concept of core and periphery is useful for understanding why certain territories may change their 'value rankings' from time to time during the course of a nation's settlement history. The value of a territory varies according to the point of view of the observer; hence Arctic Norway viewed from Trondheim in the year 1100 looked rather more valuable than when viewed from Denmark in the year 1400. In addition, territorial value varies according to the recognition or non-recognition of a region's natural resources, the technology available to the controlling state, the military or political priorities of the government of the day, the existence or lack of external threats, the organizational abilities of the government's administra-tive machinery, the personal inclinations of the monarch and many other factors. But whatever factors are in play at any one time, it is certain that there will *never* be equality of treatment for all the disparate regions or provinces which find themselves under the protective control of a particular state at a particular time. It may be argued that regional inequality is unfortunate but inevitable.

Regional inequality is also closely linked with regional consciousness and hence with regionalism. The distinctive personalities of Dalarna and Skåne in Sweden or Lappi and Vaasa in Finland have been created not only through the imprint of environment on the corporate consciousness but also through the corporate remembrance of episodes of confidence and resentment, oppression and suppression, wealth and poverty. Economic and social relationships with adjacent areas also play a part, as do the relations between province and state at the present day. These matters are treated in greater detail later in Chapters 15, 16 and 17.

Five further points are of importance in this consideration of regional consciousness, and they are all closely connected to the Scandinavian process of settlement.

1. Because of the relative inaccessibility and remoteness of the north-western fringe of Europe, the internal development of the Scandinavian countries has not been greatly influenced from outside. Since the Viking era there have been no great folk migrations into Scandinavia. In contrast, on various occasions (as in the Viking period and during the late nineteenth-century emigrations to North America), the Scandinavian environment – both natural and cultural – has prompted exploration and out-migration.

2. The evolution of the Scandinavian states was closely tied up with the intermittent development of core areas and the subsequent expansion of the settled area by means of a mobile pioneer fringe. At present, some parts of the pioneer fringe are now being abandoned, for example in Iceland and Finland, while others are so well integrated that they no longer have 'fringe' status.

3. The Scandinavian countries have not been greatly concerned with events far from the shores of the Baltic, at least since the end of the Viking era. The political history of the five states is, very largely, a history of inter-state rivalries; the development, stagnation and decline of various parts of Scandinavia can be interpreted in terms of military ambitions and political priorities as much as in terms of environmental controls.

4. The Industrial Revolution, which made such a great impact upon most of western Europe during the 1700s and 1800s, did not make a profound impact upon Scandinavia until the present century, when techniques became available for the large-scale use of water resources for the generation of hydro-electric power. Thus this chapter has made hardly any mention of industrial settlements or urban expansion based upon industry. This late development of industrialization may have been a drawback as far as the rural peasants of the last century were concerned; but in recent decades, as demonstrated in Chapters 10 and 11, it has given the Scandinavian states a distinct advantage over their industrial competitors.

5. In spite of the catastrophes – both natural and man-made – which have punctuated the settlement history of Scandinavia, the territories concerned have managed to preserve certain cultural affinities which go back 1,000 years or more. Peace and mutual respect have grown out of war and mistrust, and while each state values its own cultural heritage there is now a readily recognizable Scandinavian cultural environment. It could not have been otherwise, for the members of the Scandinavian family of nations have grown up together. Their personalities have been shaped by a multitude of shared experiences as much as by their sharing of a corner of the globe.

Suggested reading

The process of settlement

Brøndsted 1965; Foote and Wilson 1970; Graham-Campbell and Kidd 1980; Grenholm 1977; Helmfrid 1961; Jones 1964; Kirkby 1977; Magnusson, M. 1973, 1980; Magnusson, S. A. 1977; Mead 1958, 1981; Montelius 1953; Nelson 1956; Roberts 1973; Sawyer 1971; Shetelig and Falk 1978; Simpson, J. 1967; Wilson 1980.

National settlement themes

Berry 1972; Elstob 1979; Eriksson 1960; Glob 1971; Hansen 1981; Helvig and Johannessen 1966; Jones 1977; Jutikkala 1962; Leirfall 1979; Mead 1968; Moberg 1973; Newcomb 1976; Pounds and Ball 1964; Smeds 1960b; Stone 1971 a, b; Thorarinsson 1956; Werenskiold *et al.* 1957; West 1972.

Chapter 7 The cultural environment: the Viking tradition

The previous chapter was concerned with the evolution of the cultural environment of Scandinavia as reflected in settlement patterns. In many areas it is possible to see how the cultural landscape owes its origins to the nature of the physical environment, while elsewhere political and commercial factors have determined the course of development. Later in the book (particularly in Part IV), the text is closely concerned with the look and the feel of small sample communities in four of the Scandinavian countries, but so far there has been no description of any cultural landscapes in detail. There is no space here to analyse the cultural roots of field patterns, village morphology, road networks and urban zones for all of the areas discussed in Chapter 6, but in this chapter it will be instructive to look for the roots of tradition in one sample cultural landscape. These roots are perhaps most easily dug up in the Faroe Islands, and the pages which follow are devoted to an analysis of the Faroese rural lifestyle. The Viking tradition still has a surprisingly powerful influence on the Faroese way of life and the Faroese landscape. Some of the points made below also relate quite closely to our analysis of rural settlement patterns in Chapter 12.

The Faroese cultural landscape

There are three basic elements in the cultural landscape, shown in idealized form in Fig. 7.1. These are as follows:

1. The nucleated village (or *bygd*), whose form has generally remained unaltered for many centuries. Land within the village is known as *almenningur*.
2. The compact patchwork quilt of the improved infield (or *bøur*), concentrated around the periphery of the village. For the most part this consists of arable land, individually owned but subject to common winter grazing.
3. The extensive barren outfield (or *hagi*) which constitutes 94 per cent of the islands' land area and which is devoted to grazing by sheep. It is separated from the improved infield by a stone wall;

Fig. 7.1 Idealized diagram showing the main elements in the Faroese cultural landscape: *bøur*, *bygd*, *hagi* and *trøð*.

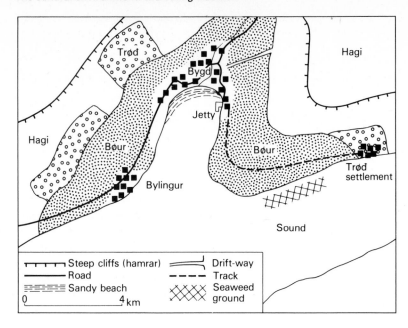

it is unimproved and supports no arable land. It is also, in most cases, owned by the farmers in common.

In the functioning at the old subsistence economy, these three elements were each vital to the community, but time has brought some measure of change. Modification of the natural landscape has been minimal in the case of the *hagi*, except in so far as continuous sheep-grazing over the centuries may have discouraged the growth of trees and shrubs. In the depths of the *hagi* there are no stone walls, and only occasional cairns to mark the carefully administered divisions of the grazing lands. Now and then one encounters rough, stone-built, turf-roofed shelters high on the moorland, or sheep-folds with guiding walls closer to the boundary of the *bøur*. The imprint of man is naturally much greater in the *bøur* itself, characterized as it is by a complex pattern of drainage ditches, small strip fields and stone walls. Often there is a walled track or drift-way which runs from the *hagi* through the infield to the centre of the village; this is used for the safe transfer of sheep (and occasionally cattle) to and from the *hagi* without danger to the hay and potato crops close to the village. A perfect example of such a drift-way may be seen today in the village of Mykines.

The Faroese village displays several distinctive Faroese features. In response to environmental factors and partly, no doubt, as a result of Viking tradition, every village (except Vatnsoyri on Vagar) is located on the coast; generally there is a small stone quay or harbour, and in favourable localities a row of boat-houses along the shore. The typical village has its small, wooden turf-roofed church, and the houses are clustered around this focal point with no clearly distinguishable pattern. The street pattern has evolved in an unplanned way, and it is clear that except in rare cases they have served more as footpaths than as routes for wheeled vehicles. The older houses are small and simple, with bases of basalt blocks surmounted by rectangular wooden structures with corrugated iron or pitch-painted roofs. The ground-floor cellars are normally used for storage rather than for livestock, and indeed the large multi-purpose barns of the other Scandinavian countries are conspicuous by their absence. Most of the farm buildings, if such they can be termed, are small single-purpose sheds; some of the older ones still have turf roofs and walls made entirely of basalt blocks.

There are two other elements which are locally important. Within the area of the infield there may be one or more secondary clusters of houses called *bylingar* (Fig. 7.1); these are morphologically similar to the *bygd* in some respects, but are inevitably smaller and simpler in plan. Where they exist they are good signs of past population pressure within the parent village. Another feature, especially on expanding settlements, may be the *trøð* land which has been won from the *hagi* and incorporated into the infield. In exceptional circumstances isolated patches of cultivated *trøð* land may be found within the *hagi* some distance away from the infield, or even more exceptionally small *trøð* settlements may be encountered. As examples, Vikar and Slaettanes on Vagar may be cited; both of these are separated from their parent villages by several kilometres, linked only by narrow tortuous paths over difficult terrain.

Settlement sites

The model settlement unit of Viking times both in Shetland and Faroe was sited according to a number of specific requirements. Among these the following were most important: (1) access to the sea, with a reasonable place to pull up a boat; (2) a patch of fairly flat, reasonably well-drained land suitable for the construction of a farmstead and with the potential for some grain cultivation; and (3) extensive grazing areas. To these requirements may be added the necessity of access to fresh water, the accessibility of bird cliffs and the proximity of shores with abundant driftwood. Strategic motives may have contributed to the location of certain villages, but it is noticeable that few villages seem to have been located on easily defended sites. Largely by chance, certain favourable sites (for example in sheltered fjords) may have been invisible from the open sea and thus less vulnerable to pirate raids during the early stages of colonization; accordingly their chances of survival may have been higher than those of sites on the exposed coast.

The Danish cultural geographer Ole Nielung has suggested a classification of Faroese villages according to site. Four major categories are recognized:

A. Isthmus (*eiđi*) villages such as Klaksvik and Viđareiđi in the northern isles and Eiđi and Eysturoy.
B. Sound and creek villages such as Tjørnuvik and Hvalvik-Streymnes on Streymoy.
C. Fjord and bay villages such as Fuglafjørđur and Skalafjørđur on Eysturoy and Miđvagur and Sørvagur on Vagar.
D. Villages on steep inaccessible localities such as Gasadulur on Vagar and Mykines village.

In addition, it is suggested that the larger towns of Torshavn, Klaksvik and Tvøroyri should be classified separately as a result of their size and exceptionally favourable sites. (It should be borne in mind, however, that these 'larger' towns are small by western European standards. Torshavn has by far the greatest number of inhabitants with just over 11,000; this is more than a quarter of the total Faroese population of 39,000. Relatively, it is the Faroese megalopolis!)

While the above classification has much to commend it, it is often difficult in practice to distinguish on the basis of site between villages in catagories B and C. The vast majority of villages are located within embayments of various sizes, and it may be more satisfactory to distinguish between (B) 'bay-head' villages with a compact *bøur* and (C) *sund* villages on the shore of a bay, fjord or sound, occasionally with an elongated settlement pattern. Bearing this in mind, the following site classification of Faroese villages seems most satisfactory:

(A) Isthumus (*eiđi*) villages.
(B) Bay-head villages.
(C) Sound villages such as Kvivik.
(D) Villages in steep inaccessible localities.

Of course there are still several villages which must be considered transitional between these types.

Systems of land tenure

The cultural landscape of the Faroe Islands cannot be fully appreciated without some understanding of the traditions of land-holding and inheritance, since these have left a more enduring imprint on the landscape than in most other parts of Scandinavia. Land on the islands is owned by the state (approximately 50%), by private individuals or cooperatively by the village communities or communes.

Most of the land known in the Faroes as *ognarjørđ* must originally have been privately owned, and was subject to an inheritance system derived from western Norway and used also in Orkney and Shetland. This is still termed *ođal* (freehold) land, and it is farmed by *ođalsbøndi* farmers. *Ođalsbøndi* farms are today generally small and of limited economic efficiency due to the tradition of division by inheritance among all the heirs. A freehold farmer may today hold twenty or thirty small strips of land scattered throughout the infield, and not all of these will be sited on productive land. Some strips will be owned in partnership with relatives or neighbours, and some will be rented out to other landowners. The problems arising from this extreme fragmentation of holdings are accentuated by the sheer physical difficulty of working the land. Strips may be no more than 30 m long by 1 m wide, and are demarcated by deep drainage ditches; consequently it is virtually impossible for a farmer to make efficient use of mechanization. *Oðalsbøndi* farmers usually have less than four cows; often they are part-time farmers possessing no mechanical equipment whatsoever, and they may not even live any longer in the village where they own their land. There are some similarities between the *oðalsbøndi* farming system and that of Scottish crofting.

Public land, in contrast, has been subject to much less fragmentation over the centuries, and is the scene of more sophisticated and profitable farming techniques. Originally this land was owned by the Church, but during the Reformation it was confiscated by the crown. It is still called *Kongs* (royal, land, and is farmed by *Kongsbøndi* farmers, although it is now owned by the state and administered by the Faroese Agricultural Council. *Kongs* land is today farmed by tenants who have to pay a nominal lease-fee. On the death of the lessee the land passes intact to the eldest male heir, or to the eldest daughter, or intact to another tenant if the Council so decides. As a result of this more rational inheritance system, *Kongsbøndi* farms remain as large, moderately efficient units where mechanization is possible and where some farmers still make a living entirely from the land. The cultural landscape of a *Kongsbøndi* village, therefore, may be different in several respects from that of a village comprised largely of *oðalsbøndi* holdings.

Trøð land falls into a third category, for although it may be well cultivated by farmers living on the *trøð* or in the main village it is economically much less viable than either *oðalsbøndi* or *Kongsbøndi* land. This is because a *trøð* farmer who was formerly landless has to pay rent (sometimes in the form of agricultural produce) to the original owner of the land, and because land-taxes to the state have traditionally been higher than with the old-established agricultural areas. In addition, small *trøð* settlements have no grazing rights on the adjacent *hagi*, so that their inhabitants are denied full participation in the well-tried integrated agricultural economy of the islands.

The use of the *hagi* is critical in the understanding of certain elements of the cultural landscape. The *hagi* is generally owned or administered by the village community as a whole, and is divided into several sections. Each section has a specific value (measured in *merkur*, according to Viking tradition), and each farmer is allowed to utilize the *hagi* in proportion to the value of his holding on the *bøur*. The system is a complex one with complex variations. For example, in a mixed community of *oðalsbøndi* and *Kongsbøndi* farmers, specific parts of the *hagi* may be designated for the use of each. In some cases farmers may actually own parts of the *hagi*; in others the land will be owned communally but the sheep flocks privately; and in others both land and sheep may be owned by the commune. Whatever the pattern of land use on the *hagi*, the number of sheep allowed to graze on each section is strictly controlled by the commune in accordance with its proved grazing capacity. Effectively, therefore, a farmer's use of *bøur* and *hagi* is strictly controlled by the commune, as is the size of his sheep flock and his number of cows. Also for every *mørk* of land he owns, he may be allowed to graze one flock of geese on the *hagi*. Certain favourable areas of the *hagi* are also designated as peat-cutting sites for the whole community.

The Faroese economy – past and present

The fluctuations which have occurred in the economy of the Faroes have quickly found expression in the cultural landscape. It must be stressed, however, that the land has always been of far greater importance to the economy than the sea. The basis of life in the Faroes was stock husbandry, with each village grazing carefully adjusted flocks of sheep on its own *hagi*. At the time of the last war there were over 80,000 sheep on the islands, but this total has since fallen to 70,000. Flocks provide mutton (nearly all for home consumption) and sheepskins and wool for both home use and export. Numbers of milking cows have fallen recently to about 3,000 and do not quite cater for all local milk consumption.

In spite of the coastal locations of villages and the prominence in the cultural landscape of stone jetties, rows of small fishing-boats on the beach, and the ubiquitous lines of boat-sheds along the sea-front, inshore fishing has never been a mainstay of the economy. Although the sea has always been of greater importance than the land for communications, the Faroese relationship with the sea has, until recently, been one of sentimental attachment rather than real economic dependence. In historical times inshore fishing in small, open Viking-style boats (Fig. 7.2) provided a welcome addition to the Faroese diet, but it was not until the late 1800s that the fishing industry attracted capital investment and began to expand. Only since the last war has the income from the growing and highly organized fishing industry been large enough to subsidize the islands' precarious agriculture.

As demonstrated by the systems of land tenure, the Faroese way of life has always presented a strange juxtaposition of private enterprise and communal control. While the farmers are themselves

Fig. 7.2 Small boats in the harbour at Torshavn. In several respects (for example the pointed bow and stern and the clinker construction) such boats preserve features of Viking boat-building methods.

responsible for the management of their own land, social convention is also seen to be responsible for certain practices – for example, the commencement of the hay harvest on *Olavsøka* (29 July) each year, and the reluctance of farmers to cut hay on the *hagi*.

The total number of crops grown in the Faroes is small, and most of the infield is devoted to the grazing of hay for winter fodder. Barley was at one time important, but declined after 1800 with the advent of imported grain and flour from Denmark and with the increasing use of the potato as a food crop. Today hardly any barley is grown, and all that remains to indicate its former significance is an occasional deserted water-mill, as at Bøur on Vagar. Besides hay, potatoes provide the only other crop of any importance in the economy (less than 10 per cent of the arable area). Potato patches are often concentrated in favourable localities, as on the shingle just above high-water mark at Sørvagur (Vagar) and Tjørnuvik (Streymoy). Rhubarb, carrots and cabbages may be grown in gardens within the villages.

Nowadays the part-time nature of farming is everywhere manifest, especially in areas of *oðalsbøndi* landholding. More and more of the family income is derived from large-scale commercial fishing operations; menfolk may be away for several months of the year on deep-sea fishing vessels, and part of the family income may be derived from the profits of commercially owned vessels. Agriculture is becoming less and less significant in the total economy, and is undertaken largely as spare-time therapy by most of the population. Many of the village infields have areas of badly managed land as a result; drainage ditches may be overgrown, plots may have reverted to rough grazing and walls may be in a state of disrepair. Often areas of *trøð* land are neglected, and the upper limit of present-day cultivation may lie well below the boundary wall of the infield.

Cattle are sometimes grazed during the summer close to the village on the infield, on land which at one time would have been jealously guarded for its hay crop. Some of these changes may have arisen in response to improved agricultural techniques, but Faroese farming is not noted for its level of technical efficiency, and most of the changes in land use are best seen as indicators of a gradual retreat from the land. Nevertheless, farming is still of considerable importance, particularly in producing supplies of milk, mutton and potatoes for domestic consumption.

The several other activities detailed below were at one time essential parts of the total economy.

1. *Fowling.*   This provided a significant element in the Faroese diet, and many young men practised the precarious art of catching puffins, guillemots, gannets and fulmars on the densely populated but precipitous cliffs of the Atlantic coasts. Fowling rights were again held by the landowners in proportion to the value and size of their holdings. Birds are still caught and consumed in large numbers, but there are now few skilled bird-catchers left except in isolated communities such as Mykines, Gasadulur and Viđareiđi. As in other aspects of Faroese economic life, the intricacies of communal control on fowling operations are considerable.

2. *Hunting the pilot whale.*   According to Willy Breinholst, this is still a national pastime, 'providing the Faroese with an irreplaceable outlet for a certain native savagery, a reservoir of untapped force, when their Viking blood boils and they go berserk on the whale-killing'. Many schools of pilot whales may be driven ashore each summer in different parts of the islands, and while whalemeat is no longer necessary for survival it is still a highly prized element of the Faroese diet. At one time the carcasses were shared out among all the inhabitants of the commune according to intricate rules

Fig. 7.3 Cutting up whale carcasses on the quayside at Torshavn after a *grindaboð* on the east coast of Streymoy.

114

(Fig. 7.3); nowadays most of the meat is auctioned. However, there is still an elaborate etiquette concerning the delimitation of coastal waters which may be hunted by different villages. Only selected shallow beaches can be used for driving the whales ashore, and provision is traditionally made in the share-out of meat for those villages with no whaling beach or with waters unfavourable for whale-hunts.

3. *Peat-cutting.* Peat has traditionally provided the bulk of fuel throughout most of the Faroe Islands, although small amounts of Tertiary lignite are mined on Suðuroy. Since the peat cover is generally thin, a careful system of communal exploitation of specific favourable localities on the *hagi* has evolved in order to conserve resources. The activities of peat-cutting, spreading and carrying were naturally concentrated into the summer months, and were vested with considerable importance for the social as well as the economic life of the community. Nowadays oil-fired central heating has largely replaced the open fire, and contemporary peat-cuttings are rarely encountered save in isolated localities like Saksunardalur on Streymoy.

4. *The gathering of driftwood.* This was once vital to the economy of a village, since it provided both building materials and fuel to supplement supplies of peat. Some villages (such as Tjørnuvik) may have been sited largely in response to the excellent quantities of wood drifting on to their beaches. Again there was an elaborate system in most villages which controlled the distribution of drift-wood among the members of the community. According to convention whole trees or branches were treated differently from timber worked by the hand of man. Nowadays imported timber and concrete form the basis for house construction; driftwood is used hardly at all for building or heating, as witnessed by the large amounts of uncollected wood in many coastal localities.

5. *Seaweed-gathering.* This was of great importance to some coastal communities with access to fertile 'seaweed grounds'. Seaweed was a vital fertilizer, and it was said that a boat-load of seaweed in spring was as valuable as a boat-load of cod. After collection the seaweed was left in shallow middens to rot for a few weeks before being spread on the land. On the island of Nolsoy there was one particularly fine seaweed ground called Stokkvik; rights to harvest it were held by certain landowners on a two-year rotation. During alternate years the landowners were instead granted the right of fowling on the best fowling cliffs of the island.

All these activities made a contribution to the economy of the old self-supporting peasant and fishing community; the only approach towards a money economy came via sales of fish, wool and knitted garments, for the most part to Denmark.

From a consideration of all these factors, it can be seen that the

Faroese village owes its morphology to a specific set of factors in somewhat unusual combination: the Viking tradition of coastal location and dependence on the sea for communications; the marginal nature of agriculture, indicated in part by the great dependence on additional food sources in the old subsistence economy; the role of communal control in the utilization of all resources; the strength of the *odal* inheritance system in restricting technical advance, especially on the infield; and the 'hidden' factors of Danish aid and income from deep-sea trawling, resulting in a standard of living which is unexpected when seen in terms of the poverty of the natural environment and the lack of commercial enterprises manifested in the landscape.

In some respects the cultural landscape bears comparison with those of Iceland and western Norway; but although there may be similarities in community organization, the effects on the landscape are very different. For example, the prominence of drainage ditches on the wet slopes of the Faroes accentuates the problems of property fragmentation and strip fields as seen in parts of Norway. Village nucleation on the Scottish Viking model is developed to a far higher degree than in either Iceland or Norway, possibly in response to the poverty of the environment. Again the clarity of the infield–outfield division is striking, whereas it has been modified severely in the well-wooded landscapes of western Norway. The Faroe Islands at present, therefore, impress with the sheer stability of their cultural landscape; many of the elements which can be seen today in Faroese villages have their origins in the Viking era, and settlements have changed little in their morphological outlines at least since the 1300s.

Traditions elsewhere

The cultural landscape of the Faroes is exceptional, for while the rural community of the islands can in no way be considered a 'peasant community' it persists in the preservation of a peasant landscape in spite of vastly improved modern conditions of living. The cultural landscape can be compared in this sense with the peasant landscapes of Greece, Spain or Italy, although of course these landscapes have grown out of quite different cultural traditions and economic circumstances.

The medieval landscapes of the other Scandinavian countries have been modified to a much greater extent over the centuries, although many 'primitive' features remain. In Sweden, for example, a large number of medieval and perhaps even older traditions are preserved in the lifestyle and landscape of Dalarna. In Norway the maritime lifestyle of the people of the fjord country certainly stretches back to Viking times, and coastal towns and villages display

Fig. 7.4 A comment on the Danish Viking tradition by a well-known Danish cartoonist – Bo Bojesen.

morphological features which are similar in many respects to the Faroese features described above. The Norwegians are proud of their Viking traditions, and in spite of the strong urbanization of the population in recent times there is a continuing affection for rural life and rural traditions. The Danes are great preservers of prehistoric and Viking relics and settlement sites, and perhaps because there is so little of the medieval cultural landscape left in their country they cultivate a sad and slightly forced nostalgia for the Viking era which has been frequently commented upon by writers and even cartoonists (Fig. 7.4). In spite of (or perhaps because of?) the disappearance of the Danish Viking landscape the Danes come closer than any of the other Scandinavians to a political tradition based upon Viking values. The country preserves a liberal and even anarchistic style of politics which is in stark contrast to the solid, introverted conservatism of the Swedish political style. In Iceland Viking landscape features do not seem to have been preserved as they have in the Faroes, although the rural economy shows some medieval characteristics. On the other hand, the Viking cultural tradition is very much alive in the country. The events of the *Landnam* period are still common knowledge, and the Icelandic sagas are still valued as the most vital components of Icelandic literature. The Icelanders are familiar with the places where the great events of the sagas took place, and many families can trace their histories back to early medieval times. They still feel a mystical relationship with the coastal sites where their forebears orginally carved out a precarious living from the land and supplemented it from the sea. Every year there are family pilgrimages to long-deserted valleys and abandoned farmhouses many kilometres away from the nearest settlement. The eleven-hundredth anniversary of the founding of the Icelandic *Thing* in 1975 was remarkable for the almost religious fervour of the pilgrims who travelled to Thingvellir and to other historic sites such as Vatnsdalsvatn in Vestfirđir.

Thus the Faroes and Iceland have managed to remain true to their cultural roots to a much greater extent than the other Scandinavian countries; probably their relative poverty and isolation has protected them from the cosmopolitan contacts which have 'modernized' the countries of the European mainland.

Suggested reading

Faroese cultural traditions

Annandale 1905; Brøgger 1929; Brøgger and Shetelig 1971; Dahl 1969; *Danish Journal* 1971; Djurhus *et al.* 1958; Hagström 1977; Joensen 1977, 1980; Johansen 1969; John 1971; Jones 1964; Jonsson and Linnman 1959; Kallsberg 1970; Kampp 1967a; Nielung 1968; O'Dell 1957; Small 1967–68; Trap 1968; West 1970–71, 1972; Williamson 1948.

Traditions elsewhere

Bjørkvik 1956; Hägerstrand 1977; Hirn 1970; Newcomb 1967; Ogrizek 1952.

Part II   Spatial expressions of human economy

Chapter 8 Primary economic activities: agriculture, forestry and fishing

Until about the year 1900 between 80 and 90 per cent of the population of Scandinavia was employed in the 'primary' exploitation of the natural environment – especially in that active and productive management of the biosphere which we refer to as agriculture. Fishing activities were carried out for the most part by farmer-fishermen, and except in a few fishing ports there were relatively few people engaged full-time in sea-fishing. Apart from the use of timber in connection with the iron industry, forestry operations were also carried out by farmers; much of the timber taken from the Scandinavian forests was for domestic use, but it was also valuable for sale as a building material, or for potash, tar, pitch and resin. Even within the 'secondary' economic sector of processing or manufacturing, the link with natural resources was a strong one; the most important industries were based upon food crops and timber.

Inevitably, the natural environment exerts a strong control over the primary exploitation of natural resources; the factors discussed in Chapter 5 determine the growth rates of trees and food crops, the abundance of sea and freshwater fish, the growth rates and health of livestock and the year-round pattern of farming and forestry operations. Soil conditions, surface moisture conditions and the duration of the winter freeze also affect the viability of farming and forestry operations, and the nature of the terrain has been an increasingly important control since the advent of mechanization on the land. It is quite possible to map a whole series of environmental and biological variables which, taken together, can give an indication of agricultural or forestry 'potential'. Two of these are shown in Fig. 8.1. As far as farming is concerned, the most significant factor of all is the length of the growing season. At the strictly local scale, factors such as aspect, slope angle, the occurrence of frost-hollows or wind-channels, accessibility and exceptionally stony or boggy surface conditions often determine what a farmer can and cannot do with his land, no matter how favourable the broader environmental circumstances may be.

In recent decades, with the increasing importance of a cash income as a part of the agricultural way of life, a variety of loca-

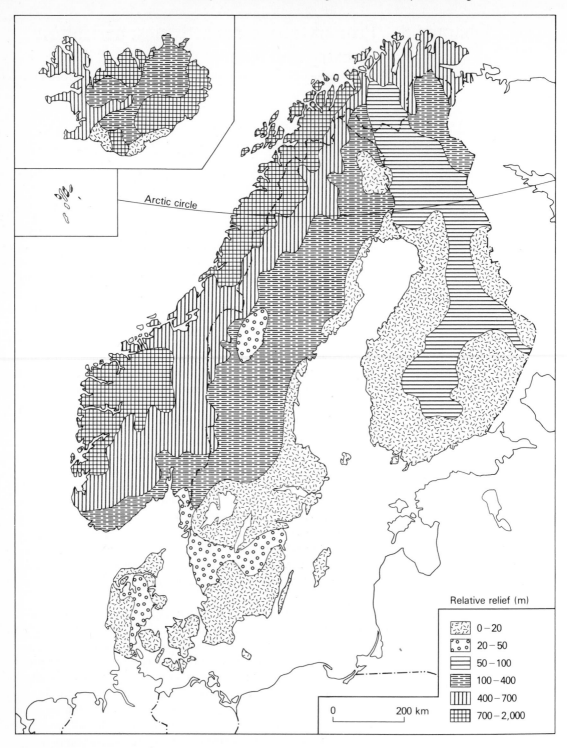

Arctic circle

Relative relief (m)

	0 – 20
	20 – 50
	50 – 100
	100 – 400
	400 – 700
	700 – 2,000

0   200 km

Fig. 8.1 Generalized maps of two environmental factors
which are of importance for agriculture and forestry. (After Sømme 1961)

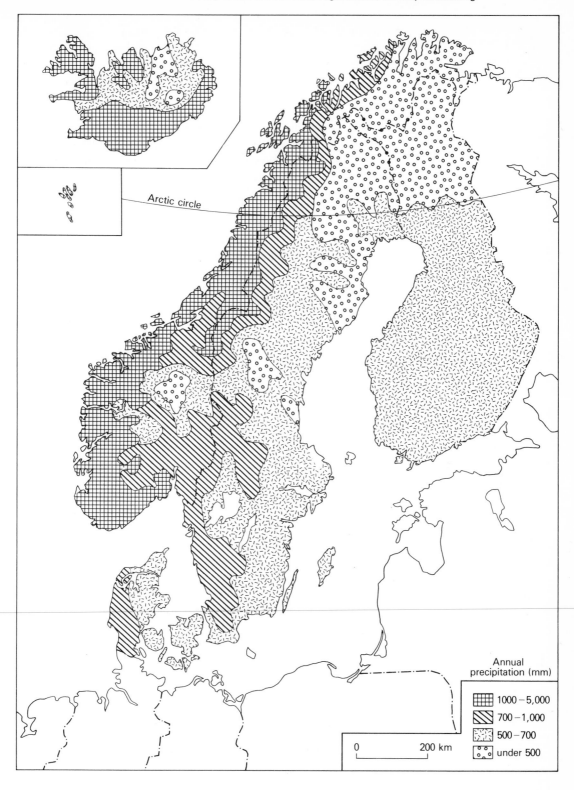

Arctic circle

Annual
precipitation (mm)

⊞	1000 – 5,000
▨	700 – 1,000
✱	500 – 700
∘∘∘	under 500

0   200 km

tional, economic and political factors have become important determinants in agriculture. Saleable agricultural surpluses are now essential to the farming economy, and a farmer's 'lowest profitable price' determines how competitive his various products are going to be in attracting sales. A farmer in a remote district in Norrland, where yields may be low even in a good year and where the quality of his produce may not compare with that of produce from Skåne, is always at a disadvantage when it comes to marketing – except in his own local or regional market-place. There are also much greater transport costs involved in getting his produce to the consumers of the main towns and cities in the historic 'core areas'. To a certain extent differences in yields and marketability, and differences in harvesting times, can be catered for by various forms of government aid in the form of rebates, subsidies and protective legislation. But different Scandinavian governments have different attitudes to agriculture; often these attitudes depend upon the relative strength of the economic and social arguments in favour of maintaining agriculture in marginal areas. Other government policies are related to the importance which they happen to attach to forestry operations. In Finland, for example, the farming *versus* forestry debate has been going on for decades, and government policies with respect to the afforestation of farmland have varied considerably.

Farming and life on the land

The main agricultural areas of Scandinavia occur in Denmark, Skåne and in a belt running from south-western Finland through the Central Lakes depression of Sweden and into the Oslofjord district of Norway. From an economic point of view agriculture is relatively most important in Denmark and Finland and least important in Sweden and Iceland. The holdings in Norway, Finland and northern Sweden are on average smaller than those of Denmark and southern Sweden. Agricultural yields also rise considerably from north to south, as does the range of crops grown. Although yields are in general low, and although the Scandinavian agricultural economy depends to a great extent upon livestock and the growing of fodder crops, the five Scandinavian states still manage to be almost self-supporting in many of the basic agricultural products such as potatoes, milk, meat and eggs.

Scandinavian agriculture, although widely dispersed throughout the countryside, is generally concentrated into pockets of productive land. For example, in Iceland there are only 130,000 ha of arable land within a land area of about 10 million ha. In Norway only 2.5 per cent of the land area is cultivated, as against 9 per cent in Finland and Sweden. In Iceland, the Faroes and western Norway

Fig. 8.2 Photo of a typical farming landscape in Skåne. In this area, as over many thousands of square kilometres in Denmark, the landscape is very largely man-made. (Photo: Swedish National Travel Association)

the cultivated area is concentrated into a narrow coastal strips, with small pockets of farmland usually located within 2 km of the sea. In contrast, Denmark has about 67 per cent of its land area under cultivation, and continuous farming landscapes created, planted and managed by man cover many thousands of hectares. On a drive across western Sjaelland, or southern Skåne, for example, the traveller sees hardly any trace of the long-lost 'wildscape' (Fig. 8.2).

During the last two decades or so the 'rationalization' of Scandinavian agriculture has been accelerating. Almost everywhere this process leads to a reduction in the number of farm-holdings, an increase in the average size of holdings through amalgamation, a reduction in manpower on the land and an increase in yields and agricultural production. Although the value of agricultural produce is rising year by year, farming activities account for a smaller and smaller proportion of each country's GNP (Gross National Product). This is because the industrial and service sectors now dominate both in terms of manpower and value in cash terms. A few figures from Finland, Iceland and Denmark will demonstrate the main structural trends in agriculture in recent times.

Fig. 8.3 Ploughing scene in Finland. Large tractors and four-furrow ploughs are now in common use. (Photo: Fiskars)

Finland

As elsewhere in Scandinavia, the character of agriculture has been transformed by mechanization (Fig. 8.3). The arable area fell from 2.7 million ha in 1967 to 2.5 million ha in 1976. At the same time there was a rise in the area of permanent pasture from 91,000 ha to 150,000 ha, and also a great increase in the area of fallow or untilled land. In the period 1950–76 there was a reduction by almost half in the number of very small holdings (under 6 ha) and holdings in the 5–10 ha range also fell from 88,000 to 78,000 in number. Holdings above 15 ha in area all increased in number during the sixteen-year period, and the number of holdings in the 50–100 ha category almost doubled. Overall, the number of holdings fell from 260,000 to 220,000. Between 1950 and 1976 the number of horses on Finnish farms fell from 410,000 to 33,000, while the number of tractors increased from 18,000 to 183,000. Cattle numbers have remained almost stable at about 1.7 million, while sheep numbers have dropped from 1.2 million to 111,000. Pigs are widely kept on Finnish farms, and chicken numbers have gone up to almost 9 million. Except for sugar beet, crop yields have gone up steadily, with the main cereal crops (in order of importance) barley, oats, wheat, rye and mixed grain. The most important crops in the farming economy are hay and other fodder crops – 5.2 million tonnes per year. As far as employment is concerned, agriculture currently employs about 15 per cent of the working population; this compares with an agricultural workforce of 67 per cent in 1910 and 32 per cent in 1960. Farm incomes are made up approximately as follows: 45 per cent from milk production, 34 per cent from meat and 11 per cent from sales of grain. In some areas 'forest money' is the most important source of income, accounting for over 35 per cent of farmers' net receipts in some of the richer forest areas of southern Finland (Fig. 8.4).

Fig. 8.4 A comment on 'modern' farming in Finland, where forestry has overtaken agriculture as the main cash-earning activity in some farming districts. (Artist: Olavi Hurmerinta)

Iceland

Somewhat surprisingly, the size of the cultivated area in Iceland has increased quite sharply between 1967 and 1977, largely because of government legislation which has led to the creation of 750 new farms and the restoration of 180 farms which had been previously abandoned. The arable area is now about 130,000 ha and several thousand hectares of newly reclaimed land are added to the cultivated area annually. (It should be noted that in Iceland the 'cultivated area' is for the most part referred to as *tun* or manured hayfield: in other countries land such as this would be called permanent pasture rather than arable land.) Fodder crop production (mostly hay) went up from 227,000 tonnes in 1950 to 3.9 million tonnes in 1977. The only other crop of any importance is the potato crop, which generally oscillates between 5,000 and 13,000 tonnes per year. Icelandic livestock-farming is based largely upon sheep, and between 1950 and 1977 numbers more than doubled to about 900,000. Poultry are now much more important than they were 20 years ago, and there are now over 63,000 cattle on Icelandic farms. Milk, butter and cheese are major products; Iceland, like the other Scandinavian countries, now attempts to be self-sufficient in dairy products. Milk production has virtually doubled in the last thirty years to a total of 132,000 tonnes per year. Overall, food production is up by 20 per cent over the last decade. In 1910 almost 48 per cent of the population were employed in agriculture, but this percentage has fallen so that today only 11 per cent are occupied on the land. Until quite recently the number of holdings in Iceland remained quite steady, somewhere between 5,500 and 6,000; but recently there has been a sharp decline to about 4,500. Although the average size of holdings is around 300 ha, the area of the *tun* is generally much less, averaging about 25 ha per farm.

Denmark

In 1938 about 3.3 million ha of land were under cultivation in Denmark, representing 76 per cent of the country's total land area. Since then the cultivated area has been reduced to less than 3 million ha, largely as a result of loss of land to urban and suburban developments, roads, airfields and industry. Most of the land lost by agriculture has been in the fertile eastern part of Denmark, leading to a reduction in the average quality of the cultivated area. Within the intensively cultivated area of 2.6 million ha grain crops for animal feed are by far the most important, being raised on 1.8 million ha of land per year. Of this, barley is more than ten times as important as any other cereal crop, accounting for 1.5 million ha. Fodder roots, hay and related fodder crops account for most of the remainder, and other crops (beet, potatoes, etc.) are relatively unimportant in terms of crop area. However, if one looks at

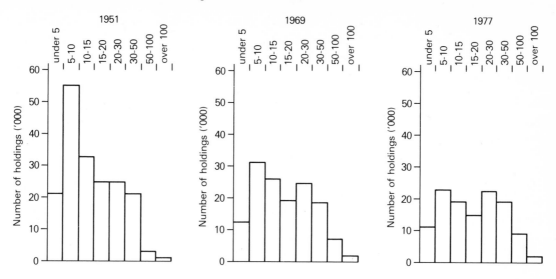

Fig. 8.5 Graph showing the changes in Danish farm sizes between 1951 and 1977. (After Nordic Statistical Secretariat 1978)

the figures for the weight of the crop harvest, it emerges that fodder roots are the most important, with an annual output of over 9 million tonnes as against 7.3 million tonnes of grain. From all points of view livestock husbandry is clearly the real focus of farming operations.

The number of farm-holdings in Denmark has dropped from 185,000 in 1951 to about 121,000 today. In 1951 there were 110,000 holdings under 15 ha; today the figure is 53,000 (Fig. 8.5). The proportion of farms in the larger-size categories has increased sharply; in the period 1951–77 the number of holdings over 50 ha increased from 4,328 to 10,705, representing 8.8 per cent of all farms. The trend towards farm amalgamation is certainly far advanced in Denmark, but it should be borne in mind that the great majority of farms are still in the size range between 5 and 30 ha.

Crop-farming in Denmark has changed quite sharply during the last thirty years. In 1950 fodder roots and potatoes were of great importance on Danish farms, but now the tonnage of the harvest has been reduced by about 50 per cent in both cases. Over the same period the grain harvest has more than doubled and sugar beet and fodder beet are now much more popular crops than they used to be. There has also been a shift in emphasis as far as cereal crops are concerned. The barley harvest has increased fivefold to over 6 million tonnes per year, while the growing of oats and rye has declined. The greatest drop in production can be seen in the figures for mixed grain – down from 682,000 tonnes in 1950 to 35,000 tonnes in 1977. Wheat production has doubled to over 606,000 tonnes over the same period. For all crops there have been sharp increases in yields per hectare, accounted for (as elsewhere in Scandinavia) by the use of improved strains of seed, better fertilizers more efficient farming practices and improved field drainage.

In the last thirty years Denmark has seen a great increase in the specialization and simplification of the farm economy. Many farmers have abandoned the keeping of cows and pigs and have begun to concentrate on less labour-intensive forms of farming such as the growing of barley or the production of beef cattle. This trend is especially marked in Sjaelland, where it is now difficult for farmers to find herdsmen and other agricultural workers. At the moment about 46,000 farms have no cattle and 32,000 no pigs. Poultry farming has also become more specialized. Relatively few farms concentrate on the production of eggs, and egg production has halved since 1950. No less than 94 per cent of the production of table birds now comes from about 300 farms.

To an increasing extent Danish agriculture is known for its concentration upon livestock. Almost nine-tenths of the total crop yield is used for livestock fodder, and about 90 per cent of the value of Danish agricultural production comes from livestock. Milk production has fallen slightly over the last thirty years, while the number of cattle has remained quite stable. Milk yields are now much higher than they were, but as more and more farmers move out of dairying, beef cattle herds are becoming commonplace. The pig population has risen steadily since 1950, and there are now 8 million pigs in Denmark. The main agricultural end-products today are (in order of importance in terms of *quantity*) milk, pork and bacon, beef and veal, cheese, butter, oven-ready poultry, eggs and lard. About a third of total Danish agricultural production goes to domestic consumption, and it is calculated that just under 3 per cent of the population produces enough food to feed the entire population of 5 million. If one includes the two-thirds of farm production which goes to export (Fig. 8.6), then one farm worker produces enough to feed 100 people on a normal Danish diet.

As in the other Scandinavian countries, the agricultural labour-force has declined steadily since the Second World War. In 1945 there were about 1 million people involved in agriculture, representing 21 per cent of the then Danish population. The farming population is now only about 400,000. Over the same period the number of farm labourers (i.e. persons who are not members of the farmer's family) dropped from 276,000 to about 30,000. The heavy reduction in farm manpower has, of course, been matched by a sharp increase in mechanization. Between 1950 and 1977 the number of farm tractors rose from 17,844 to 186,266 and in the same period the number of combine harvesters rose from 367 to 41,193. During the period 1960–65 almost 22,000 new combine harvesters were brought into use, representing a huge investment by the farming industry.

The term 'farming industry' is peculiarly appropriate in Denmark, since there has been a determined and prolonged attempt on the part of the government to develop the agricultural sector of the economy. A number of factors are responsible for this.

Fig. 8.6 Danish bacon packed in containers and ready for export to Britain. Efficient marketing has kept foreign sales of Danish agricultural produce at a consistently high level. (Photo: Pressehuset)

In the first place, Denmark is deficient in mineral resources and has never had a solid resource base for heavy industry. In the second place, the location of the country at the north-west European cross-roads makes trading links and marketing relatively easy in the adjacent heavily populated areas of the UK and the North European Plain. The country's political rapport with Britain has made marketing across the North Sea particularly straightforward. Thirdly, the process of land reform in Denmark was completed relatively early so that by 1865 there was a farming population of enthusiastic freehold farmers who were keen to apply new farming techniques to their land. The loss of Schleswig-Holstein to Germany in 1864 led to several decades of 'reclamation fever' in Jylland and also a great deal of research into agriculture. At about the same time the flooding of the European market by cheap North American grain prompted an astute shift from grain production to livestock farming in Denmark, enabling the Danes to take advantage of low grain prices for animal feed while transferring their attentions to milk and meat production. Overall, the single most important factor in the success of the Danish agricultural industry is that while the greater part of Europe was involved in an Industrial Revolution which involved the transfer of huge number of workers into industrial jobs and urban lifestyles, Denmark was involved in an Agricultural Revolution during which it learnt the skills of producing large surpluses of food.

A final point concerning Danish agriculture is that there is a long tradition of government interest and also mutual support within the farming community. The Danish 'folk high school' movement of the last century was of great importance in raising educational standards and improving farming and management techniques among country people. The Danish cooperative movement, which started in the 1850s, encouraged farmers to invest in cooperatively financed agricultural research, the processing of milk products, the purchase of machinery and the marketing of surpluses. There was also cooperation between cooperatives to ensure consistent marketing strategies and uniform produce quality. Many agricultural societies were formed, and their annual shows were of great value in improving the quality of livestock and ensuring the dissemination of new techniques. Together the agricultural societies now run a wideranging advisory service, and this supplements research and advisory work undertaken by state organizations. There are specialist associations of dairy producers, bacon farmers, and even smallholders. There are many committees which ensure that the industry is aware of market trends, new export opportunities and new developments in cropping and animal husbandry. The list could be continued. The impression may be gained that for every farm worker in Denmark there is now at least one 'agricultural bureaucrat', and this impression may not be far from the truth.

An agricultural perspective

At the present day the agricultural industry of Scandinavia appears to be relatively stable. All five countries approach self-sufficiency in potatoes, dairy products, eggs and meat, and animal feed is for the most part home-grown. The main agricultural exports are butter, cheese, bacon, canned meats and poultry, with Denmark dominating the market. Since joining the EEC in 1973 Denmark has consolidated its position as the agricultural leader of Scandinavia, and there are unfortunately few opportunities for cooperation between the five countries either in production or in marketing.

Harsh climatic conditions everywhere except in Denmark and southern Sweden make commercial arable farming precarious and not exactly profitable; and the range of options open to the agricultural community of Scandinavia is strictly limited. In effect, the countries have to *compete* with one another on the international market in the sale of any agricultural surpluses which they may have.

During the 1980s there may well be a further reduction in manpower on the land and further specialization in Scandinavian farming generally. The old-style multi-purpose farm, with its delicate balance of arable farming and livestock husbandry, is difficult to operate in the modern world. Amid a welter of government advice and government incentives to specialize and to boost production of that which is 'best suited' to your patch of land, you are a brave farmer indeed to settle for a balanced farm economy with a reasonable degree of self-sufficiency. However, the standard European solution to the problems of Scandinavia's marginal farming areas may not be entirely appropriate, and there are now signs that the *real* costs of maintaining a capital-intensive style of agriculture in areas such as Vestlandet in Norway or Jämtland in Sweden may be far too high. Denmark has already reached a position in which its agricultural production in terms of volume is falling. The EEC has 'milk lakes' and 'butter mountains', and Danish agriculture is supported by heavy EEC subsidies. The returns on agricultural investments are extremely poor, and according to conventional thinking crop yields can only be maintained or increased by greater and greater imports of fertilizer and more intensive use of the land. Fertilizer 'inputs' are already extremely high; in Denmark in 1978–79 the use of nitrogen, phosphorus and potassium totalled 582 million kg, far more than in any other Scandinavian country. The oil crisis is hitting Danish agriculture hard; some fertilizers are oil-based products, and the intensive use of farm machinery means that farm fuel costs are rising very steeply. Transport costs are also escalating, collections and deliveries of agricultural products are now so complex that few items are actually consumed in the areas in which they originate. Large centralized dairies, quality control depots, slaughterhouses and packaging or canning factories may draw farm products in from a radius of 200 km or more; nowadays the people of Hamina in Finland, or Kramfors in Sweden or Dalen in Norway find it difficult to find *local* farm products such as milk and cheese even if they want to.

If agriculture is suffering from over-mechanization, over-capitalization and over-centralization, what of the future? And what of the traditional farming community in those areas where 'agribusiness' has taken over? Among the younger generation in Scandinavia there are now a number of organizations devoted to small-scale farming, ecological lifestyles, sensible energy use, and the return of community values and loyalties. Universities and colleges throughout the five Scandinavian states are becoming the centres of radical, alternative and eminently sane thought on the ecological issues of the day. Nuclear power (see Ch. 11) is by no means the only issue of youthful concern, and there is quite a strong lobby nowadays for the more rational use of energy throughout Scandinavian society. Capital intensive farming and a highly centralized collection and distribution system make no sense at all to those who are concerned about energy conservation. They argue that agriculture should move away from specialization and back towards the traditional farming economy; this would preserve land fertility, conserve energy resources, bring people back to the land and ensure the survival of rural communities which are at present dangerously close to extinction. There are many young people who would like to move into the countryside and practise agriculture on a small scale, possibly as a part-time basis, possibly living in a communal way and using pooled resources. They are people who are concerned about lifestyles as much as economics. Generally they want smallholdings which may be less than 5 ha in area. At the moment the fragmentation of holdings is frowned upon by the Scandinavian governments, and there are many bureaucratic obstacles in the way of those who wish to take part in the 'drift to the country'. For example, in Sweden no one can purchase a viable holding unless he or she has completed a course of agricultural training and has the 'approved' qualifications. As agricultural subsidies rise, and as the energy crisis bites more and more deeply, government attitudes may *have* to change.

While concentrating on such matters as intensive pig-farming, cooperative dairies and EEC butter mountains, it is easy to fall into the trap of assuming that Scandinavian agriculture is now fully 'rational' and ultra-efficient. In fact small-scale 'peasant' farming operations are still very much a part of the Scandinavian scene. In many remote areas isolation and harsh physical conditions make large-scale commercial farming operations quite impossible, and small farmers persist in the use of techniques which may not have changed for centuries (Fig. 8.7). In the Faroes, villages like Tjørnuvik on Streymoy are surrounded by minute strips of land which are normally cultivated by hand; closely spaced drainage ditches make the use of tractors impossible, and small hand-held mechanical cultivators and mowing machines are the only engine-driven devices which can be used. The cropping traditions and the farming economy as a whole are not at all dissimilar to those of the 1700s. In western Norway remote peasant farming communities persist in the use of the mountain *seters* for the summer grazing of cattle and sheep; in Dalarna in Sweden many *fäbodar* are still in use for summer grazing and even for the cutting of summer hay crops, and there are farming families who still live in primitive conditions in what the urban world would refer to as abject poverty. In Lapland farmers still cultivate small patches of land surrounded

Fig. 8.7 Primitive farming conditions still persist in some parts of Scandinavia. This photograph shows a farming scene in Jämtland in Sweden; here sheep, goats and cattle are essential to the marginal farming economy. (Photo: Till Fjälls/SJR.)

by birch scrub, supplementing their precarious living by hunting, fishing and the collecting of wild fruits and fungi. There are those who live by reindeer-herding on the tundra, those who live in the forested areas of Norrland by farming and timber sales and those who still collect birds' eggs and seabirds from the ferocious cliffs of the Atlantic seaboard. In areas such as Härjedalen in Sweden peasant farming operations have become tourist attractions, bringing in welcome cash through guided tours and the sale of butter, cheese and eggs; sometimes (as in western Norway and southern Finland) some cash income can be gained from the letting of log cabins during the ski-trekking or hiking seasons. Some peasant communities are so remote that they are all but forgotten by the outside world; in Norway and the Faroes there are still villages and settlement clusters which have no road access and only intermittent contact by sea.

Another style of agriculture which has always been important in Scandinavia is that practised by the part-time farming community. As mentioned in Chapter 7, this is still very much a part of the modern lifestyle in the Faroes, where menfolk may work on the family farm only during their short spells at home between long-distance fishing trips. Farming/fishing operations are carried on in many districts of coastal Norway, although fishing has now more or less disappeared from most of the southern fjords. Many Finnish farmers (especially those who have to make a living in areas of marginal land) derive part of their income from farming and part from forestry operations; and the same is true in Sweden. In some areas which lie within the spheres of influence of the main towns and cities country people who have been drawn into urban employment refuse to abandon completely their links with the land. They retain ownership of their family holdings and either rent their land to neighbouring farmers or farm themselves through the use of contract labour. Elsewhere young people enter farming through part-time work on smallholdings in the more remote and inhospitable districts where land prices are relatively low. They depend, however, on income from outside jobs for their survival. The achievements of the part-time farming community are not adequately covered in the farming statistics; often they participate in a 'black economy' which is far larger and far more important than governments are prepared to admit.

It may come as something of a shock to discover that in Scandinavia in 1977 there were still 125,619 holdings under 5 ha in size; some of these are horticultural enterprises or new smallholdings such as those referred to above, but the great majority are remote places where small farmers and their families live almost as close to nature as their great-grandfathers did. They are the places where the Scandinavian environment insists upon a scale and a style of farming which the farming businessmen of Denmark have long since forgotten about.

The forest economy

As noted in Chapter 5, forestry operations are largely restricted to Norway, Sweden, Finland and Denmark. Trees are so scarce in Iceland and the Faroes that they are looked on as immensely valuable landscape resources; in the Atlantic islands planting and protection are the keywords, and felling is almost a crime.

At the present time most of the state-owned forests are located in the northern coniferous forest belt, while private forests predominate in the southern areas of mixed or deciduous forest. In Denmark about 30 per cent of the forested area is owned by the state, while at the other end of the scale, Norway has 11 per cent in state control. Overall, private forests are predominant, but there are differences between the private forests run by large companies and those owned by individual farmers; Sweden has about 75 per cent of the total 'company forest' area of Scandinavia. Table 8.1 shows the distribution of forest area by ownership group in the four countries which have forest industries. In Denmark and Norway the great majority of private forest properties (about 80 per cent and 90 per cent respectively) are managed in conjunction with farming operations. In Norway, Finland and Sweden forest management is a very important winter occupation while livestock are kept indoors and while open-air farming operations are at a standstill; timber

Table 8.1 Forests: Productive forest area by owner groups

	1,000 ha			
	Denmark 1976	Finland 1971–76	Norway 1967	Sweden 1973–77
Public				
State forests	150	4,726	699	4,126
Other public forests	32	824	428	1,675
Private				
Companies' forests	59	1,575	315	5,973
Other private forests	252	12,613	5,040	11,787
All productive forests	493	19,738	6,482	23,561

sales are now essential for the economic survival of many farmers. Overall, the forested area of Scandinavia is increasing slightly as a result of planting on previously unproductive land and old farmland, in particular in Finland.

As far as forest productivity is concerned, two factors are of particular importance. First, and by far the most critical for forest management, is the timber growth rate. In the far south of Sweden and in Denmark climatic conditions permit a growth rate of over 8 m^3 per ha per year, whereas in the extreme north the rate is only about 2 m^3. This means that harvesting of the forest can be undertaken more rapidly in the south, where the forests are of course better located with respect to the centres of demand. On the other hand, the fast-growing conifers of southern Scandinavia (where trees attain their optimum felling size in about seventy years) provide a less dense timber than the slow-growing conifers of Lapland. In the north the trees reach harvesting size in about 140 years, after which time they are still only half the height of the trees of Skåne. The following figures give some indication of the forestry resources of Sweden and Finland:

Forested area:	Sweden 23.5 million ha
	Finland 22 million ha
Total growing stock:	Sweden 2,400 million m^3
	Finland 1,501 million m^3
Annual increment:	Sweden 75 million m^3
	Finland 57 million m^3

In recent years there has been some concern that the programme of felling and thinning has been running ahead of the regeneration of the forest, particularly in Sweden (Fig. 8.8). Every year in Sweden some 300,000 ha are clear-cut; about 60 per cent of this is replanted immediately, and the rest is allowed to regenerate naturally. In addition, about 5,000 ha of farmland are afforested annually, largely because of the withdrawal of land from cultivation as the size of the dairy herd is reduced.

A second factor of great importance in the utilization or produc-

Fig. 8.8 Photograph of a forester at work in the Swedish boreal area. Although many forestry processes have now been mechanized, labour requirements are still high. (Photo: Leif Öster/Domänverket, Falun)

tivity of the Scandinavian forests is the accessibility of the forested area. A glance at the map of Scandinavia will show that few of the main forested areas are more than 200 km from the coast, in contrast to the situation in, for example, Canada and the Soviet Union. In the north of Sweden and Finland the main drainage routes converge upon the head of the Gulf of Bothnia, and timber-floating operations have in the past been relatively straightforward. In the south the situation is even more favourable, with a dense transport network of waterways, railways and roads and with many of the main centres of demand for forest products within 100 km of productive forests.

Although the location of timber-processing plants in Norway, Sweden and Finland was determined above all else by their position with respect to timber 'floatways', it is a mistake to think that floatways are still important. Twenty years ago over 11 million m³ of timber per year were floated on rivers like Dalälven in Sweden and Glomma in Norway. In Finland the tortuous pattern of waterways made river floating difficult except in the far north; consequently 'tugging' was important, and the transport problem was overcome to some extent by locating sawmills and other timber-processing plants on lake shores inland. In the heyday of floating it was about seven times cheaper to float timber than it was to transport it by road or rail, in spite of considerable losses through waterlogging. Now times have changed. Timber is such a valuable commodity that road and rail transport are widely used; for example, in Sweden about 80 per cent of the timber harvest is now carried by road, with about 10 per cent carried by rail and only 4 per cent by floating. Only eight rivers are now used for log-floating in Sweden, for it has been discovered that hydro-electric power generation and log-floating do not mix. In many cases political pressure by the government, restrictive practices by loggers' and sorters' unions, and 'ecological pressure' by conservation groups have been added to economic pressure to encourage forestry operators to abandon floatways and go over increasingly to the use of railways.

To conclude this section it is worth mentioning briefly the very important role played by company forestry operations in Scandinavia. These operations are especially important in Sweden, where there are 5.9 million ha of company forest. Twelve large companies own the greater part of this area, the biggest being Svenska Cellulose AB with 1.7 million ha. Another very large firm is Uddeholms AB, an old-established multi-purpose industrial concern based in the eastern part of Värmland. The company was established in 1668, and it has gradually built itself into one of Sweden's top twenty companies. Its activities, most of them firmly rooted in the densely forested lands to the north of Lake Vänern, include ore-mining, steel production, forestry operations, hydro-electric power production on the River Klarälven, pulp and paper production and the manufacture of chemicals. The forestry industries have always been an essential part of the company's activities, based upon some 350,000 ha of forest. The harvesting programme supplies more than the total requirements of the Uddeholm sawmills, and more than half the requirements of wood for the company's wood-pulp factories. The key plant in the use of forest products is the Skoghall works near Karlstad, built in 1914–18 and extended several times until it is now one of the largest forest industry complexes in Scandinavia (Fig. 8.9). Now Skoghall is a leading producer of sawn

Fig. 8.9 Photograph of the
Skoghall works at Karlstad,
one of the main centres for
the forestry and forest
industry operations of the
Uddeholm company. (Photo:
Lasse Olsson/Uddeholm)

timber, sulphate pulp, paper and a number of chemical products
such as trichlorethylene.

Fishing and fishermen

Fisheries have always been of great importance for the coastal
communities of the Scandinavian lands. Cod, flatfish, eels and shell-
fish were essential parts of the diet of Palaeolithic people in
Denmark, and during Viking times the range of coastal fisheries
greatly increased. In the Middle Ages herring became a staple food,
with commercial herring fisheries in many of the west-coast towns,
More recently the herring fishery was a vital part of the economy

Fig. 8.10 An old engraving showing fishing operations in the Baltic Sea, where the herring fishery was of great importance during the early decades of this century.

of the people of Åland and the Stockholm archipelago, and many other fish species were caught by net and line in the Baltic for local consumption (Fig. 8.10). Since the Second World War fishing techniques have been transformed, and purse-seine fishing and trawling have become very important activities, particularly in the North Atlantic, the Norwegian Sea and the North Sea where marine productivity (and the fish population) is high enough to sustain large-scale exploitation. The Baltic Sea, which is both brackish and quite heavily polluted, is not a major fishing area although it does provide a steady income for those involved in small-scale fishing operations, particularly for herring.

Norway has been in the vanguard of many sea fishery innovations during the last thirty years, and it is now one of the most important fishing nations in the world. It has a total catch of approximately 3.2 million tonnes per year, with a value of over 3,000 million Nkr (Fig. 8.11). In Norway there are some 33,000 fishermen and about

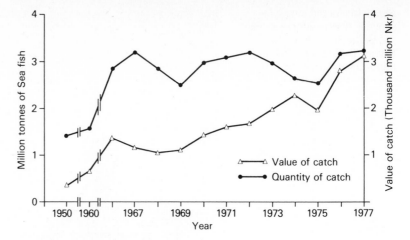

Fig. 8.11 Graph showing the size and value of the Norwegian fish catch. (After Nordic Statistical Secretariat 1979)

25,000 motor-driven fishing-boats. Most of the vessels are open boats under 25 tonnes, but the country has over 500 deep-sea fishing vessels of over 150 tonnes – far more than the total for the other Scandinavian countries combined. In terms of the size of annual catch and the manpower involved in fishing, Denmark is the second most important of the Scandinavian countries; but fishing is not in fact a great overall contributor to the Danish economy.

Relatively speaking, fisheries are far more crucial to the economies of Iceland and the Faroes. Both countries have few agricultural or other land resources, and they look upon their offshore marine resources as belonging to them by territorial right. In both countries fish and fish products account for between 75 per cent and 90 per cent of the total value of their exports, compared with about 4 per cent in Denmark and 8 per cent in Norway. Without their fish catches (currently about 340,000 tonnes per year in the Faroes and 1.4 million tonnes per year in Iceland) both countries would be virtually devoid of products which are saleable on the world market, and it is not surprising that feelings have run high on several occasions during the last twenty years or so as a result of international overfishing of the traditional Icelandic and Faroes fishing-grounds and 'poaching' within their territorial waters. During the 'Cod Wars' with Britain, Iceland has made the point quite forcibly that its very survival depends upon the protection of its fishing-grounds and the protection of its fishing industry. Now, with 200-mile (322 km) fishing-limits and a large measure of international agreement on the regulation of fish catches, both Iceland and the Faroes can attempt to conserve fish stocks which were running dangerously low. The sample studies in Chapters 20 and 21 show that fishing provides virtually the sole basis for life in some of the small coastal communities of Iceland and the Faroes; to know these communities is to see the reality behind the words and statistics of the foregoing paragraphs. It is still commonplace, in these times of scientific fish processing, to see *harðfiskur* (literally 'hard fish') hanging out to dry in and around the small towns of Iceland; the drying racks, when empty, have a spectral and skeletal quality about them.

It is appropriate to conclude this chapter with a few remarks on the Norwegian fishing industry, which still ranks sixth in the world with about 4 per cent of the commercial catch. While Norwegian vessels are active in the east Greenland, Svalbard and Barents Sea fishing-grounds, about 74 per cent of the value of the annual catch is made within 200 nautical miles (322 km) of the Norwegian coast. No less than 50 per cent of the value of the annual catch is made within the old Norwegian 12 mile (19 km) limit, with small wooden fishing-vessels fishing local waters taking the bulk of the catch. Capelin and cod are the most important nearshore fish, whereas the larger vessels which fish further away from home (for example, around the British coasts) take cod, capelin, mackerel, herring and saithe. Prawn-fishing is now increasingly important, especially in the west Greenland and Svalbard fishing-grounds. In terms of the size of the catch, capelin is by far the most important fish, being used largely for the manufacture of meal and fish oil. The fish which are used for human consumption are (in order of value) cod, saithe, prawns, haddock, herring and ling. Mackerel, which was until a few years ago used largely for meal and oil, is now becoming much more important as a food fish.

The decline of fish stocks in the North Sea and the Norwegian Sea has had a dramatic effect upon many of the fishing communities of western Norway. The number of full-time fishermen is now falling; and there has been a great decline in the number of part-time fishermen, who were more numerous than professional full-time fishermen during the 1960s. The greatest loss of fishermen has occurred in the southern districts of Trøndelag, Møre and Romsdal, and west Norway. The harshness of the fisherman's lifestyle, falling catches and the present-day trend to 'job specialization' are all partly responsible for this, and as fishing activities are increasingly concentrated in distant fishing-grounds it becomes more difficult for the part-timer to participate in the traditional seasonal fisheries – for example the winter herring fishery off the Vestlandet coast and the Lofoten cod fishery in March. The Norwegian government has a sensitive appreciation of the *social* value of fishing in small west-coast communities, and it is determined to prevent the take-over of the fishing industry by large companies and multinational food chains. It has therefore encouraged the formation of cooperatives which can finance the purchase of vessels and fishing gear, invest in new fish-finding devices, regulate local catches, fix selling prices and negotiate for subsidies. The government has prompted the building of modern processing plants, and has also encouraged the introduction of small freezing factories. Salting and drying facilities, which serve a declining sector of the international market in fish products, are gradually being phased out.

Sigurd Ekeland (1975:23), the Norwegian Ambassador to the OECD, summarized his government's attitute to the west-coast fishing industry as follows:

> 'Demographic considerations require that the fishing industry be maintained. The coast – particularly in the north – would be depopulated if a decent standard of living could not be ensured from fishing. . . . A high pressure industrialisation of the fishing industry in Norway through the use of large trawlers and fish factories would mean a concentration of fishermen in a few large ports to the detriment of the villages, which would die, slowly but surely.'

At the end of the day, however, government policies on the scale of fishing operations will only prove effective if they are matched by effective conservation measures. The 1980s may well be the decade during which man has to learn to *abandon* some of his traditional fishing-grounds in order to avoid the extermination of fish stocks. The shoals of cod in the Lofoten fishing-grounds and elsewhere off the Norwegian coast seem already to be steadily disappearing and it remains to be seen whether they have already reached the point of no return.

Suggested reading

Agriculture

Behrens *et al.* 1960;, Jensen 1975; Kampp 1975; Korst 1975; Mead 1953; Murray 1977; Osvald 1952; Platt 1957; Rørdam 1965; Rush 1970; Sinclair and Sinclair 1971; Sømme 1949–54, 1960; Varjo 1977.

Forestry

Ahlmann 1976; Arnborg 1960; Bergsten 1961; Fullerton and Williams 1975; Hedström 1977; Hofsten 1978; Smeds 1961.

Fishing

Ashwell 1963; Coull 1975; Cushing 1976; Ekeland 1975; John 1978; Kampp 1967b; Spencer 1975; Sund 1961; Vorren *et al.* 1960.

Chapter 9   Mineral resources and their exploitation

The mineral resources of Scandinavia are irregularly distributed and often difficult to exploit, and although some of these resources have a long history of use others have been under-used pending the arrival of new technologies or new economic circumstances. The Scandinavian land-mass is lacking in large reserves of either coal or oil. The most important single mineral resource is the iron ore of Swedish Lapland, concentrated in the Kiruna – Gällivare area and not exploited properly until the present century following the construction of the Kiruna – Narvik railway. Before 1902 the great difficulties involved in the shipping of iron ore from Luleå, a port greatly affected by the Baltic winter freeze, effectively kept a brake on mining and transport operations.

The exploitation of hydro-electric power resources in Scandinavia has also been subject to great locational and environmental constraints. It is in the nature of hydro-electric power that its greatest potential is in rugged terrain where heavy rainfall or heavy snow-melt can provide high discharge for rivers with a steep gradient; such areas tend to be remote from the centres of human habitation, and the electric power, once generated, has to be transported over great distances to the consumer. Until the 1970s it was not economic to utilize the more distant hydro-electric resources, since the costs involved would have been unjustifiably high in view of the relative cheapness of fossil fuels such as imported coal and oil. Now, however, with the end of the fossil fuel era in sight, it is incumbent upon the Scandinavian states to utilize every possible hydro-electric power source; the reasons for this are partly economic (brought on by the very steep rise in fossil fuel prices, and especially oil) and partly political, for continuity of oil supplies can no longer be guaranteed in the volatile modern world. The economics of hydro-electric power development, even in the far north, are now looking far better than they were a decade ago, and self-sufficiency in energy is something which every state in the western world must strive for.

As far as fossil fuels are concerned, Norway has the only large-scale resources. The minute Swedish coalfield at Höganes near Hälsingborg produces less than 2,000 tonnes per year, and production is running down. In contrast Norway can take advantage of the coalfields on Svalbard, which currently produce about 450,000 tonnes per year. In spite of the great difficulties involved in the mining and transport of the coal, it is undoubtedly a valuable resource, and some of the Svalbard coal is even exported. But by far the greatest fossil fuel resources in Scandinavia are North Sea oil and gas, and there can be no doubt about the huge incentives which exist for their exploitation. The first discoveries in the Norwegian sector of the North Sea were made in 1969 and 1970, and commercial exploitation of the Ekofisk field began in 1971. After 1975 production increased sharply with the construction of an oil pipeline running to Teesside in England and a gas pipeline to Emden in West Germany. There are now at least twenty-four oil and gas proven fields in three distinct groups in the Norwegian sector, and in 1977 Norway was a net exporter of both crude oil and natural gas. Recoverable reserves are estimated to be well over 850 million tonnes of oil and 750,000 million m^3 of natural gas. Oil and natural gas also exist within the Danish sector of the North Sea, and in 1977 crude oil production amounted to over 500,000 tonnes. As the Danish reserves are exploited they should ease Denmark's very vulnerable position as an importer of almost all the fossil fuels needed for power production.

The other power sources can also be mentioned here. One of these is uranium, the raw material needed for fuelling nuclear power-stations. Uranium reserves have been located in both Finland and Sweden, and the Swedes estimate that several hundred thousand tonnes of uranium can be recovered from the oil-bearing shales of Ranstad. Sweden has about 75 per cent of Europe's extractable uranium reserves. A uranium processing plant producing 'yellow-cake' (the nuclear power-station feedstock) has already been built and tested satisfactorily, but in view of the grave concern which now exists in Sweden about nuclear power (see Ch. 11), there must be some doubt about whether uranium will ever be mined on a large scale in the country. The environmentalist and anti-nuclear lobby is gaining in strength all the time, and although the Swedish nuclear-power referendum in 1980 produced a 'yes' vote there is a strong possibility that nuclear power will be phased out shortly after the turn of the century. At present only Sweden and Finland have nuclear power programmes. At the end of 1978 Sweden had 3,710 MW of commissioned nuclear capacity and Finland 420 MW. Twelve nuclear power-stations are planned for Sweden by 1990, and nine are already in operation.

Other power resources include peat and geothermal power. Peat (*torv*) resources are especially valuable in Finland, Sweden and Denmark, and now that the potential of renewable energy resources has been realized research is under way into the best methods of harvesting and processing peat for large-scale power production. Peat is already burnt in power-stations at Piteå in Sweden and

Fig. 9.1 The Krafla geothermal power-station, Iceland. This plant, which is of an experimental type, has not yet performed satisfactorily, but the Icelanders hope that they will obtain abundant electric power in the future from geothermal power-stations such as this. (Photo: Rafmagnsveita Reykjavik)

Tampere, Valkeakoski and Hämeenlinna in Finland, with waste heat also used for district heating purposes. Geothermal power is especially valuable to Iceland. Geothermal hot water has been used for domestic heating for many years, and its use is increasing all the time. While hydro-electric power remains the most important means of generating electricity, one experimental geothermal power-station (at Krafla, near Lake Myvatn) is already in production, and others are planned (Fig. 9.1). The potential for geothermal electric power generation in Iceland is not accurately known, but it is believed to be in the order of 5,000 MW. However, the technology of generating electricity from geothermal steam is still being developed, and the early tests on the Krafla power-station were disappointing; only 6–7 MW of electricity were produced instead of the 35 MW predicted. Additional problems at Krafla are its distance from Reykjavik (which is where the greatest demand for electricity is located) and the presence of a nearby volcano which is still active.

Following this brief introduction to the mineral and energy resources of Scandinavia it is worth looking in more detail at the most important of them – namely mineral ores, hydro-electric power and Norwegian oil. In the case of mineral ores, Sweden provides an excellent example of the relationship between the location of ore bodies and the location of metalworking; in the case of hydro-electricity, there is a long experience throughout Scandinavia of the problems and benefits of dependence upon water-power; and the case of Norwegian oil illustrates the development of a resource which may turn out to be less of a panacea than was previously thought. The following brief case studies provide some insights into the geographical impact of mineral-resource utilization.

Mineral ores

The exploitable mineral ores of Scandinavia are widely distributed and almost entirely restricted to Finland, Norway and Sweden. Finland has adequate iron-ore reserves to meet about 50 per cent of domestic requirements, although they are not of the highest grade. There are thirteen metal-ore mines in the country, of which ten are involved in the mining of non-ferrous ores. Finnish copper reserves are the greatest in western Europe; and copper and other ores including zinc, nickel and cobalt are taken from the mines at Outokumpu, Bihanti and Kotolahti. As far as Norway is concerned, the main mines are of relatively recent date; most of them are replacements for the multitude of small mines which were in operation during the eighteenth and nineteenth centuries. The new mines started operations following the appearance of modern mining techniques in the early 1900s. There are now 17 mines in operation, providing employment for about 5,000 people. They are principally involved in mining iron-ore, copper and pyrites, zinc, lead and titanium. Most of the mines are in the north of the country. The largest iron-ore mine is at Sør Varanger, close to the frontier with the Soviet Union. The annual output of iron-ore concentrates (containing about 65 per cent iron) is close to 2.4 million tonnes, and almost all of this is exported. The small quantity kept for Norwegian use goes to the Mo i Rana iron and steel works. About 800,000 tonnes of iron-ore are produced at the Rana mines, not far from the steelworks. The largest copper pyrite deposits are at Sulitjelma, on the Arctic Circle, and pyrite is also produced in the area south of Rana. Further south, along the south-western coast, there are smaller deposits of pyrite and iron; the region boasts Europe's largest deposits of ilmenite (titanic iron-ore), and the mines in the area around Sogndal produce about 500,000 tonnes of concentrates annually. The main product is titanium dioxide, used in the manufacture of paints and plastics. Most of the exploited deposits of Norway are close to the sea, which facilitates easy transport. The most easily accessible deposits and those closest to energy sources were the first to be exploited; hence many of the mines are found at the heads of fjords or close to waterfalls which can provide the power needed to make the extraction of ores an economic proposition. There is thus a close relationship between mining activity and hydro-electricity production in many cases. On the other hand the mines of Norway have not attracted industry to them; Mo i Rana is the only large metallurgical plant located adjacent to the source of one of its raw materials, although iron from Rødsand and Romsdal is used in a small ironworks at Svelgen on Nordfjord. In recent years some of the mineral resources in the interior of the country have been looked at seriously; the rich deposits of pyrites at Dovre, a remote upland region, are now being mined, and plans are afoot for the mining of copper deposits in the interior of Finnmark in the far north.

The Swedish mining industry is on a quite different scale. For example, iron-ore production amounts to about 35 million tonnes per year, and the production of sulphide ores (containing copper, lead and zinc) amounts to a further 10 million tonnes per year. At the moment there are thirty iron-ore mines and twenty-two mines winning non-ferrous ores. About 14,000 people are employed in the industry. By far the most important area as far as the extractive industry is concerned is the Kiruna – Gällivare iron-ore field in Norrland, located within the Arctic Circle. This area is considered in more detail on p. 263. The most important area for non-ferrous ores is the Skellefteå district, with large and profitable mines at Boliden and also further inland. In the upland belt along the Norwegian – Swedish frontier there are sulphide-ore deposits, and at Laisvall there is the largest single source of lead ore in Europe.

Mining in Bergslagen

Further to the south, the Bergslagen mining district, with its rich deposits of iron, copper, zinc and pyrites, was at one time the industrial heartland of Sweden. In this thickly forested region the earliest exploitation of mineral ores occurred during Viking times, and since the 1300s there has been organized mining for iron-ore in particular. In addition there are copper mines, and a number of mines which extract lead, silver, zinc and iron pyrites. The famous Falun copper mine has records which date back to 1284, and in the 1500s and 1600s it was the largest producer of copper ore in Europe.

The veins of ore in the Bergslagen ore bodies are often steeply tilted and broken by faults. Furthermore, they can often be followed down to great depths. As a result of the great difficulty of working, the old mines tended to be numerous, frequently deep and almost always short-lived. It was not at all uncommon for workings

to extend to a depth of 700 m or more. The iron-ores of Bergslagen
are of two kinds: those poor in phosphorus, and 'apatitic ores' which
contain between 0.6 and 1.0 per cent of phosphorus. The former
were at one time the only deposits of any value, since only they
could be used for iron-making with the techniques available before
1872. After that date, however, the Thomas process brought a technological revolution in the iron industry, and the previously value-
less phosphoric ores began to be mined on a large scale. Today ores
of this type account for about 70 per cent of output from the region.
The old tortuous mines have now been abandoned, and production
is concentrated in the fewer than twenty relatively large mines, for
the most part extracting their ores relatively close to the surface.
The most important centres are Grängesberg, Ställberg near
Ludvika, Norberg near Avesta and Idkerberget near Borlänge.
There are still large iron-ore reserves in Bergslagen, estimated at
about 975 million tonnes; of this, about 700 million tonnes are of
low phosporus content. The iron-ore content is generally between
32 and 60 per cent – in other words, somewhat less than the iron
ores of the Kiruna – Gällivare district.

The Swedish iron industry grew up in the Bergslagen district,
partly because of its relative accessibility with respect to the cultural
core of the country and partly because of special incentives which
were provided by the Swedish kings in the 1400s and in the
following centuries. Each privileged administrative district or
bergslag attracted miners and entreprenuers, and in the fifteenth
and sixteenth centuries there were many small furnaces and forges
located throughout the dense Bergslagen forests. Their essential
resources were iron-ores, local limestone, timber, water and charcoal, and the iron industry could never have developed properly
were it not for the tree-felling and charcoal-making activities which
went on alongside the activities of the miners (Fig. 9.2). For more
than 200 years bar-iron was Sweden's most important commercial
commodity. Later on, during the 1700s in particular, there was a
move to separate mining and smelting activities, and a body called
the *Bergslags-kollegium* granted privileges in the mining and metalworking industries. Their philosophy of decentralization was based
largely on the fear that timber resources (for charcoal) would run
out, and by 1860 large numbers of 'finery forges' had been established well away from the iron-ore mines where timber reserves
were large. At this time there were over 600 blast-furnaces and
forges in Bergslagen alone. Many of these were owned by entreprenuers who became 'iron-masters' as their businesses expanded,
and they laid the foundations for the large multi-purpose companies
which are a fascinating part of the Swedish industrial scene today.

In the latter part of the last century, as the large concerns
expanded and as iron-making was revolutionized by processes such
as the acid Bessemer and Thomas processes, the location of the
iron-ore mines again became an important factor in the siting of

Fig. 9.2 Photo of a Dalarna charcoal-burner. At its peak in the late 1800s the demand for charcoal accounted for almost 5 million m³ of timber per year, burnt in well over 50,000 charcoal kilns. Most of the old foresters of Bergslagen still have memories of the art of 'charcoaling'. (Photo: Anders Sten)

metalworking establishments. When imported coke began to take over from charcoal for smelting, many of the new works were set up quite close to the main mining centres since this involved the least bulk handling of raw materials. As the demand for iron rose with the expansion of the railways there was a further rationalization of the industry, with the larger companies such as Uddeholm, Stora Kopparberg and ASEA buying up and closing down their competitor's works. By 1920 the number of ironworking establishments in Bergslagen had fallen to 200, and most of the small plants which disappeared were those of the far west and north (Fig. 9.3). Even today the large iron and steelworks at Fagersta, Avesta, Sandviken, Hagfors and Domnarvet demonstrate the historical control of industrial location by the location of raw materials – Bergslagen is *still* the heartland of Swedish heavy industry, and industrial inertia is seen to be important even in rational Sweden.

Fig. 9.3 Korså ironworks in Dalarna, Sweden. This works was in operation for ninety years – between 1840 and 1930. (Photo: Sven Berg)

Hydro-electric power

The exploitation of hydro-electric power provided the 'power base' for the industrialization of Scandinavia. The earliest hydro-electric plants were brought into use around 1880, and by 1910 there were many small power-stations located along the rivers of the Scandinavian countries. By far the greatest water-power resources are located in Norway and Sweden. In Norway the average annual precipitation is 1,400 mm, and the annual average runoff is 1,180 mm; this latter fact, which is partly due to very low evaporation rates over most of the country, combines with rugged relief and steep gradients to provide excellent conditions for hydro-electric power generation. Most of the hydro-power potential of Norway is in the south of the country – a fact of considerable importance bearing in mind the location of the main centres of electricity demand in the Oslo–Lillehammer region and around Trondheim, Bergen, Stavanger and Kristiansand. In 1948 only 80 per cent of the Norwegian population were within reach of an electricity supply; today the figure is almost 100 per cent, with fewer than 300 households unconnected to the grid. The greatest increase in the installation of hydro-electricity plants occurred in the 1950s, and this decade was probably the most important one in Norway's history in providing a huge incentive for industrialization and urbanization. Since then the rate of hydro-electric power exploitation has slowed, largely as a consequence of the fact that the most easily utilized resources were already providing power. Nowadays, there is a tendency to build extremely large generating stations; for example, a modern hydro-electric power-station at Sima has a head of over 1,000 m and has a generating capacity of 1,120 MW. (Not so long ago a 300 MW hydro-power plant was considered to be 'large'.) The hydro-power potential of Norway is estimated to be 160 TWh (i.e. 160,000 million kWh) per year on the average. At the moment the total installed generating capacity (in some 400 hydro-electric power-stations greater than 1 MW) is about 17,300 MW, producing about 85 TWh per year. This means that about half of the hydro-electric power potential of the country is now tapped. If *all* economic hydro-power sources were to be utilized, Norway could be completely self-sufficient in energy, even without North Sea oil.

In Sweden there are substantial water-power resources, but the country suffers by comparison with Norway in that most of the large usable rivers are in the north. At present the production of hydro-electricity is about 68 TWh per year, and this accounts for over 70 per cent of all the electricity consumed in Sweden. In addition to the great distances involved in transporting power from the large hydro-power plants of Norrland to the centres of demand in the south, Swedish hydro-electricity generation suffers from two further difficulties:

1. The winter freeze, which affects lakes and rivers (especially in the north) much more severely than those on the western side of the watershed of the Caledonian Mountains.
2. The relatively low average annual precipitation (about 700 mm) compared with Norway, together with higher evaporation rates.

These two factors combine to ensure a considerable variation in hydro-electricity production from year to year; for example, the dry conditions in 1976 caused a reduction in the water held in storage in reservoirs and lakes, and this depressed hydro-electricity production to 52.8 TWh in 1977. Because some transmission lines are almost 1,000 km long, power losses in transit are also high; these may run to 9 TWh in a single year.

At the present time in Sweden about 45 per cent of electricity is generated by the state, 39 per cent by private utilities, 13 per cent by municipalities and local government undertakings, and 3 per cent by other groups. The largest hydro-power station produces

450 MW. The main part of the grid in Sweden is operated by the state, and the highest operating voltage in the network is 400 kV. This is a higher voltage than is used for most of the Norwegian grid, and it is necessitated by the very great distances involved between the main generating areas and the main areas of consumption. Plans are now afoot for a new 800 kV network to operate in southern Sweden.

As far as power-station locations are concerned, the great majority of Swedish hydro-electricity generating capacity is located to the north of Sundsvall on the Gulf of Bothnia coast. There are three main groups of power-stations in Norrland; the first, and most important, group located around the Arctic Circle and using the water of the Lule river and its tributaries (total capacity 2,652 MW), the second group based on the Skellefte and Ume rivers (total capacity 1,395 MW), and the third group based on the Ångerman river, the Indals river and the Ljungan river (total capacity 185 MW). These main groups of power-stations are shown in Fig. 17.4, together with the thermal nuclear power-stations of southern Sweden. The groups of power-stations on the Lule and Indals rivers, like most of those elsewhere in the upper parts of the main drainage basins, operate in conjunction with the careful regulation of water from lakes and storage reservoirs; some of the new plants are based upon pumped storage schemes, and the scale of the civil engineering works involved is enormous. Two of the most recent developments are at Ritsem and Vietas, in the far north of Swedish Lapland, and other extensions to the generating capacity of the Arctic power-stations include the upgrading of Harsprånget to 492 MW. This is now the largest hydro-electricity generating complex in Scandinavia, but it still has less than half the capacity of the two largest plants in Norway. The total cost of the two new Harsprånget power-stations is 67 million Skr, while the Ritsem power-station, which was commissioned in 1977–78, cost 200 million Skr. These developments are indicative of a gradual shift of emphasis in Swedish hydro-electricity production towards the far north and north-west, and some of the plans for developments in the mountain valleys of Swedish Lapland have been resisted strongly by conservationists who see this area as a last wilderness which must be left in its natural state, energy crisis or no energy crisis.

Iceland has abundant hydro-electric power potential, and recent estimates give a figure of 35 TWh per year. So far only about 7–10 per cent has been utilized; possibly about 80 per cent could be utilized should the need arise, although Iceland is of course in the extremely favourable position of having abundant geothermal energy which may be tapped more economically than hydro-power in many instances. At present only about 38 per cent of the power consumed in Iceland is hydro-electricity, and there are now considerable efforts to reduce the dependence which the country has upon imported oil for thermal power-stations and oil-heating purposes. The first large-scale developments for hydro-power supply were on the River Sog which flows via a series of rapids and falls from Thingvallavatn towards the coastal lowlands. Because the lake acts as a very effective regulator, the river has a remarkably even discharge throughout the year. The first power-plant on the River Sog, at Ljosafoss, began operating in 1937; it is rated at 15 MW. The other two Sog river plants are Steingrimsstod (26 MW) and Irafoss (48 MW). These are connected to the Greater Reykjavik area, about 40 km away, by three separate transmission lines.

By far the largest schemes to date are at Burfell and Sigalda, both on the River Thjorsa. The first stage of the Burfell scheme was completed in 1966, and following the building of a second plant in 1972 the power-station now produces 210 MW. The scheme involves the diversion of water from the Thjorsa river through sluices and canals into a new lake which can store about $6\frac{1}{2}$ million m³ of water. Very complicated dykes, weirs and canals are necessary at the diversion point because of the high quantities of sediment carried in this glacial river; sediment either has to be flushed clear or allowed to settle in deep standing water if it is not to find its way into the turbine house and do irreparable damage. From the lake the water flows in a tunnel 1 km long and 10 m in diameter to the power-station in the Fossa valley. After turning the turbines the water is released into the Fossa river, finding its way 2 km downstream back into the Thorsa river. The Sigalda power-station, 35 km from Burfell, is associated with the creation of a large lake which will be used to regulate the flow of the Tungnaa river. The power-house contains three generating units with a combined capacity of 150 MW, and there is room for a further 50 MW unit should the need arise. Apart from the five above-mentioned power-plants of southern Iceland, there is a small state-owned plant at Mjolka in Vestfirdir, and there are plans for a giant power-plant in the north-east of the country using water from three separate rivers. This latter scheme, distant as it is from Reykjavik, will only prove feasible if undertaken in conjunction with the development of some heavy industry; but the remote north-east coast is not exactly attractive to those with capital to invest in steel plants or aluminium smelters.

In Finland at the present time 27 per cent of generated electricity comes from hydro-electric plants. Annual hydro-electricity production has oscillated around 11 TWh per year (only about one-eighth of Norwegian hydro-electric production) and the installed capacity is only about 2,400 MW. These relatively low figures (compared with Norway and Sweden) are due to the generally lower discharges and lower gradients of the main rivers in Finland, and changes in weather conditions from year to year can have substantial effects on the production of hydro-power. For example, there was a drop in hydro-electricity output of 18 per cent between 1977 and 1978,

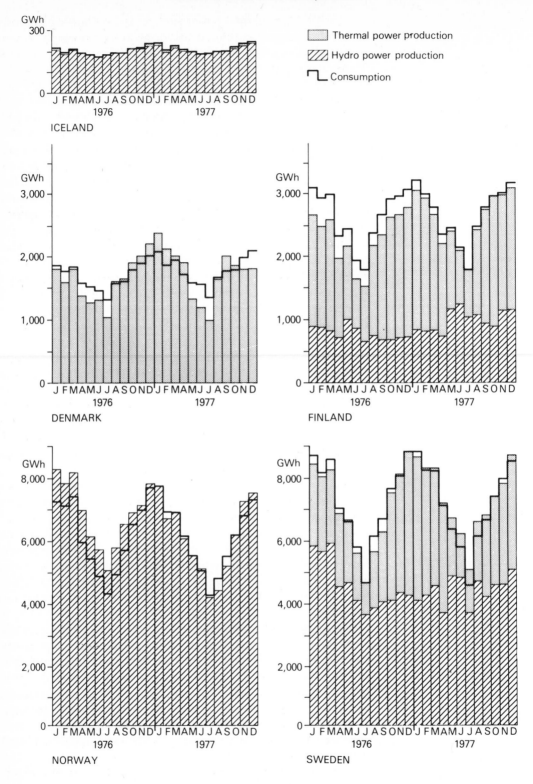

Fig. 9.4 Seasonal oscillations in electricity production and demand in the Scandinavian countries. Note that hydro-electric power production is relatively constant throughout the year in Iceland, Finland and Sweden. Where there are differences between total production and total consumption, an exchange of power between adjacent countries is usually involved. (After *Nordel Annual Report 1977*)

caused by a dry season and a drastic decline in the water reserves held in storage reservoirs. The earliest large-scale hydro-power undertaking was at Imatra, in south-east Finland, close to the border with the USSR. The power-plant here has a capacity of 120 MW, and it is still one of the largest in the country. Since the Second World War, as in Sweden, the centre of activity so far as hydro-power stations is concerned has shifted steadily northwards. The two main river basins developed so far are the Oulu and Kemi basins. The Oulu river power-stations were built for the most part in the period 1941–57. There are now thirteen hydro-power stations; most of those below the large lake of Oulujärvi were built before 1957, and most of the later developments were in the upper reaches of the river and its tributaries, concentrating in particular in the outlets of a series of lakes. The Kemi river project has been an extremely large undertaking, involving the construction of eight large power-stations and nine smaller ones on the main river and its tributaries further east. All of the power-stations lie very close to the Arctic Circle; as in Sweden, therefore, the effects of the winter freeze have to be minimized by using natural or impounded storage reservoirs which can release water beneath the ice through the winter period in readiness for refilling during the warmer part of the year. Seasonal oscillations in hydro-power production are much less marked than one might expect (Fig. 9.4), and much less than in Norway, where production drops drastically every summer. The largest hydro-electric plants on the Kemi river at present are at Petäjäskoski and Pirttikoski, both with a capacity of about 150 MW. The total output of the Kemi river plants is about 3.6 TWh per year, compared with 2.3 TWh per year by the Oulu river hydro-electric plants. Both sets of power-stations are connected up by the northern Finnish grid, and from near Oulu a double row of 400 kV transmission lines runs southwards for about 250 km to connect up with the grid of southern Finland.

Nordel

In 1962 a cooperative body called Nordel was created to advise and coordinate the use of electricity between the Nordic countries. One of the main objectives of the new body was to permit the linking-up of national power grids, and in this it has been extremely successful. There is now a substantial sale and exchange of electricity between the member countries. (Iceland is a member of Nordel, but being somewhat remote from the other members it finds it rather difficult either to buy or sell power.) Nordel acts to divide up the total production of electricity between power-stations all over Scandinavia in such a way that production costs become as low as possible; for example, hydro and thermal power-stations in Denmark, Finland, Norway and Sweden are now linked up through the grid, with surplus power being fed in at any one moment by those stations which are producing electricity most cheaply. While it is still winter in the Arctic, snow-melt may well have started in the drainage basins of southern Norway, making it feasible to use these power-stations for the export of power. In years of abundant precipitation Denmark can import large quantities of water power from Norway or Sweden; in years of drought it may be most economical for the latter countries to import thermal power from Denmark.

There is a long history of grid link-ups in Scandinavia. The earliest links were between Malmö and Copenhagen, and since 1951 the submarine cable connections across Öresund have progressively increased until today 700 MW can be transmitted in either direction. In the Norwegian – Swedish and Swedish – Finnish border regions remote communities have been provided with power from across national frontiers for many decades, but the first large-scale link-ups did not begin until 1959. By 1973 there was a 400 kV transmission line linking up the Kemi river power-stations with those of the Lule river in Sweden, and the Åland archipelago was linked into the Swedish network by a 70 kV cable. Between Norway and Sweden the first small cross-border link was made soon after 1930 in order to provide power for the Kiruna – Narvik iron-ore railway. Since then other links have followed, so that at present there are seven jointly operated connections between the two countries, including one 400 kV line. There is still quite a wide gap in Norway between the grid of the far north and that of the rest of the country. It is more cost-effective to link up the areas north of Narvik with the Swedish grid; there are two connections near Narvik already, and plans are afoot for carrying Swedish 400 kV lines across the frontier in the same region. By far the most ambitious joint projects so far have been the 'Conti-Scan' and Skagerrak projects. The former provides a link between Ålborg in Denmark and Göteborg in Sweden, involving a 250 kV d.c. cable and also a 400 kV cable which runs through Jylland to connect with the West German grid. The Skagerrak project involved two submarine cables 123 km long running from Kristiansand to Tjele in Jylland; both cables have a capacity of 250 MW d.c., and since the successful laying of the second cable in 1977 it has been possible to transmit 500 MW in either direction between Denmark and Norway. Now there are plans for laying two more 250 MW cables, thereby increasing the total transmission capacity to 1,000 MW.

In 1980 the joint capacity for power exchange in Scandinavia was as follows:

Sweden and Norway	1,500 MW
Sweden and Sjaelland (Denmark)	700 MW
Sweden and Jylland (Denmark)	260 MW

Finland and Sweden   1,100 MW
Norway and Denmark   500 MW

By common consent the cooperative operation of the Fennoscandian electricity grids has been a great success, and has saved hundreds of millions of kroner annually since the main links were established. Plans are now afoot for the Swedish 800 kV grid, and almost certainly this will also be linked, on the recommendation of Nordel, with the Norwegian grid. For a body with no permanent staff and no budget, Nordel has already achieved a great deal.

North Sea oil and gas

North Sea oil is already proving to be an immensely valuable resources as far as Norway is concerned, and as mentioned on p. 146 the huge investment in the oil industry (at least $20,000 million) is now beginning to pay dividends. Of the three major oilfields (or groups of oilfields as they should perhaps be called), the Ekofisk field is the most developed. It exports about 48 million tonnes annually by pipeline to Teesside in England, and about 11,000 million m^3 of gas to Emden in West Germany. The Frigg field, which lies approximately 200 km south-west of Bergen, is for the most part a gas field, although oil resources there may eventually prove to be exploitable. The third main field is the Statfjord field, located west of Sognefjord. Its potential has been estimated at 530 million tonnes of oil and 150,000 million m^3 of gas, and oil production during the 1980s will be between 40 and 50 million tonnes per annum. It is worth noting that the oil output from Ekofisk and Frigg represents a huge excess over domestic demand as far as Norway is concerned; total oil consumption in Norway seldom rises above 7 million tonnes per annum, whereas a country like the UK consumes about 100 million tonnes per year. Apart from the main fields mentioned above, there are a number of smaller oilfields in the Norwegian Sector of the North Sea, including the Brean and Brisling fields to the south-west of Stavanger, the Balder field just 50 km south of the Frigg field, and the Murchison field adjacent to the Statfjord field.

One great problem from the point of view of the exploitation of the Norwegian oil and gas fields is the Norwegian Trench, a deep offshore channel which plunges to a depth of 700 m and which intervenes between the oilfields and the Norwegian coast. The technical difficulties involved in laying pipelines across this trench have so far proved insurmountable, and so the supply pipelines have had to be laid to Scotland, England and Germany instead. However, it is a principle of the Norwegian government to use North Sea oil for the direct benefit of Norwegian industry, and this means bringing

Fig. 9.5 Four oil-drilling rigs under construction in a Finnish construction yard. (Photo: Rauma-Repola OY)

the oil ashore in Norway. Therefore there is no doubt that before too long new technology will make it possible to run pipelines eastwards to the Norwegian mainland across the Norwegian Trench. Until that happens all oil which is to reach Norway has to be loaded on to tankers at sea, pumped direct from the production platform into the tanker with no intermediate storage involved. This operation is difficult to achieve satisfactorily, and the disastrous blowout on the Ekofisk Bravo platform in 1977 had a sobering effect on the Norwegians, reminding them of the great dangers of operating in the North Sea environment. Nevertheless, there are hopes that a production level of about 90 million tonnes overall can be maintained through the 1980s at least.

The discovery of oil in the North Sea has given a great boost to industry, and not just in Norway. A large petrochemical plant has been built in Telemark to use Ekofisk natural gas. Norwegian companies have become expert manufacturers of drilling rigs and production platforms and Swedish, Danish and Finnish companies are also in on the act (Fig. 9.5). Many other shipbuilding activities have also been directly linked with the hectic exploratory and production work now going on in the North Sea. One highly inno-

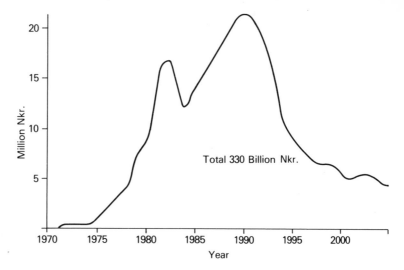

Fig. 9.6 Estimated Norwegian government income from petroleum activities in the North Sea. (Source: Aftonposten/den Norske Creditbank 1979)

vative project was the production of a huge concrete reservoir holding over 150,000 tonnes of oil and located in the Ekofisk field. This gigantic artificial island has a surface area of 9,000 m². In Stavanger, Bergen and other west Norwegian towns the impact of the 'oil boom' is readily observed, and oil-rig workers and many small companies have brought a great deal of extra wealth into the community. In some centres such as Stavanger the whole direction of economic life has been changed; it remains to be seen whether Norway as a whole will change as far as industrialization is concerned. Probably the country will be content to use the revenue from oil (Fig. 9.6) in a sane and unspectacular way; the government knows that one day even North Sea oil is going to run out, so there is little point in going wild about it.

Suggested reading

Mineral resources generally

Ahlmann 1976; Lloyd 1955; Malmström 1958; Mead 1958; Millward 1965; O'Dell 1957; Rying 1974; Sømme 1961; Vorren *et al.* 1960.

Hydro-electric power

Ahlmann 1976; *Nordel Annual Report* 1977 *et seq.*; Raitt 1958; Skog 1976.

North Sea oil and gas

Ausland 1978, Ekeland 1975; *Facts about Norway* 1978 *et seq.*; Glässer 1978; Shell Briefing Service 1979; Stenstadvold 1975.

Chapter 10 Secondary economic activities: manufacturing

The Industrial Revolution arrived late in Scandinavia, and it was not until the beginning of the present century that the advent of readily available hydro-electric power caused a wide dispersal of industrialization beyond the industrial heartlands such as Bergslagen. Many Scandinavian industries were based from the outset upon electricity as a power source, and this increased the range of options as far as industrial location was concerned. Manufacturing plants of all sorts could be market-oriented rather than 'power supply oriented', and many were located in areas with specific craft skills or specific high-value raw materials. Rural locations were commonplace for small manufacturing concerns, and the dispersed and small-scale nature of Scandinavian manufacturing has been commented upon frequently by those concerned with regional personality. However, Scandinavia has its fair share of heavy industries which are located close to their raw materials, and other locational factors come into play with industries such as the Swedish chemical industry and the Norwegian electro-metallurgical industry. Generalization is difficult, and although the image of the little glass factory hidden in a clearing in the forest is an enduring one the student should not be misled into believing that there is anything 'folksy' about manufacturing in the countries with which this book is concerned.

The roots of industrialization were planted in the middle of the last century, for the period 1860 – 1900 saw the introduction of a number of significant industrial inventions and innovations. These included the Bessemer, Siemens Martin and Gilchrist Thomas techniques in the metalworking industry, the use of dynamite in the mining industry, the introduction of both mechanical and chemical pulp-making methods in the paper industry, and the arrival on the Scandinavian scene of electricity, telephones and screw-driven ships. Communications and industrial technology were transformed, and the tempo of economic activity quickened. A multitude of new industries appeared, particularly in Sweden; these included the manufacture of machine tools of all sorts, textile machinery, dairying equipment, railway rolling-stock, cans and bottles, bricks and tiles, and electrical equipment, cables and generators. Some of these items had been produced before, but only on a small scale and without the aid of fully mechanized production lines. Thus was the base laid for the exploitation of cheap electric power and for the creation of Scandinavia's reputation for high-quality manufactured goods.

After 1900 industrialization and urbanization went hand in hand in Fennoscandia, and also to a lesser extent in Iceland and the Faroes. Sweden, with a solid industrial base in the Bergslagen iron-working industry, continued to respond quickly to the rising local and world demand for industrial products of all sorts. In Norway factory industries began to appear in widely dispersed sites before the First World War, but in Finland the early small-scale metal-working industry did not give way to widespread industrialization until political independence was achieved in 1917. The spread of industry in Denmark dates from the period after the First World War.

The crucial period in the growth of Scandinavian industries was 1945–60, and within these fifteen years there was a great increase in the industrial labour-force and a steep rise in the proportion of national incomes derived from manufacturing. Since 1960 there has been a consolidation of Scandinavian industry, but because it has been largely power-based rather than resource-based (an inevitable consequence of the shortage of Scandinavian raw materials apart from timber and iron ore) it has developed a reputation for flexibility and adaptability. These qualities are especially well marked in Sweden, which the world has seen as a leader in industrial innovation and rapid response to changing market circumstances.

This chapter concentrates on a few selected manufacturing industries in Scandinavia, while at the same time attempting to identify some of the locational and other factors involved in their development. True to the author's philosophy of examining small-scale as well as large-scale trends and events, pp. 167–175 deal with several sample industrial concerns. There is some discussion of the extent to which peculiar local circumstances are often involved in developments which might otherwise be interpreted as responses to national or international trading trends or constraints.

The role of manufacturing

Manufacturing is becoming increasingly important in terms of its contribution to the gross domestic product (GDP) of the Scandinavian states. There is, however, a current slight fall in the industrial work-force due to the world economic recession and to the increasing use of technology which reduces manufacturing labour requirements. A number of simple facts and figures will serve to demonstrate the current role of manufacturing in Scandinavia. In

Finland the percentage of national earnings in industry rose steadily if unspectacularly from 30 per cent in 1948 to 35 per cent in 1975. In the latter year industry accounted for 27 per cent of the total work-force, compared with 15 per cent in agriculture and forestry, and 42 per cent in the service sector. The recent decline in agricultural manpower has been remarked upon in Chapter 8, and some of its implications will be looked at in more detail in Chapters 12–17, but the cause is the same in all of the Scandinavian countries – a retreat from a rural lifestyle based upon agricultural employment and an advance into urban and industrial or service occupations. The same story can be told with respect to Norway, where the state income from manufacturing is rising steadily. In 1977 Norway earned 39,194 million Nkr from manufacturing, a figure far higher than that of any other economic sector and more than three times the earnings from agriculture, forestry and fishing

Fig. 10.1 Diagrams showing the estimated 1980 contribution of different sectors of the economy in Sweden to (a) employment, and (b) the gross domestic product. Note that the importance of mining and manufacturing is brought out on both diagrams. (Source: Skandinaviska Enskilda Banken 1977–78)

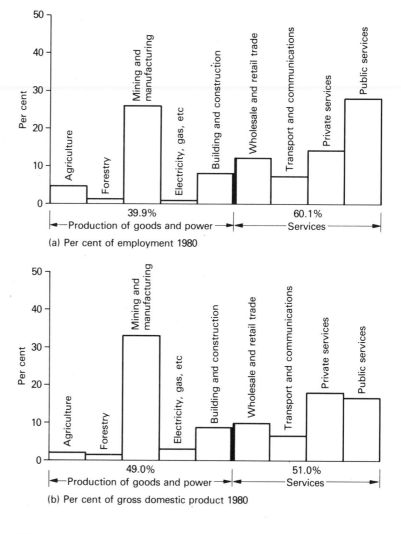

(a) Per cent of employment 1980

(b) Per cent of gross domestic product 1980

combined. About 366,000 people are engaged in manufacturing, the majority working in firms which employ less than twenty persons.

In Sweden the fall in the agricultural work-force from 13 per cent in 1960 to 4 per cent in 1980 has been balanced by a steep rise in service sector employment, while employment in mining and manufacturing has fallen from 29 per cent in 1960 to 26 per cent in 1980 (Fig. 10.1). Nevertheless, mining and manufacturing now account for about 34 per cent of the GDP, compared with 25 per cent in 1960. In Denmark the manufacturing work-force has remained almost static since 1960 at about 425,000, but the contribution of manufacturing to the GDP has risen steadily. Nowadays manufacturing makes the biggest contribution to the national product, has the biggest export earnings and yields the biggest net amount of foreign exchange. Between 1958 and 1973 the value of Danish industrial exports increased sevenfold, and the industrial share of Denmark's total exports rose from 34 to 62 per cent. In the same period Danish agricultural exports no more than doubled in value, while the agricultural work-force was halved.

The distribution of manufacturing

The early development of industry was tied quite closely to raw materials; the example of Bergslagen, cited in the last chapter, illustrates the close relationship between iron ore, charcoal resources and smelters during the 1700s and 1800s. With the advent of hydro-electricity, manufacturing was released from the constraint of the forests, and certain industries (such as the electro-chemical and electro-metallurgical industries of Norway) could now be located close to sites provided with an abundant head of water for private or state hydro-electricity generation. Elsewhere, too, manufacturing concerns set themselves up in quite remote locations where power was easily obtainable, and the small scale and wide dispersal of industrial activity through the countryside was a feature of Scandinavian life until quite recently. Since the Second World War, however, the world-wide trends towards larger-scale units of production, larger companies and a closer concentration of industry have made themselves felt. The distribution maps for the heavy engineering industry, for metal fabrication and transport engineering, for the glass and cement industries, for the chemical industry and for the textile industry all show a clear concentration in the southern part of Sweden.

The intensity of manufacturing can be used to identify an 'economic heartland' of Scandinavia (Fig. 10.2), which coincides closely with the old cultural cores discussed in Chapter 6. There are, of course, a great many incentives for industries to be located within the economic heartland; there is an abundant labour-force,

Fig. 10.2 Map of Scandinavian economic zones, showing the area covered by the economic heartland.

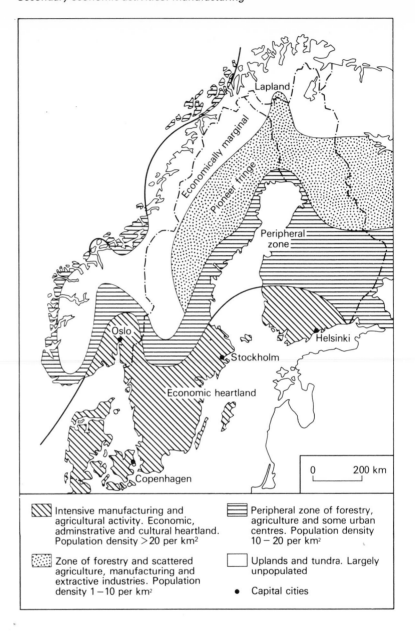

a large market, a good road and rail network, and environmental conditions are not nearly so severe as in the northern parts of Norway, Sweden and Finland. Those industries which require coastal sites are usually able to obtain them. The 'social' factors in industrial location also come into play; towns with long historical traditions and stable populations are more attractive than the raw, bleak towns of the far north, and facilities such as golf courses, theatres and sports stadiums all make for pleasing living and working environments. Besides, Swedish industrialists do not really like having their production centres too far away from Stockholm, and the Danes have been reluctant for many years even to contemplate the merits of sites distant from Copenhagen. This situation is gradually changing as a result of regional policies and a belated demand among some workers and managers for 'country' sites for their factories, but the pattern of manufacturing is now solidly established, and the relatively few manufacturing concerns located away from the economic heartland are not going to do much to disturb the solid, if recent, traditions of industrial location.

A few manufacturing concerns are more widely dispersed, and these belong to the following industries: the electro-chemical and electro-metallurgical industries of western Norway, timber processing and fabrication, wood-pulp and paper manufacture, and food processing. Certain types of chemical manufacture are also located in or close to plants involved with the processing of forestry products. All of these industries require abundant water, if not abundant energy, and all of them show a clear preference for coastal locations. As far as the pulp and paper industries are concerned, sites adjacent to river mouths are ideal. Fresh water is available for hydro-electricity generation and for the pulp- and paper-making process, and treated effluents may be released directly into the sea. In addition, factories can be given their own jetties at the coast, thereby allowing sea-going vessels to come and go with relative ease and without the imposition of port or landing dues.

Steel and metalworking in Sweden: example 1

The steel industry of Scandinavia is based upon a relatively small number of units, most of them located in the economic heartland shown on Fig. 10.2. At present there are thirty-four iron- and steelworks in Sweden, and forty-two in the rest of Scandinavia. As far as employment is concerned, the Swedish steel industry is also by far the most important, with 51,200 employees or about 5 per cent of the total industrial labour-force. Following the traditions developed in the early years of the industry the Swedish plants concentrate on high-quality products such as alloy and high-carbon steels. These latter types of steel account for one-third of Sweden's total steel production, a higher proportion than in any other country. The tonnage produced by the steel industry is relatively small, but since special steel manufacturers usually concentrate on producing a limited range of qualities and types they are often aimed at specific markets and assume a prominent position in Swedish industrial accounts because of their high earning capacity both at home and abroad. The largest special steel manufacturers are Avesta, Fagersta, Sandvik and Uddeholm. Other leading producers are Bofors and Hellefors (which are parts of the huge SKF company) and Grängesberg. Most of the Swedish production of ordinary steel is now in the hands of a new company called Swedish Steel AB

(SSAB), formed by Gränges, Norrbottens Järnverk (which operates a steelworks at Luleå in the far north) and Stora Kopparberg. Three plants produce the bulk of the SSAB output of crude steel: the Domnarvet works at Borlänge produces 1.7 million tonnes, and the Oxelösund works produces 1.3 million tonnes of crude steel rolled plate. As far as the special steels division of the industry is concerned, it is characterized by very intensive research and development, and also by the application of a number of new methods of steel-making and after-treatment. In 1977 about 3 million tonnes of special steel was produced in Sweden. Approximately one-sixth of this was exported. In terms of value, special steel is of great importance as an export, since a few kilos may sell for the same price as a tonne of ordinary steel. Thus, although Sweden imports more steel than it exports, the value of these exports is far higher.

The special steels division of Stora Kopparberg operates two steelworks at Söderfors and Vikmanshyttan, the former on the Swedish east coast and the latter in the central sphere of operations of the company in Dalarna. Stora Kopparberg is one of Sweden's oldest companies, and like others based in Bergslagen it is today a fully integrated concern with interests ranging from forestry to the mining of ore products and dolomite, from hydro-electricity generation to the manufacture of sulphuric acid and other chemicals, from steel production to farming, from wood-pulp manufacture to the making of the raw materials for disposable nappies. The special steels division uses steel scrap and alloys gathered in from all over the world, and it concentrates production on high alloy steels such as tool steel and high-speed steel. About 7 per cent of the world production of high-speed steel is produced at the two plants. Production is carefully managed so that there is close cooperation between the company's Domnarvet steelworks (which is the largest in Scandinavia) and the plants at Söderfors and Vikmanshyttan. All ingots for tool steel and high-speed steel are produced at Söderfors, along with some of the ingots to be processed into stainless steel plate at Domnarvet. The processing operations are distributed so that Söderfors rolls thin-gauge material and forges the heavier, while Vikmanshyttan rolls the heavier and forges the lighter. Söderfors also handles the final processing of stainless steel. Vikmanshyttan produces semi-finished products of tool steel and high-speed steel such as exhaust valve parts for marine diesel engines and forged rings. Stora Kopparberg has cooperated with the ASEA company to develop a new process for making powder high-speed steel. This method makes it possible to produce entirely new grades of steel which have a uniform structure. These steels have improved stability in heat treatment and they also have a much longer life than conventional steels. About 75 per cent of the production from Söderfors and Vikmanshyttan is exported, and this particular industry demonstrates the very high 'value added' element involved in the recycling of imported scrap raw materials.

The recent success of the two plants mentioned above may or may not continue in the volatile world of changing economic circumstances and global over-capacity in steel-making. World market demand and other large-scale economic factors are obviously important in explaining past success, but other more 'local' factors are also notable, such as the integrated operation of the three steel-making plants owned by Stora Kopparberg, the economic savings involved in the use of company-produced power, the cooperation with ASEA in the development of a new process, and the research and marketing operations which can be undertaken by a large and profitable concern but maybe not by a smaller independent producer. With this set of circumstances in the background, plants like Vikmanshyttan, which by reference to a map might be thought to be poorly located, can be seen to be very well located indeed. Too often geographers tend to think of industrial location strictly in terms of markets, transport costs and raw materials. There is more to it than that, and the Swedish special steel industry provides a few clues to the real reasons for economic viability (no matter how short-lived) in the competitive world of modern metalworking.

The electro-metallurgical industry in Norway: example 2

Norway occupies a pre-eminent position in the chemical and metal-refining industries that consume vast quantities of electricity. Around the fringes of the uplands of southern Norway there are deep valleys, abundant rainfall, and rivers with a great potential for the production of hydro-electricity. On the west coast of Norway in particular the fjords provide deep sheltered waterways which can be used by vessels all round the year for the import of bulky raw materials, and the export of finished products. The advent of the technology of hydro-electricity production provided the incentive for the founding of energy-hungry industries such as the calcium carbide plants at Sarpsborg (1899) and Odda (1908). Later plants emphasized the energy-based locations of related Norwegian industries, with aluminium and zinc smelters, plants producing magnesium from sea water and nitrogenous fertilizers from synthetic ammonia, and plants producing copper, nickel and ferro-alloys by electrolytic and electric smelting techniques. There are now more than thirty factories using large quantities of hydro-electricity for these industries; often they are located in very remote places, previously uninhabited valleys which are unlit by the sun for large parts of the year, or beneath the precipitous slopes of glacial troughs cut into old erosion surfaces such as Hardangervidda. Some of the plants have been developed in conjunction with housing schemes or even new towns; Høyanger and Årdal on the shores of Sognefjord are examples of 'planted' communities dominated by the aluminium industry. At virtually every site there has been huge

Fig. 10.3 Porsgrunn Fabrikker, the largest industrial site in Norway. Here there is a work-force of 4,800 people, employed by Norsk Hydro in the production of fertilizers, magnesium and PVC. (Photo: Norsk Hydro)

investment in hydro-electricity stations, dams and regulating works, tunnels and spillways. Transmission lines have had to be erected at company expense, and in addition to the factory construction projects themselves there have been great investments in shore works, roads and other installations.

Norsk Hydro A/S is one of Norway's largest industrial concerns, and its wealth is based largely on the use of hydro-electricity resources in energy-hungry industries. The company was founded in 1905 in order to utilize cheap hydro-electricity for the production of artificial fertilizers. Today the fertilizer production is based on petroleum, while the company's greatest use of electricity is in the production of aluminium and magnesium. Norsk Hydro is responsible for 15 per cent of the world production of magnesium and 35 per cent of world trade in the metal. There is a work-force of about 10,000 of whom about half work at the Porsgrunn works at Herøya in Telemark (Fig. 10.3). Of the seven large plants operated by Norsk Hydro four are concerned with the use of hydro-electricity on a large scale. The Rjukan plant, located in a remote valley in central south Norway, produces ammonia and ammonium nitrate.

Heavy water and rare gases are also produced here, and in recent years the company has expanded into the engineering field at the site. At Notodden, Hydro's oldest factory, the original emphasis on fertilizer production has now been replaced by the manufacture of laminates and furniture. There is also an engineering works and a factory producing packaging materials. At Karmøy in Rogaland a large aluminium smelter produces 120,000 tonnes of the metal per year. About half is used in the company's own rolling mills and extrusion mills adjacent to the smelter. At Glomfjord, in the far north, abundant electric power has provided the basis for the production of ammonia, fertilizers and calcium nitrate. The electro-chemical side of the Glomfjord operation is being run down, and the excess hydro-electricity will then be used for the group of aluminium smelters, each with the same capacity as the Karmøy plant. When the new smelters are in operation 800–900 new jobs will be created in the area, much to the delight of Nordland County Council who have been faced with continuous outward migration by local people for decades.

The aluminium smelter at Høyanger, on the northern shore of Sognefjord, was established in 1950. Adjacent to the works there is an attractive and mellowing 'company town' tightly clustered on the floor of a small valley and overshadowed by steep forbidding valley sides. From 1928 to 1969 there was a plant at Høyanger for extracting alumina from bauxite, but since the closure of this plant the works now concentrates entirely on the production of primary aluminium. Annual output is about 30,000 tonnes per year, and the factory consumes about 575 million kWh of electricity which comes from five hydro-electric stations in the district. During the late 1970s there were plans for the expansion of production at Høyanger, accompanied by the modernization and enlargement of the works. The planned production level will be 70,000 tonnes per year by the early 1980s. The work-force of about 500 will also rise slightly, although most of the increase in production will be achieved by the use of more modern techniques than those employed in the old plant. The Høyanger works are part of the Årdal of Sunndal Verk group, the largest producers of primary aluminium in Norway. The greater part of their output comes from Sunndalsøra on Sunndals-fjord (Fig. 10.4) and Øvre Årdal in the inner reaches of Sognefjord.

The Finnish pulp and paper industry: example 3

The industries connected with forestry are of great importance to both Sweden and Finland, with the wood-pulp industry and the paper industry especially valuable in terms of foreign earnings. In Sweden a fifth of total export earnings comes from forest products, and the pulp and paper industry represents 6 per cent of the total industrial sector's output and employment. In Finland the paper

Fig. 10.4 Sunndalsøra aluminium smelter in western Norway. It has a capacity of 120,000 tonnes per year. (Photo: Årdal og Sunndal Verk)

industry is relatively more important and 15 per cent of the workforce is employed in paper and printing. The gross value of the industry in Finland is about 21 per cent of the GDP, not far short of the percentage for the metalworking industry. The export statistics for Finland reveal the great significance of paper and wood-pulp production, for no less than 36 per cent of all export earnings come from these products, as compared with 32 per cent from metalworking. Production is concentrated for the most part in southern Finland, and a coastal location is by no means as important as it is for the Swedish industry. Most of the large plants in Finland are located on lake shores or on rivers which provide the abundant water required in all sections of the pulp and paper industry. As far as the world pulp industry is concerned, there are three types of mill: sulphate mills, sulphite mills (both producing chemical pulp), and mechanical pulp mills. In terms of production, chemical pulp is about three times as important as mechanical pulp and much more of it goes for export.

In the 1960s there was a phase of expansion in the industry, mostly involving extensions to existing plants. This emphasized the location factors which were responsible for the early growth of the industry in the immediate post-war years – a large supply of timber, possibilities for hydro-electricity generation, abundant fresh water, and (in the case of the paper industry) reasonable proximity to the main markets for newsprint, book papers and packaging materials. The mechanical pulp industry was the first to be developed, with about twenty factories mostly at water-power sites in the south of the country; these sites included four on the Kemi river and several in the Tampere area. In the early days of the chemical pulp industry the pulp factories located at sites such as Kemi, Oulu and Pietarsaari on the Gulf of Bothnia were remote from the paper industry based on factories on the south coast, along the Kemi river, and in the southern part of the Lake District. There was also a link originally between saw-milling plants and pulp-making plants. This link has now been largely replaced by a much more obvious link between pulp-making and paper-making, and the great majority of modern Finnish plants are large, integrated concerns producing pulp, paper, packaging materials and a range of chemicals. World competition and government restrictions on the amount of tree-felling have caused problems for the industry in recent years, but the Finnish pulp and paper industry is now powerful enough and resilient enough to adjust to changing demands and to hold its leading place as an exporter, especially with respect to the European market-place.

One of the largest industrial enterprises in Finland is Yhtyneet Paperitehtaat Oy (United Paper Mills Ltd), founded in 1920. Nearly 60 per cent of its turnover in 1975 came from sales of paper and paperboard, and approximately 25 per cent from sales of converted paper and board products; the balance was made up of metal and chemical products, sawn timber and shipping. Exports comprised about 75 per cent of the turnover. The company employs about 9,000 people, and it operates plants in 9 different locations which are optimistically called 'profit centres' (Fig. 10.5). These include sawmills, mechanical and chemical pulp mills, engineering works, chemical factories, printing works, forestry centres and shipping bases. One of the main centres of operation is the town of Valkeakoski, and this is where the company HQ is also located. At Kaipola, near Jämsä, in the Finnish Lake District, the United Paper Mills operations include a mechanical pulp mill and two paper mills, providing employment for about 1,000 people and producing about 350,000 tonnes of paper per year (Fig. 10.6). Building of the mills began in 1952, and there were expansion phases in 1956 and 1964. The main fibre raw materials at Kaipola are mechanical pulps and sulphite pulp which comes from the company's Tervassari and Jämsänkoski mills. Talc is also used as a 'filler', and this comes from a company plant at Sotkamo. The wood raw material comes from the surrounding districts of central Finland, being either floated to Kaipola or delivered by road and rail. The daily consumption of

Fig. 10.5 Map of the main 'profit centres' of the United Paper Mills group in southern Finland.

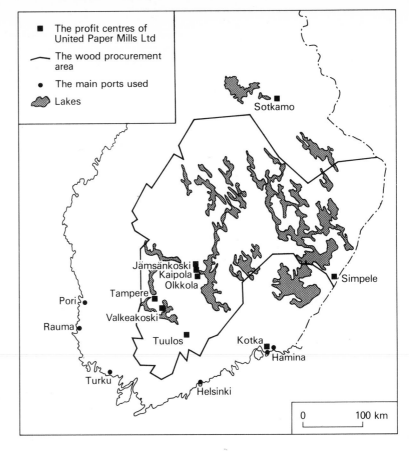

wood is about 2,000 m^3. The mills are powered by electricity; about a fifth of the requirement comes from the mill's own power plant, while the rest is delivered through the national grid. Part of the electricity purchased from the state is offset against power produced in north Finland by hydro-electric power stations partly owned by the company.

Kaipola was built from the outset as a newsprint mill, and it now specializes in various lightweight paper grades such as telephone catalogue papers. At the pulp mill there have been great developments in the manufacture of thermo-mechanical pulp, and after experiments with a pilot plant a new pulp mill was brought into production in 1977 with a capacity of 100,000 tonnes per year. This plant produces paper-grade pulp which is completely free of chemical pulp, thereby achieving considerable savings in wood raw material. About 92 per cent of the output of the Kaipola paper mills is exported, and newspapers which use Kaipola newsprint include *The Times, Daily Mail, Le Monde* and *Le Figaro*.

The operations of United Paper Mills in Finland again demonstrate the advantages of company operations on a large scale and the requirement of modern industry to cut costs by reducing

Fig. 10.6 The Kaipola Mills at Jämsä in Finland, one of the largest establishments of the United Paper Mills group. On this site there is a pulp mill and also two paper mills. (Photo: Pekka Tarvonen/United Paper Mills)

dependence on other industrial concerns as far as possible. The company controls its own forests and forestry operations; it provides some of its own hydro-electricity and sells electricity to the national grid, it provides its own raw materials such as talc and its own pulps (both mechanical and chemical), and following the production of its specialist papers it even uses some of them in its own printing works. It uses its own vessels for some of the export operations to European markets. This 'vertical and horizontal' integration of operations is a great advantage, and it enables the company to keep costs down in exactly the same way as the special steels division of Stora Kopparberg in Bergslagen.

Present-day trends

In recent decades the industrial base of the Scandinavian countries has been consolidated by a great deal of investment and development. The process is illustrated, albeit in a brief and unbalanced way, by the examples in the foregoing paragraphs. The countries of Fennonscandia now depend upon industrial production for their wealth, but there is no escaping from the problems associated with the basic shortage of raw materials. All industries which have to depend upon imported raw materials feel themselves vulnerable, and to an increasing extent the cost of raw materials is something which is difficult to control from the centre of manufacturing operations. Many Scandinavian companies have attempted to solve this problem by investing in mines and other raw-material enterprises abroad, or by making trade agreements with those states whose continued goodwill is needed for the production of bauxite, mineral ores and other items which are the consumables of Scandinavian industry. For many years the industries of Denmark have been too closely tied to food-processing, since agriculture is still the base for much of the manufacturing of the country; the industries of Finland have been too closely tied to timber products; Norwegian industry is still, to a large extent, tied to cheap hydro-electricity and Swedish industry is based upon mineral ores and abundant timber resources. The magic word as far as the four countries of Fennoscandia are concerned, is 'diversification'. This can be achieved through the greater use of high technology and a reduced dependence upon the processing of raw materials, for inventiveness and adaptability remain two of the greatest assets of Scandinavian industry. As mentioned at the beginning of this chapter, the ability to add hugely to the value of an assemblage of raw materials or semi-finished goods is essential for the economic viability of a country like Denmark. Research and development are vitally important also, as is the ability to 'read the market' and to identify trends almost before they have appeared. One of the great arts of industry is the ability to *create* market trends in order to dispose of new products and new ideas, and in this respect the Scandinavians have learnt a lot from America. The industries of all four countries are relatively new, and this is a great advantage, for there is little in the way of redundant plant or redundant labour practices to hold back development. Although the Scandinavian countries are just as likely as the rest of the world to suffer from economic recessions, over-capacity and unsold stockpiles, they are on the whole well prepared for a future in which high technology is more important than bulk production, and in which a deepening energy crisis demands the *efficient* production of everything from ice-breaking vessels to microchips.

Suggested reading

Manufacturing industries

Ahlmann 1976; Ekeland 1975; Eriksson 1957, 1960; Export Council of Norway 1979; Finnfacts Institute 1977; Fullerton and Williams 1972; Hansen 1970; Helvig and Johannessen 1966; Hadne 1975; Jones 1976; Jørberg 1970; Jörberg and Krantz 1975; Korst 1975; Mead 1958; Millward 1965; O'Dell 1957: *OECD Economic Surveys* (annual) for Denmark, Finland, Iceland, Norway and Sweden; Ølgaard 1971; Rying 1974; Scandinaviska Enskilda Banken 1977–78 *et seq.*; Schnitzer 1970; Skole 1974; Sømme 1961.

Chapter 11   The service industries

In Scandinavia, as in other parts of the western World, the service industries (which may be loosely defined as those in which there is neither any primary production of materials or any manufacture of saleable products) are becoming more and more important in terms of employment statistics and national economics. Under this heading we may include such items as shipping, transport and communications, energy supply, commerce, insurance and business services, and education. From a geographical point of view it may be considered that these sectors of the economy are 'intangible' in that they have little in the way of direct effects upon the landscape. However, a moment's thought will dispel this idea.

There can be no doubt about the effects which 'service installations' like roads and railways, airports and harbours have upon the landscape, and since developments in these fields are often of great economic or prestige value they tend to involve huge capital investments and the use of high technology in their construction. A modern airport or road bridge, just like a modern impounding reservoir, usually involves landscape modification on a grand scale, and over a relatively short space of time. There is no doubt about the landscape impact of the 400 kV transmission lines referred to in Chapter 9, and of course the generation of electric power, be it by means of hydro-electric, thermal or nuclear power stations, involves the use of buildings which are no less striking in their effects upon the landscape (and the environment at large) than factories or shipbuilding establishments. The morphology of town centres is nowadays largely determined by the needs of the service sector of the economy. In cities like Stockholm and Helsinki the commercial centres are dominated by shops and office blocks; fewer and fewer people actually *live* there nowadays, and the smaller urban settlements such as Reykjavik and Torshavn are all the more notable because houses are interspersed with commercial buildings and because inhabited flats breathe life into the upper floors and even the basements of commercial premises. Schools, colleges and universities, and urban and rural churches all add variety to the landscape and tell us a great deal about cultural traditions and social priorities. The trappings of tourism, be they small-scale developments linked to castles, museums or other cultural monuments, or large-scale coastal holiday resorts or skiing centres, also have their place within the range of man-made 'landforms' which deserve the geographer's attention.

This brief chapter glimpses a few themes from the broad headings mentioned above. The paragraphs which follow concentrate on the geographical aspects of the service sector, looking especially at the landscape impact of selected activities, the main features of distribution and the information which these service activities can provide about the 'personalities' of the countries concerned.

The significance of the service sector

It is instructive to look at the real significance of services in terms of employment and production. In Sweden, for example, about 60 per cent of the total work-force was employed in services in 1980, as compared with only 45 per cent in 1960. By comparison, agriculture and forestry only account for 5.5 per cent of the work-force, with 26 per cent employed in mining and manufacturing. In terms of the GDP, the structure of production in Sweden has changed in line with the pattern common in most developed countries. The proportion of the GDP originating from agriculture, forestry and fishing has steadily declined to about 4 per cent, whereas the share accounted for by the industrial and energy sectors has increased to about 46 per cent. The service sector's share of the GDP has dropped from 56 per cent in 1960 to 50 per cent in 1980. These figures demonstrate that while the work-force in the services is still rising, the relative productivity of this work-force is falling by comparison with manufacturing in particular. In Finland there is a similar story; nowadays the service industries account for almost 50 per cent of the work-force and about 45 per cent of the GDP. The number of people employed in private and public services (for the most part office workers) has risen from 214,000 in 1950 to over 400,000 today. Similar figures and similar trends can be identified in the other Scandinavian countries.

The cynic might remark that the growing army of office workers in Scandinavia indicates that more and more people are being employed for doing less and less of practical value (Fig. 11.1). There is no shortage of home-bred critics who complain that life in the Scandinavian countries is becoming ever more complicated, with ever more control exerted over the life of the individual by a growing army of bureaucrats. In Sweden, for example, the social services are now so all-embracing that there are forms and computer print-outs for almost everything; half the army of bureaucrats is employed in making sure that you get all the grants and payments due to you, while the other half of the army takes most of it back

Fig. 11.1 A wry comment on the activities of bureaucrats in the service sector. In transport planning, as in other matters, they have their critics. (Source: Hammarström and Hall 1979)

again. More than one cynic has remarked that you need to fill in a form in order to die in Sweden, and being born is infinitely more complicated since other people have to fill in your forms for you.

There is a certain amount of wry humour in all this, but beneath it all is a 'gut feeling' that there are too many people in offices and not enough in factories, too many unproductive people and too few productive ones. But in spite of it all the Scandinavian countries continue to prosper, with rising GDP's, rising living standards, and with rates of inflation less (except in the case of Iceland) than in most other highly industrialized countries. Perhaps the answer to the dilemma of production *versus* services lies in the remarkably small range of raw materials available for exploitation in Scandinavia. Not many people *can* find employment in primary economic activities or in manufacturing; but human skills (both physical and intellectual) are undoubtedly national resources, and the utilization of these skills goes on largely within the service sector. Hence the sale of skills becomes an important economic activity, and brainpower, inventiveness and application are qualities which can be sold abroad as well as at home. The Scandinavians realized this a long time ago, and at the present time the visitor to Scandinavia is amazed by the emphasis given to retraining. People are changing their jobs all the time, acquiring new skills to fit new circumstances while the demand for old skills drops away.

The larger the service sector becomes, the greater becomes the complexity of modern urban life. Stress becomes an inevitable by-product, caused by noise, lack of privacy, uncongenial working environments, overcrowding in city centres, commuting, job mobility and many other factors. The 'job-changing syndrome' exacerbates the stress felt by the urban worker, for it reduces the continuity of contacts with working colleagues and forces individuals to adapt constantly to new faces and new working circumstances. From the point of view of the national economy of Denmark or Sweden or Finland the status quo is no doubt convenient; from the point of view of the individual who works in the service sector the status quo is a trap with no escape, Some of the implications of the 'urban malaise' and the individual response to it are considered in more detail in Chapters 14 and 15.

Some service industries

The remainder of this chapter is devoted to a few selected service industries. There is no space to consider the impact of each industry throughout Scandinavia, so examples are taken from each state in turn. Many topics from the vast range of service industries are inadequately covered here, as in other texts, and some are hardly mentioned at all. But 'balance' is not one of the objectives of this book, and as mentioned in the Preface the principles of broad analysis and accompanying detailed description of sample localities or economic activities are thought to be appropriate. Hence topics such as internal air services, road and rail communications, and secondary education are considered but briefly; and banking, the machinery of the Welfare State and insurance are left for others to examine geographically.

Shipping in Norway

Norway has the fifth largest shipping fleet in the world, with a gross registered tonnage of 26.8 million. The country's great emphasis on the sea, both through its shipping activities and through fishing, has been built up steadily ever since Viking times, and now seafaring is very much a part of the national personality. Until about 1974 shipping accounted for over 30 per cent of Norway's total currency income, but the protracted shipping recession which has accompanied the great rise in energy prices has hit Norwegian shipowners hard. When the energy crisis broke on an unprepared western world Norway had 20 million gross registered tonnes of her shipping in oil tankers, including seventy-two tankers over 100,000 tonnes. Inevitably, with less oil to be carried round the world and with far too much tanker tonnage everywhere, a proportion of the Norwegian tanker fleet had to be laid up. In 1976 there were 100 vessels laid up, and many of them have become almost permanent features of remote Norwegian fjords, tethered together and lovingly maintained by skeleton crews who wait for the good times to return. However, the stock of laid-up ships has steadily decreased, and at the end of 1978 only forty-four vessels were not in use. The position has further improved since then.

Shipping continues to play a very important part in Norwegian life, and with over 200 shipping companies there is a wide enough range of types of vessels and scales of operation to permit the shipping industry to adapt quickly to changing circumstances. One of the strongest features of the Norwegian merchant fleet is the low average age of vessels. The average age is six years, compared to the world average of eleven years. Norwegian shipowners tend to buy and sell vessels with great regularity; for example the period 1965–75 was marked by shipping purchases totalling 25.7 million tonnes, while sales and scrapped vessels totalled 15.7 million tonnes. This tradition of rapid turnover is linked with a philosophy of constant modernization and great specialization. The merchant fleet in 1980 had over 100 specially constructed carriers designed for various oil or petroleum products, 42 special carriers for gas and 40 or so others for mixed cargo. Typically the mixed cargo vessels may transport cars outward to America and foodstuffs, machinery, tobacco or chemicals on the return journey. Only 4 per cent of the fleet's activities are nowadays connected with regular cargo routes, and many vessels are out on long-term contract work. About 93 per cent of the fleet sails between ports without ever touching Norway.

Norwegian shipping is firmly anchored in community life, with many private shipowners and a total work-force of over 28,000 men. There are few large shipping companies. Besides the 'invisible' earnings which shipping brings into the country there are, of course, well-established links with Norwegian shipbuilding concerns, manufacturers of maritime equipment, insurers and repairers, and caterers and handling agents, Many of the firms, large and small, have been involved in the oil developments in the North Sea, and although their activity has decreased since 1976 many of them made very large profits during the oil exploration period through the provision of drilling rigs, supply services and shore-based facilities.

Communications by sea, land and air

The main features of the communications network of Scandinavia are shown in Figs 11.2, 11.3 and 11.4. Sea communications are of course also important, and in addition to the vehicle ferry services shown in Fig. 11.2 there are very many ports all around the coast which participate in foreign trade. Somewhat surprisingly, in view of the size of its merchant navy fleet, Norway figures not all that prominently as a trading nation. Apart from the vast exports of iron

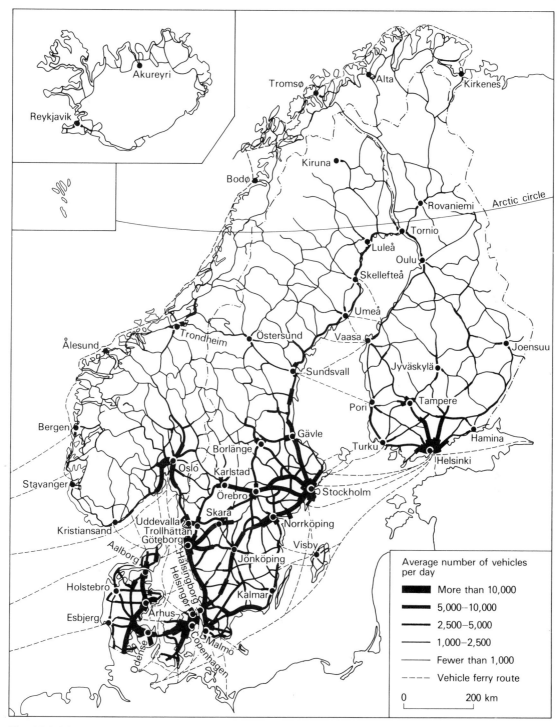

Fig. 11.2 Map of main roads and traffic volumes in Scandinavia. (After Ahlmann 1976)

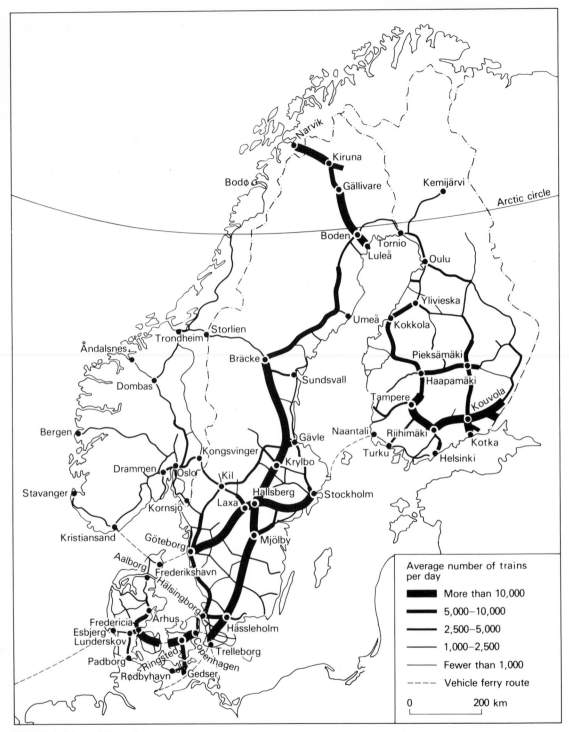

Fig. 11.3 Map of the volume
of goods traffic on the main
Scandinavian rail routes.
(After Ahlmann 1976)

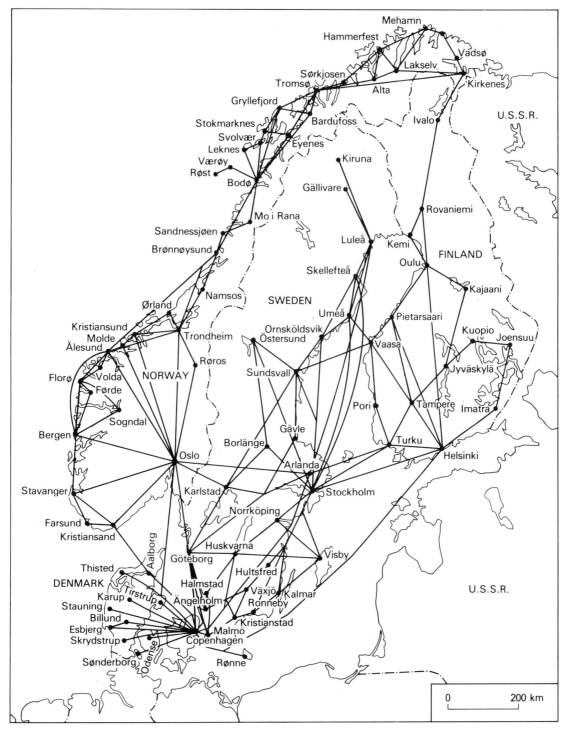

Fig. 11.4 Map of the main
domestic and international air
routes of Scandinavia.

ore from Narvik, only five Norwegian ports handle more than 2 million tonnes of goods per year: Bergen, Stavanger, Porsgrunn, Tönsberg and Oslo. The three latter are all in Oslofjord. On the Swedish coast Göteborg handles more general cargo than any other Scandinavian port, and it also handles a great deal of oil and petroleum products for its oil refineries. In all, there are 9 ports in Sweden which handle more than 2 million tonnes per year, with a further 6 in Finland and 6 in Denmark. Most of the Scandinavian port trade is import trade, although many of the smaller Baltic Sea ports specialize in the export of pulp and paper and other manufactured goods. The Baltic Sea ports in particular are subject to the environmental constraint of the winter freeze, and this topic will be dealt with in more detail in Chapter 17.

Car ferry services are particularly important between Stockholm and Helsinki, Kappelskär and Turku, Helsingborg and Helsingør and Copenhagen and Malmö. The Öresund ferries are considered in more detail in Chapter 22. Internal ferry services are of great importance in the Stockholm archipelago, and as we shall see in Chapter 18, these free services are essential if a permanent population is to be maintained on some of the more remote islands. In Denmark the most important ferry service by far is the Great Belt ferry which plies between Halsskov and Knudshoved, carrying more than 7 million passengers and $1\frac{1}{2}$ million cars per year. Norway is served by a multitude of small ferries, most of which are at work in the fjord country. The road network is gradually being improved in this difficult region through the use of tunnels and bridges, but ferries will remain important for many years to come. At present there are about 440 vessels employed in regular coastal services, and this figure includes some 250 ferries which link up sections of the road network. In 1976 the ferries carried 38 million passengers and 12 million motor vehicles. In addition to the scheduled coastal and ferry services there are a further 1,000 vessels employed in the coastal tramp trade.

The main features of the land communications system are as follows:

1. The dense road network of the economic 'core' areas of Fennoscandia and the high level of use of the main roads in these areas (Fig. 11.2). In these areas large-scale civil engineering projects are justified economically as well as socially, as in the case of the Little Belt bridge in Denmark and the Öland bridge in Sweden (Fig. 11.5).
2. The very few road crossings of the Caledonian Mountains north of Östersund and Trondheim, and the small number of roads which penetrate into the mountain valleys.
3. The relatively even spacing of main roads over most of Norway and Sweden south of the Arctic Circle.
4. The large areas of Lapland which are not served by any main road at all.

Fig. 11.5 One of the largest and most prestigious bridge-building schemes of recent years was the construction of the Öland Bridge in Sweden. (Photo: Skanska Cementgjuteriet)

5. The sparse nature of the road network of Finland, resulting partly from the difficulty of the lake areas in particular for road-building and from the dispersed population to the north of the 'core' area.

6. The very heavy use of the main railway lines by goods traffic and the small level of use of other lines. The railway lines of southern Finland are well used for goods transport, and so are the lines feeding Göteborg, Malmö and Copenhagen.

7. The significance of road transport for the movement of commodities in all the Scandinavian lands. Travellers cannot fail to notice the impact of heavy lorries with trailers even on minor unsurfaced roads. Sweden has the largest load capacity in its commercial vehicle fleet, with over 1 million tonnes, while Finland, Norway and Denmark all have fleets with capacities below 800,000 tonnes.

Iceland provides an interesting example of a country with no railways and with exceedingly difficult terrain for the building of surfaced roads. Organized road-building did not begin until about 1900, but thereafter the length of the road network increased steadily. In 1972 the ten-thousandth kilometre of road was brought into use. Although roads are now well built, graded and drained, the vast majority are still dirt roads which need constant maintenance. So far only about 200 km of road have been surfaced, by far the best being the road link between Reykjavik and the international airfield at Keflavik. Within the town centres of Iceland there is now a determined effort to provide hard surfacing, since winter mud and summer dust are sources of great irritation to local people and visitors alike. The radial pattern of large rivers draining from the interior ice-caps of Iceland towards the coast has made the completion of a ring road difficult, but it is now complete. Most of the rivers have been bridged, but a difficult section to the south of Vatnajökull held work up for several years before it could be opened to traffic in 1973. Sturdy vehicles such as Land Rovers and specially equipped tourist buses can penetrate into the interior of the country on rough tracks, but river fords are often extremely dangerous, and other hazards are quicksands, shifting river courses and quite sudden rises and falls in river-levels. Certain sections of the ring road are of far greater importance to tourism than to the people who live in isolated communities. Many of the road sections over high ground (as in Vestfirðir) are closed by snowdrifts during the winter, and towns and villages have to depend upon ships and aircraft in order to maintain their contact with the outside world.

Communications by air occupy a very special place in Iceland. Icelandair (Flugfelag Islands) operates most of the internal scheduled service, flying between Reykjavik and the main towns such as Isafjörður, Akureyri, Heimaey and Egilsstaðir. Mostly the scheduled services are based upon Fokker Friendship aircraft, but all round the country there are small aircraft companies which operate linking scheduled services to isolated communities, both for the purpose of collecting passengers and delivering mail. Tourist flights are particularly important for the small operators during the summer months. The number of passengers carried in inland flights by Icelandair since 1938 has increased at a spectacular rate. In 1955 the figure was 44,000; by 1973 this total had risen to 183,000.

Internal air communications are also of great importance in Finland, Sweden and Norway. In 1978/79 Finnair (in Finland) and SAS (in Norway) both carried over 1 million passengers and over 5,000 tonnes of freight. The traffic of SAS in Sweden was less dense, although private charter companies and short-haul operators using light aircraft are responsible for much of the air traffic, especially in the more remote districts.

Education in Denmark

Education occupies a very special place in Denmark, and

educational institutions of one sort or another make a considerable impact on the Danish way of life and on the Danish landscape. The school and college population at present is about 1.2 million, split into pre-school children, primary schoolchildren, students at two levels of secondary education, and college and university students. Primary schools are widely distributed, and their locations naturally coincide with the main centres of population in villages, towns, residential suburbs and cities. There are about 100 *gymnasiums* (upper secondary schools) in Denmark, providing education for 204,000 students between the ages of 16 and 19; but schools by no means account for the majority of young Danes in this age-group, for most 17- and 18-year-olds are involved in either vocational training or forms of apprenticeship.

The 'educational landscape' of Denmark is immensely varied, ranging from all sorts of vocational training institutions for young people to a wide range of tertiary educational establishments and adult educational centres. There are about 30 teacher training colleges with a student population of about 14,000. There are four established universities. Copenhagen University was founded in 1479, and until quite recently it was restricted to the inner-city area. However, with the growth of the university, it was moved to a suburban site. The University Park, established in 1941, remains the centre of activity, but as the range of academic and research work increases there is even greater dispersal of university buildings, with many of the teaching and accommodation blocks indistinguishable from adjacent commercial buildings set in a spacious suburban context in the northern part of the city. At present there are over 26,000 students and 1,500 teaching staff, besides a large work-force of technicians, maintenance staff and cleaners, and the economic impact of the university is considerable. Århus University, founded in 1928, has a campus on a large, spacious site to the north of the city. Here there is a real educational landscape, for almost all the university buildings have been erected in the University Park. At present the university provides education for about 14,000 students, and employment for 800 full-time teachers, many part-time teachers and about 600 full-time technical and administrative employees.

Two universities are experimenting with new forms of learning. Odense University was founded in 1966, being situated on a fine campus on the southern edge of the city. There are over 3,000 students and 200 full-time members of staff. As the university is developed it will be integrated into a new 'University Centre' which differs from a traditional University in providing education not only in traditional university subjects in the sciences, arts and humanities but also in non-academic advanced courses. There will, for example, be a large university library, a college of music, business, social studies and technical colleges, a teacher training college and a new college for physiotherapists and 'ergotherapists'. When this centre is fully developed there will 8,000 students on the site. Roskilde University Centre, the newest of the higher educational establishments of Denmark, was established in 1970 in order to reform the traditional university system through the use of more varied and flexible forms of higher education. The University Centre is being established on a large site 5 km north of Roskilde, but it will not remain an isolated campus set amid fields, The philosophy behind it is that it should become integrated into a new urban community which the municipal authorities intend to build around it. Those in charge of the centre believe that its 8,000 students should have close everyday contact with the town community around them; the buildings have been made as simple and functional as possible, and they are devoid of 'embellishments and other prestige symbols'. The University Centre idea is being extended to Aalborg and to the Ribe–Esbjerg area, and the social and environmental impact of these new centres will be similar to that of Riskilde.

Other forms of higher education in Denmark include the Technical University of Denmark at Lyngby, just north of Copenhagen the Danish Academy of Engineers at Lynby and Åalborg, and nine technical colleges in various towns and cities throughout the country. There are also technical schools and a Technological Institute in Copenhagen, together with training establishments in pharmacy, music, dentistry, veterinary science, agriculture, medicine, commerce, art and a host of other subjects. Most of these centres are in Copenhagen and the main cities.

One of the pillars of education in Denmark is the folk high school, an institution which was initially used in the education of the farming class in the mid-1800s, but which has now become a symbol of 'further education' among the whole of the Danish population. The concept behind the folk high school is that it should provide a high level of education in subjects of human and social appeal to the individual. There are at present about eighty institutions subsidized by the state, and all of them are residential. Courses last from one week to forty weeks, and many of these courses are sponsored by educational or commercial organizations in order to provide specific specialized training or to generate interest in scientific or (more particularly) arts or social science subjects. The annual intake of students is about 9,000 in long courses, and a very much higher number of short courses. There are no entrance or leaving examinations or special qualifications, and the philosophy behind the folk high school is that its courses should be educational in a broad sense and also 'personally developing'. Thus many of those who attend courses are following up a special interest, taking an educational holiday or perhaps laying the foundations for a change of job which will later involve more specialist retraining. The folk high school has changed a lot since 1844, but it still plays a very relevant role in Danish educational and social life.

Suggested reading

The service industries

Church *et al*. 1973; Ekeland 1975; Gaunt 1978; Jones 1976; Knudsen 1972; Millward 1965; Mitens 1967; Nordal and Kristinsson 1967; Schnitzer 1970; Sømme 1961.

Transport and communications

Ahlmann 1976; Bergsten 1961; Hood *et al*. 1979; Jensen 1972; Mead 1981; Ouren 1958; Schou and Antonsen 1961; Smeds 1961; Sund 1961; Thorarinsson 1961; Vorren *et al* 1960.

Education

Danske Selskab 1972; Dixon 1959; Dixon 1959; Hove 1968; Marklund and Söderberg 1967; Rørdam 1965; Rying 1974; Wizelius 1967.

Chapter 12 Patterns of living: rural settlement traditions

The man-made agrarian landscapes of Scandinavia have been evolving for 1,000 years or more, and in some areas (such as the Faroes, described in Ch. 7) there are landscape features such as field patterns, drift-ways and clusters of houses which have remained in more or less their original condition since Viking times. Elsewhere, especially in those areas which were brought under cultivation during the pioneering episodes which have affected all five countries, farming landscapes are much more recent. The most recent of all are the newly settled parts of Lappi in Finland, which have been transformed from virgin boreal forest and scrub to farming areas within the last thirty years or so. In Iceland there is another variation on the theme, for in some remote districts abandoned farmlands are now being brought into productive use again as a result of government incentives and new drainage techniques involving the use of heavy machinery.

In each of the Scandinavian countries there are several types of rural landscape, but their differences result from terrain differences and different styles of landholding rather than from great differences in agricultural practices. Except in a few areas where intensive arable farming and horticulture have become parts of the rural way of life, the basis of the farming economy is stock-raising and the production of animal feedstuffs. Before the great land reforms of the 1700s and 1800s each farmer kept just as many cattle (and, in some of the upland areas, sheep and perhaps goats) as his farmland could hold, with the benefit of upland or forest grazing areas either held privately or in common. There was a corporate or communal organization of livestock-farming, with each farmer permitted to keep only the optimum number of animals on village land. In some areas (such as eastern Denmark) this corporate management of land resources has almost entirely disappeared; in parts of Sweden, for example in Dalarna, it still exists in a few places but in a rather degraded form; and in the Faroes it is still practised in a complicated and highly traditonal way which has proved itself beautifully effective over the centuries in the management and conservation of limited grazing resources (see Ch. 7).

One consequence of the need to utilize as much grazing land as possible is the occurrence in the Scandinavian landscape – especially in Norway and Sweden – of seasonal settlement. Small groups of huts in remote clearings in the forest, or in the mountains high above the Norwegian fjords, or in coastal valleys far from the nearest villages or farms, are still very much part of the Scandinavian scene. As Chapters 14 and 19 will show, many of the old *seters* or *fäbodar* are now used as holiday cottages, but here and there they still serve their original purpose, and the seasonal movement of farming people is by no means dead. There are also seasonal fishing settlements; and on parts of the Norwegian coast there is still a substantial movement of fishermen and their families (together with ancillary workers employed in fish factories and in service activities) from one coastal zone to another, in accordance with the location of the seasonal cod or herring fishery. As mentioned on p. 143, some of the people involved in these seasonal migrations are part-time farming/fishing folk who pursue a rhythm of life through the year which is not far removed from that of their Viking ancestors.

There is also a distinct rhythm of hunting activities in some parts of Scandinavia. In Sweden and Finland the hunting of elk used to be an important part of the rural economy. Nowadays, hunting is a sport, but it also contributes greatly to the national food supply; during the short open season in September – October many thousands of elk are shot by hunters. In Sweden no less than 80,000 were shot in 1980, providing more meat than the Swedish population of beef cattle. In the thick forests the main landscape evidence for the historic roots of this activity lies in remote but well-maintained *jaktstugor* (hunting huts), some of which can only be reached on foot or by boat. In the Faroes less frivolous hunting activities also have their seasonal place; bird-cataching, egg-collecting and whale-catching still involve many people and account for the presence of a number of specific features in the cultural landscape such as bird-catchers' huts and boat-sheds and slipways near good whaling beaches.

As far as the Scandinavian phenomenon of the holiday cottage is concerned, we can speculate that its very widespread use may meet more than simply a recreational need; Norwegians and Icelanders still feel very deeply that their roots lie buried in the soil of their native valleys, even if the family farms have been deserted for many decades. In Sweden, which is now a highly urbanized country, the 'rural connection' is maintained partly because the population *was* largely rural until about 1900. The people of Sweden are still only one or two generations removed from a rural lifestyle; many older office workers remember what life was like on the land (Fig. 12.1) and many younger ones have heard all about it from their parents. These are not simply matters of interest to psychologists and sociologists; the preservation and development of old seasonal settlements, and their transformation into recreational

Fig. 12.1 The rural lifestyle is remembered or imagined with affection by many of the present generation of city office workers. (Willy Breinholst)

Deep down in his heart, there is only one dream . . .

settlements, is of profound importance from the point of view of the cultural landscape.

The settlement geography of rural Scandinavia is rooted in the natural landscape and conditioned by the environment. Chapter 8 called attention to some of the factors which originally determined the location and type of farming activities and the siting of farming settlements. At a strictly local scale the mosaic of rock outcrops and sediments, hills and valleys, lakes and bogs, forest land and clearings greatly affected the siting of farmhouses and outbuildings. These factors also determined the location of fields used for grain crops, meadows for hay, and rough fields for summer grazing. Over most of Scandinavia there is no great distance between watercourses such as lakes and rivers, so the availability of water has not normally determined the siting of settlements. In some areas such as the Faroes, north-western and eastern Iceland and western Norway fishing was originally a very important part of the rural economy, and so coastal locations were greatly valued. In Fennoscandia the roughest part of the landscape, often coinciding with patches of thick till with erratic boulders, were left forested, providing timber for buildings and fuel. Cultivable land was strictly limited in extent (except on the few fertile lowland plains), and it was needed for grain crops.

In many parts of northern and upland Scandinavia cattle had to be kept indoors and stall-fed for more than half the year, and this fact made a great impact on the cultural landscape. In the old subsistence farming economy all the best land near the farm had to be devoted to the growing of grain; winter fodder was cut from the poorer land in the infield and also from boggy areas and marshy forest clearings (Fig. 12.2). In the common lands around the farm

Fig. 12.2 A typical Finnish farm-holding. The landscape is still dominated by forest and water. Most of the clearing around the farm is used for hay and grain crops, and there is a small garden adjacent to the farm buildings. (Photo: Finnish Embassy)

other practices also affected the appearance of the forest. In some areas all the trees were ring-barked and killed in order to allow ground vegetation to flourish and provide grazing. Bark and leaf litter were collected, and so was lichen, in order to supplement the store of winter fodder. Here and there in the forest around Lake Siljan clearings were irrigated or drained as part of the community effort to provide better summer grazing and greater stocks of winter fodder. Cattle and sheep had to be found summer grazing in forest clearings up to 50 km from the home farm or above the tree-line in the mountains. In many forested areas there was a tradition (called *svedjebruk* in Sweden and *kaskipoltte* in Finland) of burning down patches of forest for cultivation (Fig. 12.3). The new clearings were used first of all for the cultivation of rye, followed by a few seasons of hay production and a few more of rough grazing. Then they became overgrown with birch and alder saplings and eventually reverted back to forest. These patches of secondary mixed forest

Fig. 12.3 An old photograph showing *svedjebruk* activity (the burning of forest clearings for short-lived agricultural use) in the central part of Sweden around the turn of the century.(Photo: Nordiska Museet, Stockholm)

can still be seen in the midst of the boreal forest in many parts of Sweden and Finland. In general the important elements of the old farming landscape – namely cultivable land, meadows, forest and clearings – were found close together; but the environment was seldom favourable for dense concentrations of farming families. Hence a wide dispersal of farms was the rule, with clusters only where extensive fertile plains or river valleys could provide food for good numbers of livestock and hence for groups of families. Where villages did develop they were often on rocky hillocks, leaving all available cultivable land clear for food production.

Since the Second World War there have been dramatic and widespread changes in farm landscapes; among the factors responsible we can count the economic advantages of 'product specialization', increasing use of farm machinery, the efficient and grant-aided drainage of previously boggy areas, improved communications, and the opportunities for buying in grain as animal feed. Improved ploughs and, later, the use of tractors have made it possible to plough even the heaviest of clay land, and much of this land has been drained through the use of deeply cut open trenches or earthenware field drains. Much of this marginal land is now used for hay crops. Hay crops are also widely grown on land which was previously devoted to the growing of barley, oats or rye, for barley can now be bought through cooperative organizations with cash from milk and stock sales. With the increased use of home-grown hay as winter fodder there is a greater need for large hay-barns; and on many farms especially in Denmark and southern Sweden silage towers have also been added to the agricultural landscape. The use of silage makes good sense, for it reduces the risk of losing the hay harvest through bad weather. With the abandonment of the margins of agriculture there has been a great reduction in the number of people living on the land; overgrown fields, derelict buildings and old meadows newly planted with conifers are just three of the morphological side-effects of the 'rationalization' of farming. In Iceland some remote areas which once depended upon both farming and fishing have now been completely denuded of people; ruined farms, abandoned churches, old gardens ablaze with wild flowers and rotting fjordside jetties are among the relics of the rural settlement pattern of another age.

Rural settlement types

Rural settlements in Scandinavia are known by a bewildering variety of different terms and it is worth defining some of them before proceeding further. In Sweden rural settlement in general is called *landsbygdsbebyggelse*. Another term is *glesbebyggelse* which means, strictly 'scattered buildings'. The term is, however, only used for areas with a low settlement density, and the related term *glesbygd* is generally used for sparsely populated areas in which the inhabitantas are engaged in farming activities. Areas where population density is greater, and where distinct settlements of 200 or more people are to be found, are known collectively in Sweden as *tätort*. Hence the *tätort* includes settlements which range in size from Greater Stockholm to loose clusters of farms and cottages. Thus *glesbygd* and *tätort* do not mean the same as 'rural' and 'urban', and the terms are looked at in more detail in the next chapter.

The fundamental unit of the old farming landscape was the family farm, which was sometimes a grouping of ten to twenty buildings housing not only the extended farming family but also a number of paid farm servants. There might be three dozen people living on the *tomt* or homestead plot. Most of the farms in difficult terrain, particularly in Iceland, Norway and western Sweden, were isolated from one another. The Norwegian word *tun* was used to describe such farms. In areas of greater settlement agglomeration, clustered farmsteads were known by the term *gård*, and still larger clusters by the term *by* in Sweden and *landsby* and *torp* in Denmark. In the Faroes, as described on p. 107, the term was *bygd*. All of these were 'agricultural villages', although it should be borne in mind that some such settlements depended partly on fishing. In Denmark nucleated villages were established for the most part in the period AD 1000–1200. They were the common forms of settlement until the commencement of agrarian reforms towards the end of the eighteenth century, since when isolated farms have become much more common. In Finland agglomerated rural settlement on the eastern Swedish model predominates in that part of the country settled by Swedes, especially where there are large continuous areas of fine-grained sediments as in southern Österbotten (Pohjanmaa). Elsewhere in Finland the single or double farm still predominates in areas of rough land, although many hill or *vaara* settlements have grown up especially in the east. Settlements of this type generally originated as single farms located on morainic hills, with later growth partly attributable to the fertility of hilltop sites in comparison with the heavy clay lands of the depressions. However, the majority of old Finnish farms are found in the lower areas, especially where fine-grained sediments occur in valleys and in lakeshore positions.

The use of farming land varied in the traditional economy according to the settlement type involved. In Norway, for example, the farm or farm cluster was generally surrounded by a cultivated infield or *innmark* and then, beyond a boundary wall or fence, by an extensive outfield or *utmark*. Strips of land on the *innmark* were generally owned by free farmers, while they used the *utmark* (and the offshore fishing grounds, if they lived in a coastal district) in common. The term *almenning* was also used for common land. After the Norwegian land reforms of the nineteenth century much of the *utmark* was brought into private ownership. However, there was by no means a uniform code of practice in the naming and use of these different elements of the farming scene; local traditions of ownership and inheritance, local population history, and the details of local land reform have combined to make generalizations dangerous.

Farm morphology and rural settlements

A typical west Norwegian *gård* of about 1870 illustrates some of the main features of farm morphology. We may assume that the buildings belonged to three property-holders. Each property was referred to as a *bruk*; and each one was linked with nearby land in the *innmark*. The buildings were all of log construction, with birch-bark and turf roofs. The largest buildings had solid bases made of stones collected from the fields, and the cellars beneath the family living-quarters were used for cold storage. Many of the smaller buildings were raised on pillars to prevent the penetration of damp and to deter mice and rats. This was particularly important in the case of buildings used for dairying or for food storage. The other buildings included cowsheds, cooking-houses (also used as bakeries and breweries), stables, goat-houses, pigsties, drying sheds and living-quarters for the farmers' dependants. The buildings were arranged in a very loose cluster with no obvious farmyards for confining animals belonging to individual farmers. This was typical of *gårdar* throughout northern and western Scandinavia, where a very communal type of farm organization of this type can still be found, for example, in Härjedalen in Sweden, in the fjord country of Norway and in the Faroes. The remote village of Mykines, in the far west of the Faroe Islands group, is an enlarged but apparently chaotic cluster of buildings similar in many respects to the west Norwegian *gård*.

Fig. 12.4 Cultural landscape regions of Scandinavia, based mainly on the agricultural settlement types of medieval times.

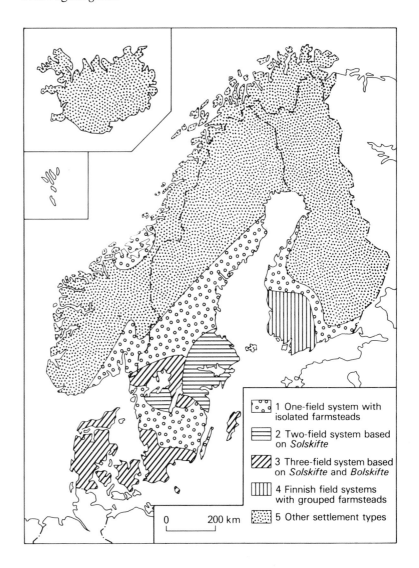

1 One-field system with isolated farmsteads

2 Two-field system based on *Solskifte*

3 Three-field system based on *Solskifte* and *Bolskifte*

4 Finnish field systems with grouped farmsteads

5 Other settlement types

0   200 km

The Swedish geographer Staffan Helmfrid has made a classification of the historic Scandinavian farm types based both on the
morphology of farms and on the 'cultural environments' in which
they existed. For the most part the classification is based upon areas
of Scandinavia which acquired their agricultural landscapes during
medieval times. It is also based upon the field systems (some of
which were of considerable complexity) used by farming communities. In effect the map in Fig. 12.4 shows the main 'cultural landscape regions' of the countryside as they were in the Middle Ages
and up to the great land reforms of the 1700s and 1800s. A number
of generalizations are made about these regions in the following
paragraphs. When reading these it should be borne in mind that the
present cultural landscape contains only relics (sometimes frequent,
sometimes rare) of the morphological features described.

1. Region of isolated farmsteads and small agglomerations

In those areas of Scandinavia subject to environmental difficulties,
settlements never developed the intricate organization of the fertile
and accessible historic 'core' areas. The basic unit was (and still is)
the isolated *tun* or *gård* such as the Norwegian example described
above. Usually the farm was owned or tenanted by a *bønde* or
yeoman farmer. Much forest remained in the settled landscape, and
until about 1900 *svedjebruk* and *kaskipoltte* were practised,
especially near the margins of settlement. Movements of animals
and people were part of farming's seasonal rhythm, and *seters* and
fäbodar were tied to the home farm by upland and forest tracks.
Where villages did occur the one-field system was the norm, as in
the Faroes. The oldest Norwegian farms and villages are in the
south, in Jaeren and around the old 'core' areas of Trondheim and
Bergen – Stavanger. In the remote forested areas of Dalarna and
Värmland in Sweden there are many settlements planted by Finnish
pioneers or *nybyggare* in the mid-sixteenth century as a result of
Gustav Vasa's interior settlement policy. There are many settlements of similar age in Norrland, although most of the pioneering
in this province took place in the period 1700–1900. Elsewhere in
Sweden (for example in Småland and eastern Dalarna) many
summer settlements were greatly expanded and transformed into
places of permanent habitation during the eighteenth and nineteenth centuries due to overpopulation and great land pressure.
Phases of expansion can be recognized through careful study; in
many parts of Dalarna, for example, there are different zones of
settlement based upon the former use of *bodland* (outlying arable
and meadow land) and *fäbodar*. As far as building styles are
concerned, the main farms were almost always built of timber, and
they were made of up to ten separate buildings ranged around a
roughly square farmyard. In the villages they were often tightly clustered, or else strung out along highways. The hayfields around the
villages were dotted with sturdy hay-barns. On the *fäbodar* build-

ings were sometimes arranged haphazardly, and sometimes constructed as replicas of the home farm.

2. Eastern Swedish farming settlements

In this region farming settlements were for the most part small, but they were nevertheless strictly organized both as to layout and the use of a two-field farming system. *Tomter* and farming strips were arranged according to strict rules within the cultivated area. The field system generally used after about 1350 was *solskifte*, in which the sequence of strip holdings was arranged clockwise and according to the passage of the sun across the sky. Farms were almost always timber-built and arranged to a rectangular plan; the elongated yard was usually divided into two, with the animal quarters around one section and the family living-quarters around the other. In the area to the south of Lake Vänern there was a modification of this type of settlement, based upon the use of the two-field and three-field systems, in early nineteenth century villages. These villages were large and irregular, with haphazard groupings of farms around a large central open space. The farms themselves were often small and of hybrid types, ranging from completely enclosed farmyards to loose clusters of buildings.

3. Region of early Swedish – Danish settlement

In the centuries after the Viking era a densely populated agricultural landscape evolved on the fertile lands of Denmark and Skåne. There were clusters of farms all over the farming landscape, and these early villages were located in the centres of their own areas of open fields. Many of them were also route centres or crossroad settlements. Each farm had its own *tomt* or plot of land, but most of the infield land was incorporated into three open fields subdivided into strips and farmed by individual tenants (Fig. 12.5). The arrangement of buildings and fields was closely regulated and the *bolskifte* field system was widespread. According to this system the ploughland was divided into strips which were allocated by lot to the various farms of the village. Farms were usually built to a rectangular plan, with a square yard almost completely enclosed by living quarters, barns and animal quarters. The enclosed yard is thought to have been based on the cattle-yards of Viking fortified settlements.

4. Settlements of south-western Finland

For the most part the earliest farming settlements were based on the Swedish *solskifte* rules for regulating landholdings and village morphology. Villages were composed of irregular groups of small farms, with the clustering most marked on the coastal plains. Further to the east, as mentioned above, the only clustered settlements were the Finnish *vaara* villages of the morainic and hilly

Fig. 12.5 Idealized plan of a Danish village with associated three-field system as it may have appeared in the sixteenth century. (After Mead 1981)

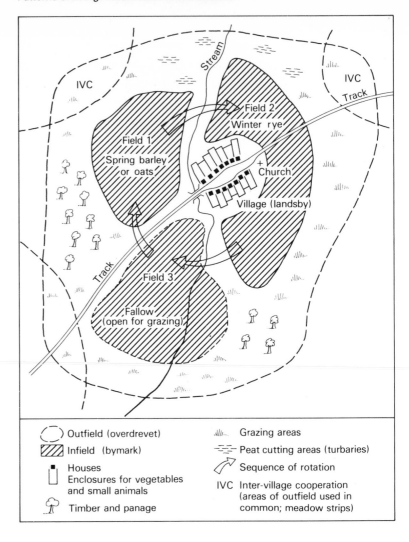

Outfield (overdrevet)

Infield (bymark)

Houses
Enclosures for vegetables and small animals

Timber and panage

Grazing areas

Peat cutting areas (turbaries)

Sequence of rotation

IVC Inter-village cooperation (areas of outfield used in common; meadow strips)

areas. These villages owed nothing to the Swedish landholding tradition.

5. Other settlement types

There were many settlement variations on the themes recorded above. For example, in Gotland there is a very old tradition of single scattered farms, with each farm using a two- or three-field system of land management. Since the 1700s stone buildings have taken over on the island from the wooden farm buildings of the early farming era. The farm types were closely related to those of the eastern Swedish mainland. In Iceland most farms were built, in the old style, as tight clusters of buildings serving all sorts of purposes under a common turf roof (Fig. 12.6). Normally farms were isolated from one another as in western Norway. Building

Fig. 12.6 A group of Icelandic farm buildings arranged on traditional lines in north-west Iceland. This 'composite building' originally had five ridges; the gable ends were made of rough planking and the internal walls were made of basalt boulders and peat.

techniques were dictated by the lack of timber as a building material and by the need to provide shelter during cold and windy winter conditions. Often the farms were built into grassy banks, merging wonderfully into the landscape. The dark rooms and interconnecting passages were contained by walls of stone blocks or peat, and windows were small and inefficient. But these farms must have been extremely warm, with grass roof, peat walls, and compact design serving to conserve the heat generated by people, animals and the smoky turf fires.

In many of the coastal districts where the community was partly dependent upon fishing, bird-catching and sealing there was little agricultural land available. In Åland, the Stockholm archipelago, Bohuslän and western Norway, for example, ancient fishing villages were often tightly clustered, and territorial rights were concerned as much with the use of fishing-grounds and remote grazing islands as they were with the use of cultivable ground.

In Norway, Finland and Sweden there were by 1750 substantial numbers of mining and metallurgical settlements. Many of them, especially in Dalarna and the adjacent parts of Östergötland and Västergötland, could trace their origins back to the thirteenth century, at which time most smelting was based on the use of bog and lake ore. The settlements of the seventeenth century were sometimes short-lived, since many forges closed down when charcoal supplies from the surrounding forest had been exhausted. But the most successful forges kept going to form the basis of the Bergslagen mining and metallurgical industry described in Chapter 9. Most of these villages had a concentrated core of dwellings with 'tributary' settlements sometimes many kilometers away. The villages were all closely dependent upon the farming community for food, fuel supplies and transport facilities. In Sweden many of the *bruk* settlements planted by wealthy landowners were carefully planned, with grid-iron street patterns, gardens and orchards introducing both geometry and aesthetics into the forested wilderness.

The manor and the church made a considerable impact upon the 'traditional' cultural landscape of Scandinavia. Every province, especially in the more densely settled areas of Fennoscandia, was dotted with churches and manors, burial grounds and religious houses. In sixteenth-century Denmark the church owned 30 per cent of the farming area, and the aristocracy 25 per cent. In 1650 no less than 45 per cent of the farmed land was in the hands of the aristocracy. Only 10 per cent of the land was actually owned by free *bønder*, the rest being farmed by tenant farmers and smallholders. There were also many large estates in Sweden, with some aristocratic families owning hundreds of farms. Large houses were springing up in the countryside, often associated with the beginnings of industry. In Finland many of the churches and monastic houses were planted during the episodes of missionary activity although in Iceland and the Faroes, where the church owned about half of the farmed area, the 'ecclesiastical' landscape was less obvious. Most priests were also farmers, and there were few large churches or manors to symbolize social stratification. Indeed the *bønde* farmer who owned his own land was responsible more than anybody else for the shaping of the cultural landscape over the centuries.

Fragmentation and amalgamation

Before the redistribution of land in Scandinavia the field parcels and *tomtar* of the settlements were intermingled, with each farmer usually holding a specific proportion of the strips in each field. In some areas the total number and size of strips was proportional to the farmer's wealth or status; in other areas inheritance and marriage settlements played a part. In areas such as Dalarna during the later Middle Ages, and indeed until the mid-eighteenth century, it was common practice to split family properties after a farmer's death between his male heirs; over the years the fragmentation of holdings eventually increased to a state in which some strips were less than 1 m wide, with some peasant farmers responsible for the upkeep of well over 100 separate small plots of land. The inefficiency of this system of holding was apparent to both landowners and tenants, and during the 1700s and 1800s there were repeated attempts to introduce land reform. The land reforms were not always welcomed; in many areas especially where farmers or *bönder* actually owned their own land, the communal organization of farm work was important both economically and socially, and there was both active and passive resistance to change.

Land reform

The redistribution or consolidation of land *Udskiftning* began in Denmark with the selling off of Crown land during the 1600s and early 1700s, and there were some instances of complete village dispersals and amalgamations of strips into compact holdings before the year 1710. The process of land reform was continued through new legislation after 1760. Although the land reforms were permissive rather than compulsory, changes were possible because most of the land was owned by large landowners, with the individual holdings farmed by copyhold tenants. Those most affected could not object violently since they had precious few rights, and indeed for the most part they looked upon the structural changes in farming as wonderful opportunities for improving their lot. The copyholders generally lived in villages or farm clusters, but the land reforms were accompanied by the decline of these villages as farmers moved out 'into the fields' to build farmhouses on their newly acquired compact holdings. There was also a transition from tenant to freehold farming, since most of the tenants were given the opportunity to purchase land of their own. Released from abject poverty and given the incentive of working their own land, Danish farmers were also able to benefit from high corn prices, and the foundations of the modern Danish farming landscape were laid. The large estates did not disappear entirely, for most of the wealthy landowners were allowed to keep their 'home farms'; much of the labour for these farms was provided by the new class of freeholders and by their sons, who could now sell their labour in order to raise cash for their own land purchases. In 1781 in the most important legislation of all, the open field system of farming was formally abolished in Denmark, and further measures were introduced to encourage the exchange of plots of land so that all farmland could be conveniently worked directly from the newly established farms. At the same time thousands of small lots, comprising patches of land with houses on them, were created on the old common lands, allowing young people and the poorer members of the old peasant class to acquire property of their own and make some sort of a living off the land.

In Sweden and Finland (which were at that time politically united) the redistribution of land began in the middle of the seventeenth century. However, the process was greatly accelerated in 1749 and 1757 with laws that reduced the number of strips in the common fields. This land reform is referred to as *storskifte*, and over half a century or more its effects were felt over most of the farming areas of the two countries. It was, however, by no means as brutal a redistribution of land as that which was affecting Denmark, for the idea was that village organization should be left undisturbed as far as possible. A further land reform called *enskifte* was instituted in 1803 by the big landowners of Skåne and the fertile plains to the south of Lake Vänern. The plan this time was to consolidate farm holdings into single blocks of land, preferably with the farms themselves located within the boundaries of the new holdings. However, there was a feeling that as few farmsteads as possible should be moved out of the villages. Before this reform could build up a strong momentum in other parts of Sweden it was overtaken by the *laga skifte* of 1827, which was much more radical and destructive in its effects. All over Sweden, during the remainder of the nineteenth century and well into the present one, old villages with their clusters of farmsteads were split up as farms were dispersed. The large nucleated villages of Skåne and the other fertile agricultural districts were especially hard hit, and many villages disappeared completely. In the areas of dispersed settlement the effects of the *laga skifte* were less severe, and some remote areas such as the Siljan region have managed to resist the complete destruction of their ancient landholding systems to this day. In the districts around Mora and Leksand, for example, land reforms according to the *storskifte* procedures were carried through in 1820–80, and while they temporarily reduced the extreme fragmentation of land, they did not put a stop to the practice of uncontrolled land division in the farmed area. Furthermore, the 'rational' subdivision of the forested areas between villages has been followed, during the present century, with further subdivision by common consent into a myriad of long, narrow strips now belonging to individual farmers! As a consequence, *laga skifte* amalgamation finally became necessary in these areas after the Second World War.

In Finland the redistribution of land under the old *storskifte* was speeded up by amendments to the law in 1848 and 1881, and then by the *nyskifte* of 1916. Now the old dense agglomerations of farmsteads on the clay plains of south-western Finland and on the fertile lands of southern Österbotten have been largely dispersed, so that villages comprised largely of farms have become extremely rare.

There have been many struggles against the breaking up of farming communities in the cause of economic efficiency. In Österbotten, for example, two parishes had their lands redistributed in 1889–1905 in the midst of great protest from local landowners. In the event 260 out of 637 farms were removed from their old sites. In Sweden some villages were involved in prolonged litigation well into the present century in their attempts to resist 'rational' change. At Kila, in Östergötland, there were 16 farms and their families in 1914, with 148 buildings. The village street was lined with granaries, cattle-sheds and out-houses and with the dwellings of the farming community. Cattle were kept on common pasture land and the arable land was divided into small strips of varying width which were ploughed, sown and harvested by cooperative effort. The farmers' 'village council' organized all common tasks, and the sixteen farming families celebrated the great festivals of the year together. Shortly before 1920 the village was partitioned, and only two of the farms were left in their original positions. By this time the legal proceedings had lasted twenty years; one farmer had gone mad, one had committed suicide, and several had been ruined through having to remove their buildings and having to install themselves elsewhere.

In Norway, Iceland and the Faroes the effects of land redistribution on the farming landscape have been much less severe. In Norway the enclosures of 1821 and 1857 did lead to a rationalization of holdings but not to the destruction of the Norwegian *gård*. In Iceland the farming landscape has for centuries been made up of single isolated farms; while many have been abandoned, those that remain have not been fragmented to any great extent. The villages and towns are for the most part non-agricultural; most of them are fishing settlements, even if a few farms may be located within and around them. The problem of farm fragmentation has not yet been adequately tackled in the Faroes. As explained in Chapter 7, crown land (administered by the Faroese Agricultural Council), has remained in viable agricultural units, but privately owned *oðals* land has been divided over the years into such small holdings that it can now be used only for part-time farming in many areas. Within the last twenty years the Faroes land registry office has been involved in the difficult task of rationalizing the ownership of the small plots of land in the infields of the coastal communities. The amalgamation of plots is proceeding slowly, gradually making village agriculture more productive and less laborious than at any other time during the present century.

Hardship and emigration

'Generation had followed generation, sons succeeded fathers at harrow and plough, and daughters took their mothers' place at spinning wheel and loom. Through ever-shifting fortunes the farm remained the home of the family, the giver of life's sustenance. Bread came from the rye field and meat from the cattle. Clothing and shoes were made in the home by itinerant tailors and cobblers, out of wool from the sheep, flax from the ground, skins from the animals. All necessary things were taken from the earth. . . . Outside of life's great events, little happened other than the change of seasons. In the fields the shoots were green in spring and the stubble yellow in autumn. Life was lived quietly while the farmer's allotted years rounded their cycle.

And so it was, down through the years, through the path of generations, down through the centuries.

On 1 January 1846, Ljuder Parish had 1,925 inhabitants: 998 males and 927 females. During the century after 1750, the population had increased almost threefold. The numbers of non-assessed persons – retired old people, cottagers, squatters, servants, parish dependants and people without permanent homes – during the same time had increased fivefold. . .'

Vilhelm Moberg (1951), in his great saga *The Emigrants*, captures the endless boredom, the unremitting hardship, the solid conservatism and the inherited defeatism of the Scandinavian peasantry of the mid-nineteenth century. This was a time of rapidly rising population and ever-increasing difficulty for small farmers. As described in Chapter 4, the Little Ice Age in northern Europe was accompanied by a number of prolonged episodes of harsh climate, forcing a retreat from the margins of settlement in Norway and Iceland and leading to crop failures all over Scandinavia. Conditions of 'acceptable hardship' on the land were replaced by conditions of famine, and the problem of feeding extra mouths was not made any easier by the archaic systems of landholding which were prevalent throughout Scandinavia. There is no doubt that land reforms were desperately needed in the early part of the nineteenth century. Social and economic distress was widespread, and there was a need to amalgamate fragmented holdings and to increase their size to dimensions of viability. In Sweden there was a rapid increase in the rural population between 1820 and 1860. This led to a tendency to increase the already widespread fragmentation of farms, and although the *laga skifte* of 1827 made many farms more compact and farming easier from a physical point of view the social repercussions were enormous. The reform of farm holding also brought into existence a large number of smallholdings; these were economically weak, for they were normally located on old common land or else in areas previously thought unfit for cultivation. Crofting or cottage farming activities appeared on a large scale; most of those involved were landless farm servants, a class that grew considerably in the pre-industrial period, and threatened many country districts with overpopulation. Most of the crofters did day work on larger farms and looked after their own pitiful patches of soil when they could find the time or the energy. Many young men could find no employment at all, and they turned into squatters or vagabonds. The *laga skifte* and its equivalents were undoubtedly necessary, but they destroyed the stability and the social coherence of country communities all over Scandinavia.

The above points provide some understanding of the background to the New World emigration which occurred in the later decades of the nineteenth century. However, it should not be assumed that the emigration was a direct consequence of land reform, for in

Norway much of the emigration occurred before the land reforms were widely implemented. The cause of the flight to the New World were related to climate, economics and demography as much as to the process of land consolidation and enclosure. Also, emigration to the virgin lands across the Atlantic appeared preferable, in the minds of thousands of farming families, to migration into the towns and cities of Scandinavia. The prospect of nineteenth century urban life was not all that inviting, for there was no guarantee of either employment or housing. The movement started in Norway around 1850, spread to Sweden and Denmark in the 1860s and 1870s and to Finland around 1890. Emigration was a fact of life in Iceland from 1861 onwards. The exodus, which was at its peak in the 1880s and 1890s, slowed gradually after the turn of the century, and it ended to all intents and purposes with the depression of 1929–30. From Norway 870,000 people emigrated between 1835–1935, a loss greater in proportion to its population than from any other Scandinavian country. Emigration from Sweden occasionally rose above 50,000 per year in the 1880s and 1890s. Between 1851 and 1923 Sweden lost 1.3 million of its people (Fig. 12.7). The peaks and troughs of emigration from Iceland and Denmark almost matched those for Sweden, although much smaller numbers were involved. Overall, the Scandinavian countries lost 2.7 million people during the emigration period, representing about 17 per cent of the total population. The areas of greatest loss were in southern Norway and southern Sweden, where some administrative districts (for example, Oppland fylke and Vest-Agder fylke in Norway and Kronobergs län in Sweden) lost over 50 per cent of their farming populations.

The 'America migration' was undoubtedly an extremely important episode in the historical geography of Scandinavia, making a deep impression upon the folk memory of the Scandinavians. It was also a sign of the times, bringing home to the geography student of today the reality of nineteenth-century rural

Fig. 12.7 Swedish emigration to America between 1850 and 1940. In the period of peak emigration (1880–95) more than 510,000 people left the country. (After O'Dell 1957)

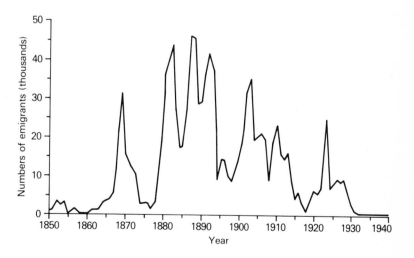

overpopulation. We are reminded, too, of the unremitting difficulties faced by the farming communities of the five countries who have to live with, or escape from, the harsh northern lands which they have inherited.

Suggested reading

Rural settlement types

Ahlmann 1976; Berg 1968; Björkvik 1956; Bodvall 1957; Grenholm 1977; Hastrup 1964; Helmfrid 1961; Holmsen 1956; Isachsen 1959; Joensen 1980; Jones 1977; Kristinsson 1973; Munch 1947; Nielung 1968; Thorarinsson 1961; West 1970–71; Williamson 1970.

Land reform and emigration

Göransson 1971; Hasselmo 1976; Helmfrid 1961; Holmsen 1961; Kampp 1972; Kero 1974; Moberg 1951; Nilsson 1970; Norman and Runblom 1980; Semmingsen 1960, 1972; Stefansson 1939; Stone 1971c.

Chapter 13   Patterns of living: urban settlement

The populations of the Scandinavian countries are at present largely urbanized, although it was not until the dawn of the industrial era of the present century that the swing from a rural to an urban life-style began to gather momentum. Urbanization has the longest history in Denmark, a country with an area of only 43,000 km^2 and a population of just over 5 million, of whom no less than 4.2 million live in towns. This means that over 82 per cent of the Danish population is to be found in urban agglomerations of one sort or another. The urban population of Sweden is proportionately about the same, but Finland and Norway still retain more of their rural traditions, with only 64.1 per cent and 65.1 per cent of their people living in towns and cities. In terms of population statistics, the Scandinavian countries with the largest percentages of urban dwellers are Iceland (87 per cent) and the Faroes (86 per cent); in the case of Iceland the overwhelming importance of Greater Reykjavik (population 120,000) is largely responsible for this state of affairs, while in the Faroes the peculiar traditions of the *bygd* (see Chapter 7) mean that many of the settlements classified as 'urban' are in fact more rural than urban if looked at from a social and economic point of view. The problem of classification is a considerable one, as mentioned in the previous chapter. Again, settlements which do not happen to fall neatly within commune boundaries are sometimes included in the urban statistics and sometimes not. Nevertheless, Table 13.1

Table 13.1 The populations of the Scandinavian countries around 1975–76, classified as agglomerated (*tätort*) and dispersed (*glesbygd*) in Swedish terminology.

	Denmark	Faroes	Finland	Iceland	Norway	Sweden
Total population	5.1 mill.	38,600	4.6 mill.	219,000	3.8 mill.	8.2 mill.
Agglomerated (*tätort*)	4.2 mill. (82.6%)	33,300 (86.3%)	2.9 mill. (64.1%)	190,400 (86.9%)	2.5 mill. (65.9%)	6.8 mill. (82.7%)
Dispersed (*glesbygd*)	882,000 (17.4%)	5,300 (13.7%)	1.6 mill. (35.9%)	28,700 (13.1%)	1.3 mill. (34.1%)	1.4 mill. (17.3%)
The metropolitan area	1.3 mill. (25.0%)	11,600 (27.7%)	880,100 (18.5%)	118,400 (53.2%)	460,300* (11.3%)	1.4 mill. (16.6%)

* Includes only the city of Oslo itself.

gives a reasonably accurate picture of the proportions of urban and rural dwellers in the six Scandinavian countries in 1975–76.

The capital cities

The capitals of the Scandinavian states have all emerged as 'primate cities', and their relative significance from a demographic point of view has increased through the period of rapid urbanization. Their locations are all coastal and all excentric; one could argue, for example, that Trondheim would make a more convenient Norwegian capital than Oslo, and that Århus would be a better capital of Denmark than Copenhagen. In spite of their locations, however, the capital cities have all attained primacy through more or less 'natural' processes, leaving a litter of ex-capitals licking their wounds and nursing their pride in other parts of their national territories. The oldest capital cities, both founded before AD 1,000, are Reykjavik and Torshavn; as centres of political and economic power for almost 1,000 years they have had ample time to outstrip all their rivals in terms of population and wealth. Reykjavik, for example, is more than six times larger than Iceland's next largest town, Akureyri. Oslo, founded in the eleventh century, did not become capital city of Norway until the fourteenth. Helsinki was not founded until 1550, and it became capital of Finland only after 1809. Copenhagen was the third capital of Denmark, having been preceded by Jelling and Roskilde; and Stockholm was preceded by Sigtuna and Uppsala as capitals of Sweden.

In the urban hierarchies of the Scandinavian states the capital cities stand well clear of all others; Greater Copenhagen, which can be referred to as the 'Scandinavian megalopolis', has about 1.3 million inhabitants or almost exactly a quarter of the country's population. In terms of population Greater Stockholm has more people, but the built-up area is not so concentrated and it includes quite distinct municipalities, such as Täby and Danderyd in the north, Huddinge and Järfalla in the south, and Nacka and Lidingö in the east. The population of Oslo is more than twice as large as that of Bergen, the second city of Norway. Helsinki is three times as large as Tampere, Finland's second city. And yet, in spite of the presence of these large urban centres, Scandinavia remains predominantly a region of small towns. For example, Denmark has only 4 towns with more than 100,000 people; Finland has 5 and Norway only 3. Sweden has a larger 'city' population than the others, and there are no less than 11 centres with more than 100,000 inhabitants. Urban geographers have remarked upon the fact that there are many medium-sized and small towns and very few large ones. It has been calculated, for example, that half of all Scandinavian towns have populations of less than 2,000 while 80 per cent have less than 10,000 inhabitants.

Migration

As in many other parts of the world, migration from the country districts to the towns has led to a drastic decline in the population of many rural areas. The consequence of this episode of population mobility, following hard on the heels of the large-scale emigration of the last century, are considered in more detail in Chapters 15, 16 and 17. Generally the migrants from the rural areas progress towards a fully fledged urban lifestyle by stages. These stages may be separated by decades or even generations, and T. Hägerstrand has identified the phenomenon of 'chain migration' in Sweden. The first stage in the chain is the movement of young people from the big towns to the metropolitan areas of Stockholm, Göteborg and Malmö. They leave behind them a vacuum which is then filled by their counterparts who migrate from smaller towns. In turn, the small-town vacuum is filled by young people from country districts with no previous experience of town life. At present the population of country dwellers seems to be stabilizing itself, but the migration process continues unabated, tending to denude the villages and small towns in particular of their most imaginative and ambitious young people. In addition, improved communications and increased awareness of urban values mean that the *rate* of movement is increasing; young people may progress from small town to large town and from large town to city within a few years. The movement of people is by no means restricted to the young; complete families and even middle-aged couples often *have* to move to the cities from the provinces in order to advance their careers. Migration on a large scale is by no means restricted to Sweden. In Oslo, for example, it is reckoned that city growth is now so rapid that four out of every five people were born somewhere else. And in Reykjavik the scale of migration from the remote country districts has been so alarming that geographers are contemplating the prospect of three-quarters of the country's population being concentrated in a single urban centre (Fig. 13.1). However, it need not necessarily be assumed that the present rate of city growth is going to continue. There are some signs, at least in Denmark and Sweden, that the rural–urban flood of migration is now beginning to ebb, leaving most of the new urban dwellers stranded in big-city life but carrying a few determined individualists back to a simpler lifestyle in the countryside. The 'drift *from* the towns' may well turn out to be a chapter in the story of Scandinavian migrations when the geographers of future generations look back at the 1980s.

Fig. 13.1 Reykjavik, Iceland's megalopolis. Greater Reykjavik now contains over 53 per cent of the country's population, and this unbalanced situation is a source of great concern for regional planners.
(Photo: Rafmagnsveita, Reykjavikur)

Urban characteristics

One feature of Scandinavian towns which strikes the visitor is their relative *cleanliness* when compared with towns elsewhere. This is partly due to the Scandinavian regard for cleanliness, partly due to careful town planning, but above all due to the fact that industrial activities are not necessarily urban in their locations. Industrialization came late to Scandinavia (see Ch. 10), and the environmental impact of large-scale manufacturing based upon the use of coal was largely avoided. The power source for the large industries established in the early 1900s all over southern Scandinavia was hydro-electric power, the generation of which produced no grime and the use of which produced no smoke. As indicated in Chapter 10, factories were released from the discipline of coalfield location and many of them grew up at raw material source sites, or on the coast, or in country districts where land was cheap. Many thousands of workers were drawn into the raw material processing plants in particular, transforming minerals or timber or producing hydro-electricity. New towns sprang up at many sites, for example, along the coast of the Gulf of Bothnia both in Finland and Sweden; and elsewhere in Scandinavia small towns were enlarged with the arrival of industry. In western Norway the movement to the new industrial centres was a healthy corrective to rural overpopulation, as it was in much of southern Sweden. The result of these developments, from the point of view of urban morphology, was that the big cities were spared from the worst excesses of industrialization. Even today there are very few industrial complexes, and towns can be classified for the most part as service centres rather than industrial centres. The wide dispersal of industry is a factor of great importance both for the social geography and economic geography of Scandinavia.

Other points which may help us to understand the urban geography of the Scandinavian countries are as follows.

1. The majority of industrial employees in Scandinavia work in concerns which have less than 100 people on the payroll. This is particularly true in Denmark, where the small 'green belt' industries of recent decades are widely scattered, in particular around the fringes of country towns.
2. Towns which may be world famous for the manufacture of specialist goods (for example, glassware, agricultural machinery or furniture) may have populations of less than 10,000.
3. The planned dispersal of population from the main metropolitan centres to 'overspill' towns such as Farsta, Täby, Skärholmen and Vällingby on the fringes of Stockholm, has been going on since the 1940s. Some of these centres, with populations well in excess of 100,000, have few if any industrial functions; they are basically service centres and dormitories, feeding thousands of commuters into the city centre every day of the working week.
4. The capital cities of Scandinavia, in spite of their overwhelming importance within their own national contexts, are quite small by world standards. The only 'million cities' are Greater Copenhagen and Greater Stockholm; physical constraints and carefully planned growth have ensured that on the whole towns and cities are spacious, with relatively low urban population densities. Central Oslo has a population density of just over 1,000 persons per km^2, while at the other end of the scale Central Copenhagen has about 8,000 per km^2.
5. The 'aesthetics' of urban life are important to the Scandinavians. By and large, town and city centres are open, spacious places in which municipal and historic buildings, trees, parks and gardens, and water all feature in the urban environment. Amenities

Fig. 13.2 The face of modern Stockholm: Västerbron, carrying one of the main bypass routes around the city centre (Photo: Swedish Tourist Traffic Association)

figure prominently, for example Tivoli in Copenhagen, the Vigeland Park in Oslo, the Folk Museum at Trondheim, and Millesgården and Skansen in Stockholm. Museums, cathedrals and churches, palaces and other historic buildings abound. For the most part they are cherished, even though some of them are overshadowed by towering modern buildings of glass and concrete, surrounded by dual carriageways and undermined by railway tunnels (Fig. 13.2). In terms of historic architecture, the richness of the Scandinavian capitals is due in no small part to the fact that there has been very little wartime destruction during the present century. Stockholm, built around the complicated waterways between Lake Mälaren and the sea, has an immensely beautiful city centre. It has a large stock of buildings which are of seventeenth-century date or older, the oldest building being the well-preserved and lovingly restored cathedral (built in about 1250). In not a few urban centres of the western world, including Rovaniemi and Oulu in Finland, the events of the period 1939–45 had more to do with destruction and re-creation than with preservation and restoration.

Urban development

The earliest towns in Scandinavia were those established by the Vikings as trading centres at Kaupang in Norway, Hedeby in Denmark and Helgö and Birka in Sweden. Of these, Birka and Hedeby were by far the most important. Birka, situated on the northern side of Lake Mälaren, was founded at the beginning of the ninth century, and it was a great centre of trade where merchants from the east met those from the west. It had a population of about 700–1,000, and it may well have had its own craftsmen including metalworkers. It declined around the end of the tenth century, and its place was taken over by Sigtuna and Gotland as the main trading centres on the east coast of Sweden. Hedeby, at the base of the Jylland peninsula, was by far the largest Viking town in Scandinavia. It covered an area of 24 ha, and its main function was as a trading centre at the focus of the east-west Baltic route and the north–south route between Norway and Sweden and the western European lands. It was also a manufacturing centre for cloth, pottery, metalware, leather goods and beads. Like Birka, Hedeby declined in the late tenth century, and after AD 1000 other towns began to take over trading functions: these included Bergen and Trondheim in Norway, Århus, Viborg and Aalborg in Denmark, and Lund, Skara and Sigtuna in Sweden. On the North Atlantic islands Reykjavik and Torshavn also served as trading centres, but on a much smaller scale.

Medieval towns

Gradually, during the early Middle Ages, towns multiplied. After about 1150 the advent of a more settled lifestyle, together with increasing prosperity, caused accelerated urban growth. Well over 100 new towns had been established by 1580, and as early as the thirteenth century towns had begun to acquire specific functions. For example, Uppsala became a religious and educational centre. as did Roskilde and Lund. In Dalarna Falun was founded as a mining town; Oslo grew quickly as a trading centre; and Trondheim was until 1380 the Norwegian capital. Bergen and Visby grew rapidly into commercial centres because of their links with the Hanseatic League. The old towns, situated for the most part in the 'core areas' of the modern Scandinavian states, waxed and waned with political shifts of power, wars and disputes, periods of prosperity and hardship, and plagues and town fires. Fires were of particular importance, for the old towns were mostly built of wood with narrow, twisting streets and buildings tightly packed together. The old town of Nyköping in Sweden was burnt down by fire in the year 1665, and many others disappeared in the same fashion.

The medieval towns of Scandinavia were for the most part located on ancient religious sites or in places used by Viking assemblies or

Fig. 13.3 The old town of Visby on the island of Gotland. The photograph shows the western part of the built-up area within the town walls. In the background we can see the harbour, and the ruin in the middle distance is St Lars's Church, one of seventeen thirteenth-century churches in the town. (Photo: Swedish National Travel Association)

tings. But commerce became more and more important for town growth, and the towns which grew most rapidly were those with the best trading sites or those with access to raw materials such as iron ore. The earliest market towns had long, narrow streets used by traders, but later on German influence in town design can be seen in the central squares which acted as the foci for different parts of the town. Probably the most important and wealthy town of the Baltic area was Visby on Gotland, which enjoyed its heyday as a trading centre in the thirteenth century. It had a population of 10,000. It was (and still is) encircled by an imposing defensive wall, and the medieval street network can still be discerned (Fig. 13.3). The town's most important features were its harbour and its huge open spaces which were designed to accommodate visiting merchants and their wares from all corners of the known world. Other important Swedish towns in the Middle Ages were Stockholm and Kalmar (both trading centres), with the latter notable because of its magnificent fortress (Fig. 13.4). Towns like Viborg, Roskilde and Lund grew up in the shadow of their monumental cathedrals, and all over southern Scandinavia great churches, castles and fortified manor-houses became the centre-pieces of the expanding towns.

Fig. 13.4 Kalmar Castle, one of the most impressive of the medieval castles of Sweden. It was built to protect the growing market town from seaborne attack, and it was also important for the defence of the country's eastern seaboard. (Photo: Swedish National Tourist Office)

Grid-iron towns

In the seventeenth century town-planning on grid-iron lines became the vogue: Göteborg and Karlskrona were founded in Sweden; in Denmark Christianshavn (which was to become Copenhagen) was founded in 1618; and the new town of Christiania (later to become Oslo) was established in 1624. New towns sprang up all over central and southern Sweden, in eastern Norway and in Finland. This was the great period of Finnish town-building, and according to W. R. Mead 'the most common feature of the established Finnish town is its grid-iron street plan'. Only five 'Renaissance' towns were built in Denmark; the reasons for this are not clear, but it may be that the country was already served by a sufficient number of urban centres which were well built and thriving at the time. It should also be remembered that by 1600 Denmark already had a substantial heritage of stone and brick buildings; there was no great need to renew these buildings, whereas in the rest of Fennoscandia timber buildings and even timber towns were occasionally levelled by fire, providing new opportunities for town-planning and development on a grand scale. Turku suffered a disastrous fire in 1827, and so did Pori and Vaasa in 1852; all three towns needed to be completely rebuilt.

Industrial towns

During the eighteenth and nineteenth centuries town planners began to realize that strict grid-iron plans were not entirely appropriate to the rough terrain and irregular coasts and waterways of many Scandinavian town sites. Consequently, a more imaginative style of planning appeared, and during the 1800s in particular between forty and fifty new towns were constructed on deliberately irregular lines. Many more were modified by rebuilding or by the addition of new suburbs. However, by far the greatest influences on town-planning in the late 1800s and early 1900s were the advent of the railways and the rise of industry. It has been calculated that in Sweden alone something like 1,000 new industrial communities came into existence during Scandinavia's belated 'industrial revolution'. The vast majority of these communities contained fewer than 1,000 people. Most of the industrial towns were developed after 1860, and they expanded after 1900. During the present century relatively few *new* industrial centres have appeared on the Scandinavian scene; modern 'new towns' are for the most part suburban developments of various types, designed to relieve the housing pressure on the big cities.

The industrial settlements of Scandinavia were scattered far and wide, particularly within regions which were rich in natural resources. In the 1860s, for example, there were over 600 blast-furnaces and forges in central Sweden, using as raw materials local iron and copper ores and vast quantities of charcoal produced in the forest. So much timber was consumed that this requirement alone caused a more or less even spacing of forges in some areas, with each forge drawing its timber (and thence charcoal) from a specified forested area. With the great rise in the demand for iron rails in the later decades of the century many of the small ironworks expanded, drawing to themselves sizeable work-forces and leading to the creation of towns or townships in quite remote locations. As mentioned in the previous chapter, small *bruk* settlements were typical of the early 'rural' period of industrialization, with larger settlements established after 1860.

A good example of a manufacturing town is Sandviken, in the northern part of central Sweden. It was founded in 1862, around Sweden's first foundry operating on the new Bessemer method. By 1865 it had attracted a population of 1,600, living to begin with in extremely primitive conditions. The works management put up

housing for the workers and their families in the style of the older
bruk housing estates – long rows of single-storey buildings, each
one with two rooms, a private entrance and a piece of garden. All
the neat, yellow-plastered wooden buildings were arranged
according to a strict grid. As the foundry continued to expand there
was a switch to two-storey apartment houses; each apartment had
its own outdoor toilet, wood-shed and shelter for the 'family pig',
which was essential to the household food supply. Apart from the
foundry, the town also had a range of services including a tailor's
shop, food store, hairdresser, chapel and coffee-house. Since 1900
the town has grown enormously. New blocks of flats have replaced
the old two-storey buildings, and the population has risen to over
15,000.

Twentieth-century town developments

As the industrial developments of Scandinavia gathered momentum more and more people were released from working on
the land. The movement to the towns and cities had been under
way for some decades before 1900, but the 'urban poor' were
condemned to wretchedly squalid living conditions on the fringes
of Helsinki, Copenhagen, Stockholm and Göteborg. For the most
part they found employment in the new industries and other businesses which were springing up on all sides, but there was little in
the way of 'industrial' housing, and the workers of the small country
towns were infinitely better off as far as living conditions were
concerned. Some 'workers suburbs' were built, for example in
Göteborg; but properly designed housing areas were frequently
talked about but seldom built because of the great cost involved.
In 1901 a quarter of the population of Stockholm lived in flats
comprising two rooms or less; 56,000 people were in lodgings, and
high rents claimed a disproportionately high percentage of the
income of even well-paid workers.

The move to the suburbs was started by the well-to-do during the
nineteenth century, especially on the fringes of Stockholm and
Copenhagen. The advent of railways and trams made it possible to
live in villas on suburban estates in the outlaying districts and to
commute daily to work in city centres. As far as the working class
was concerned, their early housing estates were often located on
privately owned land in inconvenient locations. Gradually the Scandinavian governments realized that state involvement was necessary
if the problems of suburban squalor and suburban sprawl were to
be overcome, and after 1930 municipal authorities began to play a
much more important role in town-planning. One of the largest
'overspill' schemes was the building of the satellite city of Tapiola,
to the west of Helsinki. To the west of Copenhagen the growing
city overwhelmed old farming villages by adding to them large
blocks of 'dormitory' flats. To the east south-east of Oslo new

Fig. 13.5 High-rise apartment blocks on the fringes of Stockholm. Basically these are dormitories built to contain people as efficiently and cheaply as possible, and there is now a strong reaction against this type of development. (Photo: Tiophoto)

satellite towns have taken some of the housing pressure off the city proper. As Reykjavik has grown, particularly since the Second World War, it has incorporated the towns of Kopavogur and Hafnarfjörður. All of these developments have been planned solutions to the problems of rapid urban growth.

Nowadays the problem of housing lower-income workers has been largely overcome, but mistakes have been made along the way. Some of the stereotyped housing developments of the period 1930–50 have little in the way of national identity or architectural merit. Solid blocks of four- and five-storey apartment buildings can be found on the fringes of most Scandinavian cities, similar in design to the massive apartments which have been put up in the city centres during phases of urban renewal. All over Scandinavia there are high-rise buildings linked with major housing developments (Fig. 13.5). Here and there 'special' solutions to housing problems have been found, such as the blocks of flats designed by Ralph Erskine for Svappavaara and Kiruna with arctic climatic conditions in mind. But on the whole the glossy prestige schemes such as Tensta, Vällingby and Skärholmen on the fringes of Stockholm are large and sterile, even with their carefully planned patches of greenery and their ponds and fountains. Some of them have become centres of social discontent. Large-scale developments are now

Fig. 13.6 A modern villa development in Denmark. Small schemes like this have proved immensely popular, and the demand for single-family homes is now much greater than the demand for flats in cities such as Copenhagen and Stockholm. (Photo: Skanska Cementgjuteriet)

going out of fashion, and private villa and *radhus* developments seem to be more appropriate to the needs of the moment (Fig. 13.6). But low-density housing of this type requires a great deal of space, and if the cities and towns of Scandinavia are not to destroy the environments in which they are placed the use of space must be strictly controlled. At present the urban planning problems of Scandinavia are no longer connected with matters such as poverty and housing conditions; they are, to an increasing extent, concerned with social contact, community service, stress and participation. Affluence has brought its problems and town planners and architects in Scandinavia think and write almost as much about sociology and psychology as they do about the construction and arrangement of buildings. To the urban geographer the lesson may well be that the unplanned muddle of Stockholm's medieval Gamla Stan is in many ways more satisfactory than the over-planned modern paradise of present-day Skärholmen.

223

Suggested reading

Urban geography

Åström 1967; Bidstrup 1970; Flacker and Holm 1972; Hägerstrand *et al.* 1974; Hammarström and Hall 1979; Matthiessen 1980; Mead 1971; Møller 1972; Morill 1961; Ödmann and Dahlberg 1970; Pred 1977.

The historical development of towns

Ahlmann 1976; Dodd 1971; Heineman 1975; McCririck 1976; Myklebost 1965; Paulsson 1957; Riis and Stromstad 1977.

Chapter 14 Affluence, stress and recreation

Large parts of Scandinavia can now be referred to as 'recreational areas'. These areas are neither urban nor rural in the normal sense; they contain landscapes which look different and feel different, and they also require very specialized planning techniques.

There are many different types of recreational landscape. In some places (as in Visby in Sweden and the Old Town at Århus in Denmark) complete urban environments are carefully preserved as tourist attractions and cultural monuments, and there are 'urbanized' holiday centres as on parts of the Bohuslän coast and at Tammisaari in south-west Finland. By and large, however, planned holiday resorts are few and far between, since the Scandinavians (especially those who are better off) seem to have an inbuilt reluctance to take their holidays in organized crowds – at least within Scandinavia. Those who do take their holidays *en masse* are generally those in the lower-income brackets who may spend their holidays in crowded camping-sites or in holiday chalet colonies owned by the large industrial concerns. Although there are holiday beaches which are more or less submerged by browning human flesh at the height of summer, these beaches have not attracted the urban developments typical of southern France, Belgium or southern England. Most of them have contrived to remain relatively unspoiled (Fig. 14.1). The standardized international holiday resort with its ranks of concrete and glass sea-front hotels, its clear blue swimming-pools, its trendy night-clubs and discotheques and its cosy restaurants, is peculiarly foreign to Scandinavia.

During the last decade there has been a tendency for Scandinavians to migrate during the winter and early spring in ever-increasing numbers on package-deal holidays to centres such as the Canary Islands, Gambia, Tunisia, Mallorca and Greece. For example, Swedish non-scheduled international air services (comprising holiday charter flights for the most part) carried 2.1 million passengers in 1977, compared with just over 1 million in 1970. A Danish study has shown that in the late 1970s over a third of all Danes were taking holidays abroad, with about 36 per cent of holidaymakers heading for the Mediterranean region. Rising fuel prices and air fares have caused a reduction in this traffic since 1979,

Fig. 14.1 Harbour for fishing-boats and pleasure craft at Torekov, a popular bathing resort on the west coast of Skåne, Sweden. (Photo: Swedish Tourist Office)

but the 'sunshine holiday' is still an important part of the travel scene throughout Scandinavia. Once abroad, the Scandinavians put up with gregarious holiday living as a necessary part of their mystical communion with the sun. At home, during winter skiing holidays or on long summer vacations, they have different priorities. Now the keywords are privacy, solitude, peace, independence and natural living. Summer holidays are by preference and almost by definition rural; the Swedes simply take their summer holidays *på landet* (in the country) and this little expression summarizes a Scandinavian philosophy and a recreational lifestyle.

On the other hand, the areas used by most holiday-makers for their summer holidays and their weekend breaks are not at all rural in the sense that they provide a living for country people practising the ancient arts and crafts of agriculture. Very often the holiday areas are the districts which have been largely abandoned by the farming community. Some of them are remote from the main centres of population or are so lacking in primary resources or agricultural potential that they have suffered severe (and in some cases complete) depopulation in recent decades. These 'deserted' landscapes, with their strong cultural associations, are immensely appealing from a tourist point of view. They awaken a strong sense of nostalgia and they are also areas where properties such as old farmhouses, mountain *seters* in Norway and *fäbodar* in central Sweden are available on the open market, at least for the citizens of the states concerned.

Elsewhere, closer to the main towns and cities, old farming landscapes have been transformed through summer-cottage developments. Until recently these were private developments in which virtually every summer-cottage was the result of a private decision to buy land and a private decision to build. Now, however, there are more planned developments involving large-scale investments by property companies. These companies, operating for example in the 'holiday belt' around Göteborg, create not only whole 'estates' of summer cottages but are also responsible for the infrastructure of roads and services. In the Stockholm archipelago, in the environs of Oslo and in the outer suburbs of Copenhagen, to take just three examples, 'summer-cottage settlements' are now very much a part of the cultural landscape. Although these settlements are in country environments, often with each summer-house family enjoying its own coastal outlook and its own small woodland clearing, the total impact is more urban than rural in the sense that the local authority has to provide water, mains electricity and telephones, sewage and refuse disposal services, and reasonable roads. In many areas, in spite of strict planning controls, these holiday developments have turned into extensions of suburbia. In the Stockholm archipelago, for example, many summer-cottage districts are now within one hour's driving time of the city centre. During the spring, summer and autumn many families move to the archipelago for long weekends between April and October; working men and women organize their holidays so that they have to commute only in mid-week to and from town. During the summer school holiday families move to their summer-cottages, which become their seasonal places of residence. Until recently many people were finding that their summer time environments were so congenial that they were moving into holiday cottages full-time. However, this trend has now stopped as rising petrol prices have forced commuters to opt for short daily journeys rather than long ones. Nevertheless, the permanent population of many summer-cottage districts is still rising so sharply that some Danes and Swedes refer to the 1970s as the decade when the 'drift to the towns' went into reverse. Certainly the current 'drift to the land' will have great social and economic repercussions if it continues; the countryside will acquire a new

Fig. 14.2 Finlandia Hall, Helsinki, a typically impressive modern building designed by Alvar Aalto and completed in 1971. (Photo: Finnish Embassy)

rural population made up partly of people who will wish to live *and work* in their chosen environments.

The urban malaise

One of the most important reasons for the phenomena described above is increasing dissatisfaction with an urban lifestyle. As mentioned in Chapter 13, the populations of the Scandinavian states are now urbanized to a greater extent than ever before. They enjoy a high standard of living, and slum districts have become features of ancient history. City centres are clean and well planned, although the building styles employed are not to everybody's taste. In general industrial activities have been located so that most people working in an urban context are unaffected by smoke and grime. There are abundant parks and recreational possibilities within towns and cities, and in suburban residential areas there are spacious and imaginatively designed shopping precincts and cultural centres (Fig. 14.2). And yet, in spite of the superficially attractive lifestyle of the urban inhabitants of Scandinavia, they themselves are increasingly dissatisfied. Many of them consider their environments impersonal and even hostile; in the vast high-rise housing developments of the new towns on the fringes of Helsinki, Stockholm, Copenhagen and Oslo great numbers of people feel isolated and lonely. They suffer from a lack of privacy when they want it and a lack of contact when they are in need of comfort or reassurance. Psychological problems are widespread, and social services in Sweden and Denmark, for example, are now so elaborate and so all-embracing that many people believe that community involvement and individual compassion have been killed off by the state. There is an assumption that other people's problems are the state's responsibility. On the other hand, there are few people who would like to change the system; the National Health Service, for example, is so comprehensive that people have come to look on extremely high standards of medical care as part of their birthright. Among young people there is a feeling that urban life is sterile and futile, and many of their parents are vociferous in their criticism of educational systems based upon experience rather than learning and upon the principle that 'all shall be equal even if they are not'. On many large housing estates vandalism and violence are rife, and crime rates are rising sharply. In the urban areas of Stockholm and Malmö in Sweden suicides (especially among women) are about twice the national average.

Many of the above problems are, of course, not specifically Scandinavian; urban malaise is a feature of the modern world, just as 'rural malaise' is responsible in many countries for the flight from the countryside to the towns. Furthermore, urban malaise is neither equally distributed in space or time, nor equally intense, through the countries dealt with in this book. But there are a number of features which are peculiarly Scandinavian. In the first place there is a very widespread bureaucratic control of individual liberty in Scandinavia, and many commentators have remarked that the Scandinavian brand of 'enlightened social democracy' creates frustration and disenchantment among working people just as it suppresses initiative and creativity. Bureaucratic control means that there are many thousands of non-productive office jobs; often those who fill them have profound doubts about whether they are really necessary. At the same time paperwork galore is created for the average citizen, and this paperwork is itself a source of discontent. In the industrial sector more and more jobs involve repetitive mechanical manipulations or simply the monitoring of electrical or mechanical devices; these jobs are no doubt necessary, but they involve considerable boredom and not a little stress (Fig. 14.3). Not suprisingly, many firms (with the Volvo car company a well-known example) are trying to resolve these problems by replacing produc-

Fig. 14.3 This photo captures something of the concentration and stress involved in monitoring many industrial processes in Scandinavia today. The holiday 'escape' is a psychological as well as a physical necessity. (Photo: Asea)

tion lines with 'construction teams' in which team spirit can thrive and in which each individual can develop a range of skills.

A second feature which underlines the Scandinavian phenomenon of urban discontent is the great affluence of most of the population; salaries and standards of living are so high that people have become frightened of changing the status quo. And so long as people can afford villas or comfortable flats, cars, second homes, motor-boats, sailing-boats and expensive holidays abroad, there is a tendency to pretend that the discomforts and stresses of modern urban life are really not all that serious. Scandinavian society is today intensely materialistic, and it is based upon a long tradition of hard work and just reward. The decline of religious values and the widespread breakdown of family life can both be looked on as consequences of the preoccupation with work and the pursuit of wealth.

Finally, Scandinavian people do not have a long tradition of urban living and industrial work. Very many families in the Scandinavian cities are recent arrivals, and many thousands of the present-day urban work-force were brought up in the countryside. They still feel that their roots lie outside the world of high-rise blocks of flats, inner-city offices and urban freeways. Young people

Fig. 14.4 The results of a poll showing the attitudes of young people in Sweden to city life, town life and country life. Of the sample, 96 per cent of those living in rural areas and 91 per cent of those living in small towns said that they did *not* want to move to a large city. (After Carlestam and Levi 1971)

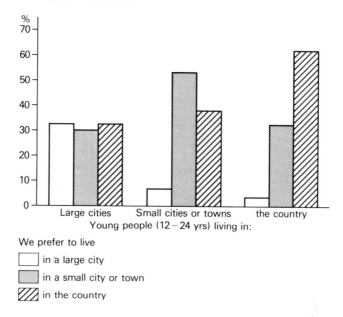

have quite a strong preference for small-town or rural life (Fig. 14.4), and urban parents feel that a temporary escape to the countryside, whenever they can manage it, is a necessary part of their lifestyle and also a spiritual necessity. In Norway in particular, the values of rural living have been transported into an urban context in a fascinating way; the people of Oslo and Bergen, for example, are far prouder of the rural past than their urban present, and features such as traditional dress, folk music and country dancing are now essential parts of the *urban* way of life. Great emphasis is also placed upon healthy outdoor pursuits; ski-trekking and mountain-hiking are activities indulged in by many thousands of urban dwellers on a regular basis (Fig. 14.5).

The impact of recreation

As mentioned above, the impact of recreation on regional land-scapes is substantial in many parts of Fennoscandia. This impact can not only be assessed in visual terms but also in terms of its economic consequences. In the Mjølfjell area of Norway, for example, an agricultural community which was declining sharply until about 1950 has been stabilized by the increasing popularity of skiing holidays. Many of the remaining farming families now obtain a good income from taking in guests particularly during the Easter skiing holiday season, and other income is derived from the letting of old farm outbuildings and *seters* as self-catering accommodation. Work is created in youth hostels and guest-houses, and incidental

Fig. 14.5 Hiking and ski-trekking are two of the most popular recreational activities in Scandinavia. The photograph shows a family ski-trekking at Riksgränsen in Swedish Lapland. (Photo: Svenska Turist-trafikförbundet)

employment is provided for carpenters, electricians and interior decorators who are involved in repair and maintenance work. During the skiing season (and also to an increasing extent during the summer) there is now a ready market for milk, dairy products and locally produced vegetables. Local roads have been improved, and electricity supplies, telephones and other services have been provided as valid components of the community's investment in tourism.

This is a pattern repeated all over Fennoscandia, and also to a lesser extent in Iceland. The latter country is not well blessed with ideal snow conditions or skiing weather, but small-scale skiing developments with ski-lifts, cafés and other facilities are now to be found near Reykjavik, in Isafjördur and at Akureyri. Developments on a much larger scale are to be found for example, at Geilo and Voss in Norway; at Sälen, Åre and Storlien in Sweden; and also at

Lahti, Jyväskylä and Kuopio in Finland. Most of these centres have modern facilities including ice-skating rinks, ski-jumps, slalom or downhill courses and many different cross-country routes. Like other large centres they have modern hotels, restaurants and also chalet developments. Chalets in these areas fetch high prices, and there is a good demand for property at or near ski resorts, particularly among families wealthy enough to own *three* houses – a town house or flat, a summer cottage and a winter chalet. In both Sweden and Norway the large skiing centres have now attracted a great deal of investment from property development companies who advertise chalets and flats for sale in the national newspapers. The impact of these developments on remote country communities is great, for in addition to the employment provided during construction projects and in the running of hotels there are opportunities for the conversion of redundant farm buildings to chalets and for taking in paying guests. Many local people are involved in the complicated web of services required by a modern holiday resort, and declining shopping centres have in some instances been given a new lease of life. Even in very remote areas there may be employment for mountain guides, coach drivers, helicopter and light aircraft operators, builders, plumbers and electrical contractors – all as a result of the tourist 'boom'. On the other hand, tourist developments create social problems which are particularly severe in the most isolated communities, where rising property values may force young people to leave even if they do not want to. Problems such as this are looked at in more detailed in Chapters 15, 16 and 17.

Countryside protection

The Scandinavian governments have, in recent years, become increasingly worried about the environmental impact of tourism. In Norway there are thirteen National Parks, but concern about tourist pressure and other developments has led to a government policy of 'keeping quiet' about their attractions. There is little publicity material for the tourist, and little encouragement for potential visitors. In addition to the National Parks many smaller areas have now been protected by law as nature reserves. In Denmark there are few 'natural' areas left, but attempts at conserving wildlife habitats and controlling tourist pressure have been made through the creation of a large number of small nature reserves. Most of these reserves have been created as a result of the Nature Conservation Act, and further protection is provided by the Environment Act and the Urban and Country Zoning Act. In Finland there is concern because the increasing scale of forestry operations has decreased the opportunities open to the public for hiking and other leisure activities in remote areas. Pressure has been building up in the nine National Parks and also in many wetland areas which are attracting ever-increasing numbers of tourists. Of the nine National Parks, the five smallest are in the centre and south of the country; none of these are more than 15 km^2. The largest are in the north – Pallas-Ounastunturi (500 km^2) and Oulanka (107 km^2). Like National Parks everywhere these are acting as tourist 'honey-pots', and there is now considerable pressure from conservationists to extend the existing Parks and to establish new ones.

The process of countryside protection is particularly far advanced in Sweden. Research into a wide range of environmental problems, and the incentives for protective legislation, came with the convening of the UN Conference on the Human Environment in Stockholm in 1972. As the host country, Sweden was determined to make the running in the field of pollution control and environmental protection, and an impressive volume of material was published by various government ministries. Some of the literature is considered in the next three Chapters, but the measures taken to reduce recreational pressure on the environment are relevant here. The critical coordinating agency in this case was the National Environment Protection Board. Maps were prepared by government departments to show areas of scientific or natural history value, areas of cultural importance and areas of national importance for open-air recreation (Fig. 14.6). The Ministry of Physical Planning and Local Government also studied the demands made by open-air recreation on land and environmental quality. The National Board of Urban Planning made a detailed survey of the Swedish coastline, showing that about half of the coastline is unsuitable for bathing and that only about 60 per cent of the remaining coast was in fact accessible for recreational use. Most of the 14,300 km of suitable and accessible coastline is found in the district between Gävle and Kalmar in the east and Svinesund and Halmstad in the west. Holiday home settlements were also studied. In 1970 there were about half a million holiday homes in Sweden, with the great majority located near the sea coast or on the shores of lakes. About 40 per cent of all holiday homes are found in an area comprising only 3 per cent of the country; the densest holiday settlements by far are in the Stockholm and Göteborg regions. It was evident from the studies that the 'wilderness' and 'cultural heritage' areas were by no means the only areas at risk from tourist pressure; in the areas of densest holiday settlement even a small increase in the building of new cottages would result in the private occupation of practically all coastal land, causing inevitable conflict with the interests of open-air recreation by the public at large. On the other hand, the Swedish tradition of *allemansrätt* is important here, allowing as it does free access to the countryside for everybody, even on privately owned property.

The Swedish studies of recreational management were concluded

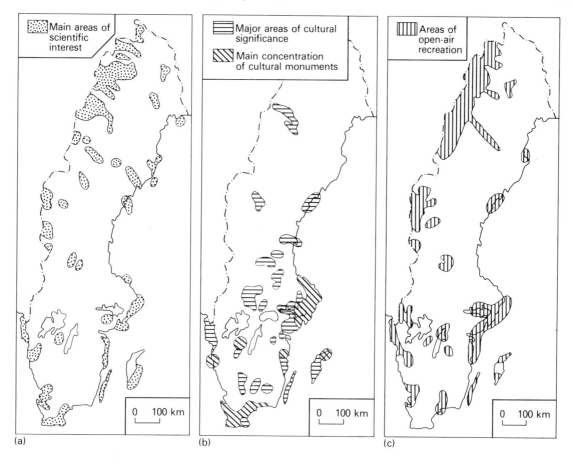

(a)   (b)   (c)

Fig. 14.6 Maps of three factors relevant for recreational planning in Sweden: (a) areas of scientific or nature conservation interest, (b) cultural heritage areas and (c) areas used for open-air recreation – in particular hiking, skiing and water sports. (After Engström 1972)

with a list of recommendations, and many of those have now been enforced by government legislation and within the context of local and regional plans. Outside the areas of holiday settlements, environmental protection is afforded by the Environment Protection Act of 1969, the Nature Conservation Act of 1964 and the Nature Conservation Ordinance of 1976. The Swedes may be guilty of 'overkill' in their attempts to save the country's beautiful areas from the attentions of tourists, and some of their measures have been widely criticized because they effectively 'shut out' certain sections of the Swedish public (for example the old and infirm) from wild places where road and chalet developments are refused. Sarek in Swedish Lapland is an example, difficult of access and yet immensely popular not only with Swedish hikers but also with foreigners. In a 1980 survey it was found that on part of the Kungsleden long-distance trail 40 per cent of all the hikers were foreigners. Is it right that this wilderness area should be open to healthy young Germans and Englishmen but effectively closed to most Swedes? The problem is unresolved.

But the Scandinavians all agree that they do not want overcrowded wildernesses, and they have not forgotten that holidays should present a range of opportunities for *re-creation*. In the last resort peace and quiet, solitude and seclusion, which are so important to the soul of Scandinavia, are worth legislating for.

Suggested reading

The geography of recreation

Ahlmann 1976; Aldskogius 1967, 1978; Barđarson 1976; Caraman 1969; Carlestam and Levi 1971; Håkansson 1980; Helle 1970; Kidson 1974; Ljungdahl 1938; Marsden 1976; Møller 1972; Moore 1980; Nelson 1973; Nicol 1975; Nyquist 1977; Ogrizek 1952; Scherman 1976; Scott 1967; Simpson 1966; Sund 1949; Turner 1976.

Part III   Regional inequalities

Chapter 15   The Scandinavian heartland today

This chapter, together with Chapters 16 and 17, constitutes a short section of the book devoted to regional inequalities in Scandinavia. As indicated in earlier chapters, these inequalities are important historically, geographically and economically. Their root causes have been intensively studied and the governments of the six countries have devoted a great deal of effort to the 'ironing out' of differences in regional incomes, industrial production, recreational use and many other factors. As in other parts of Europe, regional planning policies have been formulated in order to hold remote rural communities together and to prevent excessive out-migration to the traditional and economically strong 'core areas' which were defined in Chapter 6. It will have been apparent from Chapters 10–14 that the Scandinavian heartland attracts the great bulk of both private and public investment in the provision of power, in manufacturing and the service industries, in housing and social services, in transport and communications, and even in recreation and tourism. The heartland is the zone of 'comparative advantage' from an economic point of view (Fig. 10.2, p. 166), while the peripheral zones are clearly areas of 'comparative disadvantage'.

This is a typical statement of regional policy issued by one of the Scandinavian governments (Engström 1972):

'Regional policy must be instrumental in:-

The creation of a distribution of prosperity such that people in different parts of the country are given satisfactory economic, social and cultural conditions.

The promotion of rapid economic progress by assisting in a location of enterprises such that capital and labour resources are fully utilized.

Ensuring that structural changes take place in such a way that the security of the individual is safeguarded.

Guiding development in such courses that a better regional balance is achieved and that the rising prosperity is distributed more evenly in different parts of the country. Such a distribution is warranted also by environmental policy considerations.

It is a central task of regional policy to influence the

geographical distribution of activities and the population in such a way that the weaknesses inherent in the present urban structure are counteracted.'

There is a considerable emphasis in this statement, as always in regional planning policies, on geographical *distribution*, and it is worth looking at some of the evidence used by the Scandinavian governments in attempting to identify their regional problems.

Economic features of the heartland

Much of the discussion in the foregoing chapters of this book brings out the environmental and economic inequalities between heartland and periphery. For example, a map of the cultivated area would show that the heartland is an area of relatively intensive agricultural use, and most dairy-farming and milk-processing is concentrated in the same broad belt across Denmark, south-east Norway, southern Sweden and south-western Finland. Hydro-electricity production is, of course, widely distributed, based as it is upon the occurrences of streams with high gradient or discharge or both; but the production of power from thermal or nuclear power-stations is concentrated within the zone of densest settlement and greatest power demand (Fig. 15.1). The majority of manufacturing industries are also located within the heartland, which is the centre of demand for manufactured products of all sorts. The exceptions here are the electro-metallurgical and electro-chemical industries of Norway and the pulp, paper and related chemical industries of Sweden and Finland; the former are located in areas with large hydro-electricity surpluses, and the latter in areas favourable for the harvesting of forestry resources and the use of large volumes of industrial process water. One map which brings out the strength of the heartland particularly effectively is the map of transport engineering establishments. The activities concerned include shipbuilding, railway engineering, automobile engineering and the aerospace industry. All of these require large work-forces, considerable research and development investment, nearby markets and the application of high technology. The industries themselves are highly mechanized and capital-intensive, and in the terminology of economic geography they are 'market oriented' rather than 'resource oriented'.

From the point of view of population and settlement density the strength of the heartland is again apparent. An atlas map of main settlements brings out clearly the concentration of the urban population within the area under consideration, and it is also true that the great majority of the *rural* population lives here. Overall, the average population density of the heartland is over 20 persons per km^2; in the peripheral belts around the main cities, and even

Fig. 15.1 Nuclear power-station at Oskarshamn. (Photo: Gösta Nordin)

in some rural areas such as southern Skåne, Sjaelland and Fyn the population density is well in excess of 50 persons per km². In the three Swedish counties of Stockholm, Göteborg and Bohus and Malmöhus the average population density is 163 persons per km² with 36 per cent of the country's population living on 3 per cent of the land area.

A study of population and settlement trends is also highly instructive as a means of demonstrating the attractions of the heartland. Throughout Scandinavia the scattered population in agricultural and forestry areas has become sparser and sparser, and even small towns have stagnated in their development or begun to decrease in

241

size. In contrast, the large urban areas and their suburban peripheries have grown considerably. Examples of towns experiencing a growth rate of between 2.5 and 5 per cent per annum are Lahti and Lappeenranta in Finland, Växjö and Uppsala in Sweden, Skien and Kristiansand in Norway, and Roskilde and Herning in Denmark. Reykjavik and Torshavn, the capital cities of Iceland and the Faroes respectively, have also experienced rapid growth; Torshavn now contains over 30 per cent of the population of the Faroes, and no less than half of the Icelandic population now lives in Reykjavik. The towns with the greatest growth rates are those with populations between 30,000 and 100,000. The migration statistics show that there is not only a drift into the towns but also a drift towards the south throughout Scandinavia. For example, all of the northern counties of Finland are experiencing a population decline while metropolitan Finland is experiencing population growth. In southern Sweden more than 70 per cent of the population now lives in urban centres, and the biggest centres are attracting people from

Fig. 15.2 Net migration flows into the three metropolitan regions of Sweden in 1966. By far the greatest drift of population was into the Stockholm region, with particularly severe consequences for Norrland. (After Ödmann and Dahlberg 1970)

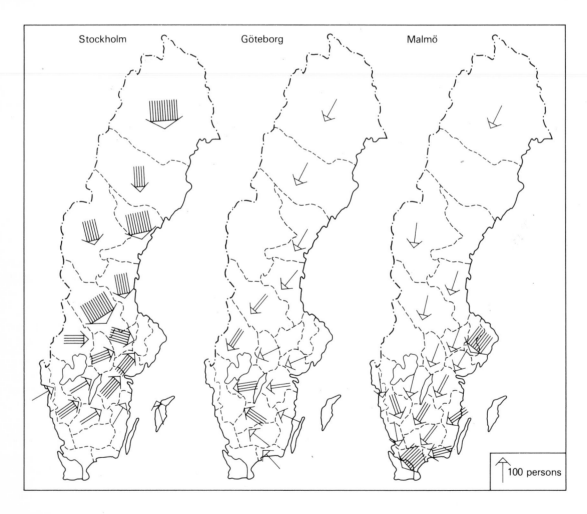

all over the country (Fig. 15.2). At present relatively few people in southern Sweden live more than 30 km from an urban centre with at least 10,000 people, and this fact is brought out very effectively in a series of studies by T. Hägerstrand. A series of his maps published in 1970 demonstrate clearly the pre-eminent place occupied by the ancient core area in the population geography of Sweden.

The statistics for immigration to the Scandinavian countries give another clear impression of the attractions of the balmy south. Most immigrants come from southern Europe, western Europe (especially West Germany and the UK) and from Asia. There are also considerable numbers of political refugees, particularly from the Soviet Baltic republics. In order of importance the greatest immigrant centres are Copenhagen, Stockholm, Göteborg and Malmö, and Oslo. However, there are detailed figures for Sweden which show that up to 3,000 immigrants per year are also attracted to the other southern counties (Fig. 15.3). They come in search of urban and industrial jobs, and many find employment in the service sector. Except for centres like Bergen, Stavanger, Kiruna and Gällivare, no more than a few hundred immigrants per year are attracted to those parts of Scandinavia which we refer to as 'peripheral' areas. The four areas which now have long-established immigrant communities are the Stockholm–Mälaren area, with a population of over 2 million; Ostergötland, with a population of about 380,000; western Skåne, with a population of 746,000; and the Göteborg area. with a population of over 900,000. In these areas over 6 per cent of the population is composed of immigrants. It is no coincidence that they are also the areas of highest per capita incomes in Sweden, over 5 per cent above the national average.

Social indices

There are many factors which can be classified as having 'social relevance' for a study of regional inequality. The occurrence of holiday homes has already been considered as an indicator of affluence or social status, and distribution maps of holiday-home settlements show that the densest concentrations are near the main cities and also within the areas of highest incomes. It goes without saying that they are also within the heartland. The map of cultural monuments (Fig. 14.6, p 235) shows that the southern part of Sweden is not only relatively wealthy but also well endowed with cultural riches such as fine buildings, parks, museums and archaeological sites. The Danish part of the heartland is similarly well endowed (Fig. 15.4).

Maps for the distribution of higher education centres and hospitals emphasise the distribution of settlement in Scandinavia and also

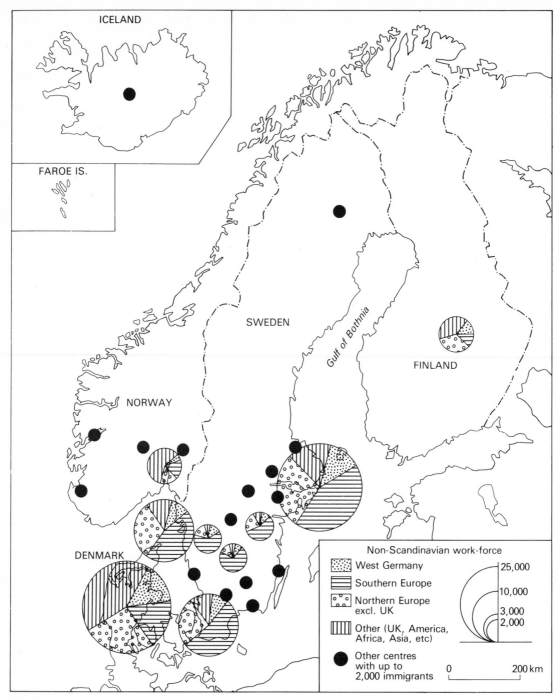

Fig. 15.3 The immigrant work-force (excluding Scandinavian people working in countries other than their homeland) in 1973–4. Note the very strong attraction of the heartland as a labour market. (After Ahlmann 1976)

Fig. 15.4 Aerial photo of the Frederiksborg Castle in northern Sjaelland – one of the greatest Renaissance castles in northern Europe. As a famous cultural monument it is now a museum of natural history. (Photo: Pressehuset)

some of the advantages of living in the heartland. In southern Finland, southern Sweden, south-east Norway and Denmark there are few rural or urban areas which are more than 50 km from the nearest hospital. The accessibility of other services has been analysed by Swedish geographers; in domestic matters such as trips to the dentist, trips to the nearest chemist and trips to the nearest library the inhabitant of southern Sweden is clearly in a position of comparative advantage over his provincial neighbours. The concentration of persons employed in the 'quaternary sector' (i.e. in the production of ideas rather than goods or services) shows the same bias; artists, writers, public administrators, and scientists and technologists employed in research are much more common in the main urban areas of Scandinavia than they are elsewhere. In Sweden about 52 per cent of politicans and civil servants are found in the Stockholm region, and approximately half of the country's writers, actors and artists live and work in the city.

The list of mapped evidence for Scandinavian regional imbalance could be continued *ad infinitum*, and the specialist literature is full of maps of traffic flows, private housing expenditure, municipal investments in schools and hospitals, new shopping centres and recreational developments which show broadly similar distribution patterns. The message comes through time and time again – the regional imbalance between the heartland and the rest of Scandinavia is becoming more severe with every year that passes. The heartland is the zone of increasing wealth, increasing concentration, increasing centralization. It is also being realized – none too soon – that it is the zone of increasing problems.

Regional policies for the heartland

The tendency for institutions, manufacturing concerns and offices to cluster together in the economic 'core' areas has been a cause of concern to the Scandinavian governments for several decades. T. Hägerstrand wrote in 1967 of the changing nature of dependence 'from contact with the soil to human interaction', decribing the technical, industrial and social reasons for recent urbanization. This is his analysis of the changes which have taken place:

'Bit by bit, and at an accelerated pace since World War II, society has managed to cut loose from many of the binding ties which once made the siting of work-places and homes something regulated by natural circumstances. Because of its limited manpower requirements, agriculture has become less and less of a leading sector where distribution of settlement and population is concerned. Energy can be transported over long distances and indefinitely divided up into small portions. Apart from some exceptions, manufacturing industry has

become less and less dependent on proximity to sources of energy and raw materials. In employment terms the service sector has become the dominant one. Service industries are predominantly people-orientated. At the same time the advent of motorization has liberated large groups of people from the earlier compulsion to live very close to the work-place. . . . Telecommunications have rendered the movement of messages almost wholly independent of distance and time.'
(*The National Settlement Pattern as a Political Problem, Plan Habitat 1976*)

He also referred to the reasons for the reinforcement of the urban lifestyle once established, including the ease of contact between bureaucrats, industrialists and technologists; the economics of scale; the more and more richly differentiated supply of goods and services available to urban dwellers; and 'the profuse and variegated supply of workplaces for gainful employment'.

On the other hand, a highly concentrated and urbanized society is not necessarily a contented society. Many people have written of the problems which arise as a result of regional inequalities in opportunities and incomes, and at a deeper level there is concern that the cooperation and compassion of rural societies tend to be replaced by the competition and self-interest of urban societies. As noted in Chapter 14, urban societies have their own special sources of stress, in spite of their wealth as measured in terms of material possessions and opportunities for education, entertainment and self-fulfilment. In Sweden there has been a great deal of research into the effects of urbanization both from an economic and a social point of view, and the disadvantages of the present regional imbalance in the country have had a good airing. During the last two decades successive governments have, in theory, been committed to decentralization policies, and a number of measures have been brought in to relocate government agencies in remote areas, to encourage firms to follow suit and to discourage any further movement of either companies or private individuals from the country districts to the main urban areas. But real decentralization is easier talked about than achieved, and in spite of a few determined efforts to decentralize Civil Service establishments and higher education centres the government has found that, by and large, staff who are used to the Stockholm lifestyle do not take kindly to a move into the country. For example, when the National Road Administration was moved to Borlänge in 1980 about 700 staff were required to move with it. Only 30 per cent agreed to this, and the remaining 70 per cent left their jobs and found other employment. In Norway, too, there is a regional policy which involves the greatest possible distribution of development throughout the country. This policy has not been a marked success, and Oslo continues to attract both people and investment; but the strong regional loyalties of Bergen,

Trondheim and Tromsø have ensured that local developments are often fought for and obtained. In Finland, Denmark, Iceland and the Faroes regional policies are not so hotly debated as in Norway and Sweden, even though their problems are similar.

A final matter which is closely related to the overdevelopment of the heartland of Scandinavia is the problem of environmental pollution. As mentioned in the last chapter, concern about the environment reached its peak around 1972 with the holding of the UN Conference on the Human Environment in Stockholm, and although 'the energy crisis' has now replaced 'pollution and conservation' as the great issue of the day, all of the Scandinavian states have enacted environment legislation designed to minimize the undesirable side-effects of urbanization and industrialization. For example, the Danish Ministry of the Environment (created in 1971) enforces the Conservation Act as well as a broad range of legislation aimed at combating every form of pollution. Similar legislation is in force in Norway and Finland. In Sweden the word *miljö* (environment) is frequently used in everyday conversation, and government and voluntary organizations are active in their pursuit of effective conservation and anti-pollution measures. There is a constant monitoring of air, water and land pollution, and in Sweden direct action is taken against pollution in the following fields:

1. Physical planning at national, regional and local scales.
2. Direction of industries which have 'special' requirements to favourable locations.
3. Preservation of landscape resources through the regulation of 'sparse building development,' i.e. in areas classified as *glesbygd*.
4. Regulation of sewage discharge and also of effluents by industry.
5. Prohibition of dangerous industrial goods, chemicals and food products.
6. Encouragement of effective cleansing and refuse collection services.

To a large extent legislation under these headings is of course designed to ameliorate the worst effects of the overconcentration of both people and industry. It would be pleasant to believe that the now considerable range of laws and regulations available for pollution control in Sweden will be used to encourage the decentralization of industry and the development of previously neglected areas beyond the boundary of the 'economic core' of the country. This is, however, by no means assured; it is more likely that the anti-pollution measures will be used probably with the backing of local residents, to *restrict* developments in remote communities in the interests of environmental conservation. As a result most large developments, in all likelihood, will be concentrated instead in areas of existing dense settlement and existing industry. It is interesting to reflect that the overconcentration of toxic materials in air or water is thought of as pollution, whereas the overconcentration of people is still quite acceptable. To echo the words of

T. Hägerstrand: 'Concentration is a self-propelling process; dispersal on a national scale is not.'

Suggested reading

Regional policies

Aintila 1972; Berg 1971; Coates *et al.* 1977; Brofoss 1968; Ekeland 1975; Elbo 1975; ERU 1974; Godlund *et al.* 1978; Hägerstrand 1970; Hansen 1981; Levi and Andersson 1976; Lorendahl 1969, 1974; Näslund and Persson 1972; Nilsson 1980; Stenstadvold 1975; Strömdahl 1979; William-Olsson 1960.

The heartland

Åström 1967; Carlestam and Levi 1971; Church *et al.* 1973; Hägerstrand 1976 and 1977; Hall 1957; Linzie and Ericsson 1980; Matthiessen 1980; Roberts 1979; Thunberg *et al.* 1979.

Chapter 16   Towards the fringe

The 'peripheral zone' of Fennoscandia, shown in Fig. 10.2 (p. 166), is an area beset by its own peculiar problems. In general these problems are more severe than those of the heartland and less severe than those of the economically marginal zone of the uplands and Lapland. For the most part the populations of the intermediate areas shown on the map are not separated by large distances from the heartland. Only the Narvik–Tromsø area in north Norway is more than 600 km from the 'core area' of its own country, and much of the area dealt with in this chapter is quite accessible from the heartland in terms of both distance and travelling time. Except perhaps in western and north-western Norway and around the head of the Gulf of Bothnia *remoteness* (measured in terms of distance from the nearest metropolitan region) is not one of the great problems of the peripheral zone; it would be truer to say that *isolation*, *neglect* and *political insensitivity* are causes for much greater concern.

Environmental costs

It is worth looking at some of the most important environmental characteristics of the peripheral zone. For the most part this is the zone in which environmental difficulties combine with the problem of isolation to create a situation of 'relative disadvantage'. As will be appreciated from Fig. 10.2, this zone experience a very wide range of environments. The southern tip of Norway is quite different climatically from the south-eastern corner of Finland which lies more than 1,200 km towards the north-east. Other extremes of climate are experienced on the Norwegian west coast between the oceanic and relatively warm coasts around Stavanger and the harsh Arctic waters of Tromsø. Perhaps the greatest feeling of isolation is induced by the winter freeze, which exerts a particularly pervasive influence in the coastal lands around the Gulf of Bothnia and in central Finland. In their book *Winter in Finland* W. R. Mead and H. Smeds look at the impact of winter in a variety of different ways, and three of their maps are shown in Fig. 16.1. In

Fig. 16.1 Three maps which demonstrate the impact of winter in Finland. (a) Means of absolute minimum temperatures for January; (b) the retreat of the snow cover. Inside the Arctic Circle the snow lies for more than a month longer than in the south-west; (c) the average date of lake-ice disappearance for the period 1892–1941. (After Mead and Smeds 1967)

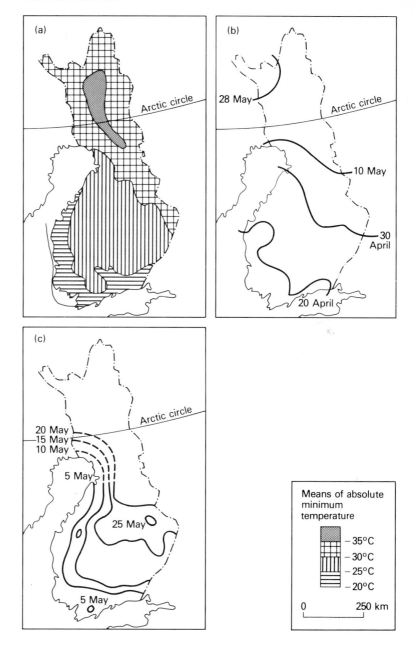

the north of the Gulf of Bothnia winter begins around 10–20 November each year with the first snowfalls which remain on the ground, and after 20 November most days have a daily mean temperature of 0 °C or less. The number of days with sub-zero mean temperatures may be as high as 180, and there may be 40 days with means of –10°C or less. Absolute minimum temperatures fall below –30°C, and the mean temperature for February (the coldest month) is about –16°C immediately inland of Tornio and

Kemi. In this area winter snows are on average 70 cm deep, and the period of lasting snow does not end until mid-May. Summer (defined as the time when daily mean temperatures are 10°C or more) does not begin until early June, and it lasts for only three months. The length of the growing season is only about 140 days, compared with 160 days in the Central Lake District, and 180 days in the extreme south-west.

Winter conditions at sea, in the Gulf of Bothnia, are responsible to a large degree for the feeling of isolation experienced by the coastal communities of the inner Gulf. Sea ice starts to form at the beginning of November in the northernmost harbours, and ports such as Luleå, Kalix, Kemi and Oulu may be closed by thick ice by the middle of December. Usually they remain closed until late May, and during the five to six month period of port closure pack ice which may be more than 1 m thick makes access impossible for all except the strongest ice-breaking vessels. During mild winters the ice-covered area of the Baltic can be as little as 60,000 km², but the total may rise to 400,000 km². Well offshore, in the widest section of the Gulf between the Åland archipelago and Kvarken, open pack ice composed mostly of floes permits shipping operations to continue during averages ice years, but close to the shore land-fast ice may be very difficult to penetrate. During severe years thick, fast ice may cover the whole surface of the Gulf of Bothnia and the

Fig. 16.2 The Finnish ice-breaker *Urho* on station in a field of broken pack ice in the Baltic. This vessel, completed in 1975, was at that time the largest of the many ice-breakers made by the Finnish company Wärtsilä. (Photo: Wärtsilä)

Gulf of Finland, also encompassing Stockholm and the islands of the Stockholm archipelago. Ice-breaking vessels remain in constant use through the sea-ice period, keeping open the shipping lanes close to the coast of south-west Finland and also to the ports of the inner Gulf if sea-ice conditions permit (Fig. 16.2). When conditions are too severe to justify ice-breaking efforts on behalf of the most northerly ports, the ice-breaking vessels move south in order to keep the southern sea-ways open. Those ports which are abandoned to the tender mercies of the winter freeze quickly become overloaded with export goods and also with timber and other products normally transported by sea to the ports of metropolitan Finland. This problem is, however, lessened to some extent by the payment of subsidies for the transport of goods by road or rail to the nearest open port. Large quantities of goods are transferred to the railway, and the volume of rail traffic swells to about four times that of the summer. Stockpiling costs money, and so do rail–ship transfers; and delays in exporting in the competitive modern world can mean the difference between customer satisfaction and customer frustration. The cost of winter, as far as the commerical and industrial managers of Finland's peripheral zone are concerned, can be measured in time and effort as well as in cash terms.

Geographical features

Some of the geographical characteristics of the peripheral zone have already been described in Chapter 15. The population density of the zone is between 10 and 20 persons per km², although in smaller pockets in the more fertile river valleys (for example, around Härnösand and Umeå in Sweden and around Lillehammer in Norway) the density rises to over 40 persons per km². The great majority of towns in the peripheral zone have populations of less than 10,000. Most of the larger towns have coastal locations; these are Trondheim (population 135,000), Bergen (211,900) and Stavanger (88,000) in Norway; Sundsvall (94,400), Umeå (75,000) and Luleå (59,000) in Sweden; and Oulu (93.400) and Vaasa (53,800) in Finland. Other large towns include Kajaani, Kuopio, Joensuu, Jyväskylä, Imatra and Lappeenranta. In the Finnish Lake District there is a more even spread of population than in the Swedish and Norwegian sections of this economic belt.

The economic characteristics of the peripheral zone are quite varied from place to place. As we can see from the map of the Swedish coasts of the Gulf of Bothnia (Fig. 16.3), this area is classified as 'intermediate' from the point of view of its primary economic activities; agriculture predominates but forestry is also important, and Swedish planners recognize that 'there are prospects of developing agricultural units and combined agricultural and

Fig. 16.3 Agriculture and forestry areas in northern Sweden.(After Engström 1972)

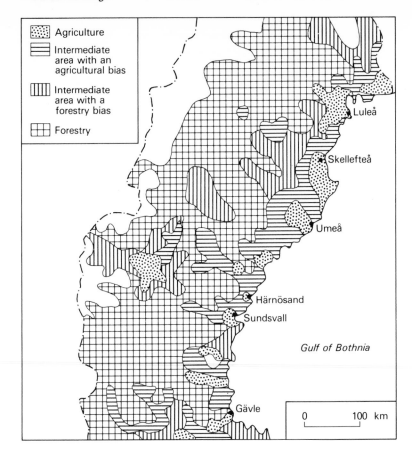

forestry units'. Most of the urban centres along this coast depend upon the processing of forestry products; there are now thirty pulp mills and fourteen paper mills between Gävle and Luleå. Centres like Sundsvall and Luleå have developed a wide range of manufacturing and service activities; and Härnösand, Umeå, Piteå and Boden are classified as service centres. Skellefteå, Luleå and Raahe are among the few towns which have draw wealth from metalworking industries. Most of the towns along the western shore of the Gulf of Bothnia were founded after 1900, and this means that there is no deep-rooted cultural loyalty among urban dwellers to their place of residence. This is one of the problems faced by most urban centres outside the cultural core areas considered in the last chapter. Average incomes are modest in Swedish terms, and in most parts of this region there is a shortage of employment opportunities. Transport opportunities are good, with the main E4 road following the coastine for most of the distance between Gävle and Luleå; but this road is a mixed blessing in that it not only permits easy contact with the heartland but also acts as an encouragement to migration. Air links with Stockholm are also good. Out-migration rates are still a source of concern (Fig. 15.2, p. 242), even though the rates of loss have slowed down during the last decade. Social services are by no means as well developed as in the heartland, nor so accessible to those who live outside the main towns.

Difficulties and solutions

T. Hägerstrand has identified a number of reasons for the 'relative disadvantage' of the areas which are classified as falling within Fennoscandia's peripheral economic zone. In general, access to large, well-equipped service centres is difficult, and the range of employment opportunities available to householders (men and women) is restricted. Should existing jobs disappear it is often extremely difficult to find new ones without migrating. The use of facilities such as libraries, cinemas, sports centres, medical centres and indoor shopping areas often requires the expenditure of much time and money in travelling. Those who work in the towns and live in the country often have to face round trips of 60–80 km per day; and those forestry workers who are not ensconced in caravan camps have to commute even greater distances between their homes, works depots and actual places of work in the forest. As far as firms are concerned, they hesitate to set up new plants or offices in areas which have neither a pool of varied occupational skills nor an abundant supply of the specialist services which they need. Small traffic volumes cut down competition between transport operators, and so firms have little flexibility in the movement of raw materials or finished products. Executive employees have to incur big sacrifices of travelling time if their place of work does not lie close to an airport. Many of the companies which have established works in the 'provinces' insist on keeping their head offices in Oslo, Stockholm or Helsinki, so that provincial executives spend much time away from home when they have to attend top-level meetings. Promotions often involve movement from one plant to another or from a regional centre of operations to the company headquarters in the capital; the prospects and the facts of promotion often lead to family stresses and divided loyalties.

It is something of a myth that in all three of the countries discussed in this chapter large sections of industry have been decentralized by moves away from the main population centres. Four examples of major provincial investments are often quoted in discussions of regional policy. These are the steel-making plants established with government aid at Mo i Rana in Nordland (established in 1946), at Luleå in Norrbotten (established in 1940 and recently greatly expended) and at Tornio in Lappi (established in 1900) and Rautarukki in Pohjanmaa (established in 1967). All four were planned attempts to create growth centres and to provide a greater range of job opportunities for local people. Other industrial enterprises sponsored by government agencies are the softwood-processing plants at Kalix and Piteå in Sweden and at Kemi and Kemijärvi in Finland. All of these industrial concerns have been beneficial from a social and an economic point of view, but we should remember that they were motivated above all else by *political* considerations. During the troubled decade of the 1940s in particular, the need for 'effective occupation' of national territory was vital if the expansionist policies of Germany and the USSR were to be resisted. As far as private industry is concerned, only the most straightforward manufacturing functions have been decentralized (sometimes, but only rarely, into the 'provinces'). Examples are the establishment of component plants by firms such as Scania-Vabis, L. M. Eriksson and Atlas-Copco in the Luleå – Piteå area, and the building of an aluminium smelter and a nylon fabric factory at Mosjøen to the south of Mo i Rana. On the other hand the managerial, marketing, planning, research and product development sections of industry have more and more come to be merged into a few centres and into the capital cities in particular. In all of the countries of Scandinavia the decision-making and information-handling élites are now largely concentrated in the capital cities; only a few large firms stand against this trend. Manufacturing establishments in the outlying centres, and particularly those which lie a long way from the heartland, suffer increasing frustration because they are in control of their own destinies only to a limited extent and because they depend upon support of one sort or another in order to provide employment and generate local wealth. Managers and production staff feel that they are net exporters of wealth (in the form of forestry products and hydro-electricity in particular) and that they do not get the returns they are entitled to expect in the way of social facilities and state investment in education and employment.

Regional aid programmes and regional plans are designed to correct some of the economic and social imbalances between heartland and periphery. In Finland the country has been divided up into twenty regional planning districts, and 'general plans' are also in force for most of the urban areas and for some rural communes also. In Norway the greater part of the country is covered by plans of one sort of another, and in the north these have taken over where the major development plan for Arctic Norway left off in 1961. In Sweden most of the detailed planning so far has been in the south of the country. There is no national plan, and most regional plans have been concerned with urban areas or with urban hinterlands. There have been very few exercises anywhere in Scandinavia in the matter of *rural planning*; as in other parts of north-western Europe, many of the rural inhabitants of the peripheral zone feel that the planners have no sympathy for the rural lifestyle and for rural values. The help which has been given to them so far is mainly in the form of grants and subsidies within the Swedish 'development

Fig. 16.4 Transport subsidy zones in Sweden, designed to assist industries which are remote from the 'core areas' of the country. (Source: Percivall, 1979)

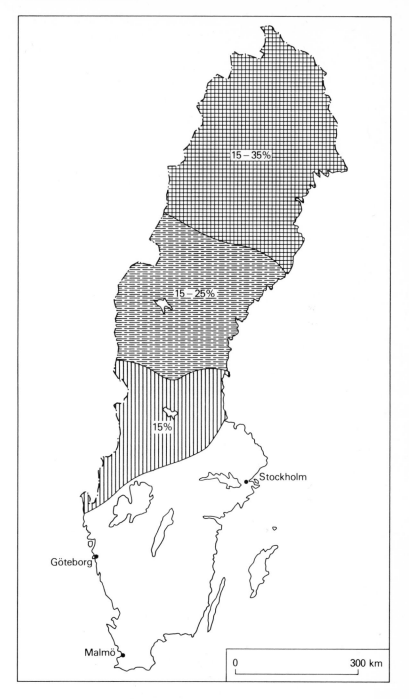

area' and in the form of transport subsidies which vary according to distance from the heartland (Fig. 16.4). In addition, as described in the last chapter, a number of government agencies have been relocated in the provinces, drawing about 11,000 workers and their families out from Stockholm in the process and leaving many more behind. Examples are the establishment of a new forestry institute in Umeå and the siting of the Geological Survey HQ in Luleå. But most of the relocation has been in the heartland, in centres such as Linköping and other towns with populations over 50,000. Only a small number of firms have either built new plants or invested in expansion programmes in the long coastal belt north of Gävle.

Large-scale industrialization is not in any case appropriate, for it would be out of keeping with the basically rural lifestyle of the area and the small size of most urban centres. By and large, industrialists have no great desire to locate here, and from a planning point of view there is already great concern about the scale of coastal pollution associated with the discharge of oxidizable organic substances and total phosphorus from pulp and paper mills directly into the sea. Long stretches of the coast have only limited water exchange, and during the summer months the total phosphorus content of sea water is too high for the comfort of either marine biologists or fish. Further industrialization (unless based upon small 'workshop' developments) would be both unpopular and ecologically unsound.

At present the trend in regional planning policy in all three countries is away from direct government involvement in major developments and towards a form of local planning with financial assistance from the state. This is partly in response to the never-ending demands in the northern areas in particular for greater local autonomy. Recent research has dampened some of the former enthusiasm for the relocation of government agencies in 'needy' areas, and the emphasis is now on the creation of a balanced hierarchy of settlements with an adequate range of services and employment opportunities. The 'patchwork' solution which was based on the planting of large industrial enterprises or bureaucratic institutions in selected locations has now been modified, and the world recession of the early 1980s is causing new developments in the peripheral zone to be few and far between.

Suggested reading

The problems of the fringe

Aldskogius 1960; Brofoss 1968; Enequist 1959; Fullerton and Williams 1972; Hansen 1972; Hellmann *et al.* 1977; Knox 1973; Lorendahl 1969; McCririck 1976; Mead 1959; Öström 1980; Paget 1960; Stone 1962, 1965.

Chapter 17 The Northern Problem

The problems of overdevelopment and underdevelopment which have been looked at in the last two chapters have been sources of great concern to the Scandinavian governments, but it is probably true to say that the area which has exercised the greatest fascination from a 'regional development' point of view is Nordkalotten – the extreme north of the Fennoscandian peninsula. In the words of W. R. Mead, 'Nordkalotten bristles with problems'; these problems are environmental, political, demographic, adminstrative and technological. Some of them are mirrored in parts of Iceland and, on a very small scale, in the Faroes. In this chapter we look at the nature of 'the northern problem' and discuss some of the solutions tried out in isolation and in cooperation by the governments of Norway, Sweden and Finland.

Nordkalotten

Nordkalotten (which means, strictly, 'the Northern Cap') comprises those parts of Norway, Sweden and Finland which fall within the Arctic Circle. The administrative areas concerned include some areas to the south of this mythical line: Nordland, Troms and Finnmark in Norway, Norrbotten in Sweden, and Lappi in Finland (Fig. 17.1). Parts of Västerbotten in Sweden and Oulu province in Finland are also included in Nordkalotten by some authors, but in this book some settlements around the head of the Gulf of Bothnia have already been dealt with in the previous chapter as a part of Fennoscandia's peripheral zone. Certainly there is little uniformity in Nordkalotten, either from a physical or an economic point of view. The area is vast. The counties of Nordland, Troms and Finnmark (about 112,000 km²) are as large as Wales and Ireland put together; Norrbotten (99,000 km²) is larger than Scotland, and so is Lappi (94,000 km²).

The landscape is for the most part bleak and inhospitable, varying from the broad high *vidder* (barren plateau) of the Norwegian–Swedish border to the glaciated alpine terrain of Sarek

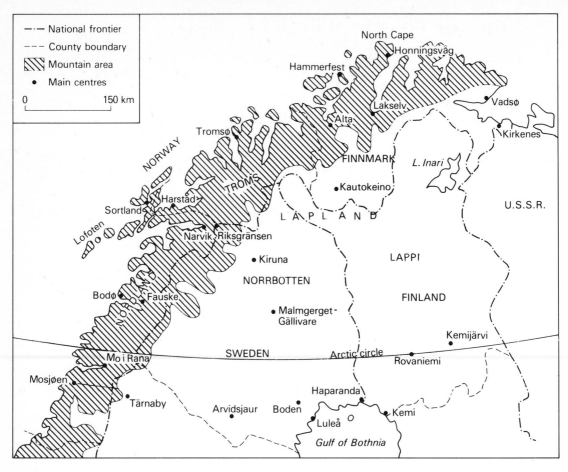

Fig. 17.1 Map of Nordkalotten, showing the main administrative districts, towns and natural resources.

and the wide gently undulating lowlands of Lappi. Much of the region is covered with boreal forest, but on the flanks of the uplands and also in the extreme north in the county of Finnmark the coniferous trees give way to an irregular patchwork forest of gnarled and tangled birch. Around the north coast and in the uplands above an altitude of 500 m there is a largely treeless subarctic terrain; on the plateaux tundra vegetation predominates, while steeper slopes and peaks are barren rocky areas where snowfields, glaciers and frost-shattered rock keep the land in the constant thrall of winter. The main rivers which drain the land surface of Nordkalotten are the two Lule rivers, the Muonio, Torne, Ounas and Kemi; they all converge upon the head of the Gulf of Bothnia, adding large volumes of fresh water to this already brackish branch of the Baltic Sea. The largest rivers which drain northwards to the Arctic coasts of Nordkalotten are the Tana and Alta rivers, both of which reach the sea amid the fjords and peninsulas of Finnmark.

Lapland and the Lapps

The area referred to by politicians and academics as Nordkalotten is known – much more widely – as Lapland. The Lapps or *Sami*, as they call themselves, have been settled in this area since the pre-Christian era, and among early travellers a considerable mythology grew up about them and the country they inhabited. They never organized themselves to a condition in which they could claim nationhood, and their territory was eventually occupied and incorporated into the states of Norway, Sweden, Finland and Russia. At present there are between 40,000 and 50,000 Lapps, distributed roughly as follows:

Norway: 25,000
Sweden: 15,000
Finland: 4,000
USSR: 2,000

The traditional Lapp economy was based on reindeer-herding, with hunting and fishing as subsidiary activities. For the most part Lapp family groups lived a nomadic lifestyle, following the reindeer herds between their upland and lowland grazing areas. This style of life was particularly prevalent in the mountains; in the forested lowland areas the reindeer did not migrate over great distances, and so a more sedentary type of reindeer husbandry grew up. Both of these lifestyles persist, but nowadays only a small proportion of Lapp people can still be thought of as nomads and reindeer herders (Fig. 17.2). In Norrbotten, for example, only about 2,500 Lapps (about 600–700 households) are currently involved in reindeer-herding; this is only about one-sixth of the Lapp population of the region. Other Lapps are now strictly sedentary in their habits, finding employment as farmers, fishermen, electricity linesmen, forestry workers, miners and even office workers. Most of them are urban dwellers, but even those who live in the small towns of Lapland feel that their personal territory extends over the horizon. Traditionally they have little respect for national frontiers; movement between the different parts of Nordkalotten was of course a natural part of the way of life when there were reindeer herds to be followed, and nowadays seasonal movements across frontiers in search of employment are also looked upon as perfectly natural.

For those who are involved in reindeer-herding there is a good living to be made. There are at least 600,000 semi-domesticated reindeer, and with the rise in the popularity of reindeer meat the cash incomes of breeders and herders have never been higher. Those family groups who have the largest herds are nowadays very wealthy people; they employ light aircraft, helicopters and snow-mobiles in locating and driving their herds, much to the delight of the cartoonist (Fig. 17.3) and the disappointment of the tourist in search of a primitive Lapp lifestyle.

Fig. 17.2 Lapp reindeer-herding activities in northern Finland. (Photo: Finish Embassy)

Fig. 17.3 A comment on the affluence of the modern Lapp reindeer herder. (Artist: Olavi Hurmerinta)

Population and resources

The Lapps now account for less than 5 per cent of the population of Nordkalotten. At the moment some 928,000 people live in the region; of these about 467,000 live in the three northern counties of Norway, 266,000 in Norrbotten and 195,000 in Lappi. Approximately two-thirds of the population can now be classed as urban, and the rural population is declining all the time. Urbanization and centralization are facts of life here in the remote Arctic wastes just as they are amid the fertile lands of Denmark and southern Sweden. The rate of natural population increase has been slowing down for several decades now, and the excess of emigration over immigration between 1951 and 1977 was 141,000; overall the population is now approximately in a state of balance. Of the total work-force only about 20 per cent are now engaged in agriculture, forestry and fishing, as against 28 per cent in services and 20 per cent in mining, manufacturing and electricity production.

The natural resources of Nordkalotten are considerable, especially with respect to minerals, timber, fish and water power. The mineral wealth of the region has been recognized since about 1700, and among the early exploitation efforts were iron-ore mining at Malmberget in Sweden and at Dunderland in Nordland, and copper-mining at Kåfjord in Alta and at Gravberget in Norrbotten. The 'iron-ore mountain' at Kiruna has been worked since 1900, although commercial large-scale mining of iron-ore began ten years earlier at nearby Gällivare – Malmberget. The crucial boost to the mining enterprise was the completion of the railway line from Luleå to Kiruna in about 1900 and the extension to Narvik in 1903. This outlet to the Atlantic was of great importance, for as indicated in Chapter 2 shipping operations at Luleå have to be of a distinctly seasonal nature because of the severe winter freeze-up of the inner parts of the Gulf of Bothnia. Since 1960 a new open-pit mining operation has been operating at Svappavaara, some 40 km south-east of Kiruna, and there is another small mine at Tuolluvaara. Current production of iron-ore is about 22 million tonnes in the Kiruna area, about 5 million tonnes at Gällivare – Malmberget, and about 4 million tonnes at Svappavaara. More than 95 per cent of Swedish iron-ore exports comes from these mines, and reserves are vast – 3,000 million tonnes of high-grade ore according to recent estimates. Exports of ore from Narvik mostly come from the Kiruna mines, carried by up to twenty-eight ore trains per day; annual exports are sometimes over 20 million tonnes per year, and in 1975 Narvik shipped out its 500 millionth tonne of ore. Most of the ore from the Malmberget – Gällivare area goes to Luleå; a variable proportion is used in the NJA steelworks and the rest is exported.

Other mining localities in Nordkalotten include the copper mine at Aitik (south-east of Malmberget); the valuable iron-ore workings at Sør Varanger in the far north of Norway; the Finnish iron-ore fields at Raajärvi and Kolari; the copper mines at Sulitjelma and Repparfjord in north Norway; and the lead and zinc workings at Bleikvassli in Nordland. The most important of the mining districts in northern Västerbotten (strictly outside Nordkalotten) is the Boliden – Laisvall district, in which sulphide-ore deposits are mined at a number of different sites. The earliest and most important workings were at Boliden (1826–1967), but now the largest mine is at Laisvall, the biggest single source of lead ore in Europe. Copper, silver, gold and nickel also come from this ore field, and most of the smelting is done at Rönnskär on the coast near Skellefteå.

Hydro-electric power is a great resource in Nordkalotten (Fig. 17.4), and there are still considerable untapped reserves. Lappi is Finland's most important district for hydro-electric power generation, with the Kemi river predominant. There are now five large generating stations along the river, and discharge is controlled increasingly through the regulation of the large lakes in the upper reaches of the river. In Norrbotten the Lule river is by far the most important for power production, with no less than eleven generating stations strung out between its headwaters and the town of Luleå. The installations at Porjus, Harsprånget and Ligga involved huge civil engineering works in very difficult terrain, and indeed most of the developments on the Lule river have been inside the Arctic Circle.

Among the other economic resources of Nordkalotten, farming is of local rather than national importance, although efforts are being made through the introduction of new seed strains and new farming methods to reduce the region's dependence on imported foodstuffs. In addition, part-time farming makes a great contribution to the local economy. Fisheries are much more important, especially to the small coastal communities of north Norway. Approximately 10,000 people are still employed in the fishing industry, and many more depend upon it indirectly through their work in fish-processing plants, ship-repair facilities and so on. Traditionally, the cod fishery has been the most important along the Troms and Finnmark coast, with herring-fishing further south. However, part-time seasonal occupation in fishing has always characterized the way of life here, with herring fishing in the fjords during the summer, inshore fishing for saithe, offshore fishing during the winter and spring for cod, and fishing on the Norwegian Sea banks for fish such as cod, haddock, and halibut. As in Iceland, small communities have been hit drastically in recent years by overfishing (by Norwegian as well as foreign boats using new techniques), and by the still unpredictable migrations of fish which have now left some fjords almost devoid of herring. Forestry is a very valuable industry as far as Nordkalotten is concerned, and both in Finland and Sweden the forests above the Arctic Circle are largely

Fig. 17.4 The main power resources of Sweden. Note that the great majority of hydro-electric plants are in Nordkalotten. The most important rivers are the Lule river in Sweden and the Kemi river in Finland.
(After Nordic Statistical Secretariat, 1978)

The figures after the names state the electric capacity in MW

The figures in brackets state the electric capacity after extension

The names underlined refer to stations owned through subsidiaries

state owned. There has been a great deal of investment in forestry operations in this region, since both governments see the harvesting of slow-growing coniferous trees (and, to a lesser extent, birch trees) as holding the key to the viability of remote rural communities. On the other hand, there will never be a great growth of the pulp and paper industry in Nordkalotten since more suitable timber resources are abundant further south.

The nature of the problem

Nordkalotten's 'problem' is many-sided. It is underlain by the unremittingly harsh nature of the environment. The rhythm of day and night, summer and winter imposes stress even on those who have been born into this world of darkness and twilight, snow and ice; and those who come to the area from the south often experience great difficulty in adjusting. When winter lasts for nine months of the year all sorts of economic activities are handicapped, and in calculating the viability of enterprises ranging from farming and forestry to mining and manufacturing the 'cost of winter' has to be added to the cost of isolation. Transport costs are high, building costs are high, heating costs are high, and salaries have to be high if qualified technicians and other skilled workers are to be encouraged to stay. There is still a feeling of the pioneer fringe about much of Nordkalotten, even if pioneering has now come to a halt except in Finland. Towns such as Gällivare and Malmberget, with their wide dusty streets, stunted trees and unfinished buildings, look slightly uncomfortable when seen in bright summer sunshine, as if they are waiting for the first winter snows to bring a return to normality.

Agriculture is exceedingly difficult, and things have not changed much since these words were written by the religious revivalist Petrus Laestadius around 1830.

'This is a grim place, lying behind a sky-high snow-mountain.
... The land consists mainly of stone slabs with hardly any soil
at all. Around us are cold marshes. This seems to be the
mosquito capital and their proper home. Innumerable billions
of gnats dance in the air, forming a continuous haze through
the short summer. On the first autumn night a cold fog rises,
enveloping the vegetation in a white sheet of hoar-frost, There
are forty frightful miles to the church, all through entirely
uninhabited country. In summer it is often difficult to travel
because of storms; in winter it is practically impossible to drive
a horse because of the deep snow or the water on the lake ice.
In this Hell my parents settled, but they soon found that no-
one could live there....'

If Nordkalotten is lacking in uniformity it is also lacking in unity. The Lapps never attained nationhood, and the mixed population of today includes Finns, Swedes, Norwegians and the descendants of Muscovites who used to move freely between Russia and Finland before the present-day frontier between those two states was drawn with an impenetrable line.

Those who have their roots in Norrbotten know that large-scale investments have been made as much for political motives as for economic or social ones. There is no doubt that the local economy is unbalanced. Superficially, there now seems to be a reasonable manufacturing base, and more people than ever before are employed in manufacturing industry. But like most marginal areas this is a region of *export* – export of iron-ore and other minerals, export of forestry goods, export of hydro electricity, and nowadays export of people. Soon the people of north Norway will also see the export of North Sea oil and gas from their stormy offshore waters. From the point of view of industrial structure there are a number of long-term problems:

(a) A large part of resource-oriented production is state owned. And nationalized industries are, in Scandinavia as elsewhere, 'sluggish operators'.

(b) Many of the manufacturing concerns in Nordkalotten are there because of incentives. If, due to a change of government policies, the area loses its comparative advantages, many new industries – and some of the old ones – will drift instead to the south.

(c) Many of the northern firms are subcontractors owned by, or dependent upon, larger firms in the south. They are dependent upon the profitability of these firms and are increasingly vulnerable because of the modern tendency of parent companies to subcontract abroad.

Emigration is a severe problem, particularly in the northern counties of Norway which have been losing young people particularly fast. The problem is exacerbated by the present-day impact of the oil industry. For many years there has been a steady movement of people from isolated farmsteads, hamlets and villages into the towns, and a loss from the towns to the core areas of the three states concerned (Fig. 15.2, p. 242). Seasonal migrations of people are still quite marked, especially in conjunction with the cod fishery off the north Norwegian coast, and with the seasonal demand for forestry labour. There is also a considerable migration of Finns across the border into Norrbotten (and often thence to Stockholm), attracted by secure jobs, good housing and high wages. In this part of Sweden there is a demand for labour, but the scale of the Finnish involvement in the labour market has caused much ill feeling.

There is a basic conservatism among the people of the far north even if there is a tradition of radical politics. From a political point of view the three state governments have to face resentment from those who feel that change – in whatever direction – is undesirable. There are those who argue that their rulers are 'urbanizing' Nordkalotten too rapidly, those who feel that their area gets inadequate government aid, and those who see every development as a threat to the beauty and the wildlife of one of Europe's last great wildernesses. There is also a strong pro-Lapp lobby which urges the estab-

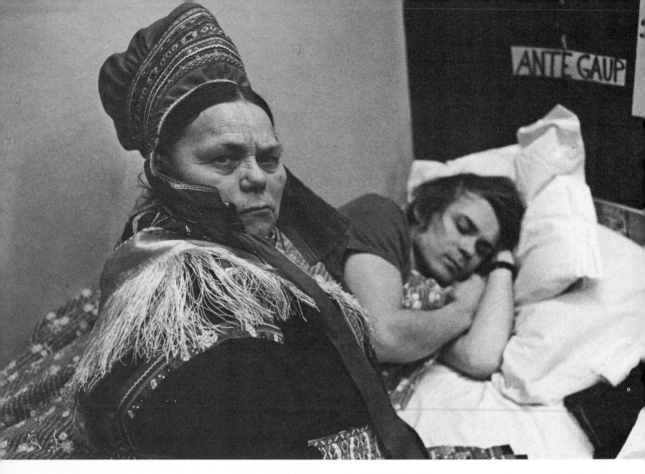

Fig. 17.5 Brita Gaup and her son Ante during one of the protest hunger strikes which took place in Oslo in February 1981. The photograph was taken on Ante Gaup's twenty-fourth day without nourishment, in protest against the Norwegian government's plans to use the Alta valley for a large-scale hydro-electricity project. (Photo: Bernt Eide)

lishment of a Lapp or *Sami* parliament, more Lapp schools, the increased use of Lapp place-names, and the protection of the traditional Lapp reindeer-grazing areas.

Some of these issues came to a head in 1979–80 when the Norwegian government proposed to construct a new hydro-electric dam across the Alta valley. This would have entailed the flooding of a reindeer-calving area, the disturbance of the Alta salmon spawning grounds. and the construction of roads and pipelines across reindeer migratory routes. Most significantly, the plan was interpreted by the Lapps not in economic terms but in spiritual ones. As far as they were concerned, the government intended to rape their cultural heartland, which is centred on the three valley settlements of Kautokeino, Masi and Alta. They responded to the threat with demonstrations, deputations and hunger strikes (Fig. 17.5). It was widely claimed that the government was behaving with complete insensitivity to local interests, and that it was callously prepared to sink a scalpel into the heart of the *Sami* people.

These emotional claims were accompanied by widespread practical resistance. The local councils at Alta and Kautokeino decided to oppose the plans, supported by every single Lapp organization in Scandinavia, by fishing and farming interests, by the Norwegian

Nature Conservancy, by university student groups, and by environmental and anti-nuclear bodies. Support for the resistance campaign came from all over northern Europe. In spite of this the government was quite determined to press ahead with its construction plans, and a start was made with the building of the road from Alta to the dam site. The leadership of the protest campaign was then taken over by Folkaksjon (People's Action), whose single objective was to stop the building of the Alta dam by non-violent means. In July 1979 6,000 people from 20 countries demonstrated their support on the Alta site; by the end of 1980 Folkaksjon had 20,000 paid-up members. The motto *elva skal leve* (the river shall live) began to ring through the country. The military authorities in Finnmark responded to public pressure by refusing to cooperate with the police. Eventually the Norwegian government, faced with maintaining the largest police operation in the nation's history, and with mounting revulsion throughout the country, was forced to back down. At the end of the day the symbolism became more important than the reality; the issue crystallized into a conflict between the legitimate interests of an ethnic minority and the insensitive and pig-headed determination of a national government to implement an unwise and unnecessary policy decision. The Alta dam became a symbol of suppression and oppression, bureaucracy and technocracy, and the Norwegian people, not being used to such things, were deeply shocked by the episode.

It would be a mistake to imagine that the Lapps feel themselves to be suffering from repression on a large scale. All three of the governments involved in Lapland make efforts to meet the demands of the Lapp leaders through investments in Lapp schools and through the provision of radio and television programmes for Lapp speakers. And while this goes on other inhabitants of Nordkalotten claim that these measures, designed to please the Lapps and their vociferous supporters, give a disproportionate amount of attention to what is after all a very small cultural minority!

It is generally recognized that economic and social life in Nordkalotten is dependent upon outside help and support – mostly from central government in the form of subsidies, tax incentives, direct grants and industrial and other investments. The important decisions are made over 1,000 km away in Oslo, Stockholm and Helsinki by people who do not know, and who do not apparently greatly care, what goes on in Lapland. This may be an unjustifiably cynical attitude, but it is widely held and it gives rise to a consistently high Communist vote among the Nordkalotten electorate. Southern naiveté is summarized in the old story of the farmer from southern Skåne who expressed surprise at the fact that good crops could be grown at Lund, so very far to the north. . . .

Another factor in the complex web of perceptions of the far north concerns military strategy. The area is a sensitive one from a military point of view; much of Lapland was devastated during the Second

World War, and near Kirkenes the NATO forces of Norway stand face to face with the forces of the Soviet Union. Lappi is a province which the Finns are determined to keep Finnish, but its long and easily breached frontier with the Soviet Union is a source of concern to both the Finnish government and the NATO Alliance; this frontier will only remain safe as long as Finnish – Soviet relations remain friendly and as long as the Soviet leaders see the need for a military buffer zone on their country's north-western flank.

Nordkalotten's 'Northern Problem' is multi-faceted, and it is no easy problem to solve. The harsh environment of this remote and socially complicated zone has, according to some theorists, caused man to 'live assertively'. It is held that the environment, far from holding back development, has stimulated innovation and technical investment. True, there are many examples of high technology and of sophisticated lifestyles in Nordkalotten, but at what cost? And to what purpose? W. R. Mead's 'principle of comparative disadvantage' is perfectly valid here, eliciting a government response which is in some respects reasonable and sensitive to the needs of the community.

In Finland the Regional Development Fund finances or subsidizes industries such as tourism, fishing, fur-farming, export industries and industries which provide substitutes for imports. In Norway small-scale or workshop industries have been encouraged, and as mentioned on p. 255 there has been a great deal of state investment in industry. The Regional Development Fund, created in 1961, is designed to assist in the creation of employment in 'regions with special employment difficulties' such as north Norway. But it is difficult for the Norwegians to maintain a sense of balance when the arrival of the oil industry has caused many people to leave the land and seek highly paid employment on oil rigs, service vessels and shore bases. These 'market forces' are difficult for the individual to resist in a free economy, but local and national politicians know that those who have left farming and fishing in pursuit of high salaries in the new service industries will not return to their former occupations when the oil boom ends. In Sweden the government has invested a great deal of money in the north, for example in improvements to the road network. There are also subsidies of all sorts to encourage investment in Norrbotten, together with a whole range of other devices for attracting manufacturing and service industries. Short-term and long-term settlers are enticed to the north by houses, subsidies and incentive payments.

On matters of specifically Lapp concern there is now a new government-sponsored Commission on Lapp Affairs, and it has become Swedish policy to treat the Lapps as a common ethnic group deserving of special legislation in many instances. The three governments are also working together in an attempt to solve the Northern Problem. The universities of Tromsø, Oulu and Umeå are cooperating in research projects concerned with life above the Arctic

Circle; there is a Joint Nordic Centre for labour-market training at Övertorneå and an Institute for Laplanders at Kautokeino. The Nordkalott Committee (with three representatives from each country) is working for a greater measure of cooperation in regional policy and labour-market policy; there are proposals for a joint Norwegian–Swedish–Finnish Fund for the Development of Nord-kalotten; and the Nordic Council has promoted improved road and air communications in the area.

There is no doubt about the commitment of the three governments to the cause of Nordkalotten. Their commitment is of course paternalistic, and this paternalism is encouraged not only by a system of centralized state control but also by the demands and pleas for help which come from the community leaders who reside above the Arctic Circle. The Northern Problem is so complicated that there can never be a 'final solution'; there are so many conflicting interests involved in social and economic matters that any measures taken by the three governments, independently or jointly, inevitably lead to at least some undesirable side-effects. And there are plenty of people who are prepared to point these out. In the remote wilderness of Nordkalotten, it seems, there is no action, however well intentioned, without reaction; whatever else can be said about the region, its people are determined not to be forgotten, and determined to have their say.

Suggested reading

The Northern Problem

Bosi 1960; Bylund 1966; Helle 1970; Hilton 1972; Ingold 1973; Knox 1973; Landmark *et al.* 1959; Lundquist 1954; Manker 1963; Mead 1947; Mead and Smeds 1967; Pantenburg 1968; Rönn 1961; Tietze 1971; Ruong 1967; Siuruainen and Aikio 1977; Stone 1971a; Teal 1954; Thunborg and Andersson 1960; Vorren and Manker 1962; Vorren *et al.* 1960.

Part IV Local landscapes and sample studies

Chapter 18   Rödlöga Skärgård in the Stockholm archipelago

The setting

The Stockholm archipelago is reputed to have at least 24,000 islands. These islands, ranging in size from some which cover hundreds of square kilometres to others which are mere bedrock knolls projecting through the surface of the Baltic Sea, are arranged in a mosaic of infinite complexity just off the eastern tip of Svealand. The archipelago extends from near Arholma in the north to near Landsort, 150 km away in the south. The greatest east – west extent of the archipelago is about 80 km; its total area is about 6,000 km², of which a fifth is land. The gradation from land to sea is subtle in the extreme, and many of the inland areas around Lake Mälaren have the feel of the archipelago about them. The concept of a 'coastline' has little meaning here, for the archipelago is simply a part of the downwarped Baltic Shield where the peneplained Pre-Cambian rocks (mostly schists and gneisses) are very gently tilted beneath sea-level. In the inner part of the archipelago most of the rock surface is still above sea-level; in the middle part the sea has invaded old valleys and other low points in the landscape; and in the outer part most of the old landscape lies beneath sea-level, with but a few old hill summits projecting as islands. Here there are broad open sounds separating small clusters of islands, and here it is more appropriate to talk of 'seascape' than it is to talk of landscape.

Throughout the whole of the archipelago the bedrock surface has been scoured and smoothed by ice, and deep ravines or *tunneldalar* have been excavated along lines of geological weakness. In the inner archipelago some parts of the eroded bedrock surface are thickly covered with sands, gravels and marine clays, but sediments become scarcer and scarcer towards the east, and the outer islands are for the most part barren and inhospitable patches of smooth bedrock. From the point of view of marine processes this is in an area of low energy expenditure, at the other end of the scale from the north-west coast of the Faroes (p. 42) which is constantly battered by Atlantic storm waves. Processes of marine erosion are not of great importance in the fashioning of the landscape, and

275

there are few sea-cliffs or sandy beaches. Of much greater importance is the process of isostatic uplift. As mentioned in Chapter 4, the Stockholm archipelago is still rising from the sea at a rate of 50 cm per century; this means that many areas which were submerged in 1880 are now above sea-level, and it also means that in many areas coastal configuration is gradually changing as emerging islands are enlarged. Because the Baltic Sea is not a tidal sea, true tidal currents are not an important feature of the marine environment; but the water surface rises and falls through more than 1 m in response to changes in wind direction and air pressure.

The climate of the archipelago enjoys the benefits of a maritime environment, but continental influences are strong. Annual precipitation is below 700 mm. On the island of Möja the mean air temperature of the coldest month (February) is about –3 °C, and during the months of January – April the sounds, bays and straits between islands are often covered with thick ice. During particularly severe spells the whole archipelago is bound together by a continuous sheet of sea ice, and the outer islands can be reached by ice skaters and even by motorists. During the summer months there are long spells of calm, dry, hot weather, influenced above all by the continental high-pressure systems which extend eastwards from the USSR and Finland. At Möja the mean air temperature in July is 16 °C; daily maxima often reach 25 °C. Fronts from the west lose much of their energy before they reach the archipelago, and the islands seldom suffer the thunderstorms and torrential downpours that affect the inland parts of Sweden in the high summer. If it were not for the mosquitoes and horse-flies the summer climate would be ideal.

From the point of view of natural resources we can conveniently divide the archipelago into an inner and an outer zone as defined by the Swedish planning authorities. The inner islands have relatively lush woodland vegetation with stands of spruce and pine interspersed with deciduous patches in which alder, rowan, oak, birch and aspen are common species. There are many open spaces which have been managed over the years as rich meadow land, and in other clearings in the woodland there are wild strawberries, raspberries and bilberries in abundance. Shallow coastal embayments are usually filled with dense growths of reeds. Throughout the inner archipelago there are relatively prosperous agricultural communities, together with some old fishing villages such as Möja and Furusund. Here and there old holiday resorts with their elegant buildings are reminders of the early days of tourism. For example, Köpmanholm on Yxlan was popular before the turn of the century as a summer resort; one of its regular visitors was the author August Strindberg. Communications are relatively good; there is a well-maintained road network, and the narrowest straits between the islands are connected by road bridges. Where straits are wider free vehicle ferries operate a scheduled service at least once an hour during the day, for example between Furusund and Köpmanholm and between Roslags Kulla and Ljusterö. The most important element in the farming economy is dairying, but the long sunny days of the summer permit some arable farming and even market-gardening near the main towns such as Åkersberga, Norrtälje and Nynäshamn.

In contrast, the outer archipelago is a world dominated by water and sky. When you are in the outer islands you spend a great deal of time looking at the sky, for weather changes have a critical and rapid effect upon wave conditions on the wide open stretches of water which lie between you and the distant mainland. The islands of the outermost archipelago have no roads and no motorized vehicles; all transport must be by water in the summer and over the sea ice in the winter. Closer to the mainland there are a number of larger islands with roads and scattered small settlements; these include Blidö, Ljusterö, Runmarö, Nämdö, Ornö and Utö. The largest settlement is at Sandhamn, an old holiday resort which is now a famous sailing centre. At Möja the community is much involved in strawberry-growing; Möja *jordgubbar* (literally: little old earth-men!) are sold throughout the Stockholm region in late June and July. Throughout the archipelago there are too many shoals for large vessels (except along the main shipping routes), and rough weather and fog often create problems for small boats and for the passenger vessels which link the outer islands with Stockholm.

Until the 1920s there were well-organized and tightly knit communities in the outer archipelago. There were permanent settlements on the larger islands such as Svartlöga and Långviksskär, and groups of farming and fishing folk habitually travelled by small open boat to the remote outer islands during the summer. The expeditions were for fishing, bird-catching, seal-hunting and for the gathering of hay crops from some small sheltered meadows. People lived a life which was marginal in the extreme, and barrels of salted herring were almost the only items which families could sell to provide cash incomes. The harsh maritime environment and the sheer remoteness in time and space of these communities from commercial centres like Norrtälje, Stockholm and Uppsala made it inevitable that their way of life would disappear. And so it *has* disappeared, leaving behind little besides memories.

Rödlöga and its islands

Rödlöga Skärgård is a group of scattered islands in the outer archipelago about 15 km to the east of Blidö. The main island of Rödlöga is about 1.2 km long and 500 m wide, and the other islands

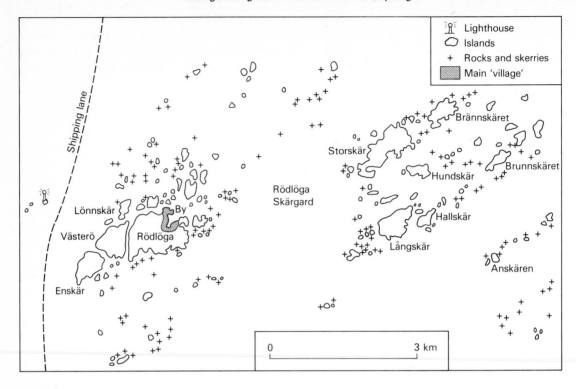

Fig. 18.1 Map of Rödlöga Skärgård, showing the location of the main island and its *by*, and also the outer islands belonging to the community.

are much smaller. The road network ends on Blidö, and so all contact with Rödlöga has to be by sea (Fig. 18.1). The main quay on the northern side of the island is the centre of local life, just as it always has been. Near the quay there is a cluster of well-built wooden houses and smaller huts, together with a few boat-houses at the shore. Other small huts are scattered over the island, mostly in coastal locations. The outermost islands of the *skärgård* are separated from Rödlöga by a wide stretch of open water, and they have never supported any clustered settlements. There are, however, several groups of small huts known as *fiskestugor* and traditionally used by fishermen. On some islands and islets cairns, sea-marks and small stone and timber jetties are the only signs of human interference. Otherwise this is a landscape which still looks largely 'natural'; it is also breathtakingly beautiful.

The old way of life

During the 1700s the population of Rödlöga Skärgård was approximately 200. By 1800 most families owned their own land, having bought plots which had previously been leased from the state. Some of these plots were *tomter*, on which building and permanent habitation was allowed. Most of the *tomter* and homesteads were on the main island of Rödlöga, where they made up the *by* or township. Most families owned additional plots on Rödlöga for agricultural use, and patches of land were owned on the outer islands also; these latter were used for summer grazing, hay-cutting and as bases for fishing trips and sealing expeditions. Some land, labelled *samfällighet* on the old maps, was owned in common, including especially valuable areas such as sheltered harbours and also small rocky islets and shoals which were not of any great value. Rödlöga community was assessed as one *mantal*. Each family owned a proportion of the *mantal*, and the old land register showed that each owner held a certain percentage of the *mantal* land. The ownership and organization of land was originally discussed at community meetings, but matters were formalized by the *laga skifte* of 1873–74. Figure 18.2 shows the pattern of land ownership on Rödlöga Storskär in 1873–74, and the inset map shows the quite sophisticated mapping of land units (some of them no more than 5 m long) which was completed at the time of the *laga skifte*. All of the mapped plots were numbered in the land register, and these basic units have remained the same ever since. Many plots, however, are no longer in the hands of the original Rödlöga families; some have been split between children, some have been amalgamated, and others have been sold to new owners who have no land interest in Rödlöga By.

As late as the 1940s the people of Rödlöga township persisted in the old ways of life. Their homesteads were on the main island, and here they had their small hayfields, their gardens, their jetties and their boat-houses. They kept a few cattle, pigs and chickens in other small wooden huts, but space was at a premium since the island's woodland had to be maintained as a firewood source and as vital shelter against winter gales. The outer islands still played an important (but declining) part in the economy, and they were used above all as bases for fishing herring and other sea fish and for shooting seabirds and seals. In earlier decades eggs were collected, especially from eider duck colonies. Those families who owned meadows in the outer archipelago used them for cutting hay, and sometimes animals were transported by boat to those meadows where they could graze during the later part of the summer. Occasionally whole family groups would move out to islands such as Röder, Skarv and Långskär, taking with them pigs and poultry as essential parts of their food supply. Some of their time was spent on cutting hay, but the 'summer places' were used above all else as fishing bases. Each summer the herring catch was salted down into barrels for transport back to Rödlöga at the end of the season. The *fiskestugor* used by these family groups can be looked on as the equivalents of the *seters* of Norway or the *fäbodar* of the Swedish uplands; mostly they were used seasonally, but a few of them were permanently inhabited by single men who owned no land in Rödlöga By. At the end of the summer season the barrels of salted herring were taken back to Rödlöga, where they were sorted out and then transported in larger sailing vessels to Uppsala and

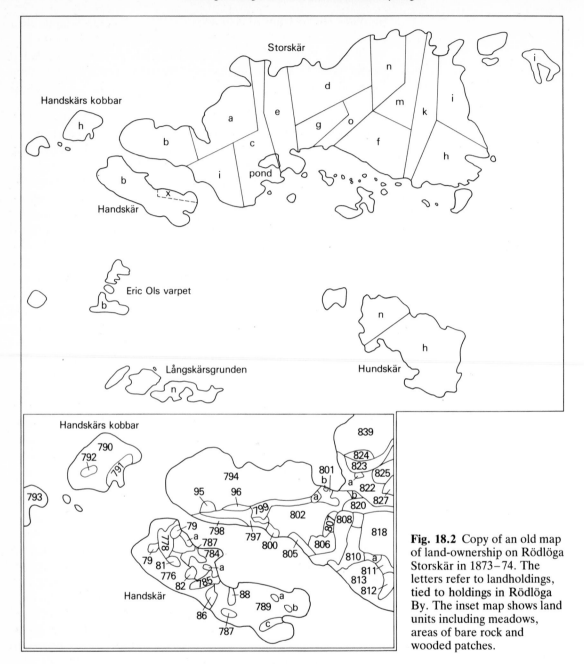

Fig. 18.2 Copy of an old map of land-ownership on Rödlöga Storskär in 1873–74. The letters refer to landholdings, tied to holdings in Rödlöga By. The inset map shows land units including meadows, areas of bare rock and wooded patches.

Enköping for sale. Sometimes several families would combine for this marketing operation, and each community had its traditional destination for disposing of the herring catch.

Modern conditions

Within the last forty years the population of Rödlöga has declined sharply. The keeping of animals has been abandoned, and after decades of emigration there were only a few people resident in Rödlöga By during the 1970s. There were no children. During the winter of 1979–80, for the first time in over 400 years, there was not a single soul in residence on Rödlöga. Yet another archipelago community was dead; yet another island lay lifeless in the grip of the winter ice.

The last fisherman to live in the outer archipelago left his little hut on Rödlöga Storskär in 1976 after a severe illness compounded by an excessive zeal for alcohol. Cut off from all contact with the outside world during the winter months and beginning to suffer the effects of old age, his family and friends convinced him that his life of peaceful isolation was becoming a threat to his health and safety. Now he lives in Rödlöga By during the summer and on the mainland during the winter. The last married couple on Rödlöga own the shop, which does a roaring trade throughout the summer with those who have huts in the archipelago and with those who spend their holidays afloat in sailing boats and cabin cruisers. They operate the petrol and diesel fuel pumps, sell bottled propane and paraffin, and act as postmen and agents for goods ordered and sent out from the mainland. They know everybody and everybody knows them. The shopkeeper even owns a car, a small status symbol which stands rusting away beneath the trees near the shop; it has never been used, since Rödlöga has no road.

The end of the old way of life really began in the 1920s as herring stocks declined in the traditional Rödlöga fishing-grounds. At the same time, as in other parts of the outer archipelago, a few rich Stockholm families began to explore beyond the traditional holiday centres such as Ljusterö, Köpmanholm, Sandhamn and Vaxholm. They flocked out to the archipelago by steamer, and Fig. 18.3 gives a vivid impression of the seething activity on Strömkajen, Stockholm, on a summer weekend in 1926. Some people even started to use the area for sailing holidays. Some of them bought abandoned fishing-huts or plots of land, and many new houses were built by the new affluent summer residents. By 1935 there were 17,000 summer-houses in the archipelago. As the tourist use of the area increased local people were able to derive some income from the direct sale of vegetables, eggs, milk and fish, but the simplest way of making money was to sell the old *fiskestugor* of the outer archipelago. There was also a good income to be made in the 1920s and 1930s from smuggling operations. Local fishermen became professional smugglers; they bought alcoholic drinks from passing ships in the 'outer lead' or off the outermost skerries, and sold their contraband either locally or in the main towns. Nearly all archipelago people were involved in the trade. But family incomes remained low, and after the Second World War more and more families left the area.

The great majority of huts in Rödlöga Skärgård are now used for

Fig. 18.3 Crowds about to depart for the archipelago by steamboat in June 1926. The quay is Strömkajen. (Photo: Törnbloms/Waxholmsbolaget)

recreational purposes only, although a few huts near the shop on the main island are used by fishermen during the summer. Their herring nets hanging out to dry are a last reminder of a past lifestyle. Increasingly the area is being used by sailing-boats and motor cruisers, and Rödlöga has become a centre for water-skiing, windsurfing and skin-diving. Planning controls have to be strictly enforced if the outer archipelago is not to be destroyed through overuse. Part of Rödlöga Skärgård has been declared a national nature reserve, and during the bird nesting season no landings are allowed on certain islands. Shooting of ducks and seals is now prohibited. No new buildings are allowed, and old buildings can be replaced but not enlarged. Greater and greater use is being made of good anchorages such as Åsmansboda, and at the height of the holiday season, between late June and the end of August, there are up to thirty sailing-boats and motor cruisers tied up here for the night. This sort of pressure brings with it a need for toilet facilities and rubbish disposal centres, and Norrtälje Kommun (the local authority responsible for this part of the archipelago) has put up wooden toilet huts and large dustbins in strategic locations. A special boat calls to collect the full toilet containers and rubbish bags at regular intervals, and a charge is also levied on summer-cottage owners who wish to make use of this water-borne refuse collection service. This service is essential if the beauty of the archipelago is to be preserved; without it the most popular anchorages and beauty spots would by now have become heavily polluted.

In recent years there has been a great change in the social character of archipelago tourism. Twenty years ago only the wealthy could afford pleasure boats, and there was a rather exclusive 'club' of sailing-boat owners who habitually visited their own parts of the archipelago and who met up with one another summer after summer. Nowadays boats are looked upon by people from all income groups as good investments and also as pieces of property which can be purchased with tax-allowable loans; so the level of boat ownership has increased enormously. As mentioned in Chapter 14, large-scale boat rental has further increased the possibilities for water-borne summer holidays, and there are now at least 50,000 boats in the archipelago which have facilities for sleeping and cooking. The archipelago now attracts large numbers of people who know nothing about navigation and very little about boat-handling. Some of the 'new' sailors have scant regard for private property in the archipelago and they are not greatly concerned about the protection of the environment. They tie up at private jetties, trample old meadows which are now botanically important sites, light fires and leave litter and broken glass, and pick flowers and wild berries close to summer cottages which are carefully and lovingly maintained. Another problem arises out of the sailing tours organized by Kryssarklubben, one of the Swedish sailing clubs. At intervals through the summer fleets of 30 or more sailing boats containing well over 100 people descend upon sheltered anchorages which may have no toilet facilities or litter bins. Peaceful havens are transformed and localized pollution is inevitable. To an increasing extent, and reluctantly, landowners are having to put up fences around their property and notices on their jetties. The planning authority is trying to control the free public use of this environmentally valuable area, but the Swedish *allemansrätt* (the right of free public access) is something that is not easily tampered with. The sailing public cannot be banned any more than the summer-cottage owners, and there would be an outcry if too much of the archipelago was reserved for the exclusive use of wild life.

A lot of people benefit from the current boom in archipelago tourism, but only a handful are natives of Rödlöga, and even they no longer live permanently on the island. Unless a few young families come along in the next few years with the vision and the motivation to regenerate the community by becoming permanent Rödlöga residents, yet another isolated archipelago settlement will be wiped off the map of permanently settled places.

Through the more remote parts of the Stockholm archipelago the old way of life has disappeared, leaving but a few survivors and a few relics for the amusement of the new summer inhabitants. These are

Fig. 18.4 Holidays afloat are now part of the Swedish lifestyle and sailing boats such as this move around the Stockholm archipelago in their thousands during the summer. (Photo: Fiskars)

the second-home owners and boat-owners of Stockholm who spend their long summer days in this maritime wilderness, well away from the cares of the high-pressure urban world (Fig. 18.4). With their exotic sailing-boats and their fast cabin cruisers, with their sunburnt wives and their healthy well-fed children, they now use as a playground a region which was, only fifty years ago, inhabited by people who looked on it as a world to be endured or, if possible, left behind. To the archipelago folk the comforts and delights of Stockholm were heard about second- or third-hand, dreamt about and talked about but seldom encountered. Most of them were trapped by family responsibilities and by the innate conservatism of peasant communities everywhere. Now that large parts of the archipelago have been emptied of permanent residents the people of Stockholm and Uppsala look on it as their idyll and their dream world – a world in which problems, troubles and responsibilities cease to exist. As mentioned in Chapter 14, escapism becomes a factor of great geographical importance.

Suggested reading

Archipelago life and landscape

Håkansson 1980; Hedenstierna 1948, 1960; Hustich 1964; Jaatinen 1960, 1978; Jones, Mead and Jaatinen 1975; Mead *et al*. 1964; Nordenstam *et al*. 1970; Smeds 1950; Smeds, Jaatinen *et al*. 1960; Tapsell 1969.

Chapter 19 Fjaerland, a Norwegian fjordside settlement

Fjaerland is one of the northern arms of Sognefjord, in the heart of the Norwegian fjord country. It is also located more or less centrally in the county of Sogn and Fjordane (Fig. 19.1), and from a planning point of view it is considered to be a part of the inner Sognefjord region. The centre of community life in Fjaerland is Mundal village near the head of the fjord. It is not connected to the road network of Sognefjord, and all contact with the outside world is by means of the ferry-boat which is based at Balestrand on the north shore of Sog-

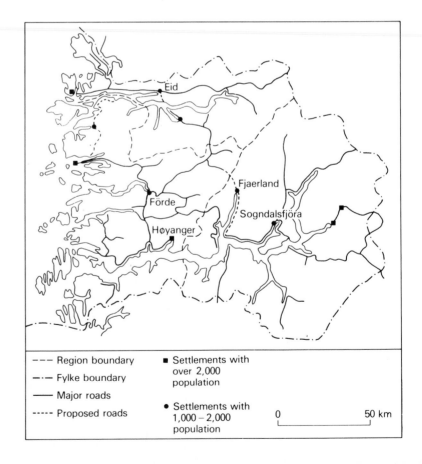

Fig. 19.1 Map of the *fylke* (county) of Sognog Fjordane, western Norway, showing the location of Fjaerland, together with the main towns and roads.

nefjord proper. The nearest small towns are Høyanger some 60 km to the west and Sogndalsfjöra about the same distance to the east. Bergen is the nearest large town, visited by local people only on rare and special occasions.

The Norwegian fjord country is immensely appealing to the visitor but none too easy to live in as far as the average resident is concerned. On the flanks of the fjords the land rises steeply, and in places precipitously, from sea-level to altitudes approaching 1,000 m. There are very sharp contrasts in topography between the coastal skerries and strandflat, the long deep fjords, and the undulating and harsh fjell country above the 800 m contour. In places there is a sharp break of slope between steep valley sides and the flat coastal terraces of sand and gravel raised isostatically after the end of the last glaciation. Many glacial valleys also have thick fills of sand and gravel of fluvioglacial origin, in addition to intermittent banks and ridges of moraine. W. R. Mead has pointed out that in this region features such as vegetational types, agricultural practices and settlement distribution are controlled more by vertical factors than by horizontal ones. The climate of the Fjaerland area is oceanic but nevertheless severe. There are over 200 rain-days per year. Winter is long, dark and dismal, but there is not a great deal of snowfall at sea-level and the fjords are very seldom iced up. Annual rainfall totals are over 2,500 mm on the coast and on the high fjells, but at the heads of tributary fjords and in some of the interior valleys annual rainfall is under 500 mm. The heads of the fjords are pockets of warmth during the summer, especially where there are south-facing valley sides which can obtain maximum benefit from the sun. In contrast, north-facing valley sides are dark, cool and damp throughout the year.

From the point of view of resources, Mead has described the fjord country as a region made up of three different components as follows:

1. The flat rock terraces, raised beaches and fluvioglacial terraces beneath the 200 m contour, which make up the 'intensively cultivated homestead'.
2. The steep slopes on the flanks of fjords and glacial valleys, constituting the 'extensive background of summer pastures and woodland'.
3. The fjords themselves and the inner waters of the skerries, which make up the 'extensive foreground of fisheries'.

Fjaerland and Mundal

Around the head of Fjaerlandsfjord is a little world fashioned by glacier ice. On the high plateau to the north and west, visible and oppressive, the Jostedalsbre ice-cap dominates the landscape. Four

Fig. 19.2 Map of the inner reaches of Fjaerlandsfjord, showing the converging valleys and their physical features which form the basis of the community's economic life.

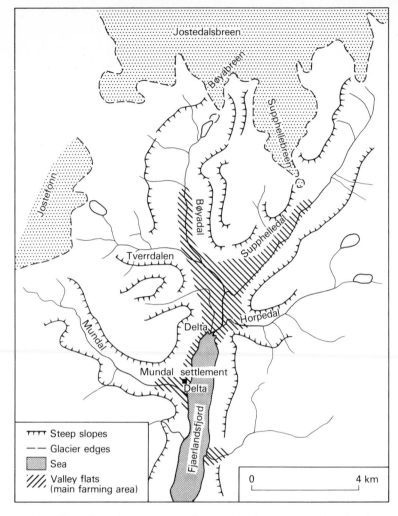

main valleys have been carved by outlet glaciers carrying ice from Jostedalsbreen; these are Mundal, the Bøya and Supphelle valleys, and Horpedal (Fig. 19.2). These, and several other valleys such as Uppsetedal, have been excavated so deeply and widely that they are now separated only by narrow ridges and isolated pyramidal remnants of the old plateau. Where the valleys converge near Mundal the combined force of the confluent glaciers was sufficient for the excavation of Fjaerlandsfjord proper – a more or less straight and very steep-sided gash cut through the undulating plateau country for a distance of 20 km. In places the fjord sides are broken by hanging glacial valleys, by steep river valleys and gullies, and by alluvial fans and trails of landslide debris. The lower slopes are heavily wooded with mixed deciduous and coniferous trees and along the shore there are wild raspberries and blackcurrants in profusion among moss-covered boulders and in small sunny clearings. At the head of the fjord there is a broad, fertile lowland made for the most part of outwash sands and gravels and marine silts and clays. As isostatic recovery proceeds, the deltaic flats are still being extended seawards. This lowland, the area's most valuable agricultural area, extends for some way up the Bøya and Supphelle valleys also. There is another valuable agricultural area, based largely on raised terraces of sand and gravel, at the mouth of the Mundal valley.

The landscape around the head of the fjord is dramatic; glimpses of the Jostedalsbre and the small outlet glaciers of Bøyabre and Supphellebre, together with dark valley sides and spectacular pyramidal peaks, combine to create scenery which was tailor-made for the Victorian traveller in the days when intrepid and pictures-que explorations were in vogue. Times have changed, and so have tastes, but here the way of life of the farming community is still dominated by the landscape. In addition, tourism was and is an important part of the local economy. The landscape may be a difficult one to live in, but it is also a major resource for Fjaerland people.

The community economy

At present the population of the whole Fjaerland area is approximately 400; of these, about 100 people live in Mundal village which is the stopping point of the ferry-boat from Balestrand. Mundal has a church, a large hotel which has been popular with tourists for over 100 years, a guest-house and various other holiday establishments, two or three shops specializing in groceries, household essentials and tourist goods, an agricultural machinery repair shop, a post office, a commercial bank branch office, and a small leather workshop making shoes. In the 1970s there was also, somewhat surprisingly, a workshop producing large Christmas bells out of expanded polystyrene! In the surrounding area there are more than twenty small farms, and in the higher parts of the main valleys some small groups of *seters* are still in a good state of repair. A number of small fishing-boats are kept at the main quay at Mundal, and several of the farmers own open rowing-boats which are used only in the immediate vicinity. Fishing is not a significant local occupation nowadays, and only one man catches fish for sale; in contrast fishing was, until about the time of the Second World War, an essential part of the economy for most Fjaerland families.

Bøya Farm, at the mouth of the Bøya valley, is typical of the other farms in this area. The farmland, of about 40 ha, is not consolidated into one block but is split into four strips, each one located successively higher up the valley, and separated by blocks of land owned by neighbouring farms. Nevertheless, this farm is unusually large, and it has the benefit of reasonably flat and fertile land. On the typical west Norwegian pattern the farmer (who carries the name of the valley as his family name) utilizes resources of three different types:

1. *The innmark*. This is the cultivated area which is located (albeit in four different sections) relatively close to the home farm or *gård*. The arable land is used above all else for hay crops, but other crops which are grown in rotation on the small fields are oats, barley, potatoes and turnips. In the hayfields the hay is dried in the fields on long wire fences, as elsewhere in the fjord country. The greater part of the farm produce is used as animal feed on the home farm. Hardly any of it is sold. The *innmark* fields are protected by stone walls and wire fences. The *gård* itself is typically Norwegian, with the family home close to a multi-purpose barn and a few smaller outbuildings. The barn is used for the storage of fodder, timber and farm implements, but its most important purpose is for the winter shelter of farm animals. New features include machinery sheds, silos and larger barns for the larger breeds of dairy cattle which are now stall-fed for much of the year.

2. *The woodland area.* Partly on the valley floor and partly on the valley side, this is used for firewood and fencing materials, and also for the rough structural timbers needed in the farm buildings. Birch and alder are used for firewood; generally the trees are felled during the winter when tractor-drawn sledges can be used for timber haulage. Part of the woodland is a coniferous plantation of spruce which is well managed with professional help in felling and replacement planting. Most of the timber is sold for conversion to wood-pulp.

3. *The utmark*. This is the open grazing land on the valley sides and in the upper part of the valley above the cultivated area. In the case of Bøya Farm the *utmark* is divided into two by a fence running across the valley; each section has a little cluster of traditional wooden *seters* known collectively as a *støl*. Unlike some other valleys, Bøyadal is shared by several farmers, each of whom owns one *seter* in the upper *støl* and one in the lower *støl*. The *utmark* is used for the summer grazing of about 15 milk cows, 25–30 heifers and bullocks, and 20 sheep belonging to Bøya Farm, and also by other animals belonging to neighbouring farms. In the old days the farmers' daughters used to stay for weeks at a time at the *seters* with the cattle and sheep; they were expected to milk the cows and use all the milk for the making of butter and cheese. Nowadays nobody stays at the *seters*, for twice-daily milking journeys can be made by tractor from the farm. The huts are falling into disrepair, and because of the problems of cooperative management of the two sections of the *utmark* the farmers have now divided and enclosed certain parts for private use. However, the *utmark* is still used in the traditional way. In the spring the animals are moved to the lower *støl* as soon as there is warmth in the air and growth in the grass. At the height of summer they are moved to the lush grass of the upper *støl*, leaving the grass on the lower *støl* to recover ready for another session of grazing during the autumn when the weather

begins to deteriorate. Occasionally nowadays hay is cut on parts of the *utmark* to supplement the hay crops of the *innmark*; this is one of the reasons why some farmers wish to divide and enclose the land immediately above the *innmark* boundary wall.

From the above it will be apparent that the economy of Bøya Farm, in common with all the other farms of Fjaerland, is based upon dairying. Sheep are not of great importance, and the greater part of the farm income comes from the sale of fresh milk. Milk is collected from every farm by a tanker lorry three times a week. During the summer months in particular there is a ready market for butter and cheese. There is some income from the sale of timber, and some from the sale of special items such as eggs and potatoes to Hotel Mundal and the local guest-houses. But times have changed enormously since the early decades of the century; in place of the old broad-based and largely self-sufficient way of life the farmers of Fjaerland now depend almost entirely for their livelihood upon small-scale and heavily subsidized dairying operations. Among recent innovations the advent of silage production is one of the most important, since this eliminates the risk of losing the hay crop. But the making of silage requires new machinery and also silage towers, and these things require investments and subsidies.

It is difficult to calculate the real value of tourism to the community economy of Fjaerland. During the summer season Fjaerland welcomes its tourist invasion; in 1980 at least 5,000 holiday-makers stayed at Fjaerland. Very many more came by the ferry on day-trips. The hotel and the guest-house provide seasonal employment for more than thirty people, and other employment is provided in the local shops and in 'incidental' jobs such as painting and decorating, electrical contracting and vehicle maintenance. Some farmers are beginning to let holiday accommodation, and in the Mundal Valley some of the old *seters* are being renovated for holiday use. The gross income derived from tourism in Fjaerland may not be very great, but for a small community it is of inestimable value.

The wider context

Fjaerland is representative of the more remote fjordside communities in the Bergen hinterland. Its isolation is a severe handicap, but like the members of many isolated communities the people of Fjaerland cling to their traditions determinedly (Fig. 19.3) and feel a strong sense of local loyalty. But from an economic point of view Fjaerland is not well blessed. Elsewhere in the fjord country, for example around Leikanger on the sunny north shore of Sognefjord and along the northern shore of Hardangerfjord, farmers can supplement their income from dairying with fruit and vegetable production. Elsewhere, for example in the region inland of Stavanger

Fig. 19.3 Traditional dress is still worn by the women on special occasions such as weddings. This photo was taken after a wedding in the little church of Mundal.

where relief is more subdued, farms are clustered together into small villages which provide a much greater range of services than is available at Mundal. In many areas there has been a marked reduction in the number of sheep in recent decades; this has reduced the 'grazing requirements' of many farms, and through the increased use of fertilizers which can be easily imported by road or sea improved hay yields on the *innmark* have made it possible to keep cattle close to the *gård* throughout the summer. The farmer at Bøya is by no means the only one keeping heavier cattle which are fed largely on imported feedstuffs and which have greater milk yields than the lighter animals kept in previous decades. Consequently the *utmark* is not fully used, and many of the more remote and inaccessible *seters* fall into disrepair. Shrubs and trees spread over the old grazing areas, reducing their stockholding capacity greatly and fundamentally altering the character of the landscape. In some areas the old grazing lands of the *utmark* are being turned over to forestry, and large plantations of spruce are appearing in fenced enclosures, served by new forestry roads and drained by new open ditches and covered drains. As in many parts of Finland and eastern Norway, 'forest farming' is becoming a vogue, and many farms are discovering that it is somewhat easier than farming on traditional west Norwegian lines.

As far as Fjaerland is concerned, it is still true that the farm economy is oriented almost entirely towards the fjords. Beyond the local road network all movement of people and goods has to be by sea. The fjord steamers carry vehicles, passengers, cattle and sheep, mail, goods for the local shops, supplies for hotels and guest-houses, milk for delivery to the fjordside dairies and a host of other things. The dairying activities of the farmers are a world apart from the activities of the Danish dairying industry; and farm efficiency is limited by the small size of holdings, the fragmentation of the *innmark*, the lack of investment capital and by the low fertility of arable land which is a consequence of the physical limitations of the environment.

Prospects for the future

As the depopulation of the remoter parts of Vestlandet continues, and as small family farms continue to be abandoned, there is little prospect of the immediate revitalization of a farming economy which is, in spite of subsidies, in a very poor state of health. But no one, least of all the Norwegian government, wants to see whole fjordside communities disappearing, and there are perfectly valid social reasons why investment in a number of different forms should be pumped into the fjord country for the benefit of Fjaerland and a host of other small settlements. Already there are a number of developments which should have far-reaching effects.

1. Communications are improving all the time in Sognefjord and the other fjords of the region. Ferries are larger and more efficient than before, new roll-on/roll-off landing stages are being built and sailing schedules are much improved. The road network is being extended, and by the time this book is published Fjaerland will be connected with the Sognefjord roads through the building of a road along the east shore of Fjaerlandsfjord. This new road is also being connected via a tunnel which runs for 6 km under Jostedalsbreen to link up with the Sunnfjord road network.
2. Hydro-electric power resources in the fjord country are being developed, bringing construction jobs to many male workers both from within and outside the fjord country. As new electro-chemical and electro-metallurgical plants are completed these will also bring new jobs and lead to the creation of new communities similar to Årdal and Høyanger. Many men are also finding employment in connection with the North Sea oil industry.
3. The process of farm rationalization, started during the *skifte* of the late nineteenth century, continues today. Small scattered holdings are being consolidated into more compact units, and inefficient field patterns are being replaced by more regular patterns of larger fields which allow farmers to mechanize many of their farming operations. This process results in depopulation, but it also results in a more stable farm economy and perhaps, in the long term, in a more stable community life.
4. Tourism is increasing in importance all the time. As the cost of holidays in Norway rose sharply during the 1970s the number of tourists (especially from the UK) declined. However, the gross income from tourism continues to increase, and the British, Germans and Americans continue to make up the bulk of visitors to the fjord country. Hotels and guest-houses are fully booked

every summer, and package-deal holidays in chalets and farms are increasing. During the summer some 2,000 old *seters*, farm buildings and even abandoned farmhouses are let out on a self-catering basis. Several shipping lines have summer cruises to the fjords, and cruise holiday-makers spend a great deal of money on their shore visits. The Norwegian Tourist Board is making a determined drive to attract 'active' holiday-makers in walking, fishing, camping and climbing holidays.

5. As urban populations increase in the fjord country the demand for fresh fruit and vegetables rises, allowing many of the farmers in reasonably accessible locations to increase their production of apples, cherries, pears, raspberries and plums. Vegetable production is also rising close to the main towns. In parts of Hardangerfjord the process is so well advanced that some old farming districts have approached a state of monoculture with fruit or vegetables the entire basis of the economy. Even Fjaerland has benefited from the fruit and vegetable business, and produce such as cauliflowers, cabbages and strawberries are collected from local farmers during late summer and autumn for processing in a new freezer plant in Laerdal.

6. Farming cooperatives are becoming more widespread and more efficient. Milk collection is much better organized than a decade ago, and bulk purchasing of feedstuffs and fertilizers brings great benefits to the individual farmer. Cooperatives and specialized forestry management groups have also made the management and utilization of timber resources less destructive and far more profitable. The marketing of farm products is also much more efficient, bringing the farmer better prices and a steady demand for his milk, butter and cheese.

7. The farm economy is now diversifying in some areas with the introduction of enterprises such as egg production, silver fox farming and mink-farming. Some of these enterprises fail, but others succeed, bringing local jobs and increased community stability.

8. There is now considerable investment on the part of the Norwegian Ministry of Agriculture in capital projects designed to increase the country's cultivated area. For example, a 6 million Nkr scheme for river control and land reclamation is currently under way in the Fjaerland delta. When complete, this will bring into use about 300 ha of new, highly productive arable land.

9. Guaranteed farm incomes (which are tied to industrial wage levels), together with subsidies on farm products, are making capital investments less risky than they used to be from the point of view of the farmer. New farm buildings and machinery are appearing on the farming scene even in the most remote districts.

Overall, the future for the fjord country of western Norway appears reasonably bright, even though rural depopulation will probably continue for some time yet. The fjord economy is adjusting itself gradually to modern circumstances, and in spite of the tourist ships and the smoking chimneys at Odda and Årdal the fjords retain much of their character. For many people this region of long deep fjords, plunging valley sides and snow-capped mountain peaks is still the epitome of Norway.

Suggested reading

The Norwegian fjordland economy

Bjørkvik 1963; Evans 1958; Gray 1938; Mead 1947, 1958, 1981; Myklebost and Strømme 1963; Sund 1960; Symes 1968; Walling 1966.

Chapter 20   The north-west peninsula of Iceland

The national context

After three cod wars and a great deal of international bitterness the world has come to recognize that the Icelanders feel strongly about their fish stocks. The people of this remote North Atlantic island have more than a sentimental attachment to deep-sea fishing as a way of life; they have a desperate dependence upon fish. To them the survival of culture, economy and nation is at stake; this survival can only be guaranteed through the maintenance and controlled management of fish stocks within the Icelandic fishing-grounds. It is difficult for other nations to appreciate the almost symbiotic relationship which exists between people and fish in Iceland. However, for many years now fish and fish products have made up more than 75 per cent of all Iceland's exports. And of course the people of Iceland look upon the Icelandic fishing-grounds as natural extensions of their own territory. To them, the case for a 200 mile (322 km) fishing-limit is self-evident, and they have been disillusioned by the reluctance of other nations to accept the principle of such a limit. Eiður Guðnason has summarized the Icelandic position in these terms:

> 'Other nations have their resources on land under firm control where no outsiders can interfere. Iceland's position is totally different. It is relatively easy for outsiders to interfere with the fish stocks that seek the nutrient-rich waters close to Iceland. Therefore this all-important resource needs special control and care, because its depletion would simply sweep away the basis of human life in Iceland.'

The Icelanders do not think that this is overstating the case, and in this short chapter we examine the relationship between one regional community and the resources which lie beyond its coastline.

The local context

Vestfirðir – the western fjords – is a region of about 8,600 km² which is scenically unique in Iceland. It is a penisulated peninsula, projecting into the icy waters of Denmark Strait and connected to the main island by a neck of land about 10 km wide. The northernmost tip of the peninsula lies only 10 km south of the Artic Circle. Geologically, as indicated in Chapter 3, the region is a Tertiary basalt plateau, older and more stable than the central parts of Iceland. The overall altitude of this undulating plateau is 600–800 m, although there are some areas where summits approach 1,000 m. By far the most impressive of the topographic features are the fjords which cut deep into the heart of the peninsula from the north and west coasts. The largest of the fjords is Isafjarðardjup, 75 km long and with an impressive array of tributary fjords on its southern flank. Of the other fjords Arnarfjörður is 40 km long and the Jökulfirðir (glacier fjords) system in the north is 30 km long. Like the rest of Iceland, the north-west peninsula has been greatly affected by glacier ice, and at the present day there are still a number of small cirque glaciers and one ice-cap in the uplands.

Overall, Vestfirðir has an environment which is extremely harsh. Mean annual air temperatures are about 4 °C. and summer temperatures seldom rise above 10 °C. Gale-force winds are common, particularly during the winter months. Drifting pack ice, carried southwards by the East Greenland Current, is never far away from the north coast even during the summer. Snow and frost can occur in any month of the year. Winter can last for seven months, with heavy snow, sub-zero temperatures and high winds effectively preventing all outdoor work and cutting road communications over the high passes. There are few low-level roads, and most of the settlements of Vestfirðir are isolated by road during the winter.

There is little land suitable for agriculture, and yet as in the other fjord areas of northern and eastern Iceland, settlements were established during the *Landnam* period of AD 870–950 even in coastal locations which nowadays seem to be singularly uncomfortable. The basis for settlement was originally as much maritime as agricultural; settlers established homesteads in coastal locations which had fresh water, a little farming land, nearby summer pastures, a beach for hauling up a boat and offshore waters where fish stocks were plentiful. The region was occupied by powerful feuding families during the early Middle Ages, and it was renowned for its remoteness and for the harsh lifestyle which it imposed upon the early generations of settlers. Some of the remoter farming and fishing settlements have now disappeared, but most of them still remain. Those with the most favourable sites have grown into the fishing towns and villages of the present day.

Population change

At present there are thirteen towns and villages in Vestfirðir, located for the most part in the western fjords (Fig. 20.1). Most of

Fig. 20.1 Map of Vestfirðir.
showing the main fjords,
settlements, plateau areas and
roads.

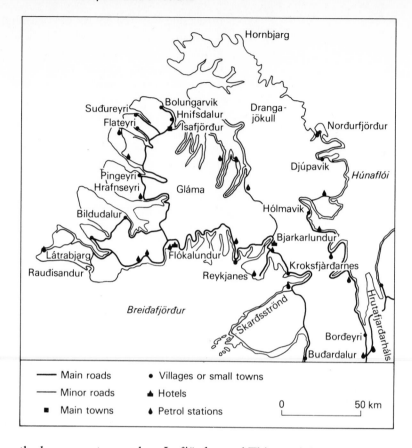

the larger centres such as Isafjörður and Thingeyri developed in the
decade 1850–60 with the abolition of the Danish trade monopoly
and the growth of the commercial fishing industry. Others, such as
Bolungarvik, owe most of their growth to the present century.
Outside the urban districts there are some 250 farms, scattered
around the coastline and almost always located beneath the 100 m
contour. Most of the settlement sites have been continuously occupied for over 1,000 years, but in this extremely marginal environment man is very much at the mercy of nature and there have been
a number of phases of violent population change. Unlike other parts
of Iceland, Vestfirðir has been free of volcanic eruptions and
catastrophic floods in historical time, but other factors have precipi-
tated population change just as effectively. In particular, periods
of prosperity and growth, hardship and decline can be related to
climatic oscillations. The most dramatic fluctuations of population
occurred during the Little Ice Age (see Ch. 4). Each of the smaller
climatic deteriorations of the period 1500–1840 was accompanied
by widespread famine and depopulation, and during this period the
Icelandic population was decimated. From a peak of 75,000 in about
AD 1200 the population of the country dropped erratically to its
lowest ebb of 34,000 in 1709. As in other parts of Iceland, many of

the remoter farmsteads of Vestfirđir were abandoned. In the country as a whole at this time there were about 3,500 assessed farms and about the same number of abandoned ones. Later on some of the deserted territories, which had been ravaged by volcanic eruptions or floods but also by overgrazing or mismanagement, were reclaimed and revitalized. In the later part of the nineteenth century the Icelandic population grew to a total of 78,000. The position remained stable until about 1930, but then rural decline set in again, and the flight from the land has continued to this day.

The flight from the land

To an outsider the scale of Vestfirđir's rural depopulation might seem insignificant, for the population is small even by the standards of north European marginal areas. Out of a total of about 8,500 persons, some 86 per cent live in towns or villages. The largest town, Isafjörđur, has a population of 3,100, while the two next largest (Bolungarvik and Vatneyri) each have a population of about 1,000. All of the other towns have populations of less than 500.

The rural population is widely scattered, and it is in the rural community that the most distressing numerical decline has been experienced. While the population of the towns and villages has remained almost static over the last 40 years, approximately 2,000 people have left the land. Most of these have been young people, and most of them have migrated to Reykjavik, the Icelandic megalopolis. Between 1932 and 1970, over 330 out of 561 farms were abandoned. There was a drastic decline in the rural population of the peninsula west of Patreksfjörđur, and also around the inner parts of the Isafjarđardjup fjord country. On the south shore of Arnarfjörđur, and in the southern fjords around Kollafjörđur, the population declined by more than 70 per cent between 1940 and 1973 (Fig. 20.2). In some of the country parishes the 1973 population was less than half that of the early eighteenth century.

The reasons for the decline of the rural population have been relatively straightforward. In recent decades in particular the traditional subsistence economy failed to give an income as high as that which could be obtained in the towns or on deep-sea fishing vessels. The sheer hardship and boredom of life in the country districts was in sharp contrast to the relative comfort and the social delights of towns like Isafjörđur and Patreksfjörđur. And in some areas the rural decline can be linked to the end of small-scale fishing operations in the fjords. Many of the farmers of Önundarfjörđur, Dyrafjörđur and Arnarfjörđur depended upon the local cod and herring fishery for their livelihood, and many of them had inadequate land to provide even self-sufficiency in agriculture. In Arnarfjörđur, for example, large-scale farm abandonment occurred during the period 1935–50 as a direct result of the start of shrimp

Fig. 20.2 Map of population change in Vestfirđir during the period 1940–73. (After Sigfus Jonsson)

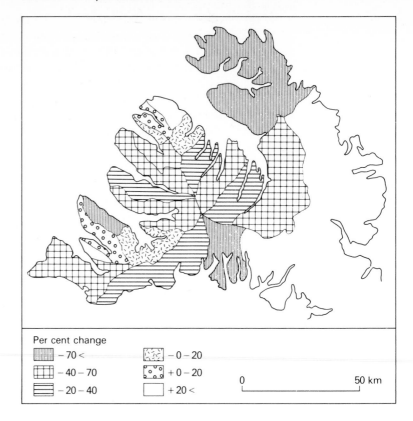

Per cent change

	– 70 <			– 0 – 20
	– 40 – 70			+ 0 – 20
	– 20 – 40			+ 20 <

0   50 km

fishing in the fjord based at Bildudalur. There was an unanticipated mass slaughter of young cod in the shrimp-nets, and the way of life of the fjordside farming – fishing community was accidentally and tragically altered within the space of a few years. With no fish to catch, and with inadequate land for the growing of winter fodder, very many farmers were forced to sell up and leave their family homes. Their small patches of land were incorporated into the other farms which now had enough land to make farming operations viable.

The case of Norđur – Isafjarđarsysla

The most severe population decline of all has occurred in the province of Norđur – Isafjarđarsysla, centred upon the harsh territory around Jökulfirđir. Here, in the period 1932–70, 82 out of 88 farms were abandoned. Now there is no permanent habitation north of Unadsdalur on the east coast of Isafjarđardjup and no settlement north of Ofeigsfjörđur on the coast of Hunafloi. Hornstrandir, the most magnificient coastline of Iceland, has been left to the birds. In fertile valleys and inlets throughout this area there are small deserted settlements such as Ađalvik and Grunnavik. In some, the old farm buildings have been maintained by families who feel that these are the places where their roots lie; they return like pilgrims every summer from their modern homes in Reykjavik and Isafjörd-ur to enjoy a solitude and a sense of history which is theirs by right. Elsewhere dereliction has set in, and groups of farm buildings which were vibrant with life just thirty years ago are now reduced to disintegrating skeletons of concrete and timber clothed only with bits and pieces of corrugated iron, broken stone and blocks of turf. There are old trackways, drainage ditches, gates and fences, bridges and sheepfolds – now all but covered by a mantle of green. Where sheep once devoured everything edible there is now wild unin-habited growth and a lush flora of unexpected beauty.

Probably the most dramatic single event in the recent settlement history of Vestfirðir was the abandonment of Hesteyri. This village, established in about 1894 on the northern shore of Jökulfirðir, was based initially upon a whaling station built by a Norwegian company. Following a drastic decline in whale stocks, shore stations were banned in 1916 and the factory was turned over to the processing of herring. In 1930 there were three herring vessels based at Hesteyri, and the factory was also supplied by upwards of twenty other vessels. There were abundant herring stocks in Isafjarðardjup and in Jökulfirðir, and the factory was a thriving concern. The population of Hesteyri was about 180, of whom 80 were permanent inhabitants and the rest temporary workers at the factory. Besides the factory accomodation there were seventeen houses, mostly made of good Norwegian timber, as well as numerous outbuildings and a small church. The population of the whole district around Jökulfirðir (i.e. the parishes of Slettuhreppur and Grunnavikur-hreppur) was about 650, and there were other small communities also further to the east, notably at Furufjörður (population 82) and

Fig. 20.3 The little church at Furufjörður is still kept in good repair almost fifty years after the abandonment of the settlement.

Reykjafjörður (Fig. 20.3). After 1936 the herring stocks declined, and although there was a boom year in 1940 the factory did not reopen at the beginning of 1941 season. It never opened again. Hesteyri declined rapidly, and the harsh living conditions in this remote and difficult area caused a sharp increase in migration from the small farms also. One by one they were abandoned, and in 1952 the last inhabitants left Hesteyri and Aðalvik. Grunnavik was abandoned in October 1962. Not for the first time, a complete Icelandic community was dead.

Towards the future

Today the people of Vestfirðir enjoy greater prosperity than ever before. The spectre of famine no longer stalks the land; those families who have remained in farming make a reasonable living, helped by grants and loans for land drainage and agricultural improvements. Farming is now a strictly commercial operation, based upon the supply of milk, butter, meat and eggs to the towns and villages. In Isafjarðardjup and Breiðafjörður regular ferryboats collect milk and other produce from the farming community and also deliver mail, spare parts for agricultural machinery, groceries and a host of other goods. The *Fagranes* of Isafjörður calls several times a week at remote farms and isolated jetties (Fig. 20.4), and it even takes passengers and milk-churns aboard from small open boats which pull alongside. But while the rural community seems to be stabilizing, the visitor to Vestfirðir cannot fail to see the dereliction in the countryside. There is a deep-seated fear that this dereliction will spread to the towns, which are at present the real centres of prosperity. Everybody knows about the

Fig. 20.4 The ferry-boat *Fagranes* delivering stores and picking up milk at one of the small jetties of Isafjarðardjup.

Fig. 20.5 (a) The small 'harvester' used for collecting help from the shallow waters of Breiðafjörður; (b) the drying cabinet in the Reykholar seaweed-drying plant. Locally collected kelp is dried and milled before shipment to Scotland, where it is processed for the extraction of alginate.

life and the death of Hesteyri, and everybody suspects that the root cause of the abandonment of the village was the mismanagement and eventual extermination of local herring stocks.

The most fundamental of Vestfirðir's problems is its desperate shortage of resources. The region has no exploitable minerals, hardly any sources of geothermal power and very little potential for hydro-electric power generation. It is not even self-sufficient in agricultural produce, and 1 million litres of milk for human consumption has to be flown in from Reykjavik each year. The only new industry is a small seaweed-drying plant using geothermal power at Reykholar, on the south coast (Fig. 20.5). Probably the most valuable resource in Vestfirðir is its scenery, for its spacious fjord country compares favourably with that of western Norway. But tourism has not been promoted on any scale, and the communities of Vestfirðir remain utterly dependent upon a single resource and a single way of life. That resource lies at sea, and the way of life is fishing.

If it were not for the continuing employment provided by the fishing industry several of the region's towns and villages would by now have disappeared. Isafjörður, the regional capital, is least dependent upon fishing; out of a total working population of 1,437 only about one-third is employed in fishing and fish-processing, and there is a sizeable group of service sector employees. Elsewhere fishing provides virtually the whole basis for life. The small towns and villages generally have their own communally owned trawlers and privately owned smaller inshore vessels, and they have their own fish-processing plants. At Tunga (Talknafjörður) the working population of 118 includes no less than 77 persons employed in fishing or fish-processing. At Suðureyri the working population of 281 includes 211 in the same sector. This is repeated over and over again in the other settlements. All of the towns are deficient in alternative sources of employment. All of them have over-capacity in terms of fishing vessels, and the twelve fish-processing plants in the region could handle 90,000 tonnes of fish per year instead of the current catch of about 50,000 tonnes. At Thingeyri the processing plant is currently used at less than 20 per cent of its capacity, and there is severe under utilization of the plant at Bildudalur also. Some of the slack has been taken up by increasing scallop fishery in recent years, and shrimp-fishing is also important in some of the fjords; but there is no guarantee that these activities will continue for more than a few seasons. The fish stocks which supplied the Heysteyri factory disappeared over the space of four years, and this could well happen elsewhere.

There is a widespread recognition among both local and national government officials that the economy of Vestfirðir is much too dependent upon fishing – but what is to be done? To ensure the survival of the fishing towns some say that there must be virtually exclusive use of the local fishing-grounds by local vessels. The fishing banks around Vestfirðir are capable of providing 140,000–180,000 tonnes (mostly of cod) per year, and yet up to 66 per cent of the annual catch has traditionally been taken by foreign vessels or Icelandic vessels from other fishing ports. Local people believe that they must be allowed to use their own vessels more efficiently close to home, and that they must be allowed to handle the majority of the catch even if landed by 'outside' vessels. However, while Iceland now has greater control than ever before upon the fisheries within her 200 mile (322 km) limit, the tough conservation measures needed over the next few years will hit the communities of Vestfirðir hard. For the moment profits are high, but the local economy is as unstable as ever, and the future is uncertain. Ghost towns are not pleasant places, and the Icelanders do not want any more of them. To keep towns like Flateyri and Bildudalur alive, they would undoubtedly go to war again.

Suggested reading

The outer districts of Iceland

Gislason 1973; Griffiths 1969; John 1978; Kidson 1974; Magnusson 1977; Nordal and Kristinsson 1967; Phillips 1980; Shepherd 1867; Stefansson 1974; Stone 1971b.

Chapter 21   Vestmanna, a Faroese town

Vestmanna, one of the larger settlements of the Faroe Islands, has a population of over 1,200. The town is located in the north-west of the island of Streymoy on the north side of Vestmannasund, and it enjoys the benefit of a magnificent natural harbour (Fig. 21.1). The built-up area covers a sweep of hillside on the north-west side of the harbour, and the southerly aspect was no doubt originally of great importance for the success of farming operations in the town's *bøur* (cf. Ch. 7). Deep water runs into the harbour from Vestman-

Fig. 21.1 The site of Vestmanna on the island of Streymoy. The town enjoys the advantages of one of the best harbours in the Faroe Islands.

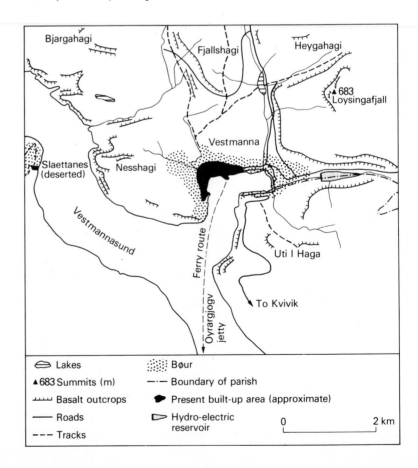

nasund, enabling ships of 10 m draught to approach the town's jetty. The sheltered deep water and the convenient location of the fjord near the north-west coast of the Faroes were important factors in the growth of Vestmanna, and it has always been known as a 'good winter harbour' well placed for vessels seeking shelter from westerly or northerly gales. The town is the base for the small ferry which plies acrosss Vestmannasund, linking the islands of Vagar and Streymoy. All passengers and traffic moving between Torshavn and the airport have to use this ferry and pass through the town. The town is thus well located within the Faroese network of route-ways. However, its growth has been somewhat restricted as a result of the lack of level building land for industrial, commercial and housing developments. The lower slopes around the harbour are best suited for modern building and for the use of agricultural machinery, and inevitably the town has developed most rapidly along the shoreline towards both the south and the east of the original *bygd*.

The economy

Agriculture

The main features of land use are typical of many Faroese in settlements. The *bøur* extends round the fjord, but the north-west section is better kept than those parts close to the town; this section was enlarged by a new intake from the *hagi* during the eighteenth century when the restriction on fishing and trade under the Danish trade monopoly caused the population to come perilously close to famine. At the same time terraces were constructed on parts of the *bøur* in order to increase and improve the cultivated area. These terraces are now in a poor state of repair; their soils are leached and denuded, and they are overgrown with weeds. The old wall of the *bøur* can still be seen, and outside it there are still a few potato patches as reminders of the period of agricultural expansion. The land to the east of the town is of moderate slope but here the cultivated area has declined sharply in recent years. The small fields have been badly kept, and glaciated rock knobs projecting through the thin soil indicate how difficult cultivation must always have been.

Nowadays agriculture provides a full-time occupation for only two *Kongsbøndi* farmers who lease much of the land in the central and north-western parts of the *bøur* and who run most of the sheep on the *hagi*. The rest of the land is owned by *oðalsbøndur*, who keep their land out of tradition and interest, but who do not regard it as an important source of income. In the 1930s their previously complicated ownership of small strips of land was rationalized by *utskift* legislation, and the resulting more compact parcels of land enabled many farmers to double their head of cattle and use modern agricultural machinery for the first time. For a while there was a great increase in farm productivity, but in recent decades there has been a decline in farming and a reduction of the cultivated area as the town has grown. Many of the lower and more fertile plots have already been used as housing sites, and many more are earmarked for building development. The *Kongsbøndi* farmers who remain are somewhat restricted in their ability to improve their productivity because of the unwillingness of the *oðalsbøndi* landowners to part with their land.

The agricultural traditions of Vetnmanna die hard. Hay and potatoes are the only crops, and no proper rotation is practised. Cattle are very few in number, and since most dairy products have to be imported they are scarce and expensive in the town. In contrast, before the Second World War every family owned its own cow, so that milk, cream, butter and cheese were plentiful. Nowadays 3,000 sheep are run on the *hagi* with an annual cull of about 1,000. Many carcasses are sold locally, and mutton is one of the main items in the family diet. The carcasses are hung up whole in cold stores in households to provide meat during the winter. Agricultural innovations have been few and far between in recent years, although small mechanical cultivators and mowing machines have taken much of the drudgery out of farming on small plots and terraces. Norwegian-style hay-drying racks are quite commonplace in the fields. Some of the hay crop is turned into silage, but agriculture on such a small scale as this cannot support the major investments needed for harvesting machinery and silage containers.

Fishing

The sea has now become completely dominant as far as the economy of Vestmanna is concerned. The man who makes a living at sea is no longer desperate to return home for the haymaking after 29 July, although for those who do remain behind the Olavsøka festival is still a time of great family get-togethers and prolonged merriment. For the majority of families the fishing industry and its associated activities are all-important as the providers of employment and the sources of income. Vestmanna has been in the forefront of the fishing industry since Faroes Jack, a Faroese who learned the techniques of trawling while working with the Scottish fleet, introduced trawling to the town in the 1930s. It was not until after the Second World War that other settlements began commercial fishing with trawl-nets. The village owns an 800 d.w.t. trawler (with a crew of forty-five) and a German seine-net. There are also smaller trawlers which provide employment for about fifty men. During the summer months as many as 100 men are away for periods of up to 6 months in Greenland waters, fishing intensively from small boats to stock the larger vessels which call at the Greenland base ports. About twenty men are employed at sea on smaller fishing vessels, and about the same number work with foreign fishing and merchant fleets. The smallest family boats are now used only in local waters for private purposes, and the fish caught from them provides only a small part of the total catch.

The Vestmanna fish factory provides regular work for up to twenty persons, but many more are employed in season. The herring fleets of other countries land catches, and in 1967 36,000 barrels were handled. Dried cod and salted herring are exported directly to Catholic countries. In the shipyard the facilities for shipbuilding and ship-repairing are slow and outdated, but there is always repair and maintenance work to be done on home-based vessels or on visiting trawlers damaged at sea. About sixty men are employed in the yard, but the weather is a serious hazard and there are few facilities for indoor work.

Employment

As indicated above, most of the job opportunities in the town are associated with the sea and the fishing industry. The only other significant employment is provided on building and road-making projects, domestic and commercial services such as carpentry and plumbing, and in shops, banks and offices. These activities provide about 200 jobs in total. Probably the town's labour-force is in the region of 500, although accurate figures are difficult to obtain because there is much casual labour and part-time working.

The economy of the town has developed along typical Faroese lines. The service sector is important, but Vestmanna lacks the broad base of service activities found in the capital, Torshavn. The income from the sea is high; fishermen in the town earn at least £5,000 a year, and skippers can earn very much more. The cash inflow has stimulated the service sector, and there are three banks and several modern general and specialized stores. The men seek employment during their months on land, and work in road-making, building (often in Torshavn) or in the fish factory. These extra jobs all provide a better income than the returns on the small family plots of land in and around the town. A few additional jobs are provided in local workshops dealing mostly with imported semi-finished products which need to be assembled or packaged. There are no proper manufacturing concerns.

The population of 1,200 has increased rapidly in recent decades, but employment opportunities have not kept pace. The proportion of young people in the town is very high, and the new school can hardly accomodate the growing numbers. Seasonal unemployment is caused by the return of men from the sea, and in part by the sociological impact of new wealth in an isolated society which reduces the need for young people in particular to work hard and

Fig. 21.2 Vertical air photograph of Vestmanna, showing the street pattern and other morphological features. (Photo: Reproduced with permission (A.425/83) of Geodaetisk Institut, Denmark).

earn a living. The employment situation is also affected by the town's meagre natural resources. Fishing, the mainstay of the economy, needs few special skills and only a turnover of labour. Young people are brought up to expect something more from life than Vestmanna can offer, and many now desire an income from a less exacting occupation than deep-sea fishing. Many leave school to finish their studies or to train in Copenhagen, and they seldom return. The usual pattern is for young people to go first to Torshavn and then to Denmark. The social impact of the standard of living is visible in new status symbols such as motor cars, which on the rough roads last on average two years and provide ample opportunities for motor mechanics to practise their craft! Taxi drivers find that more of their trade comes from the ferry across to Vagar than from the local inhabitants, and this is an indication of the high level of car ownership.

The morphology of the town

The modernization of the economy has gone hand in hand with great morphological changes within the town. The early growth was in an area near the harbour, where the roads and alleys are still narrow and winding despite the almost complete reconstruction of the town since the Second World War. The major streets run parallel to the shore, and the street pattern shows close similarities with some of the towns and villages of western Norway. The town was once quite a compact bay-head settlement, but it has now become much more elongated in form. The southward and eastward extensions of the built-up area display a natural preference on the part of the householders for fjordside sites; but the alignments of streets are also restricted by the terrain and partly determined by the availability (or lack of it) of agricultural land within the *bøur*.

Most of the town's new houses have been built on the sites of older buildings, but few of them have made use of the original bases of basalt blocks. Some of the building materials come from a local concrete-block factory. Only one old turf-roofed house remains, towards the upper edge of the town, but turf roofs are now becoming popular again among wealthy local people who are building new architect-designed houses. A recent morphological development has been the extension of gardens at the back of the houses where public land or *bøur* once existed. Potatoes, rhubarb and some vegetables are grown, and poultry are kept. Some expensive new housing has been built on the high road and round the shore. The harbour area was given a new jetty in 1952, but the family boat-houses remain in position along the shore, occupying sites that have been in continuous use for 1,000 years, or so.

The council has recognized the dangers of haphazard growth in the restricted physical setting of Vestmanna and has prepared plans for a phased zonation of building. Future building developments will take place in three stages. Public and service buildings have been concentrated along the shore road, with the consequent beginnings of a high street (Fig. 21.3). It can be seen from the map that the public buildings are still clustered in the harbour area, maintaining the original nucleus as the town centre. New enterprises are opening along the shore, while residential building has spread on to small, level areas behind and above the shore road. There is a complicated and interwoven relationship between the unaltered *bøur* and the built-up area; the extent of the *bøur* has played a large part in restricting development to a belt along the shore. The town plan is designed with the intention of preserving as much cultivated land as possible by regulating expansion, and it emphasizes the existing trend towards an elongated shoreline settlement.

Problems and prospects

At the present time Vestmanna is changing far more rapidly than many of the smaller Faroese settlements. The economy has altered out of all recognition as a result of the rise of large-scale commercial

Fig. 21.3 Map of services along the shore road of Vestmanna, showing how this road is becoming the main shopping and business street of the town.

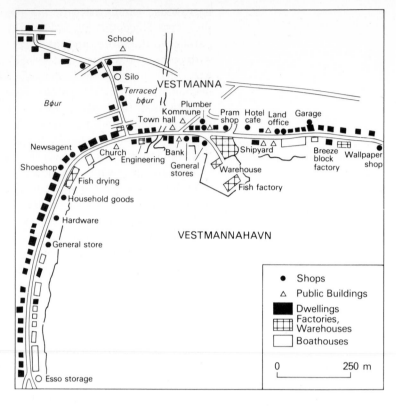

fishing, and traditional farming and other communally organized activities have declined sharply as cash incomes have risen. Hence the traditional activities of a Faroese *bygd* (see Ch. 7) play a minor and diminishing role in the town as the community's real wealth is obtained from the sea. Some local people are frightened by the new economic vulnerability which has come with the rise of the fishing industry and the abandonment of a broad-based and largely self-sufficient way of life. The eventual death of the North Atlantic fishing industry, which many people half expect as a result of over-fishing, could well lead to the death of the town. The older people argue the merits of a broad-based economy but they fear that it is too late to return to the old Faroese lifestyle. The affluent young seamen of today are quite aware of what is happening. Most of them are well educated and widely travelled, and they recognize the problems of exporting fish to countries such as Spain which are intent on building their own fishing industries and increasing home supplies. They know that the local fishing industry has to be increasingly adaptable in its methods of catching and processing fish if it is to remain competitive.

At the present time, the income of the town is essentially 'imported', for many heads of families have to leave the community (whether to fish off Greenland or to work in Torshavn or Copenhagen) to obtain a good living. It does not seem possible to generate more local wealth through services, for the town is too small to sustain a great growth in this economic sector. The decline of agriculture and the spectacular rise of living standards indicate an increasingly urban – industrial outlook within the community, and local councillors believe that the time is ripe for investment in manufacturing concerns. Vestmanna is in a good position to participate in the manufacturing sector of the Faroese economy because of its location, the experience of the work-force, the presence of local capital, the nearby hydro-electric power plant, and the small industries which already exist. Communications are also good, and Vestmanna is easily accessible both from Torshavn and from the airport on the island of Vagar. There is also easy access to the open sea. New entrepreneurial ability, such as was seen in the fishing industry during the 1930s, could make a great difference to the town.

The council has recognized most of the local problems, but solutions are not easy to find. The local population is basically conservative; the older generation, which has already seen the old way of life almost swept away by the tide of progress, does not feel any sense of urgency to change the local economy more rapidly than is absolutely necessary. After all, local incomes are high by Faroese standards, and emigration, although publicly lamented, has long been accepted as a part of the Faroese way of life. There are still a few people who believe that the traditional activities of Faroese people and the traditional values of Faroese society, as described in Chapter 7 of this book, had a great deal to commend them. With the international energy crisis and its associated economic recession beginning to make an impact, it is as well that the Faroese virtues of self-reliance and corporate responsibility, and the Faroese skills of community self-sufficiency, are not forgotten. The Viking tradition may prove to be as useful in the year AD 2000 as it was 1,000 years ago.

Suggested reading

Faroese urban and rural economy

Guttesen 1970; Jacobsen 1953; Joensen, 1980; John 1971; Kampp 1967b, 1973; Landt 1810; Magnusson 1973; Nielung 1968; O'Dell 1957; Phillips 1980; Rying 1965; Small 1967–68; Trap 1968; West 1970–71, 1972; Wheeler *et al.* 1978; Williamson 1948.

Part V Unity and stress

Chapter 22 Scandinavian expressions of unity

Once upon a time an oil-rig foreman was asked if it was true that several Swedes were at work on his platform. 'How many Swedes work here?' he was asked. He thought about it long and hard. 'Well', he replied eventually, 'about half of them, maybe.'

'Have you heard about the Norwegian who was so stupid that even his own countrymen noticed it?'

'Do you know how to recognize a Swede who's working on a North Sea drilling rig? No? He's the one who throws breadcrumbs to the helicopters.'

The Norwegians and the Swedes obtain endless amusement from telling jokes about one another. And there are plenty of jokes doing the rounds in Scandinavia about the Danes, the Finns, the Icelanders and the Faroese as well (Fig. 22.1). Some of the jokes are barbed while others are quite innocent, but they are very seldom malicious. The Scandinavians are friends, relatives and neighbours, and jokes about one another are as inevitable as the jokes bandied back and forth between the English, the Scots, the Welsh and the Irish.

Scandinavia deserves its unofficial title as 'the quiet corner of Europe'. The five countries dealt with in this book have contrived to live at peace with one another since 1814, and they have also managed, for the most part, to avoid disharmony with their non-Scandinavian neighbours. The 'special relationship' which was propagated by students all over Scandinavia during the middle part of the last century has survived so far for 166 years, in spite of severe stresses and strains at various times. The most serious events were the Prussian–Austrian invasion of Schleswig-Holstein in 1864 during which the Danes expected, but did not receive, military support from Norway and Sweden; the Norwegian declaration of independence of 1905, which brought Sweden and Norway to the brink of war; and especially the events of the Second World War. During the Finnish Winter War many Swedes, acting as individuals, helped the Finns to resist the Russian invasion, but during the final phase of the war both Sweden and Norway refused to allow Anglo-French forces to pass through Scandinavia to the relief of Finland.

317

Fig. 22.1 Gentle jokes at the expense of the Norwegians, the Icelanders and the Finns. Like all good jokes, they contain more than a few grains of truth. (Courtesy Willy Breinholst)

As the world's foremost whalers Norwegians never say no to a whale steak . . .

The Icelander's capacity for exploiting his hot springs is remarkable . . .

The terrors of the Sauna are of vital importance to the Finn . . .

From 1940 to 1945 both Norway and Denmark were occupied by the Nazis, while Iceland was occupied by Britain and then by the United States. In both Denmark and Norway resistance movements were active, and severe hardships were experienced by both peoples. Finland suffered most of all, finding herself first of all at war with Russia as an ally of the Nazis, and then attempting to expel the German troops who adopted a 'scorched earth' policy which devastated Finnish Lapland. Throughout the war Sweden remained neutral, unoccupied and unharmed, and the huge resentment which this caused among her neighbours has still not entirely disappeared.

But in spite of everything the 'Northern Fellowship' survives and even thrives. Five countries which differ greatly in their size, geographical characteristics and historical traditions have found sufficient in common to bind themselves together by an ever more complex web of invisible ties; at the same time each one has managed to preserve and even enhance its own feelings of individuality and independence. This may seem, to a non-Scandinavian, to be something of an enigma, and in the remainder of this chapter it is worthwhile to examine some of the expressions of Nordic unity.

Nordic cooperation

In 1856 King Oscar I of Sweden declared to a mass meeting of students in Uppsala: 'Henceforth, war between Nordic brothers is impossible.' War has been staved off, not just because of the cultural links between the Scandinavian states but because of a determination to look for unity through *practical* measures. Practical Nordic cooperation has a history which stretches back to 1872, when a customs agreement was made between Denmark, Norway and Sweden. At the same time a conference of lawyers initiated the cooperation in the fields of law and legislation which has grown steadily ever since. Later on there was cooperation in the fields of labour relations and social policy. The scale of cooperation increased after the First World War; government bodies began to cooperate on all sorts of matters, and at a different level informal and formal cultural links were established, for example with the formation of 'Norden associations' in each country. In spite of the divisive effects of the Second World War links were established again soon after the return to peace, and the war provided a spur for the creation of a common approach to foreign policy matters. As it became apparent that the Soviet Union was in an expansionist mood there was a strong feeling in the Nordic countries that they should form some sort of political or military alliance, but from a military point of view this proved impossible. Sweden was determined to pursue its policy of 'strong neutrality' which had carried it unscathed through two world wars; Finland could do nothing which might upset its communist neighbour and eventually signed a pact of mutual aid and friendship with the Soviet Union; and Denmark, Norway and Iceland felt that the only route towards a lasting peace was through membership of NATO. In 1972 Denmark joined the EEC, thereby apparently shifting its centre of interest from Scandinavia to the European mainland.

Hence the arrangements for Nordic cooperation are apparently very superficial and informal. There is no military alliance, no federation, no political grouping similar to that of the EEC and no pooling of resources. The ties between the five countries are remarkably easy to untie, and most of them are of a strictly informal nature. Maybe the most important feature of Nordic cooperation is its embodiment of a great mutual respect for national sovereignty, and this means much to the 'young' countries of Iceland and the Faroes, Norway and Finland. With national autonomy guaranteed and unimpeded, the web of cooperation which now exists in Scandinavia offers no threats and involves few sacrifices, and it is not only accepted but also elaborated throughout a wide cross-section of society. The range of cooperative activities is so large that a comprehensive listing of them would be a daunting task; in Iceland, for example, a small country widely separated from Fennoscandia by both distance and language, there are at least 150 organizations specifically devoted to Nordic links of one sort or another, ranging from scientific bodies to associations for contact between students, from trades union associations to cultural exchanges, from twin towns to farming societies.

Government cooperation

One of the best-known bodies which exists to foster good relations between the Scandinavian states is the Nordic Council, set up in 1952. This is an advisory body of the Nordic parliaments and governments (including the Faroes and Åland), and it deals with questions concerning cooperation in the economic, legislative, social and cultural fields and also regarding environmental protection and communications. It acts by adopting recommendations on the advice of standing committees and by using national delegations to see that various cooperative measures are actually implemented out by the member governments. The Nordic Council is no mere talking shop; its meetings (normally held for one week per year) are attended by prime ministers and foreign ministers as a matter of course, and ministerial sessions and a whole range of informal contacts between delegations take place throughout the year. It would be most unusual for any of the Scandinavian governments to shelve a matter raised by the Nordic Council. Matters discussed by the Council include projects such as the Öresund bridge, new roads between Norway and Sweden, and common ferry services. By tradition the Nordic Council has abstained from discussing foreign policy or military affairs, but during the 1970s touched on a number of controversial issues with wide implications, such as the Finnish President Kekkonen's plan for a nuclear-free zone in Scandinavia.

The general objectives for Nordic cooperation were laid down in the Helsinki Agreement of 1962. This was revised in 1971, when the decision was taken to set up the Nordic Council of Ministers. The Council is now well established, and it is a powerful decision-making body at a Nordic level. Its jurisdiction extends over the whole area of Nordic cooperation, and its resolutions can be binding on the member governments. Its composition varies according to the matters being discussed, but each member state has a Minister for Cooperation. Under the Council of Ministers there are committees of senior officials, and the civil servants involved are guaranteed their independence under an agreement signed in 1973. There is now a permanent secretariat with offices in Oslo (for general affairs) and in Copenhagen (for cultural affairs).

The results of Nordic cooperation in the legislative field are impressive. In some areas the laws of the five countries have been almost completely harmonized, whereas in other areas agreement has been reached on certain basic legal rules or principles. Cooperation has been particularly fruitful in the fields of private and commercial law. Parts of the law concerning families (e.g. concerning parentage, marriage and inheritance) have been harmonized. Laws concerning matters such as contracts, purchase of goods, instalment purchases, insurance policies and bills of exchange are now virtually identical in Denmark, Norway, Sweden and Finland. The same can be said of the laws on copyright, patents, trademarks and industrial design and of the laws on transportation and maritime activities. Progress is being made on the harmonization of criminal law also, although this is an area in which differences of philosophy on crime and punishment give rise to formidable obstacles. Consumer protection laws are being given a high priority. A citizen of one Nordic nation can obtain citizenship of another Nordic nation with relative ease. Immigrants can exercise political influence in the country of their adoption; even though they may be citizens of another country they may vote, and stand as candidates, in the municipal elections of the country where they are now living. A convicted person may choose to serve his or her sentence in a country different from that in which the sentence was made.

Since 1954 there has been a common Nordic labour market, giving citizens the right to work in another Nordic country on exactly the same terms as that country's national work-force. No work permit is needed. There is a continuous exchange of information between government bodies on job vacancies, training schemes, seasonal unemployment rates, the provision of technical and other skilled jobs, and employment problems concerning young people and those of retirement age. There is a joint declaration to the effect that equality between men and women is one of the most important goals in labour policy. There are on-going studies of the movement of capital and labour between one country and another, and it is widely recognized that these movements can create severe stresses between adjacent Nordic countries in particular. Since 1954 over one million migrations between the Nordic states have been registered, most of them between Finland and Sweden. Over 60 per cent of all foreign workers in Sweden come from the other Nordic countries, and Finns constitute the largest national group by far. In 1976 there were 118,000 of them working in Sweden.

Labour market and social policies have been matched by a Nordic Passport Union, which since 1954 has allowed Nordic citizens to travel between the Scandinavian countries without presenting passports. The Nordic countries are also committed to the coordination of customs regulations. The frontiers between Sweden and Norway and Sweden and Finland (the only land frontiers within Scandinavia) are remarkably 'open'; at road crossings there is only one group of customs officers on duty, carrying out customs control on behalf of both countries at the same time. Joint rules also regulate the control of road traffic, traffic shipped between Nordic countries and cargoes carried between one country and another. As far as possible, export and import procedures have been simplified, and common Nordic customs forms are now widely used.

Cultural cooperation

The far-reaching similarity of Nordic cultural traditions, language and forms of government has been the mainspring of the cooperation on cultural matters which has existed for over 150 years both at an official and an unofficial level. A Nordic Cultural Commission was established in 1947, and in 1971 a Cultural Agreement was signed with the aim of developing cultural contacts of all sorts – for example in the fields of education, research, literature, theatre, cinema and television. There is now a common fund for cultural cooperation, administered via the Secretariat of the Nordic Council of Ministers in Copenhagen. In the educational field there is now coordination of syllabuses and agreement on the status of national examinations as qualifications for jobs in other countries. Permanent educational institutions include the Nordic People's Academy and the Nordic Institute for Community Planning. Joint scientific research is undertaken by, for example, the Nordic Institute for Theoretical Atomic Physics in Denmark and the Nordic Institute for Vulcanology in Reykjavik. There are Nordic Council prizes for literature and music. Finance is available for the exchange of artists and the translation of modern literature from one Scandinavian language to another. Permanent cultural institutions include Norden House in Reykjavik (Fig. 22.2), the Lapp Institute at Kautokeino in Norway, the Nordic House in Torshavn and the Nordic Arts Centre in Helsinki. Each year the Nordic Cultural Fund

Fig. 22.2 Norden House in Reykjavik, a cultural centre paid for by the Scandinavian countries jointly. (Photo: Nordic Council)

disburses over 8 million Dkr aiding spontaneous initiatives over the whole field of cultural activity. Since 1958 a jointly funded organization called Nordvision has helped to promote the exchange of programmes for TV and radio, and has also been involved in many joint productions. Attempts are also being made to increase the making of programmes for linguistic minorities (such as the Lapps and Faroese), and plans are afoot for the use of satellites in beaming television programmes simultaneously to all the viewers of the five countries.

Cooperation in industry and trade

In the immediate post-war period the Scandinavian states had far-advanced plans to dismantle all internal tariffs and form a Nordic common market or customs union. These plans were never realized, and Denmark, Norway and Sweden joined the UK, Portugal, Switzerland and Austria in the formation of the European Free Trade Association (EFTA). Finland became an associate member in 1961 and Iceland joined in 1970. Tariff walls for industrial products were dismantled within EFTA in 1967, in effect bringing into being a desired 'Common Nordic Market' which happened to include four non-Nordic states. Much more far-reaching cooperation, in a new economic union called NORDEK, was planned in the years 1968–70, but it never came into being. Although Denmark is the only Scandinavian state to belong to the EEC, the other Nordic countries have concluded EEC trade agreements, and in effect the tariff walls between the EFTA and EEC countries have now been largely removed. The only commodities still protected by tariff walls are certain sensitive items including paper products. In January 1980, Iceland completed the removal of its tariff walls which had restricted the import of EEC goods. In effect the Scandinavian states have managed, by one means or another, to built up intra-Nordic trade at an impressive rate (Table 22.1). Nowadays each Nordic country sends out at least a quarter of its total exports to other Nordic countries, and many firms have factories and subcontractors abroad but within the Scandinavian region.

In view of the overall shortage of raw materials and energy sup-

Table 22.1: Figures for intra-Nordic Trade: value of imports and exports in millions of US dollars. (After Nordic Statistical Secretariat, 1978)

Imports from	Year	Total	Imports to				
			Denmark	Finland	Iceland	Norway	Sweden
Denmark	1970	872.2		77.8	21.1	230.4	542.9
	1977	2,379.6		200.3	61.9	744.8	1,372.6
Finland	1970	578.6	128.5		4.3	88.0	357.8
	1977	2,045.4	413.3		11.4	439.6	1,191.1
Iceland	1970	27.3	10.6	4.2		2.5	10.0
	1977	46.5	11.4	11.3		10.2	13.6
Norway	1970	652.4	172.9	62.6	8.7		408.2
	1977	2,126.2	626.1	280.7	60.6		1,158.8
Sweden	1970	1,876.3	700.1	424.2	8.0	744.0	
	1977	5,124.0	1,738.1	1,017.3	42.6	2,326.0	

Exports to	Year	Total	Exports from				
			Denmark	Finland	Iceland	Norway	Sweden
Denmark	1970	947.4		94.2	11.3	176.6	665.3
	1977	2,676.0		291.6	10.1	569.3	1,805.0
Finland	1970	566.1	77.2		2.6	60.4	425.9
	1977	1,594.8	189.4		10.1	254.5	1,140.8
Iceland	1970	38.2	19.2	3.4		8.3	7.3
	1977	182.4	75.7	9.8		59.5	37.4
Norway	1970	1,058.1	235.4	85.2	2.4		735.1
	1977	3,604.4	744.3	417.1	9.3		2,433.7
Sweden	1970	1,311.5	555.5	348.5	9.8	397.7	
	1977	3,756.8	1,439.8	1,206.8	12.1	1,098.1	

plies in Scandinavia there is a strong incentive for cooperation in industrial consumption and production. As we have seen in Chapters 9 and 10, the discoveries of oil and gas off the Norwegian coast have given rise to a number of industrial cooperative ventures, and there is now an elaborate exchange of electric power via the distribution grids of the various states, coordinated by NORDEL. There is cooperation in the building industry, and industrial firms of all sizes have a multitude of contacts with other Scandinavian firms in matters to do with design and technology, production and investment, and marketing at home and abroad. One of the most influential cooperative enterprises is the Nordic Investment Fund, set up in 1973 to encourage the effective use of resources, and the elimination of duplicated effort, in the fields of environmental technolgy, energy research, transport technology and the use and conservation of natural resources.

A relatively recent addition to the web of contacts in the fields of business and industry is the Nordic Investment Bank, established in 1976. It is situated in Helsinki, and its function is to strengthen the economies of the Nordic states by granting loans for investments, making guarantees for investment projects and backing export initiatives.

Cooperation in communications

For many years agreements have existed to encourage cheaper and safer communications between the Nordic states. A treaty of cooperation in the field of transport and communications was brought into force in 1973. It is a general framework establishing the administrative machinery for cooperation, and the national transport ministers, operating under the umbrella of the Council of Ministers, are responsible for executing the treaty. A multilateral road transport agreement, signed in 1971, eliminates most obstacles to the free movement of goods by road and ferry between the five states. There are now uniform tariffs for the international movement of goods by rail. One of the best-known of all Scandinavian institutions is SAS (the Scandinavian Airlines System), formed by a merger of the airlines of Denmark, Norway and Sweden in 1951. It is now financed by both private and public capital from the three countries.

A postal union is in operation between the Nordic states. It costs no more to send letters and cables between the countries than within any of the countries. Nordic telephone charges are reduced, and there are also reductions in telex fees within Scandinavia.

Regional development

Nordic cooperation in the field of regional development aims at a consistent policy and the consistent use of planning methods especially in areas which are of interest to more than one state. For many years there has been an exchange of information in community planning matters, and also coordination of government grants for regional developments in adjacent communes which may be separated by national frontiers. As already mentioned in Chapter 17, the problems of Nordkalotten have encouraged considerable cooperation between the governments of Norway, Sweden and Finland in the far north, and other areas are now also demanding international attention in matters of planning. One of these is the so-called *ARKO-region* which runs from Kongsvinger in Norway to Arvika in Sweden, and which has a long history of cross-frontier contacts between Norwegians and Swedes. Communities on both sides of the frontier (but particularly in Sweden) in the ARKO-region have felt genuine grievance against their own governments for neglect in regional planning and investment, and many contacts between adjacent local authorities (dating in particular from the period since 1965) have been strengthened. For example, there is local cooperation in the provision of social services, the movement of labour, in tourism planning and in road policy. Another area which demands atention is *Midjebältet,* which lies astride the frontier between Trøndelag in Norway and Jämtland in Sweden. Here there is no large built-up area as in the ARKO-region, but remoteness from the centres of control in Oslo and Stockholm, and the natural contact which has always existed between Trondheim and the east via the natural routeway through the mountains, has given rise to local demands for coordinated planning particularly in the field of road transport. At the level of country planning there is already active cooperation, and the central governments of Norway and Sweden are backing the local attempts to coordinate industrial, transport and physical planning over a broad belt of country stretching from Trondheim to Östersund.

Örestad – an international vision

In the extreme south of Fennoscandia the Öresund region has become the centre of an elaborate vision. The vision is the new megalopolis of Örestad, and it typifies some of the problems confronting those who believe in large-scale cooperation between neighbour states in the fields of regional and transport planning and civil engineering.

The Danish–Swedish metropolitan region which encompasses Öresund contains some 2.8 million inhabitants. At its narrowest point the Sound is only 4 km wide, and during exceptionally hard winters it is possible to walk on the sea ice between Copenhagen and the shores of Sweden. Kastrup Airport, just outside Copenhagen, is one of the busiest international airports in the world, recording almost 164,000 take-offs and landings in 1977. There is another air-

Fig. 22.3 Motor vehicles transported by the Öresund ferry services between 1967 and 1977. Note the particularly steep rise in traffic on the Helsingør–Helsingborg route (Source: Nordic Statistical Secretariat 1978)

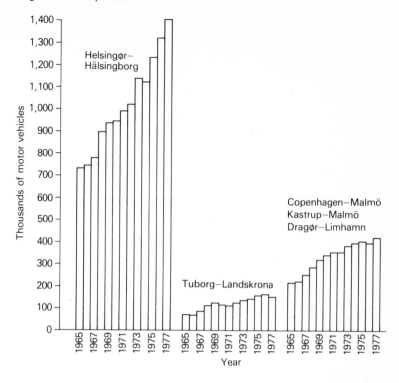

port at Sturup near Malmö. The Sound is one of the most congested waterways in the world. In 1977 more than 30,000 vessels passed through it, many of them calling at the main ports of the region – Copenhagen, Tuborg, Kastrup and Helsingør on the Danish side, and Malmö, Limhamn, Landskrona and Helsingborg on the Swedish side. But the greatest volume of traffic by far is cross-channel traffic on four main routes; Helsingør – Helsingborg in the north, Copenhagen – Landskrona in the middle part of the Sound, and Copenhagen – Malmö and Dragør – Limhamn in the south. In 1977 the ferries carried 25.5 million passengers between them, the great majority being carried between Helsingør and Helsingborg. In the same year about 2 million motor vehicles were transported, and the cross-channel ferries also carried 49,000 tonnes of goods traffic in railway wagons and 51,000 tonnes in lorries and trailers. Motor vehicle traffic is rising year by year on all the main ferry routes (Fig. 22.3).

Culturally and historically the Öresund region had a common background until 1658, with Skåne part of the core area of the Danish state. Later, the frontier was drawn along the Sound, and Skåne came increasingly to look upon itself as part of Sweden. There can be no doubt where its loyalties now lie, in spite of the very strong regional spirit which marks Skåne as very different from the northern parts of the country. However, in recent years the growth of the economy and the population of this metropolitan region has

327

Fig. 22.4 Maps showing how the villages to the west of Copenhagen were caught up by the spread of suburban development in the century 1860–1960. Since 1960 the rate of development has increased still further. (Source: Hansen 1960)

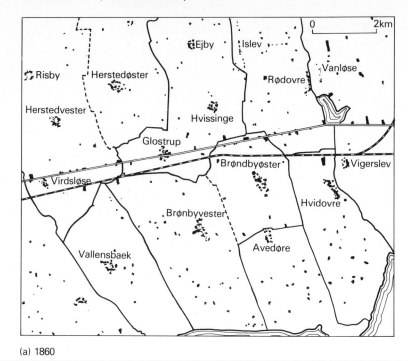

(a) 1860

(b) 1960

brought Greater Copenhagen and the Malmö district closer together, and there is now a multiplicity of links across the Sound.

Much of the incentive for a more formal linking of the two sides of the Sound has come from Denmark. Greater Copenhagen has grown so rapidly (Fig. 22.4), and its economy is now so strong that in some ways its links across the Sound are more important to its business community that its links across the Great Belt channel which separates Fyn from Sjaelland. The area now contains 40 per cent of the economically active population of Denmark, and there is a work-force of about 880,000 involved in manufacturing and the service industries. The centrifugal momentum of Copenhagen has now ensured that towns like Køge, Roskilde, Frederikssund, Hill-erød and Helsingør have been caught up in the 'dormitory belt'; the original aims of the Danish 'finger plan' for the capital (involving the preservation of green areas between fingers of development projecting westwards and northwards) have been largely abandoned under the inexorable pressure for development between the southern fingers in particular.

On the Swedish side of the Sound the Malmö–Lund area has now become a metropolitan region, containing over 1 million people and almost 13 per cent of the country's economically active population. Malmö itself is not only the centre of a rich agricultural area but also a manufacturing and business centre. Since the turn of the century it has spread at alarming speed across top-quality agricultural land towards the south and west, more than quadrupling its area in eighty years.

The historical traditions of Öresund, the demographic and economic characteristics of the area, and in particular the huge importance of the Sound itself from transport point of view, have combined to create a planner's paradise. In the 1960's the Nordic Council recommended that there should be joint Danish–Swedish planning in the Öresund region, and it also recommended a permanent traffic link between Copenhagen and Malmö and a new international airport – to serve both cities – on the small island of Saltholm. Planning bodies got to work, and the grand scheme gradually became more and more grand. The region acquired a new working name – Örestad. After site investigations, plans were made for a road tunnel from Copenhagen to Saltholm and a bridge from the island to Malmö. A rail tunnel was planned for the Helsingør–Hälsingborg crossing. Other important features of the plan included new motorway links running along both sides of the Sound, extensions of the built-up areas between Copenhagen and Helsingør and between Malmö and Lund; green belt or countryside conservation areas especially on the Swedish side of the Sound; and a joint nuclear power-station on the island of Ven (Fig. 22.5). The Danes made plans for the abandonment of Kastrup Airport and, hopefully, a move to the new Saltholm Airport around 1985. Various agreements were drawn up between the Swedish and Danish governments

Fig. 22.5 Map of the main planning proposals for Öresund.

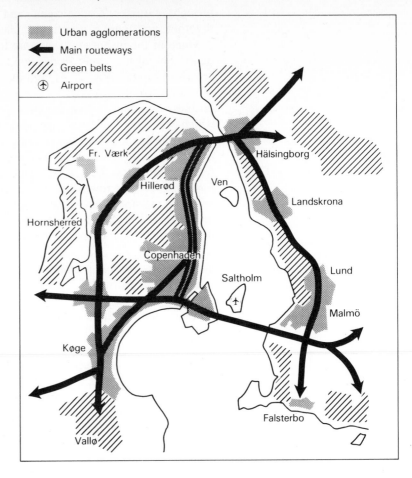

to cover these developments with the Swedes proving originally to be the most enthusiastic partners. However, while the arrangements were ratified (prematurely) by the Swedes, the Danes decided at the last moment to withhold their approval. A new joint report on the future of Örestad was prepared, and this was presented to the two governments in March 1978. However, as the economics recession has deepened the initial enthusiasm for the great scheme has started to wane, and the signs are that Örestad will never come into existence.

There are many reasons for the difficulties experienced in translating the Örestad vision into reality. In the first place, the cost of the various civil engineering projects proposed by the planners would be enormous. There is cynicism about the grandiose designs of the planning fraternity, and about the involvement of the powerful civil engineering and industrial lobby. In the second, place, the world energy crisis has put a question mark over the future of large-scale cheap air travel; the use of Kastrup Airport is not increasing at the predicted rate, and the *necessity* for a new airport on Saltholm is now in doubt. In addition, the Swedes have built a new airport at Sturup, and nobody believes that yet another airport in the southern part of the Öresund region would make economic sense. In the third place, broader strategic issues are involved. The Swedish government is genuinely worried about the implications of an integrated Öresund region; Malmö is already advantageously placed in comparison with many other Swedish industrial areas, and it is also somewhat remote from the historic 'core area' of the Stockholm region. It already lies under the very powerful influence of Greater Copenhagen, and new bridges and tunnels would undoubtedly draw the whole metropolitan region of south-western Skåne more closely still into the world of Danish commerce. In the fourth place, there are genuine fears on both sides of the Sound about the environmental impact of a south Scandinavian megalopolis; for example, the people of Lund can see themselves being incorporated into the commuter belt of Copenhagen, and they know that this would greatly increase the erosion of the rural area which has already suffered through the expansion of Malmö. Fifthly, there are philosophical reasons for the abandonment of the Örestad plan. Communities on both sides of the Sound feel that the existence of Örestad would threaten their own local individuality and reduce the opportunities for local decision-making in local affairs. The Swedes wonder how a scheme as gigantic as this can be equated with their government's protestations on decentralization and local autonomy. Also, there are differences of opinion in crucial matters of public debate. For example, the Danes have declared themselves to be anti-nuclear, and there is no way that they would accept a nuclear power-station on the island of Ven. The list of problems and worries could be continued.

It seems that schemes involving physical changes on the scale of those proposed for Örestad are, for the time being at least, just too exacting and too ambitious to obtain the backing that they need. It appears that national and local priorities are, at the end of the day, greater than supranational ones, and it appears that in the public mind schemes such as the Örestad project are just too vast and too dehumanizing to contemplate seriously. In spite of the multitude of supranational contacts referred to above, the Swedes and the Danes still prefer their lives to be lived at a 'human scale'. The vision of Örestad was just too grand.

Cooperation and national personality

The foregoing paragraphs have been largely concerned with non-geographical factors, involving politics, law, employment, culture and economics. Much of the content of the chapter may be considered irrelevant in a geography text, but it should be borne in mind that a central concern of regional geography (as defined in Ch. 1) is the recognition of regional personality. The character of Scandinavia is affected just as much by factors which have a non-spatial dimension as by those which are conventionally considered to be 'geographical'. There can be no doubt that the corporate identity of the Scandinavians is not only affected by environment and history but also by the legal and unofficial links forged, over the past few decades in particular, between the peoples concerned. The peoples themselves have required the forging of these links; and because they have not been imposed upon them from above they are likely to survive. And as these links persist and strengthen, more and more of them will begin to have an effect upon the landscape. The Scandinavian geography texts of the future may well light upon such matters as the geography of supranational town and country planning, the geography of educational cooperation or the geography of the international labour market.

It only remains to ask whether this apparent sinking of national interests in favour of supranational ones will eventually reduce the individuality of the five states considered in this book. Has the 'personality of Scandinavia' now become so easy to recognize and define that the personalities of Sweden or Norway or Finland have become somehow less attractive? Is a geographical synthesis of Scandinavia more appealing and challenging than a geographical study stressing national and regional individuality? The text of this book must be seen as a negative answer to both these questions, and the next (and final) chapter confirms that Scandinavian unity, in its broadest sense, is still a long way off.

Suggested reading

Nordic cooperation

Anderson 1967; Andrén 1967; Breinholst 1960; Connery 1966; Karvonen 1977; Lorendahl 1969; Malmström 1965; Mead 1981; Miljan 1977; Pederson 1954; Sletten 1967; Solem 1977; Sundelius 1976.

Chapter 23 National and supranational interests: present and future

The impressive list of Scandinavian cooperative ventures contained in the last chapter may give a slightly misleading impression of the extent to which national interests have been submerged by supranational ones. Earlier chapters have shown that there is no lack of 'national identity' in any of the five states considered in this book, and patriotism of a particularly proud sort burns in the breasts of the Swedes no less than in the breasts of the Norwegians and Finns. In Finland that source of great national pride, the sauna, is both a cultural indicator (Fig. 23.1) and a valuable export. In Sweden there is much flying of national flags, and days like Midsummer, 7 August (the opening of the crayfish season) and 13 December (Lucia Day) are celebrated with due regard to ancient traditions. In Norway there is a great affection for folk culture, and 17 May (the day on which the National Assembly adopted the constitution in 1814) is by far the most important day in the year. In the Faroes the great national festival is Olavsøka, on 29 July. And the other countries have their national events as well. There is no sign of them disappearing, and no sign that the international sporting rivalries (for example between Sweden and Finland) will disappear either.

In this final chapter it is worth stressing the individuality of each of the states of Scandinavia. Having looked at their physical environments, their cultural traditions, their economic activities and settlements, their regional inequalities and local idiosyncracies, the reader should be in no doubt at all that huge differences of landscape and lifestyle exist throughout the Nordic world. This book has been much concerned with the individual characteristics of each state, seen in glimpses through text and illustrations, and the text has never strayed too far away from the twin objectives of regional geography as defined in Chapter 1 – namely the study of process – form relationships and the search for 'regional personality'. In the various chapters of the book history and geography have been brought together on innumerable occasions, and a great stress has been placed upon landscapes as the records of moments in time. There have been many deliberate changes of emphasis from chapter to chapter between the small scale, the medium scale and the large scale, for generalizations, no matter how wisely made, are seldom

Fig. 23.1 The sauna, an institution of which the inhabitants of Finland are fiercely proud. It is an essential part of their lifestyle, and it is now increasingly popular in the other Scandinavian countries also. (Photo: Finnish Tourist Board)

relevant to all scales through all time. Thus, although the reader will have seen a multitude of common characteristics when viewing Scandinavia as a whole (or, to use the terminology of Ch. 1, at a very low level of resolution) differences and contrasts become so overwhelming when *small* regions are compared that one wonders whether they have anything in common at all.

Bearing in mind the above points, it is important to recognize the extent to which landscapes and land-use policies can be affected by conditions created a great distance away. Local communities may find themselves forced to transform their traditional cultural landscape, as happened when the *storskifte* and especially the *laga skifte* brought land reform to country folk all over Scandinavia. Economic factors such as grain prices can cause complete shifts in agricultural policy, as happened when in the 1800s the Danes moved from cereal-growing to livestock-farming in order to take advantage of low-priced grain as animal feedstuff. Military events such as the devastation of Finnish Lapland in 1945 may cause the renewal of virtually every man-made feature in the landscape, with 'modernization' projects taking place at a vastly greater rate than normal. Political agreements may also lead to landscape transformations; an example is the Peace Treaty of 1940 between Russia and Finland, by which Finland ceded 11 per cent of its territory and had to settle 422,000 refugees within its new frontiers. The 'cold farms' transformed the forest and extended the cultivated area throughout southern Finland. Government policies and incentives can cause small communities to become fired with 'reclamation fever' or 'drainage fever'; the latter is affecting many of the cultivated parts of Iceland at the present day, and the effect of the long, straight drainage ditches upon the landscape is striking indeed. Many more examples could be cited of landscape change initiated by external forces, but it should also be remembered that for every transformed landscape there are ten which are but slightly affected and twenty which remain quite unaltered. Also, the nature of the Scandinavian landscape, in which cultural landscapes exist only in small isolated pockets, means that the world of nature retains its hold over by far the greatest part of the Scandinavian land area. And it is by no means unusual for landscapes tamed by the hand of man to revert to the natural state again when economic, political or social circumstances demand a withdrawal of human beings from the margins of settlement.

The human environment of Scandinavia

The human environment of the states of Scandinavia (i.e. the environment created by political, social and other institutions) is controlled and conditioned by a number of non-human factors. The physical environment, discussed in detail in Part I of this book, is one such factor. Another is the relatively small range of commodities which can be obtained from the natural resources of these northern lands. Each of the Scandinavian states has had to struggle to escape from undue dependence upon a restricted range of products. In the case of Finland and Sweden, forest products have predominated; in Norway, Iceland and the Faroes, fish and fish products; and in the case of Denmark, agricultural produce. Nowadays each of the Fennoscandian countries manages to build its fortunes on a fairly wide economic base, but large volumes of imports are required if the manufacturing industries in particular are to keep going. Hydro-electric power, which is a major resource in Norway, Sweden, Finland and Iceland, is by no means an unmixed blessing, for a high degree of inventiveness is needed in order to maintain power supplies in the winter, when river flows are at their lowest and when demand is at its greatest. The Baltic Sea, which is a valuable resource allowing shipping to penetrate right into the heart of Fennoscandia, also has its fair share of problems associated with the

Fig. 23.2 The 'control of winter' in Finnish Lapland. Here the long snowy winter affects the farming landscape in all sorts of ways, and also has a profound effect upon the lifestyle and economy of the farming community. (Photo: Finnish Embassy, London)

winter freeze. In analyses of resources and of the constraints which exist on their use, the geographer returns time and again to the nature of the physical environment. Little wonder that the Scandinavian region was very popular among old-fashioned determinists. Even today, with more enlightened attitudes to the relations between man and nature, one cannot avoid talking about 'the control of winter' over and again in considerations of Scandinavian geography (Fig. 23.2).

Another fact which arises from the overall shortage of natural resources in Scandinavia is the competitive nature of the Scandinavian economies. The five states compete with one another for the sale of fish and fish products; the two 'forested states', Sweden and Finland, compete with each other for the sale of timber and forestry products such as pulp and paper; there is competition in dairy products and other agricultural goods; the shipbuilding industries of the four Fennoscandian countries are in direct competition with one another; and there is also competition among merchant marines and in a wide range of manufacturing and service industries. The competitive element in the Scandinavian economy is not often talked about, and indeed various of the cooperative ventures mentioned in the last chapter are designed to counteract its effects. But in the background national interests often prove to be more powerful than supranational ones; the failure of the NORDEK scheme, and the failure to establish a proper customs union, are quite revealing in this respect.

In spite of the great success of the Scandinavian economies since the Second World War, as measured in terms of the level of affluence and the standard of living of the average inhabitant, there is considerable concern about the small size of the market demand within the Nordic world. All of the Scandinavian states have small internal markets and they therefore have to depend upon exports for their livelihood. To a certain extent the need to export is catered for by the build-up of 'intra-Nordic' trade (see Table 22.1, p. 324), but each one of the countries with which this book is concerned normally has a balance of trade deficit. Each one is vulnerable to a world economic recession, and the greatest fear among the managers of the Scandinavian economies is the appearance of widespread tariff barriers designed to protect home industries from outside competition, be it from Scandinavia or elsewhere. This fear was no doubt one of the main reasons for the Danish decision to join the EEC even though the Danes knew that this would make the full economic integration of Norden that much more difficult to achieve.

Geography, politics and military strategy

Earlier chapters have included some consideration of the stresses and strains that have affected Scandinavia as a result of the events of the Second World War. The post-war strategic situation has also caused a few stresses in Nordic relationships, since the five states have all pursued military policies of self-interest involving very few concessions to the supranational ideal of Norden. The long-continued Soviet shadow over Finland has been a source of disquiet to the free world since 1945 in particular. The deployment of nuclear weapons has increased the strategic importance of Scandinavia, for it lies between the industrial heartland of the USA and the industrial heartland of the USSR. Norway flanks the exit from the Arctic Ocean to the North Atlantic, while Denmark and Sweden control the exit from the Baltic to the North Sea. Iceland and the Faroes are both located in strategically important parts of the North Atlantic – a fact fully appreciated by both the Germans and the Allies during the Second World War.

The events of the Second World War, together with the post-war political situation, convinced both Norway and Denmark that the traditional style of Scandinavian neutrality was outdated, since their corner of the world was no longer remote from the centre of affairs. After much thought, and no doubt after much pressure from the USA and the UK, both countries opted for strong defence through membership of NATO. Nowadays both states have small, full-time armed forces, but they also have compulsory national service and large military reserves. Although their armies, navies and air forces are small in terms of manpower, they have sophisticated military equipment in the form of conventional weapons, radar installations, and ships and aircraft. Both countries refuse to permit foreign troops to be stationed on their soil, and there is a firm commitment to exclude nuclear weapons also.

Sweden, considered by many to be militarily the strongest state in Scandinavia, is determined to defend her neutrality vigorously. The country refuses to align itself with any political or military alliance, and this is largely why no Nordic military alliance has ever come into being. For the same reason it refuses to join the EEC. Swedish defence policy and foreign policy find an outlet particularly through the work of the United Nations, and in active UN participation Sweden declares itself dedicated to the support of national independence movements, economic and social equality, and world peace. In order to retain global respect for Swedish neutrality the country has built up the strongest defence system of any small European state. There is compulsory national service, with a total armed force of over 750,000. Largely for philosophical reasons, the country's defence is based entirely on its own financial resources; arms are manufactured entirely by Swedish industry, and fuels and other essential military goods are stockpiled for use in the event of any blockade whether in peace or war. Tanks, armoured personnel carriers and guns are made for the most part for exclusive Swedish use, as are all naval ships, submarines, torpedoes and other missiles. The air force has thirty-five squadrons, mostly of all-weather fighter and attack units, and the Draken and Viggen fighters, built by the Swedish company Saab, are among the most efficient aircraft in military service anywhere (Fig. 23.3). All services have underground installations blasted out of rock, the philosophy being that it is rather absurd to have *anything* of military importance visible at the surface. Many of the underground installations also have nuclear blast and fall-out protection. There is a Civil Defence Force of about 300,000 men and women, and in the main urban areas there are radiation shelters (for the most part located beneath large blocks of flats) capable of holding 5 million people. There is a large Economic Defence Force trained in the management of stockpiles of fuel, food and other materials, and there is even a National Board for Psychological Defence whose purpose is to maintain and strengthen the will to resist an aggressor and to counteract enemy propaganda.

Finland provides yet another variable on the theme of defence, largely because of its position in what Roy Millward calls 'the twilight world of the states on the Soviet Union's western border'. The

Fig. 23.3 The Viggen fighter, one of the aircraft developed in Sweden and built by Saab primarily for the defence of Swedish national territory. (Photo: Saab-Scania)

disastrous events of the Second World War at least ensured that Finland did not become an *occupied* country, but the price of collaboration with the Germans has been a high one to pay. The armistice with the Russians after the war left Finland with a mutual defence pact and a ludicrously small army; the country was allowed to maintain a defence force of only 42,000 men, only 60 aircraft, and a naval tonnage of only 10,000 tonnes. The reparations which were to be made to the Soviet Union were huge, amounting to over $1,000 million, to be paid for the most part in industrial goods. This involved the complete rebuilding of the Finnish steel industry and the establishment of a wide range of metalworking and manufacturing concerns. The reparations were not completed until 1952. According to the 1948 Treaty of Friendship, Cooperation and Mutual Assistance with the Soviet Union, Finland is committed to repel any attack against its neighbour through or across Finnish territory, and the country has to remain outside military alliances which may be anti-Soviet in intent. Finland may be 'assisted' by the Soviet Union through military occupation in the case of a direct outside threat, but only by mutual agreement. Finland has declared its intention to remain apart from any conflicts of interest between the Great Powers, and for obvious reasons it has to tread with extreme caution in the whole field of foreign affairs.

As far as Iceland and the Faroes are concerned, they are solidly involved within the western military alliance. There is a large NATO airbase at Keflavik, not far from Reykjavik, and although it remains quite apart from the mainstream of Icelandic life it is looked upon by many of the people as an unwelcome intrusion of American culture. From an economic point of view the base is valuable, however, providing employment for many Icelanders and contributing to the Icelandic economy through purchases of goods and services. The Faroe Islands, through their links with Denmark, are also involved in the NATO Alliance, and although there is no large-scale military activity in and around the islands radar installations figure prominently on the skyline. These installations are part of the western European early warning defence system.

Far from being united in their commitment to Nordic values and Nordic strategic interests, the five states find themselves split three ways. In the west Iceland, the Faroes, Norway and Denmark are firmly wedded to NATO: in the centre Sweden maintains a position of powerful neutrality; and in the east Finland is an uneasy neighbour of the Soviet Union, wedded by a shotgun marriage to the Soviet bloc and also dependent upon Soviet goodwill for its continued survival as a free state. From the point of view of politicians and military strategists, this is an acceptable state of affairs, providing a gradual transition between east and west and involving only one small strip in the far north (along the Norwegian – Soviet border) where NATO and the Soviet Union confront one another face to face. The 'Nordic Balance' suits most of the parties concerned, and the maintenance of the *status quo* is a priority both for the superpowers and the Scandinavian states. Shielded by this balance Nordic cooperation has been able to advance along a broad front: maybe the balance is more of a unifying factor than a divisive one. It certainly ensures that feelings of mutual respect are not allowed to lapse; from a military and strategic standpoint real political union between the five states is impossible, but it is in everybody's interests to ensure that national inviolability remains a guiding principle.

Scandinavia and the EEC

When the negotiations for a European free-trade area broke down in the late 1950s it was inevitable that the Scandinavian countries should look to EFTA as a framework for economic cooperation. By 1970 all of the Scandinavian states were either full or associate members of EFTA, but there were certain weaknesses in the arrangements from the point of view of Norway and Denmark in particular; the main weakness was that EFTA arrangements did not cover such important economic sectors as agriculture and fishing. There was a genuine fear that as the EEC grew it might prove exceptionally difficult to sell fish and agricultural produce within the European community of nations. Both Norway and Denmark sought to join the EEC, and in 1973 Denmark became a full member after a referendum. Norway, having completed negotiations, also held a referendum before becoming fully committed to the EEC; somewhat to the surprise of the other European nations, there was a substantial majority *against* membership.

In 1973 there were great fears that Europe would be split apart economically by the divided loyalties of the European states, but since the EEC was happy to make free-trade arrangements with the EFTA countries (in other words, all the Scandinavian states except Denmark, which was now a full EEC member) there were no great obstacles to economic growth in the northern lands. The EEC/EFTA Trade Agreement was signed in May 1973, and since that time there has been a gradual movement towards free trade in industrial and many other products. The main source of concern in Scandinavia has been the exclusion from the agreement of certain 'sensitive' products such as pulp and paper, and the very slow removal of import duties on a whole range of other goods. For example, the EEC tariff on frozen fish fillets was reduced only gradually, reaching zero in 1977, and there were other transitions in respect of ferro-alloys, aluminium and other metals. The Scandinavian states which still belong to EFTA are concerned about the possible temporary imposition of EEC tariffs on certain of the products which they need to sell. But they know that they cannot expect complete free trade with the EEC countries, thereby enjoying all the economic advantages they might wish for, without also taking on the economic and political responsiblities of full membership. And in spite of everything, Nordic trade with the rest of Europe continues to rise at a very satisfactory rate, while intra-Nordic trade rises even more steeply.

The member states of the EEC recognize that strong national economies in Scandinavia are of mutual benefit. They have agreed that Denmark's membership of the EEC should not exclude continued Nordic cooperation, and certainly trade has not been greatly inhibited so far. The Nordic countries still aim for full participation in the broad European market. They believe that they have many values in common with the rest of Europe, and they believe that they have evolved a style of living and a human environment which can influence the future shape of the world. They know that they can never hope to influence the rest of the world by isolation, and cooperation and fellowship are words which mean a great deal in Scandinavia. The five states, whatever their military and political priorities, have a set of human values, and an underlying respect for civilized behaviour, which the rest of the world will do well to imitate.

Postscript

While global military strategy and matters of European political and economic importance may seem suitably profound topics on which to end this book, it is worth recalling that most of the people of Scandinavia, and the landscapes which they inhabit, are only marginally affected by the decisions made in Moscow and Washington, Brussels and Strasburg, Helsinki and Copenhagen. For most of them life goes on through the passage of the years, punctuated by great events and insignificant incidents, enlivened by moments of joy and hushed by moments of sadness. And the perennial values persist in spite of the complexities of the modern world. At heart Scandinavia has not changed all that much since Jon Jonsson, an Icelandic farmer, wrote (in English) around the year 1866:

The winter approached as usual in the month of October, and the frosty weather and drift of snow came on. My manservant was charged to take care of my little herd of sheep, which were then in number (the lambs included) 60, but I myself that had no liking for herdsmanship, went to the lake every day fishing, and had much pleasure in this work, especially when the weather was fine, and when I fished well. In the winter I had generalli 6 nets under the ice. . . .

In the spring I lost some of my sheep for wanting of provender, which is a most lamentable accident that befals the Icelandish farmer, to see his most usefull animals starving for wanting of food, around his farm, as it is searching on the snow covered pasture land. Yet it is a heartrending sight to looke on it, when the poor animals go so very slowly to their cotes and caves, almost unable to support themselves for hunger. But nobody can help it when all the hay is consumed and there is nothing to be done, but kill the animals. This occurs almost annuali in the severe Winters and Springs which now successively visit Iceland . . . (Fig. 23.4)

This year we had a good crop of juniperberries, and I wandered some days a great distant from my home in eastward direction to gather these berries. . . .

As usual I hold the Christmass and New Year with our rural festivity and joifulness, and regaled my family with coffi and fine bread, besides smok-dried mutton, which is only given on feast days at Myvatn, and is very nutritive food. I gladdened myselv by a little of brandy, and played on these holy evenings on the fiolin. . . .

The first of March, when I had almost emptied my haybarn, I sent my servant with 20 sheep to the peasants around Myvatn that had hay yet, but the 22 in same month I slaughtered 10 ewes, they could not support themselves for meagerness. I wandered every day to the bushes, and carried on my back great bundles of the small branches, trying to support my remanent flock, but it could

Fig. 23.4 The harshness of
the Icelandic winter is
captured in this engraving by
Edward Whymper showing an
Icelandic funeral in the late
nineteenth century (Source:
Howell 1893)

not help them. I lost them every day, and when this ever
memorable winter was ended, I had lost 65 sheep and goats. . . .
The 2d. and 3d. of May I sowed my potatoes, as we had by this
time very fine and serene weather, so we had even fine grass in
the middle of May. . . . By all opportunities, I was occupaid by
the building of a stone wall around my tun. . . . The calamity
occurred in the middle of the hatching time, that our islands and
holms were visited of immense swarms of ravens, which robbed
and carried almost every egg that the ducks laid in the nests, so
we lost thus a third part of the collection of eggs we formerly got
in the former summer seasons. . . .

Some days after we perceaved a dens smoke in the air that
showed that a Volcano was in eruption. We at last got the news
from the Southland that it was in a glacier, which burnt for a part
of the summer, and it was, indeed, the main cause for the rainy
and cold summer season we then had.

This autumn I got not one single potato from my gardens, they
had all perished and gone in rottenness in the frosty summer, but
I got about 6 bushels of turnips, and digged them from the snow
that covered my garden.

How charmful day! It is noon, and the sunbeams fall on the
calm and plain surface of the lake, and many birds of passage that
have lately arrived are cheerfully chattering on the calm water,

and some are coming, huriing, flying on the air, and fling themselves on the lake between their companions. The midges are now recovering, and swarm gently in the warm and brighte sunshine near the beach of the water. Now and then a trout ascend to the level surface in order to snatch a midge, and move a little the surface and disappir in the same moment. A holy peace is prevailing in this rural scenery, and a divine rejoice is awakened in every bosom. . . .

Jon Jonsson knew all about adversity. To him every day was an adventure, every moment an opportunity. People like him created the modern Scandinavia.

Suggested reading

Nordic geography and politics

Anderson 1967; Åström 1977; Chabot *et al.* 1958; Cole 1877; Fredborg 1978; Friis 1950; Griffiths 1969; Gröndal 1971; Haupert 1959; Karvonen 1977; Magnusson 1977; Malmström 1965; McCririck 1983; Mead 1958, 1968; Nickels *et al.* 1973; Phillips 1977; Rying 1974; Sletten 1967; Sømme 1961; Sparring 1972; West 1972; Wizelius 1967.

Bibliography

Abler, R., Adams, J. S. and Gould, P. 1972: *Spatial Organiation*. Prentice-Hall, London, 587 pp.

Aftonposten/Den norske Creditbank 1979: *The Norwegian Market*. Oslo, 31 pp.

Ahlmann, H. W:son 1919: 'Geomorphological Studies in Norway, *Geog. Ann.* **1**, 3–148 and 193–252.

Ahlmann, H. W:son (ed.) 1976: *Norden i text och Kartor*. Generalslabens Litografiska Anstalts Förlag, Stockholm, 116 pp.

Aintila, S. 1972: *De regionalpolitiska medlen: Finland*. Nordiska arbetsgruppen för regionalpolitisk forskning, 1972:4

Aldskogius, H. 1960: 'Changing land use and settlement development in the Siljan region', *Geog. Ann.* **42** (4), 250–61.

Aldskogius, H. 1967: 'Vacation house settlement in the Siljan region', *Geog. Ann.* **49**, 69–95.

Aldskogius, H. 1978: 'Leisure time homes in Sweden', *Current Sweden* No. 195 (Swedish Inst. Stockholm). 9 pp.

Andersen, J. L. and Sollid, J. L. 1971: 'Glacial chronology and glacial geomorphology in the marginal zones of the glaciers Midtdalsbreen and Nigardsbreen, south Norway', *Norsk Geogr. Tidss.* **25**, 1–38.

Andersen, B. G. 1965: 'The Quaternary of Norway', in Rankama, K. (ed.), *The Quaternary*, vol. I. Interscience, New York, pp. 91–138.

Anderson, M. S. 1954: *Splendour of Earth*. Philip, London,

Anderson, S. V. 1967: *The Nordic Council – a study of Scandinavian regionalism*. Univ. of Washington Press, Seattle, 194 pp.

Andrén, N. 1967: *Nordic Integration, Cooperation and Conflict*.

Ångström, A. 1958: *Sverige's Klimat*. Stockholm,

Annandale, N. 1905: *The Faroes and Iceland: Studies in Island Life*. Oxford, 238 pp.

Appleton, J. 1975: *The Experience of Landscape*. Wiley, London, 293 pp.

Appleton, J. 1979: *The Aesthetics of Landscape*. Univ. of Hull, 95 pp.

Arnborg, T. 1960: 'The forests from the tree limit to the coastline', in Mannerfelt, C. M:son, *A Geographical Excursion through Central Norrland*. IGU, Stockholm, pp. 66–76.

Åse, L-E. 1979: *Spår efter isen*. Svenska Turistföreningen, Stockholm, 64 pp.

Ashwell, I. Y. 1963: 'Saga of the Cod War', *Geog. Mag.* **45** (8), 550–8.

Åström, K. 1967: *City Planning in Sweden*. Swedish Institute, Stockholm, 160 pp.

Åström, S. 1977: *Sweden's Policy of Neutrality*. Swedish Institute, Stockholm, 99 pp.

Ausland, J. C. 1978: 'Norway's oil adventure', *The Norseman* **5**, 131–3.

Bailey, E. B. and Holtedahl, O. 1938: 'Northwestern Europe Caledonides', in Andrée, K. *et al.* (eds.), *Regionale Geologie der Erde*, vol. 2. Leipzig

Barđarson, H. 1976: *Ice and Fire: Contrasts of Icelandic Nature*. H. Barđarson. Reykjavik, 171 pp.

Behrens, S. *et al.* 1960: 'Regional geography of southern Sweden', *Svensk Geog. Årsbok* **36**, 7–57.

Berg, A. 1968: *Norske Gardstun*. Universitetsforlaget, Oslo, 340 pp.

Berg, P. O. 1971: *Regionpolitikk i Norge*. Nordiska arbetsgruppen för regionalpolitisk forskning, 1971:3.

Bergsten, K. E. 1961: 'Sweden' in Sømme, A. (ed.) *The Geography of Norden*. Heinemann, London, Ch. 12, pp. 293–349.

Bergsten, K. E. 1976: *Jordytan*, Liber-Läromedel, Lund, 173 pp.

Bergthorsson, P. 1969: 'An estimate of drift ice and temperatures in Iceland in 1,000 years', *Jökull* **19**, 94–101.

Berry, E. 1972: *The Land and People of Iceland*. J. B. Lippincott, Philadelphia, 158 pp.

Bidstrup, K. 1970: 'The face of Denmark', *Danish Jnl* (special edn), 25–31.

Bjørkvik, H. 1956: 'The old Norwegian peasant community: the farm territories', *Scand. Econ. Hist. Rev.* **4**, 33–61.

Bjørkvik, H. 1963: 'Norwegian *seter*-farming', *Scand. Econ. Hist. Review* **11**, 156–66.

Bodvall, G. 1957: 'Periodic settlement, land-clearing and cultivation'. *Geog. Ann.* **39**, 213–256.

Bosi, R. 1960: *The Lapps*.

Ancient Peoples and Places, London, 220 pp.

Bout, P. *et al.* 1955: 'Geomorphologie et glaciologie en Islande Centrale', *Norois* **2**, 461–572.

Breinholst, W. 1960: *The North from A to Z*. Copenhagen, private pub., 32 pp.

Brofoss, E. 1968: 'Regional problems in Norway', in *Conference on Regional Policies under the Auspices of the European Movement*, Oslo.

Brøgger, A. W. 1929: *Ancient Emigrants*. OUP, Oxford.

Brøgger, A. W. and Shetelig, H. 1971: *The Viking Ships – their Ancestry and Evolution*. C. Hurst, London, 192 pp.

Brøndsted, J. 1965: *The Vikings*. Penguin, London, 347 pp.

Bunge, W. 1962: *Theoretical Geography*, Lund Studies in Geography, Series C, No. 1.

Buttimer, A. and Seamon, D. 1980: *The Human Experience of Space and Place*, Croom Helm, London, 199 pp.

Caraman, P. 1969: *Norway*. Longmans, London, 226 pp.

Carlestam, G. and Levi, L. 1971: 'Urban conglomerates as psycho-social human stressors', *Contrib. to UN Conference on the Human Env.* Royal Ministry of Foreign Affairs, Stockholm, 74 pp.

Chabot, G. *et al.* 1958: *Finlande et les pays Scandinaves* (2 vols). Paris.

Church, R. J. H. *et al.* 1973: *An Advanced Geography of Northern and Western Europe* (2nd edn). Hulton, London, 480 pp.

Coates, B. E., Johnston, R. J. and Knox, P. L. 1977: *Geography and Inequality*. OUP, London, 292 pp.

Cole, G. R. F. 1877: 'Jon Jonsson's Saga–a genuine autobiography of a modern Icelander', *Fraser's Magazine* **15** (85).

Connery, D. 1966: *The Scandinavians*. Eyre &

Spottiswoode, London, 590 pp.

Coull, J. 1975: 'Faroese fish for prosperity', *Geog. Mag.* **47** (4), 224–7.

Cushing, D. H. 1976: 'The impact of climatic change on fish stocks in the N. Atlantic', *Geog. Jnl* **142** (2), 216–27.

Dahl, E. 1946: 'On the origin of the strandflat', *Norsk Geogr. Tidss.* **11**, 159–72.

Dahl, S. 1969: 'Ancient monuments' in Nyborg, A. (ed.), *Welcome to the Faroes.* Anders Nyborg A/S, Copenhagen, pp. 79–82.

Danish Journal 1971: *The Faroe Islands* (special edn).

Dansgaard, W. *et al.* 1975: 'Climatic changes, Norsemen and modern man', *Nature* **255**, 24–8.

Danske Selskab 1972: *Schools and Education in Denmark.* Copenhagen, 160 pp.

Davis, W. M. 1909: *Geographical Essays.* Dover, New York, (reprint 1954), 777 pp.

Denton, G. H. and Karlén, W. 1973: 'Holocene climatic variations – their pattern and possible cause', *Quat. Res.* **3**, 155–205.

Dickinson, R. E. 1976: *Regional Concept: the Anglo-American Leaders.* Routledge & Kegan Paul, London, 408 pp.

Dixon, W. 1959: *Education in Denmark.* London, 233 pp.

Djurhus, N. *et al.* (eds.) 1958: *Faerøerne*, vol. I. Dansk–Faerøisk Samfund, Copenhagen, 309 pp.

Dodd, G. 1971: 'From *bygd* to Torshavn – and then?' *Danish Jnl* (special edn.), 13–17.

Dons, J. A. (ed.) 1960: 'Excursions in Norway', 21st Int. Geol. Congress, *Norges Geol. Undersøkning* **212**, Oslo.

Einarsson, Th. 1963: 'Pollen analytical studies on the vegetation and climate history of Iceland in Late and Postglacial times', in A. and D. Löve (eds.), *North Atlantic*

Biota and their History. Pergamon, Oxford, pp. 355–65.

Einarsson, Th. 1971: *Jardfreidi.* Heimskringla, Reykjavik, 254 pp.

Einarsson, Tr. 1962: 'Upper Tertiary and Pleistocene rocks in Iceland', *Visindafelag Islendinga* **36**, 197 pp.

Ekeland, S. 1975: *Norway in the Modern World*, Royal Ministry of Foreign Affairs, Oslo, 64 pp.

Elbo, C. 1975: Chapter on Denmark in Clout, D. (ed.), *Regional Development in Western Europe.* Wiley, London, pp. 287–297.

Elstob, E. 1979: *A History of Sweden*, Boydell Press, Ipswich, 224 pp.

Enequist, G. 1959: 'Geographical changes of rural settlement in N. W. Sweden since 1523', *Uppsala Univ. Geog. Inst. Medd.* No. 143.

English, P. W. and Mayfield, R. C. 1972: *Man, Space and Environment.* OUP, London, 623 pp.

Engström, A. (ed) 1972: *Management of Land and Water Resources*, Royal Ministry of Foreign Affairs, Stockholm, 74 pp.

Eriksson, G. A. 1957: 'The decline of the small blast furnaces and forges in Bergslagen after 1850', *Geog. Ann.* **39**, 257–75.

Eriksson, G. A. 1960: 'Advance and retreat of charcoal iron industry and rural settlement in Bergslagen', *Geog. Ann.* **42**, 267–84.

ERU (Expertgruppen for regional utredningsverksamhet) 1974: *Orter i regional samverken*, SOU (2 vols), Allmänna Förlaget, Stockholm.

Evans, E. E. 1958: 'The Atlantic ends of Europe', *Adv. Sci.* **15**, 54–64.

Evers, W. 1962: 'The problem of coastal genesis, with special reference to the "strandflat", the "banks" or "grounds", and "deep channels" of the Norwegian and Greenland coasts', *J. Geol.* **70**, 621–30.

Eyles, J. D. and Smith, D. M. 1978: 'Social geography', *American Behavioral Scientist* **22** (1), 41–58.

Eyre, S. R. 1964: 'Determinism and the ecological approach to geography', *Geography* **49** (4), 369–76.

Eyre, S. R. and Jones, G. R. J. 1966: *Geography as Human Ecology*. Edward Arnold, London, 308 pp.

Eythorsson, J. 1949: Variations of glaciers in Iceland 1930–1947. *J. Glaciol.* 1 (5), 250–252.

Eythorsson, J. and Sigtryggson, H. 1971: 'The climate and weather of Iceland', *The Zoology of Iceland* **1** (3), 1–62.

Export Council of Norway 1979: *Norway 79*. Oslo, 72 pp.

Finnfacts Institute 1977: *Finland as a Trading Partner*. Finnish Foreign Trade Assoc., Helsinki, 86 pp.

Flacker, Å and Holm, L. 1972: *Urbanization and Planning in Sweden*. Royal Ministry of Foreign Affairs, Stockholm, 66 pp.

Foote, P. G. and Wilson, D. M. 1970: *The Viking Achievement*. Sidgwick & Jackson, London, 481 pp.

Fredborg, A. 1978: 'Finland – the unknown country', *International Background* **6** (7), 1–22.

Friis, H. 1950: *Scandinavia between East and West*. Ithaca, New York, 388 pp.

Fullerton, B. and Williams, A. F. 1972: *Scandinavia* (2nd edn), Chatto & Windus, London, 375 pp.

Gale, S. and Olsson, G. 1979: *Philosophy in Geography*. D. Reidel, Netherlands, 469 pp.

Gaunt, D. (ed.) 1978: *Chance and Change. Social and Economic Studies in Historical Demography in the Baltic Area*, London.

Geer, G. de 1912: 'A geochronology of the last 12,000 years', *Comptes Rendus,* 11th Int. Geol. Congress, Stockholm, pp. 241–53.

Gilbert, E. W. 1960: 'The idea of the region', *Geography* **45**, 157–75.

Gislason, G. Th. 1973: *The problem of Being an Icelander: Past, Present and Future*. Almenna Bokafelagid, Reykjavik, 92 pp.

Gjessing, J. 1966: 'Some effects of ice erosion on the development of Norwegian valleys and fjords', *Norsk Geogr. Tidss.* **20** (8), 273–99.

Gjessing, J. 1967: 'Norway's Paleic Surface', *Norsk Geogr. Tidss.* **21**, 69–132.

Glässer, E. 1978: *Norwegen*. Wissenschaftliche Buchgesellschaft, Darmstadt, 289 pp.

Glob, P. V. 1971: *The Bog People*. Paladin, London, 142 pp.

Glückert, G. 1974: 'Map of glacial striation of the Scandinavian ice sheet during the last (Weichsel) glaciation in northern Europe', *Bull. Geol. Soc. Finland* **46**, 1–8.

Godlund, S. *et al.* 1978: *Att forma regional framtid*. Publica (Liber Förlag), Stockholm, 298 pp.

Göransson, S. 1971: 'Village planning patterns and territorial organization: studies in the development of the rural landscape of eastern Sweden (Öland)', *Acta Univ. Upsaliensis* **4**, 18 pp.

Graham-Campbell, J. and Kidd, D. 1980: *The Vikings*. British Museum, London, 200 pp.

Gray, D. 1938: Farming in western Norway', *Geography* **23**, 24–7.

Gregory, D. 1978: *Ideology, Science and Human Geography*. Hutchinson, London, 198 pp.

Grenholm, G. (chief ed.) 1977: *Den Svenska Historien*, 15 vols. Bonniers, Stockholm.

Griffiths, J. C. 1969: *Modern Iceland*. Pall Mall, London.

Gröndal, B. 1971: *Iceland: From Neutrality to NATO Membership*. Universitetsforlaget, Oslo, 106 pp.

Guttesen, R. 1970: 'Faerøernes migrationer 1961–65, med on kort befolkningsbeskrivelse', *Geog. Tidss.* **69**, 1–27.

Hägerstrand, T. 1970: 'Tidsanvändning och omgivningsstruktur', Ch. 4 in *Urbanisering i Sverige*, ERU, Stockholm, pp. 4.1–4.135.

Hägerstrand, T. 1976: 'The geographer's contribution to regional policy: the case of Sweden', in Coppock, J. T. and Sewell, W. (eds.) *Spatial Dimensions in Public Policy*. Pergamon, Oxford, pp. 243–256.

Hägerstrand, T. 1977: 'On the survival of our cultural heritage', *Ethnologia Scandinavica*.

Hägerstrand, T. *et al.* (eds.) 1974: *The Biography of a People: Past and Future Population Changes in Sweden*, Royal Ministry of Foreign Affairs, Stockholm, 204 pp.

Hagström, B. 1977: The Faroese language, *Faroe Isles Review* **2** (1), 31–7.

Håkansson, B. (ed.) 1980: *Bohuslän i vår Hjärtan*. Göteborgs-Posten, Göteborg.

Hall, W. 1957: *The Finns and their Country*. Max Parrish, London, 224 pp.

Hammarström, I. and Hall, T. (eds) 1979: *Growth and Transformation of the Modern City*, Byggforskningsrådet, Stockholm, 278 pp.

Hansen, J. C. 1972: 'Regional disparities in Norway with reference to marginality', *Trans. I.B.G.* **57**, 15–30.

Hansen, J. C. 1981: 'Settlement pattern and population distribution as fundamental issues in Norway's regional policy', in Webb, J. W. *et al.* (eds.) *Policies of Population Distribution*, Oulu, pp. 107–124.

Hansen, S. A. 1970: *Early Industrialisation in Norway*. Copenhagen.

Hansen, V. 1960: 'Some characteristics of a growing suburban region', *Geog. Tidsskrift* **59**, 124–225.

Hartshorne, R. 1960: *Perspective on the Nature of Geography*. John Murray, London, 200 pp.

Harvey, D. 1969: *Explanation in Geography*. Edward Arnold, London, 521 pp.

Hasselmo, N. 1976: *Swedish America – an Introduction*. Swedish Int. Service, New York, 70 pp.

Hastrup, F. 1964: *Danske andsbytyper. En geografisk analyse*. Århus.

Haupert, J. S. 1959: 'The impact of geographic location upon Sweden as a Baltic power', *Jnl Geog.* **58**, 5–14.

Hedenstierna, B. 1948: 'Stockholm's Skärgård', *Geog. Ann.* **30**, 1–444.

Hedenstierna, B. 1960: 'Geographic features of Stockholm's Skärgård', *I G C Norden*. Stockholm.

Hedström, B. S. (ed.) 1977: *Swedish Forest*. National Board of Forestry, Jönköping, 88 pp.

Heineman, H.-E. 1975: *New Towns and Old*. Swedish Institute, Stockholm, 184 pp.

Helle, R. 1970: 'Tourism in Lapland', *Nordia* **2**.

Hellman, B. *et al.* (eds.) 1977: *Byggnader och Kulturmiljöer i Västernorrland*. A.B. Svensk Byggtjänst, Stockholm, 407 pp.

Helmfrid, S. (ed.) 1961: 'Morphogenesis of the agrarian cultural landscape' (IGC 1960), *Geog. Ann.* **43**, 1–328.

Helvig, M. and Johannessen, V. 1966: *Norway – Land, People, Industries*. Tanum Forlag, Oslo, 135 pp.

Herbertson, A. J. 1905: 'The major natural regions', *Geog. Jnl* **25**, 300–10.

Hilton, K. D. 1972: 'Subarctic mining communities: the Swedish experience', *Musk-Ox* **10**, 46–56.

Hirn, M. 1970: *Pictures of Vanishing Finland*. Weilin and Göös, Helsinki, 145 pp.

Hodne, F. 1975: *An Economic History of Norway, 1815–70.* Bergen.

Hofsten, E. V. (ed.) 1978: *The Domänverket Story.* Domänverket, Karlstad, 63 pp.

Holmsen, A. 1956: 'The old Norwegian peasant community: general survey and historical introduction', *Scand. Econ. Hist. Rev.* **4**, 17–32.

Holmsen, A. 1961: 'The transition from tenancy to freehold peasant ownership in Norway', *Scand. Econ. Hist. Rev.* **9** (2), 151–64.

Holtedahl, H. 1967: 'Notes on the formation of fjords and fjord valleys', *Geog. Ann.* **49**, 188–203.

Holtedahl, H. 1975: 'The geology of the Hardangerfjord, West Norway', *Norges geol. unders.* **323**, 87 pp.

Holtedahl, H. and Sellevoll, M. 1972: 'Notes on the influence of glaciation on the Norwegian continental shelf bordering on the Norwegian Sea', in Dahl, E. *et al.* (eds.), *The Norwegian Sea Region: Its Hydrography, Glacial and Biological History* (*Ambio*, Special Report No. 2), pp. 31–8.

Holtedahl, O. (ed.) 1960: *Geology of Norway.* Norges geologiske Undersøkelse, Oslo, 540 pp.

Hood, M. *et al.* 1979: 'Report on Scandinavia', *Fairplay Int. Shipping Weekly* (3 May), 43–76.

Hoppe, G. 1959: 'Glacial morphology and inland ice recession in northern Sweden', *Geog. Ann.* **41**, 193–212.

Hoppe, G. 1972: 'Ice sheets around the Norwegian Sea during the Würm glaciation', *Ambio*, Special Report No. 2, 25–9.

Hove, O. 1968: *The System of Education in Norway.* Tanum, Oslo, 70 pp.

Howell, F. W. W. 1893: *Icelandic Pictures Drawn with Pen and Pencil.* Religious Tract Society, London, 176 pp.

Hultén, E. 1950: *Atlas över växternas utbredning i Norden.* Stockholm.

Huntingdon, E. 1927: *The Human Habitat.* Van Nostrand, New York, 293 pp.

Hustich, I. 1964: *Finlands Skärgård*, Borgåa.

Ingold, T. 1973: 'Social and economic problems of Finnish Lapland', *Polar Record* **16**(105), 809–26.

Isachsen, F. 1959: 'Rural settlement in Norway', *Norsk Geogr. Tidss.* **17** (1–4), 187–96.

Isachsen, F. 1961: 'Norden', in Sømme, A. (ed.) *The Geography of Norden.* Heinemann, London, Ch. 1, pp. 11–17.

Jaatinen, S. 1960: 'Expansion and retreat of settlement in the southwestern archipelago of Finland', *Fennia* **84** (2).

Jaatinen, S. 1978: 'Identitet och överlevande i en insulär miljö: ett exempel från en nordåländsk utskärgård', in Aldskogius, H. (ed.), *Regional identitet och förändring i den regionala samverkans samhälle.* Univ. of Uppsala, pp. 83–100.

Jacobsen, J-F. 1953: *Faerøerne, natur og folk* (2nd edn). Torshavn.

Jacobsen, N. K. (ed.) 1960: *Guidebook Denmark* IGC, Copenhagen, 272 pp.

Jacobsen, N. K. 1976: 'Natural-geographical regions of Denmark', *Geog. Tidss.* **75**, 1–7.

Jensen, E. 1975: *Danish Agriculture – Past and Present* Danish Farmers Organization, Copenhagen, 28 pp.

Jensen, N. 1972: *Danske jernbaner 1847–1972.* Copenhagen, 270 pp.

Joensen, J. P. 1977: 'The Faroese boat', *Faroe Isles Review* **2** (1), 6–11.

Joensen, J. P. 1980: *Färöisk Folkkultur.* Liber Läromedel, Lund, 228 pp.

Johansen, V. 1969: 'The Faroese

vessel', in Nyborg, A. (ed.), *Welcome to the Faroes*. Anders Nyborg A/S, Copenhagen, pp. 53–62.

John, B. S. (ed.) 1971: *Village Studies from the Faroe Islands*. Univ. of Durham, Geog. Dept. Occasional Papers Series, No. 12, 49 pp.

John, B. S. 1978: 'Fish for survival in Vestfirðir', *Geog. Mag.* (Oct.), 63–6.

John, B. S. and Sugden, D. E. 1962: 'The morphology of Kaldalon, a recently deglaciated valley in Iceland', *Geog. Ann.* **44**, 347–65.

Johnston, R. J. 1978: 'Paradigms and revolutions or evolution; observations on human geography since the Second World War', *Prog. Hum. Geog.* **2** (2), 189–206.

Johnston, R. J. 1979: *Geography and Geographers: Anglo-American Human Geography since 1945*. Edward Arnold, London, 232 pp.

Jones, G. 1964: *The Norse Atlantic Saga*. OUP, London, 246 pp.

Jones, H. G. 1976: *Planning and Productivity in Sweden*. Croom Helm, London, 212 pp.

Jones, M. 1977: *Finland – Daughter of the Sea*. Dawson, London, 247 pp.

Jonsson, S. and Linnman, N. 1959: *Faröarna – fåglar och fångster*. LT's Forlag, Stockholm, 111 pp.

Jörberg, L. 1970: 'Industrial development of Scandinavia, 1850–1914', in Cipolla, C. M. (ed.), *Fontana Economic History of Europe*, Collins, London, **4** (8).

Jörberg, L. and Krantz, O. 1975: *Scandinavia 1914–1970* (trans. by Paul Britten Austin). Fontana, London, 87 pp.

Jutikkala, E. 1962: *A History of Finland*. Praeger, New York, 291 pp.

Kallsberg, E. 1970: 'The Faroes today', in Williamson, K. (ed.), *The Atlantic Islands*. Routledge & Kegan Paul, London, Ch. 13, pp. 305–21. (2nd ed.)

Kampp, Aa. H. 1967a: *Laer selv Faerøerne*. Hassings Håndbøger, Denmark, 112 pp.

Kampp, Aa. H. 1967b: 'The Faroes – today's problems', *Inter-Nord*. **9**, 83–97.

Kampp, Aa. H. 1972: 'Changes in the distribution of land in Denmark: village, manor, smallholding, joint operation', *Geog. Tidss.* **70**, 22–28.

Kampp, Aa. H. 1973: *Faerøerne*. AB Håndbøger, Copenhagen, 124 pp.

Kampp, Aa. H. 1975: *An Agricultural Geography of Denmark*. Akademiai Kiado, Budapest, 88 pp.

Karlén, W. 1973: 'Holocene glacier and climatic variations, Kebnekejse Mountains, Swedish Lapland', *Geog. Ann.* **55**, 29–63.

Karvonen, L. 1977: 'Economic relations in the Nordic area: failures and achievements', *Yearbook of Finnish Foreign Policy 1977*, Finnish Inst. of International Affairs, Helsinki, pp. 52–9.

Kero, R. 1974: *Migration from Finland to North America in the Years between the United States Civil War and the First World War*. Turku, 260 pp.

Kidson, P. 1974: *Iceland in a Nutshell*. Iceland Travel Books, Reykjavik, 242 pp.

Kiilerich, A. 1928: 'Geography, hydrography and climate of the Faroes', in Jensen, A. S. *et al.* (eds), *Zoology of the Faroes*, vol. 1. Copenhagen, pp. 1–51.

Kjartansson, G. 1969: *Jarðfreiðikort* (geological maps of Iceland). Landmaelingur Islands, Reykjavik.

Kirkby, M. H. 1977: *The Vikings*. Phaidon, Oxford, 207 pp.

Knox, P. L. 1973: 'Norway's regional policies and prosperity', *Scottish Geog. Mag.* 89 (3), 180–195.

Knudsen, O. 1972: *Norway at Work: A Survey of the Principal Branches of the*

Economy. Tanum, Oslo.

Korst, M. 1975: *Industrial Life in Denmark*. Det. Danske Selskab, Copenhagen, 175 pp.

Kristinsson, V. 1973: 'Population distribution and standard of living in Iceland', *Geoforum* **13**, 53–62.

Kristjansson, L. (ed.) 1974: *Geodynamics of Iceland and the North Atlantic Area*, Proc. NATO Advanced Study Institute in Reykjavik, Reidel, Holland, 323 pp.

Landmark, E. *et al*. 1959: 'Northern Norway – nature and livelihood', *Norsk. Geogr. Tidss*. **17** (1–4), 138–67.

Landt, J. 1810: *A Description of the Faroe Islands*. London, 440 pp.

Leirfall, J. 1979: *West over Sea*. Thule Press, Shetland, 159 pp.

Levi, L. and Andersson, L. 1976: *Population, Environment and the Quality of Life*. Allmänna Förlaget, Stockholm, 142 pp.

Lewthwaite, G. R. 1966: 'Environmentalism and determinism: a search for clarification', *A.A.A.G* **56**, 1–23.

Linzie, J. and Ericsson, B. 1980: *Behövs Stockholms – regionen?* Länsstyrelsen i Stockholms Län, Stockholm, 96 pp.

Linden, F-K. and Weyer, H. 1974: *Iceland*. Robert Hale, London, 224 pp.

Ljungdahl, S. 1938: 'Sommarstockholm', *Ymer* **58**.

Lloyd, T. 1955: 'Iron-ore production at Kirkenes (Norway)', *Econ. Geog*. **31**, 211–33.

Lorendahl, B. 1969: *Regionalpolitik i Norden*. Ystad p.

Lorendahl, B. 1974: *Nordisk regional-ekonomi*. Föreningarna Nordens Förbund, Stockholm, 352 pp.

Lowenthal, D. and Prince, H. C. 1965: 'English landscape tastes', *Geog. Rev*. **55**, 186–222.

Lundquist, G. 1954: *Lapland*. Bonniers, Stockholm, 128 pp.

Lundqvist, J. 1965: 'The Quaternary of Sweden', in Rankama, K. (ed.), *The Quaternary*, vol. 1. Interscience, New York, pp. 139–98.

Lundqvist, J. 1972: 'Ice-lake types and deglaciation patterns along the Scandinavian mountain range', *Boreas* **1**, 27–54.

McCririck, M. 1976: *The Icelanders and their Island*. Bangor, private pub., 169 pp.

McCririck, M. 1983: *Jón Jónsson of North Iceland*. Bangor, private pub., 88 pp.

Magnusson, M. 1973: *Viking Expansion Westwards*. Bodley Head, London, 152 pp.

Magnusson, M. 1980: *Vikings!* Bodley Head/BBC, London, 320 pp.

Magnusson, S. A. 1977: *Northern Sphinx: Iceland and the Icelanders from the Settlement to the Present*. C. Hurst, London, 261 pp.

Malmström, V. H. 1958: *A Regional Geography of Iceland*. Nat. Acad. of Sciences–Nat. Res. Council Pub. No. 584, 255 pp.

Malmström, V. H. 1965: *Norden: Crossroads of Destiny and Progress*. Van Nostrand, New Jersey, 128 pp.

Mangerud, J. 1970: 'Late Weichselian vegetation and ice-front oscillations in the Bergen district, western Norway', *Norsk Geogr. Tidss*. **24** (3), 121–48.

Mangerud, J. 1976: 'Fra istid till nåtid', in Hartvedt, G. H. (ed.) *Hordaland og Bergen*. Gyldendal Norsk Forlag, Oslo, pp. 111–51.

Mangerud, J., Andersen, S. T., Berglund, B. E. and Donner, J. J. 1974: 'Quaternary stratigraphy of Norden, a proposal for terminology and classification', *Boreas* **3**, 109–28.

Manker, E. 1963: *People of Eight Seasons*. Watts, London, 231 pp.

Mannerfelt, C. M:son 1945: 'Några glacial morfologiska

Formelement', *Geog. Ann.* **27**, 1–239.

Marklund, S. and Söderberg, P. 1967: *The Swedish Comprehensive School.* Longmans, London, 119 pp.

Marsden, W. 1976: *Lapland.* Time-Life, Amsterdam, 184 pp.

Martin, A. F. 1951: 'The necessity for determinism', *Trans. IBG* **17**, 1–12.

Matthiessen, C. W. 1980: 'Trends in the urbanization process: the Copenhagen case', *Geog. Tidss.* **80**, 98–101.

Mead, W. R. 1947: 'Sogn and Fjordane in the fjord economy of western Norway', *Econ. Geog.* **23** 155–66.

Mead, W. R. 1953: *Farming in Finland.* Athlone Press, London, 248 pp.

Mead, W. R. 1958: *An Economic Geography of the Scandinavian States and Finland.* Univ. of London Press, London, 302 pp.

Mead, W. R. 1959: 'Frontier themes in Finland', *Geography* **44**, 145–56.

Mead, W. R. 1968: *Finland.* Benn, London, 256 pp.

Mead, W. R. 1971: *The Scandinavian Northlands.* OUP, London, 48 pp.

Mead, W. R. 1981: *An Historical Geography of Scandinavia.* Academic Press, London, 313 pp.

Mead, W. R. and Hall, W. 1972: *Scandinavia.* Thames & Hudson, London, 208 pp.

Mead, W. R. and Jaatinen, S. J. 1975: *The Åland Islands.* David & Charles, Newton Abbot, 183 pp.

Mead, W. R. and Smeds, H. 1967: *Winter in Finland.* Hugh Evelyn, London, 144 pp.

Mead, W. R. *et al.* 1964: 'Saltvik – studies from an Åland parish', *Geog. Field Group Reg. Study* No. 10, 63 pp.

Miljan, T. 1977: *The Reluctant Europeans.* C. Hurst, London, 325 pp.

Millward, R. 1965: *Scandinavian Lands.* Macmillan, London, 487 pp.

Minshull, R. 1967: *Regional Geography: Theory and Practice.* Hutchinson, London, 168 pp.

Minshull, R. 1970: *The Changing Nature of Geography.* Hutchinson, London, 160 pp.

Mitens, E. 1967: *Facts about the Faroe Islands.* Føroya Banki, Torshavn, 34 pp.

Moberg, V. 1951: *The Emigrants.* Popular Library, New York, 383 pp.

Moberg, V. 1973: *A History of the Swedish People*, Heinemann, London, 2 vols, 210 pp and 268 pp.

Møller, S. E. 1972: 'New critical attitude to housing', *Danish Jnl* **72**, 30–7.

Møller, S. E. 1971: 'Their own house – the Danish dream', *Danish Jnl* **71**, 8–13.

Montefiore, H. C. and Williams, W. W. 1955: 'Determinism and possibilism', *Geog. Studies* **2**, 1–11.

Montelius, S. 1953: 'The burning of forest land for the cultivation of crops', *Geog. Ann.* **35**, 41–54.

Moore, R. (ed.) 1980: *Fodor's 1980 Guide to Scandinavia.* Hodder & Stoughton, London, 519 pp.

Morill, R. L. 1961: 'The development and spatial distributions of towns in Sweden – an historical– predictive approach', *AAAG* **53**, 1–14.

Munch, P. 1947: 'Gård, the Norwegian farm', *Rural Sociology* **12**, 256–363.

Murray, J. W. 1977: *Growth and Change in Danish Agriculture.* Hutchinson, London, 64 pp.

Myklebost, H. 1965: 'Urbanization and rural depopulation in Norway', *Proc. 4th N.Z. Geog. Conf. 1965*, pp. 167–76.

Myklebost, H. and Strømme, S. (eds) 1963: *Norge*, vols 1–4, Cappelens, Oslo.

Näslund, M. and Persson, S. 1972: *Regional politik, i går, i*

dag, i morgon. Stockholm.
Naturgeografisk region-indelning av Norden 1977: NU:B, 34 (Gotab., Stockholm), 130 pp.

Nelson, H. 1956: 'Seasonal wanderings in Sweden in the nineteenth century', *Folk Liv.* **20**.

Nelson, N. 1973: *Denmark.* Batsford, London, 195 pp.

Newcomb, R. M. 1967: 'Geographic aspects of the planned preservation of visible history in Denmark, *A.A.A.G.* **57**, 462–480.

Newcomb, R. M. 1976: *Episodes or Continuity? Culture Changes on the Landscape of N. E. Jutland, Denmark.* Geog. Inst. Univ. of Århus, Denmark, 28 pp.

Nickels, S. *et al.* (eds.) 1973: *Finland – an Introduction.* Allen & Unwin, London, 377 pp.

Nicol, G. 1975: *Finland.* Batsford, London, 216 pp.

Nielung, O. 1968: 'Bygdetyper på Faerøerne', *Kulturgeografiske skrifter* **2**, 149–84.

Nilsson, E. 1960: 'The recession of the land-ice in Sweden during the Allerød and the Younger Dryas Ages', *21st Int. Geol. Congress (Norden)*, Report 4, pp. 98–107.

Nilsson, F. 1970: *Emigrationen från Stockholm till Nordamerika 1880–1893.* Norstedt & Söner, Stockholm, 392 pp.

Nilsson, J. E. 1980: 'Problem och strategier för regional utveckling under 80 – talet', *Plan* **3**, 99–108.

Nordal, J. and Kristinsson, V. (eds) 1967: *Iceland.* Central Bank of Iceland, Reykjavik, 390 pp.

Nordel Annual Report 1977 *et seq.* Copenhagen.

Nordenstam, A. *et al.* 1970: *Skärgårdsboken.* Förlags AB Baltic, Stockholm, 240 pp.

Nordic Statistical Secretariat (ed) 1972 *et seq: Yearbook of Nordic Statistics*, Nordic Council/Nordic Statistical Secretariat, Stockholm.

Norman, H. and Runblom, H. 1980: *Nordisk Emigrationsatlas* (2 vols). Cikada AB, Uddevalla.

Nyquist, F. P. (ed.) 1977: *Jotunheimen, Challenge of a Mountain Wilderness.* North Sea Press, Grøndahl, 200 pp.

O'Dell, A. C. 1957: *The Scandinavian World.* Longmans, Green, London, 549 pp.

Ödmann, E. and Dahlberg, G.-B. 1970: *Urbanisation in Sweden.* Allmänna Förlaget, Stockholm, 256 pp.

Ogilvie, A. G. 1957: *Europe and its Borderlands.* Nelson, London, 340 pp.

Ogrizek, D. (ed.) 1952: *Scandinavia.* McGraw-Hill, New York, 438 pp.

Okko, V. 1955: 'Glacial drift in Iceland: its origin and morphology', *Bull. Comm. Geol. Finl.* **170**, 1–133.

Ølgaard, A. 1971: 'The Faroese economy', *Danish Jnl* (special edn.), 21–7.

O'Riordan, T. 1983: *Environmentalism.* Methuen, London, 409 pp.

Ostenfeld, C. H. and Gröntved, J. 1934: *The Flora of Iceland and the Faroes.* Williams & Norgate, London, 195 pp.

Ostenfeld, C. H. 1901: 'Geography and topography' and 'Climate', in Warming, E. (ed.), *Botany of the Faroes based upon Danish Investigations.* vol. 1. London, pp. 6–20 and 32–7.

Østrem, G., Haakensen, N. and Melander, O. 1973: *Atlas over Breer i Nord-Skandinavia*, NVE & Stockholm Univ., 315 pp.

Østrem, G. and Ziegler, T. 1969: *Atlas over breer i Sør-Norge*, NVE, Oslo, 207 pp.

Oström, K. 1980: 'On periferins problem', *Plan* **3**, 127–31.

Osvald, H. 1952: *Swedish Agriculture.* Swedish Inst., Stockholm.

Ouren, T. 1958: *The Port Traffic of the Oslofjord region*. Oslo.

Paget, E. 1960: 'Comments on the adjustments of settlements in marginal areas', *Geog. Ann.* **42**, 324–6.

Pantenburg, V. 1968: 'Europe's northern cap', *Musk-Ox* **3**, 24–38.

Paulsson, T. 1957: *Scandinavian Architecture*. London, 256 pp.

Pedersen, P. T. 1954: 'Four nations break down the barriers', *Danish Foreign Office Jnl* **14**, 18–19.

Percivall, M. 1979: *Special Issue – Sweden*. If HP News Sheet 1979 No. 2, p. 17.

Phillips, D. (ed.) 1977: *Jon Jonsson of Vogar: His Life 1829–1866* (fascimile reprint). private pub., Nenthead, 32 pp.

Phillips, D. 1980: *Check-list of Principal Books on Iceland and Faroe*. private pub., Nenthead, England, 27 pp.

Platt, R. R. 1957: *Finland and its Geography*. Methuen, London, 510 pp.

Pocock, D. C. D. 1981: *Humanistic Geography and Literature*. Croom Helm, London, 224 pp.

Pounds, N. J. G. and Ball, S. S. 1964: 'Core areas and the development of the European States system, *A.A.A.G.* **54**, 24–40.

Pred, A. 1977: *City Systems in Advanced Economies*. Hutchinson, London, 256 pp.

Preusser, H. 1976: *The Landscapes of Iceland: Types and Regions*. W. Junk, The Hague, 363 pp.

Relph, E. 1981: *Rational Landscapes and Humanistic Geography*. Croom Helm, London, 231 pp.

Raitt, W. C. 1958: 'The changing pattern of Norwegian HEP development', *Econ. Geog.* **34**, 217–144.

Riis, T. and Stromstad, P. (ed.) 1977: *Scandinavian Atlas of Historic Towns*, Odense.

Roberts, M. 1973: *Sweden's Age of Greatness, 1632–1718*. Macmillan, London, 314 pp.

Roberts, M. 1979: *The Swedish Imperial Experience*. Cambridge Univ. Press, London.

Robinson, G. W. S. 1953: 'The geographical region: form and function', *Scot. Geog. Mag.* **69**, 49–58.

Rönn, G. 1961: *The Land of the Lapps*. Saxon & Lindström, Stockholm, 111 pp.

Rørdam, T. 1965: *The Danish Folk High Schools*. Det Danske Selskab, Copenhagen.

Roszak, T. 1981: *Person/Planet*. Paladin, London, 350 pp.

Rudberg, S. 1954: 'Västerbottens berggrundsgeologi', *Geographica* **25**, 457 pp.

Rudberg, S. 1961: 'Geology and morphology', Ch. 3 in Sømme, A. (ed.) *The Geography of Norden*, Heinemann, London, pp. 27–40.

Rudberg, S. 1965: 'Reconstruction of polycyclical relief in Scandinavia', *Norsk Geogr. Tidss.* **20**, 65–73.

Rudberg, S. and Bylund, E. 1957: 'From the Bothnian Gulf through southern and central Lapland to the Norwegian fjords', *Geog. Ann.* **41**, 261–88.

Ruong, I. 1967: *The Lapps in Sweden*. Swedish Inst., Stockholm, 116 pp.

Rush, F. A. 1970: *Denmark Farms On*. Danish Agricultural Producers, London, 127 pp.

Rutherford, G. K. 1982: *The Physical Environment of the Faroe Islands*. The Hague, 148 pp.

Rying, B. (ed.) 1965: *The Farthest Shore*. Royal Danish Ministry of Foreign Affairs, Copenhagen, 38 pp.

Rying, B. (ed.) 1974: *Denmark – an Official Handbook*. Royal Danish Ministry of Foreign Affairs, Copenhagen, 902 pp.

Sauer, C. O. 1963: *Land and Life: A Selection from the Writings of Carl Ortwin Sauer* (ed. by J.

Leighly). Univ. of Calif. Press, Berkeley, 435 pp.

Sawyer, P. H. 1971: *The Age of the Vikings*. Edward Arnold, London, 275 pp.

Scherman, K. 1976: *Iceland: Daughter of Fire*. Gollancz, London, 364 pp.

Schnitzer, M. 1970: *The Economy of Sweden: A Study of the Modern Welfare State*. Praeger, New York, 252 pp.

Schou, A. 1949: *The Landscapes*, vol I of *Atlas of Denmark*. Hagerup, Denmark, 129 pp.

Schwartzbach, M. 1971: *Geologen Fahrten in Island*, Karawane-Verlag, Ludwigsbur, 104 pp.

Schytt, V. 1959: 'The glaciers of the Kebnekajse massif', *Geog. Ann.* **41**, 213–27.

Scott, G. W. 1967: *The Swedes – a Jigsaw Puzzle*. Sidgewick & Jackson, London, 163 pp.

Semmingsen, I. 1960: 'Norwegian Émigration in the nineteenth century', *Scand. Econ. Hist. Rev.* **8**, 150–60.

Semmingsen, I. 1972: 'Emigration from Scandinavia', *Scand. Econ. Hist. Rev.*

Semple, E. C. 1911: *Influences of Geographic Environment*. Constable, London, 683 pp.

Shell Briefing Service 1979: *North Sea Progress* (Dec.), 9 pp.

Shepherd, C. M. 1867: *The North-West Peninsula of Iceland*. London, 162 pp.

Simpson, C. 1966: *The Viking Circle*. Hodder & Stoughton, London, 366 pp.

Simpson, J. 1967: *Everyday Life in the Viking Age*. Batsford, London, 208 pp.

Sinclair, J. D. and Sinclair, M. 1971: 'Danish bacon in the balance', *Geog. Mag.* **43**, 684–5.

Siuruainen, E. and Aikio, P. 1977: *The Lapps in Finland*. Soc. for the Promotion of Lapp Culture No. 39, Helsinki, 60 pp.

Sjörs, H. 1956: *Nordisk Växtgeografi*. Scandinavia Univ. Books.

Skandinaviska Enskilda Banken

1977–78 *et seq: Some Data about Sweden*, Stockholm.

Skog, J. 1976: 'Blessings of harnessed water', *The Norseman* **4**, 105–8.

Skole, R. 1974: 'A heart of steel', *Sweden Now* (special issue) **5**, 21–7.

Sletten, V. 1967: *Five Nordic Countries Pull Together*. Nordic Council, Copenhagen, 92 pp.

Small, A. 1967–68: 'The distribution of settlement in Shetland and Faroe in Viking times', *Saga-Book* **7** (2–3), 145–55.

Smed, P., Meesenburg, H. and Tongaard, S. 1966: *Det Danske Landskab*. H. Meesenburg, Tønder, 179 pp.

Smeds, H. 1950: 'The Replot Skerry Guard – emerging islands in the northern Baltic', *Geog. Rev.* **40**, 103–33.

Smeds, H. 1960a: 'Post-war land clearance and pioneering activities in Finland', *Fennia* **83** (1), 1–31.

Smeds, H. 1960b: 'Three faces of Finland (Guidebook IGU Congress)', *Fennia* **84**.

Smeds, H. 1961: 'Finland', in Sømme, A. (ed.) *The Geography of Norden*. Heinemann, London, Ch. 9, pp. 149–202.

Smeds H., Jaatinen, S. *et al.* (eds.) 1960: *Text till Atlas över Skärgårds – Finland*. Nordenskjöld-Samfundet, Helsinki, 179 pp.

Solem, E. 1977: *The Nordic Council and Scandinavian integration*. Praeger, London, 197 pp.

Sømme, A. 1949–54: *Jordbrukets geografi i Norge*, 2 vols. Geog. Avh., Bergen.

Sømme, A. (ed.) 1960: *Vestlandet – Geographical Studies*. IGC Norden 1960, Bergen, 84 pp. (Geog. Avh. No. 7).

Sømme, A. (ed.) 1961: *The Geography of Norden*. Heinemann, London, 362 pp. (2nd ed, 1968)

Sparring, A. 1972: *Island, Europa och NATO*. Raben & Sjögren,

Stockholm.

Spate, O. H. K. 1957: 'How determined is possibilism?' *Geog. Studies* **4**, 1–10.

Spate, O. H. K. 1966: *Let me Enjoy*. Methuen, London, 303 pp.

Spencer, A. 1975: *The Norwegians: How They Live and Work*. David & Charles, Newton Abbot, 147 pp.

Stefansson, U. 1974: 'The Icelanders and the sea', *UNESCO Courier* (Feb.), 26–30.

Stefansson, V. 1939: *Iceland – The First American Republic*. Doubleday, New York, 275 pp.

Steindorsson, S. 1935–37: *Contribution to the Plant Geography and Flora of Iceland*. Reykjavik.

Steindorsson, S. 1962: 'The age and immigration of the Icelandic flora', *Soc. Scient. Isl.* **35**, 1–157.

Stenstadvold, K. 1975: Chapter on Scandinavia in Clout, H. (ed.), *Regional Development in Western Europe*. Wiley, London, 328 pp.

Stone, K. 1962: 'Swedish Fringes of settlement', *AAAG* **52**, 373–393.

Stone, K. 1965: 'Finnish fringe of settlement zones', *Tijd, voor Econ. en Soc. Geog.* **57**.

Stone, K. 1971a: 'Regional abandoning of rural settlement in northern Sweden', *Erdkunde* **25**, 36–51.

Stone, K. 1971b: 'Isolations and retreat of settlement in Iceland', *Scot. Geog. Mag.* **87** (1), 3–13.

Stone, K. 1971c: *Norway's Internal Migration to New Farms since 1920*. European Demographic Monographs, The Hague, 68 pp.

Strand, T. and Kulling C. 1972: *Scandinavian Caledonides*. Wiley, London, 302 pp.

Strøm, K. 1949: 'The geomorphology of Norway', *Geog. Jnl* **62**, 19–27.

Strøm, K. 1960: 'The Norwegian coast', *Norsk. Geogr. Tidss.* **17** (1–4), 132–7.

Strömdahl, J. 1979: *National Physical Planning*. Ministry of Housing and Phys. Planning, Stockholm, 51 pp.

Sund, T. 1949: 'Sommer-Bergen', *Norsk Geog. Tidss.* **12**.

Sund, T. 1960: 'Fjord land and coast land of western Norway', *Norsk. Geog. Tidss.* **17**, 176–86.

Sund, T. 1961: 'Norway' in Sømme, A. (ed.), *The Geography of Norden*. Heinemann, London, Ch. 11, pp. 235–92.

Sundelius, B. 1976: *Nordic Cooperation: A Dynamic Integration Process*. Denver, Colorado, 78 pp.

Symes, D. G. 1968: 'Vågsøy, a west Norwegian Island', *Geog. Field Group, Reg. Study No. 13*, 125 pp.

Tamm, O. F. 1950: *Northern Coniferous Forest Soils*. Oxford Univ. Press.

Tapsell, A. 1969: *Northward but Gently*. Stockholm.

Teal, J. J. 1954: 'The rebirth of North Norway', *Foreign Affairs* **32**, 123–35.

Thorarinsson, S. 1937: 'The main geological and topographical features of Iceland', *Geog. Ann.* **19**, 161–75.

Thorarinsson, S. 1944: 'Present glacier shrinkage and eustatic changes of sea-level', *Geog. Ann.* **26**, 131–59.

Thorarinsson, S. 1956: *A Thousand Years' Struggle against Ice and Fire*. Reykjavik.

Thorarinsson, S. 1961: 'Population changes in Iceland', *Geog. Rev.* **51** (4), 519–33.

Thorarinsson, S. 1969: 'Glacier surges in Iceland, with special reference to the surges in Bruarjökull', *Can. Jnl Earth Sciences*, **6** (4), 875–82.

Thorarinsson, S. Einarsson, T. and Kjartansson, G. 1959: 'On the geology and geomorphology of Iceland', *Geog. Ann.* **41**, 135–69.

Thoroddsen, Th. 1905–6: *Island – Grundriss Der Geologie und Geographie*. Peterm. Mitt.

152, 153, Gotha.

Thunberg, B. *et al.* (eds) 1979: *Miljö och miljövård i Sverige.* Statens Naturvärdsverk, Solna, 160 pp.

Thunborg, F. and Andersson, B. 1960: *Norrbotten – Land of the Arctic Circle.* Norstedt & Söner, Stockholm, 193 pp.

Tietze, W. (ed.) 1971: 'The European north calotte', *Geoforum* **5**, 3–74.

Trap, J. P. 1968: *Faerøerne* (vol. 5 of *Danmark*). GEC Gads. Forlag, Copenhagen, 375 pp.

Tuan, Yi-Fu 1974: *Topophilia; A Study in Environmental Perception, Attitudes and Values.* Prentice-Hall, New Jersey, 260 pp.

Tuan, Yi-Fu 1980: *Landscapes of Fear*, Blackwell, Oxford, 262 pp.

Turner, B. 1976: *Sweden.* Batsford, London, 158 pp.

Turnock, D. 1967: 'The region in modern geography', *Geography* **52**, 374–83.

Varjo, U. 1977: *Finnish Farming – typology and Economics.* Akademiai Kiado, Budapest, 146 pp.

Varjo, U. 1982: *Norden: Man and Environment*, Univ. of Oulu Press.

Vasari, Y., Hyvärinen, H. and Hicks, S. (eds) 1972: *Climatic Changes in Arctic Areas During the Last Ten Thousand Years.* Oulu, Finland, 511 pp.

Virkkala, K. 1963: 'Ice marginal features in south-western Finland', *Bull. Comm. Géol. Finlande* **210**, 76 pp.

Voksø, P. 1980: *Norge sett fra Luften.* Det Beste, Oslo, 384 pp.

Vorren, Ø. *et al.* 1960: *Norway North of 65.* Univ. Press, Oslo, 271 pp.

Vorren, Ø. and Manker, E. 1962: *Lapp Life and Customs: A Survey.* London, 183 pp.

Wallén, C. C. 1961: 'Climate', Ch. 4 in Sømme, A. (ed.) *The Geography of Norden*, Heinemann, London, pp. 41–53.

Walling, D. E. 1966: 'Field studies in Fjaerland, Norway, Summer, 1965', *Exeter Geog. Mag.* **2**, 7–23.

Werenskiold, W. *et al.* 1957: *Norge-vårt land* (3 vols). Gyldendal, Oslo.

West, J. F. 1970–71: 'Land tenure in a Faroese village', *Saga-Book* **18** (1–2), 19–46.

West, J. F. 1972: *Faroe – The Emergence of a Nation.* C. Hurst, London, 312 pp.

Wheeler, P. T. *et al.* 1978: *The Faroe Islands* (Geog. Field Group Regional Study No. 21). Univ. of Nottingham, 27 pp.

Whittlesey, D. S. 1949: *Environmental Foundations of European History.* Appleton, New York.

Whittlesey, D. 1954: 'The regional concept and the regional method', in James, P. E. and Jones, C. F. (eds) *American Geography: Inventory and Prospect.* Syracuse, pp. 19–68.

William-Olsson, W. 1960: *Stockholm, Structure and Development.* I.G.U. Norden, Uppsala, 96 pp.

Williamson, K. 1948: *The Atlantic Islands* (1st edn). Routledge & Kegan Paul, London, 385 pp. (New edition 1970)

Wilson, D. (ed.) 1980: *The Northern World.* Thames & Hudson, London, 248 pp.

Wizelius, I. (ed.) 1967: *Sweden in the Sixties.* Almqvist & Wiksell, Stockholm, 296 pp.

Index